FALLEN VAMPIRE

Big Mortar shows up in this volume. Drawing that is as disgusting as it is fun, and I hope that comes across.
—*Yuri Kimura*

Artist Yuri Kimura debuted two short stories in Japan's *Gangan Powered* after winning the Enix Manga Award. Shortly thereafter, she began *The Record of a Fallen Vampire*, which was serialized in Japan's *Monthly Shonen Gangan* through March 2007.

Author Kyo Shirodaira is from Nara prefecture. In addition to *The Record of a Fallen Vampire*, Shirodaira has scripted the manga *Spiral: The Bonds of Reasoning*. Shirodaira's novel *Meitantei ni Hana wo* was nominated for the 8th Annual Ayukawa Tetsuya Award in 1997.

FALLEN VAMPIRE

STORY BY: KYO SHIRODAIRA ART BY: YURI KIMURA

4

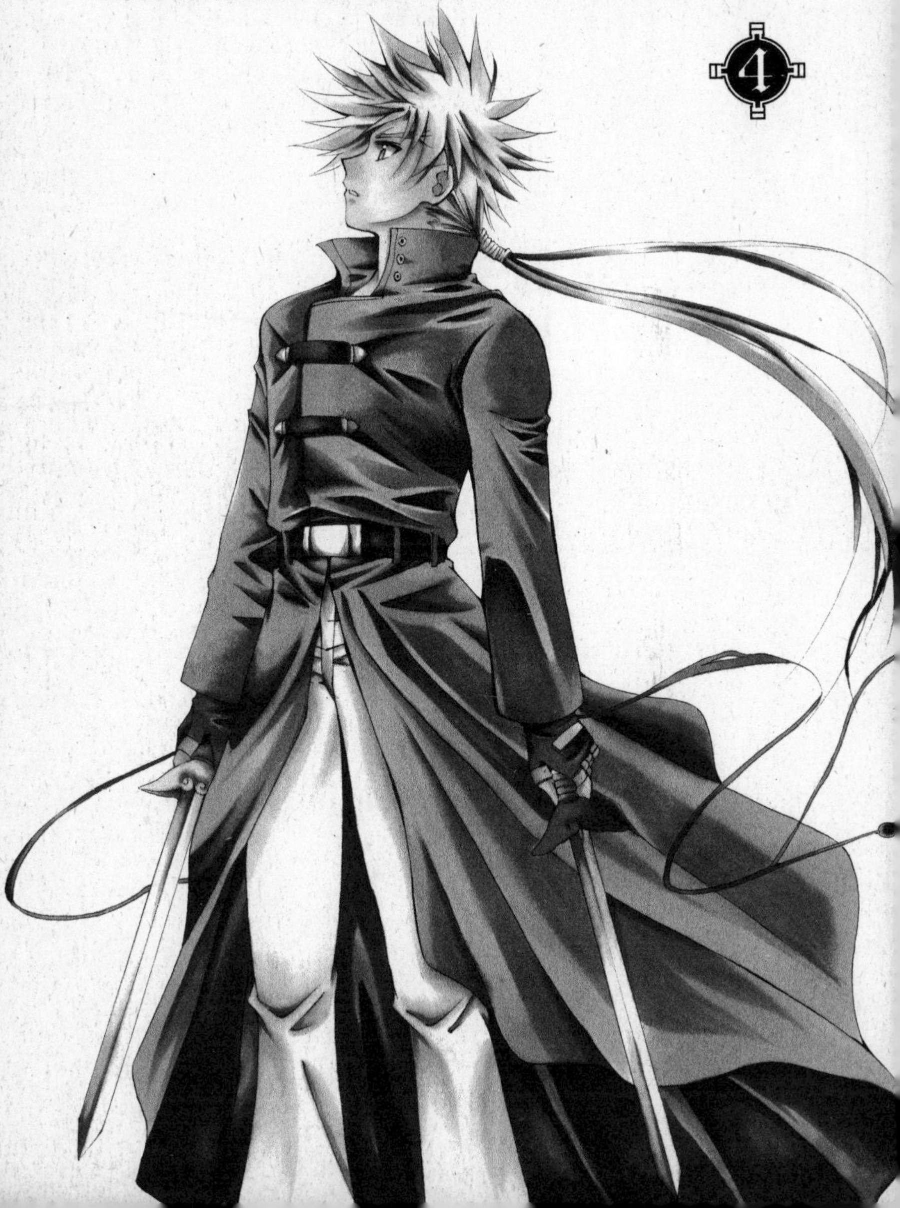

of vampires,
"Night Monarchy"
ty.
beginning of

This is the legend the history of the and its last Majes A story about the vampires' agony...

Story : Kyo Shirodaira

Art : Yuri Kimura

CONTENTS

CHAPTER 14 Tonight the Sky Falls..............7

CHAPTER 15 History's Largest Invasion.....43

CHAPTER 16 Shoot the Invaders...................79

CHAPTER 17 Eternal Goodbye 113

CHAPTER 18 Phantom Lady 151

Chapter 14: Tonight the Sky Falls

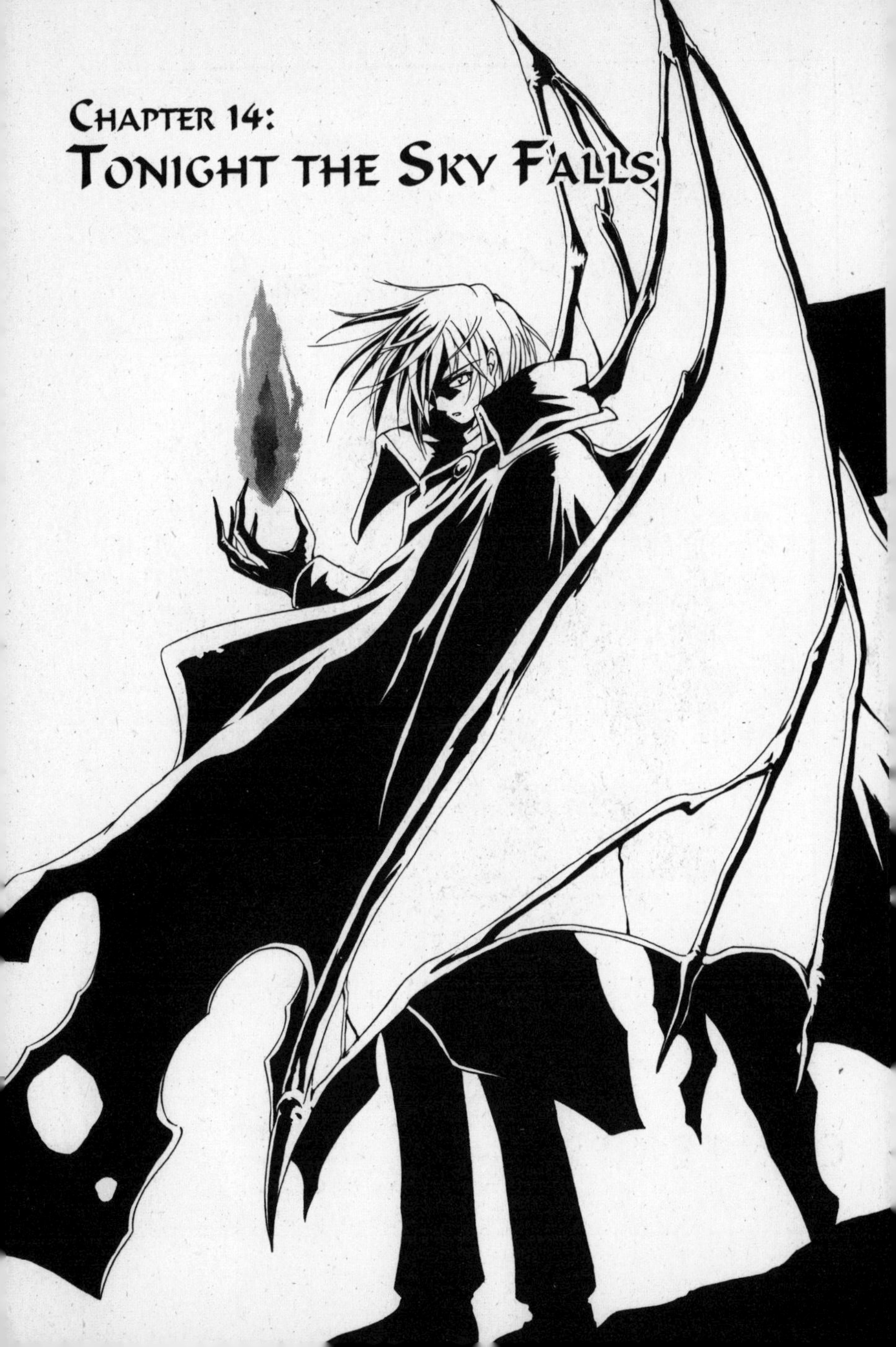

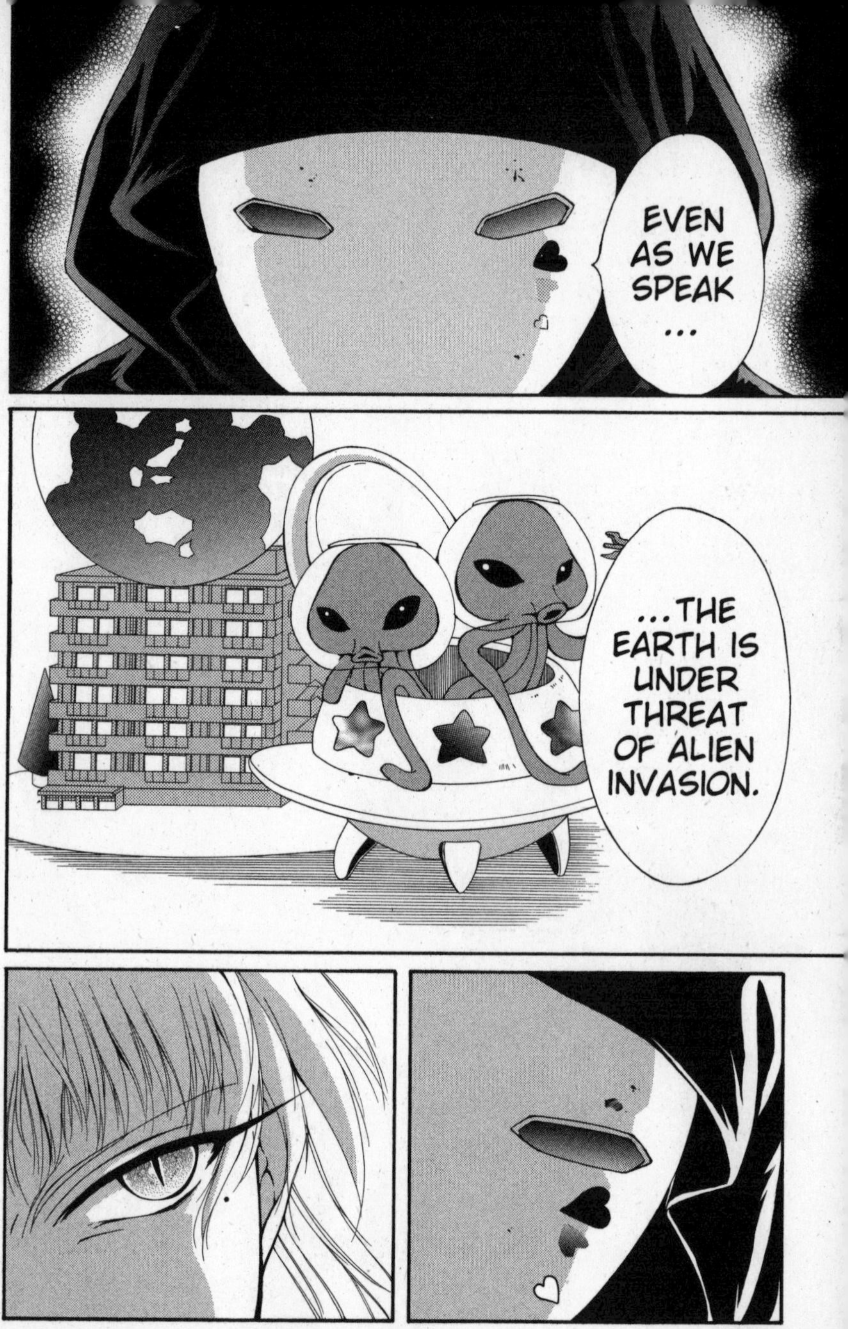
EVEN AS WE SPEAK ...
...THE EARTH IS UNDER THREAT OF ALIEN INVASION.

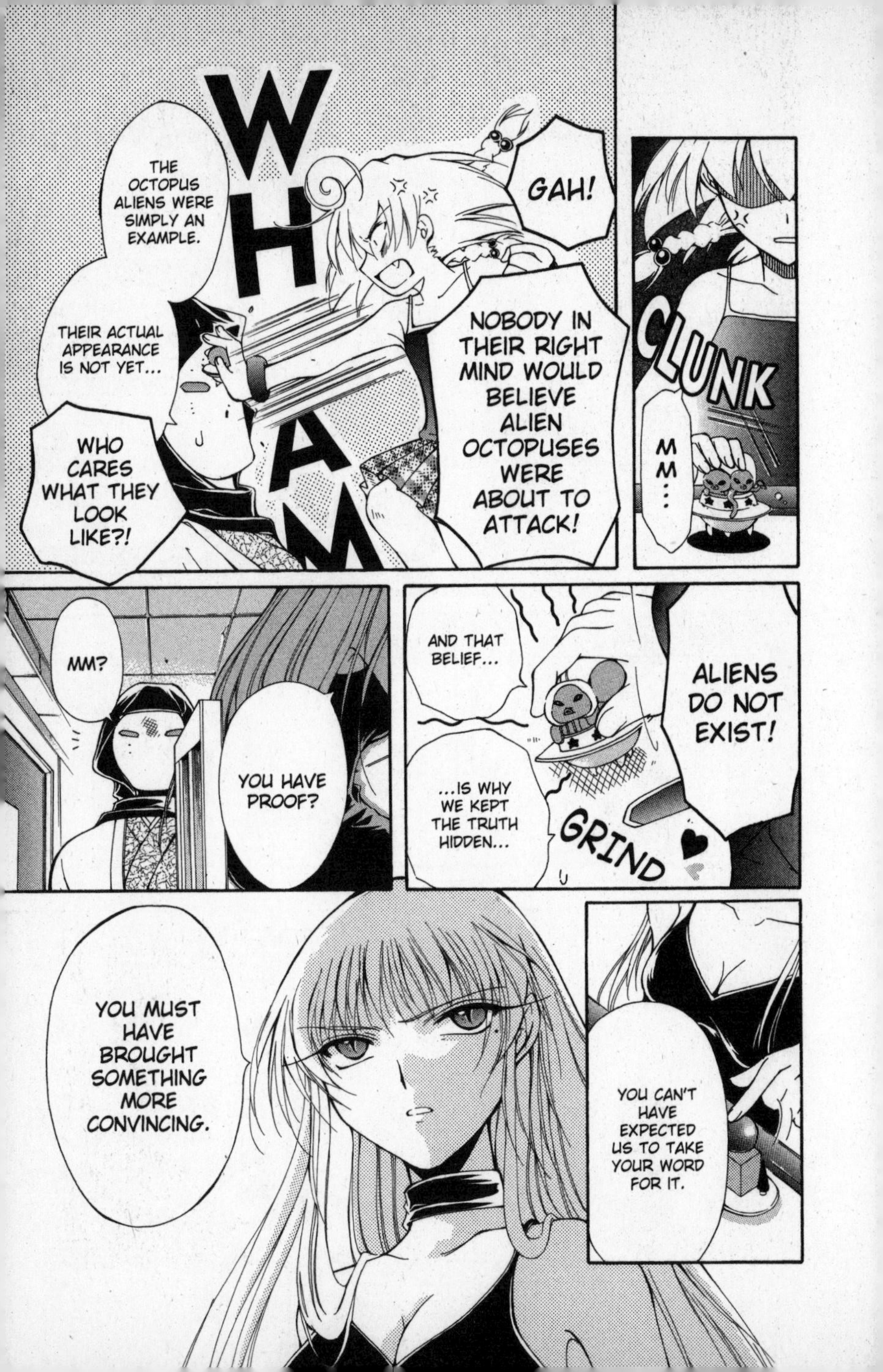
CLUNK
MM...
THE OCTOPUS ALIENS WERE SIMPLY AN EXAMPLE.
THEIR ACTUAL APPEARANCE IS NOT YET...
WHO CARES WHAT THEY LOOK LIKE?!
WHAM
GAH!
NOBODY IN THEIR RIGHT MIND WOULD BELIEVE ALIEN OCTOPUSES WERE ABOUT TO ATTACK!
ALIENS DO NOT EXIST!
AND THAT BELIEF...
...IS WHY WE KEPT THE TRUTH HIDDEN...
GRIND
MM?
YOU HAVE PROOF?
YOU CAN'T HAVE EXPECTED US TO TAKE YOUR WORD FOR IT.
YOU MUST HAVE BROUGHT SOMETHING MORE CONVINCING.

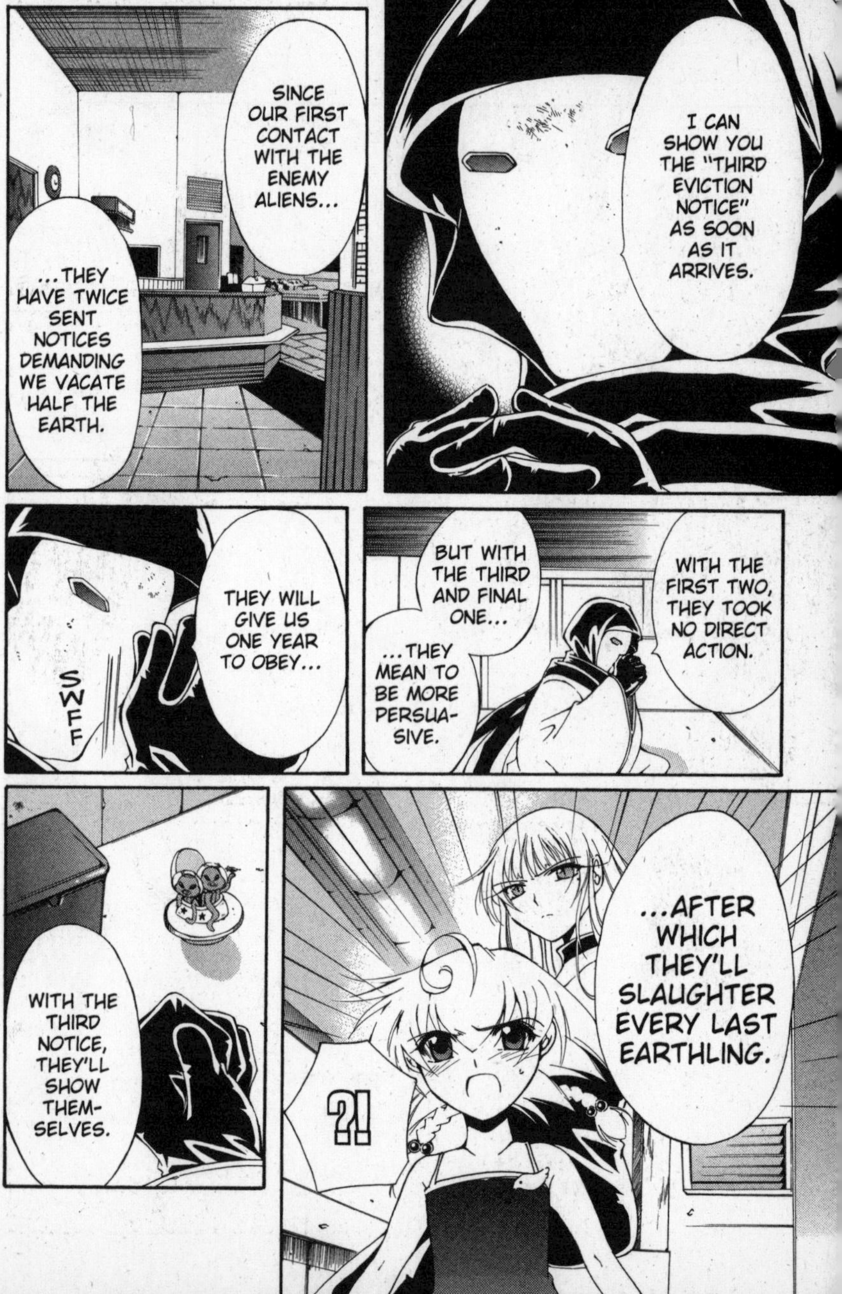
I CAN SHOW YOU THE "THIRD EVICTION NOTICE" AS SOON AS IT ARRIVES.
SINCE OUR FIRST CONTACT WITH THE ENEMY ALIENS...
...THEY HAVE TWICE SENT NOTICES DEMANDING WE VACATE HALF THE EARTH.
WITH THE FIRST TWO, THEY TOOK NO DIRECT ACTION.
BUT WITH THE THIRD AND FINAL ONE...
...THEY MEAN TO BE MORE PERSUA-SIVE.
THEY WILL GIVE US ONE YEAR TO OBEY...
SWFF
...AFTER WHICH THEY'LL SLAUGHTER EVERY LAST EARTHLING.
?!
WITH THE THIRD NOTICE, THEY'LL SHOW THEM-SELVES.

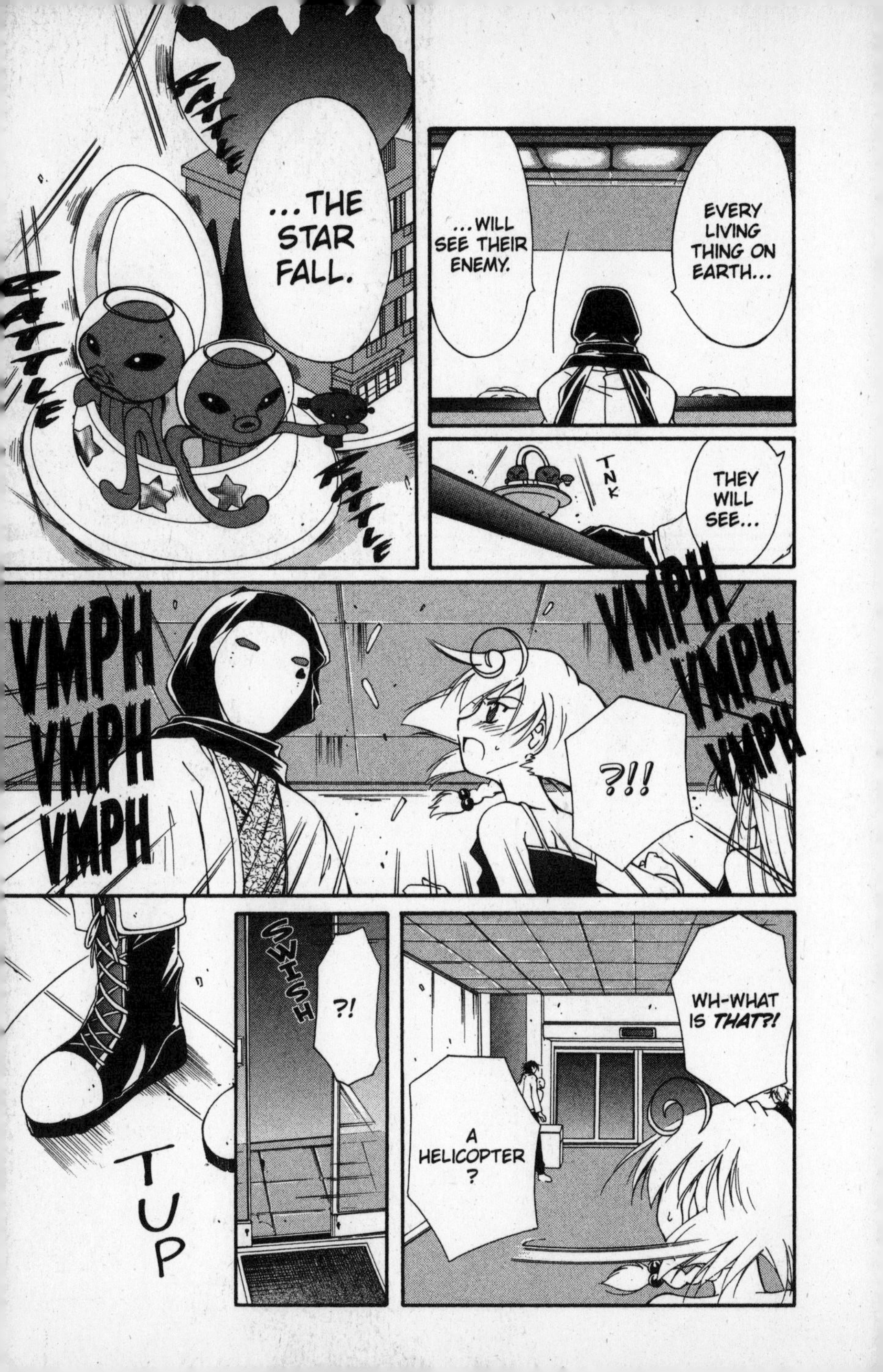
EVERY LIVING THING ON EARTH...
...WILL SEE THEIR ENEMY.
THEY WILL SEE...
TNK
RATTLE
...THE STAR FALL.
RATTLE RATTLE
RATTLE
VMPH VMPH VMPH
?!!
VMPH VMPH VMPH
WH-WHAT IS *THAT?!*
A HELICOPTER ?
SWISH
?!
TUP

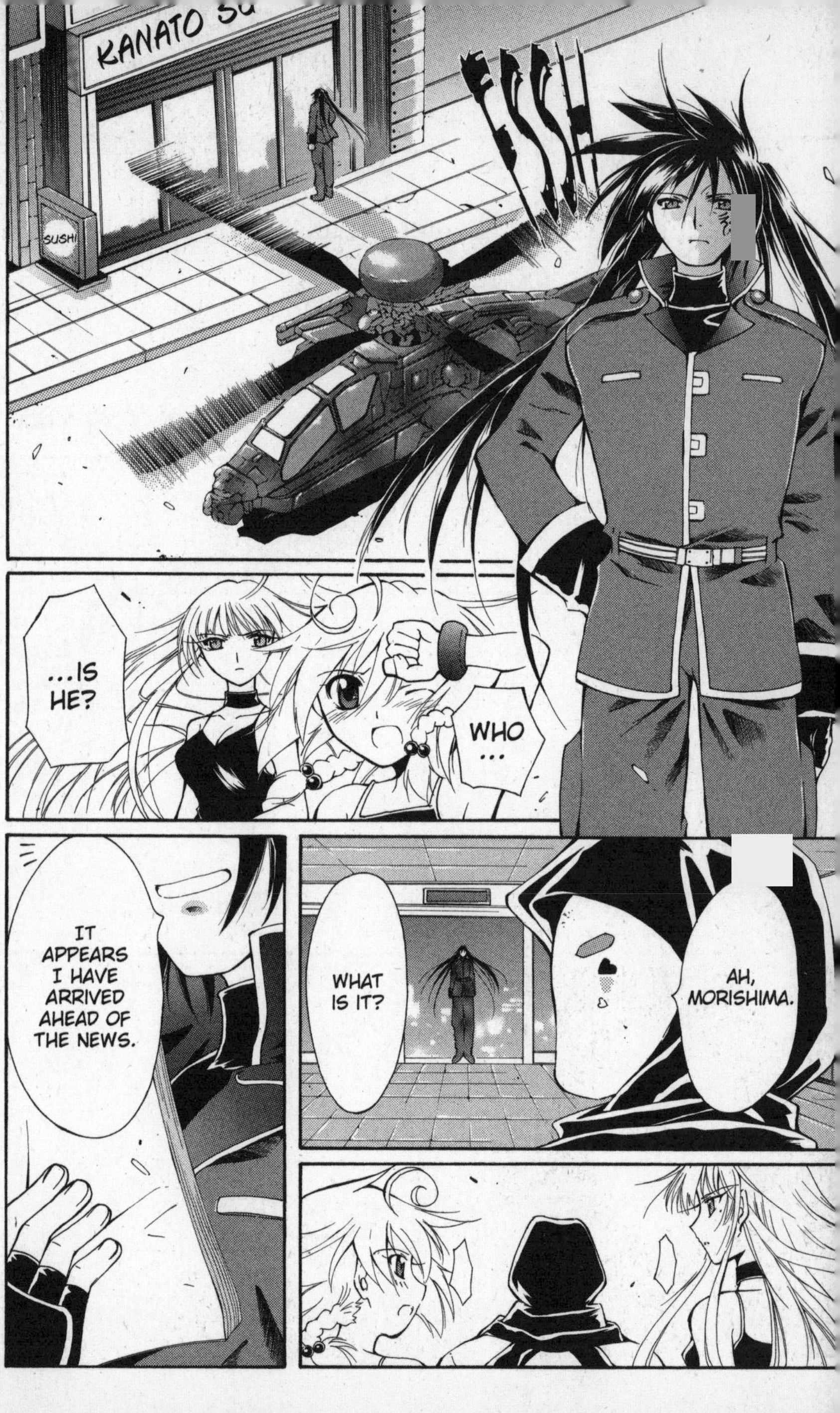
KANATO SU
SUSHI
FSSH
WHO ...
...IS HE?
AH, MORISHIMA.
WHAT IS IT?
IT APPEARS I HAVE ARRIVED AHEAD OF THE NEWS.

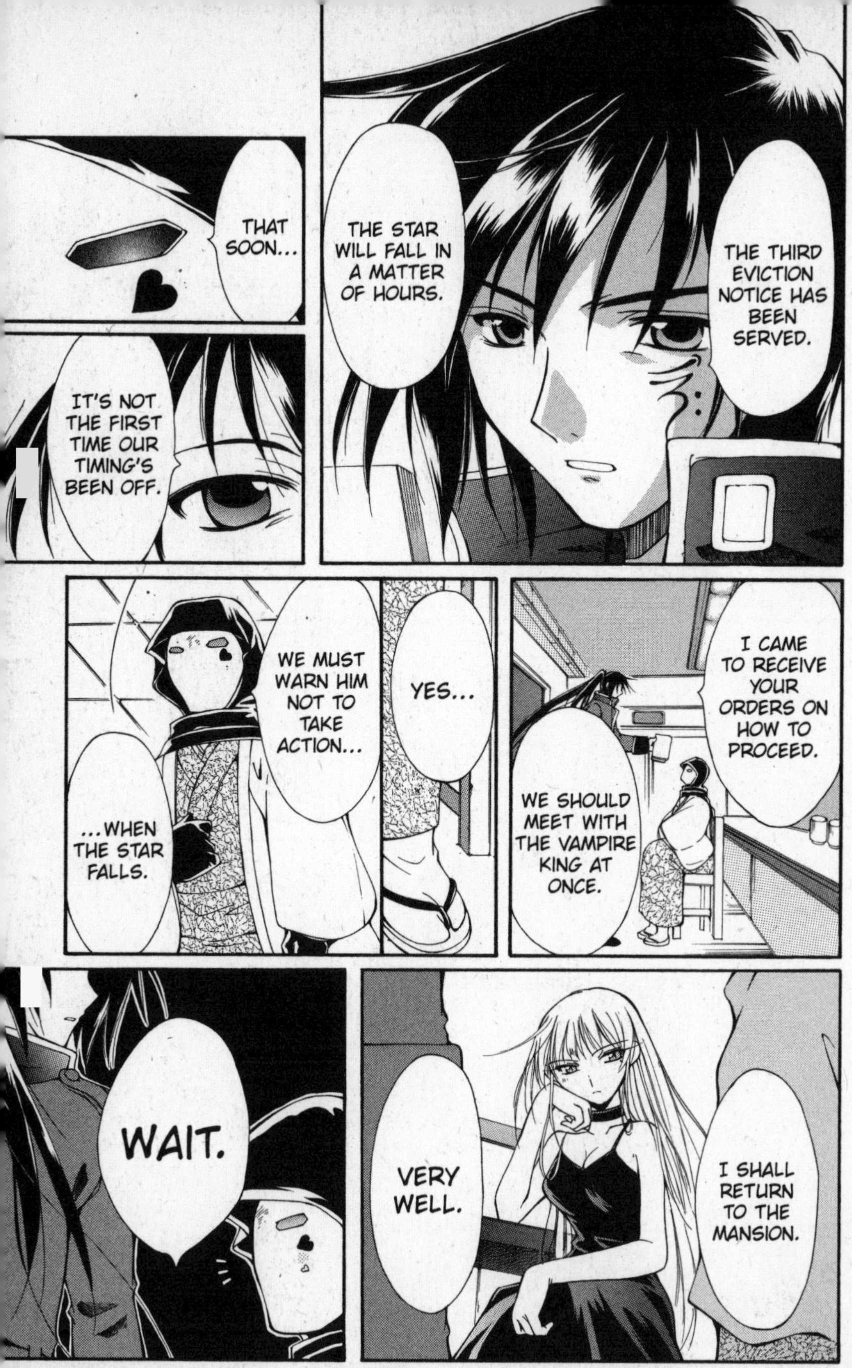
THE THIRD EVICTION NOTICE HAS BEEN SERVED.
THE STAR WILL FALL IN A MATTER OF HOURS.
THAT SOON...
IT'S NOT THE FIRST TIME OUR TIMING'S BEEN OFF.
I CAME TO RECEIVE YOUR ORDERS ON HOW TO PROCEED.
WE SHOULD MEET WITH THE VAMPIRE KING AT ONCE.
YES...
WE MUST WARN HIM NOT TO TAKE ACTION...
...WHEN THE STAR FALLS.
I SHALL RETURN TO THE MANSION.
VERY WELL.
WAIT.

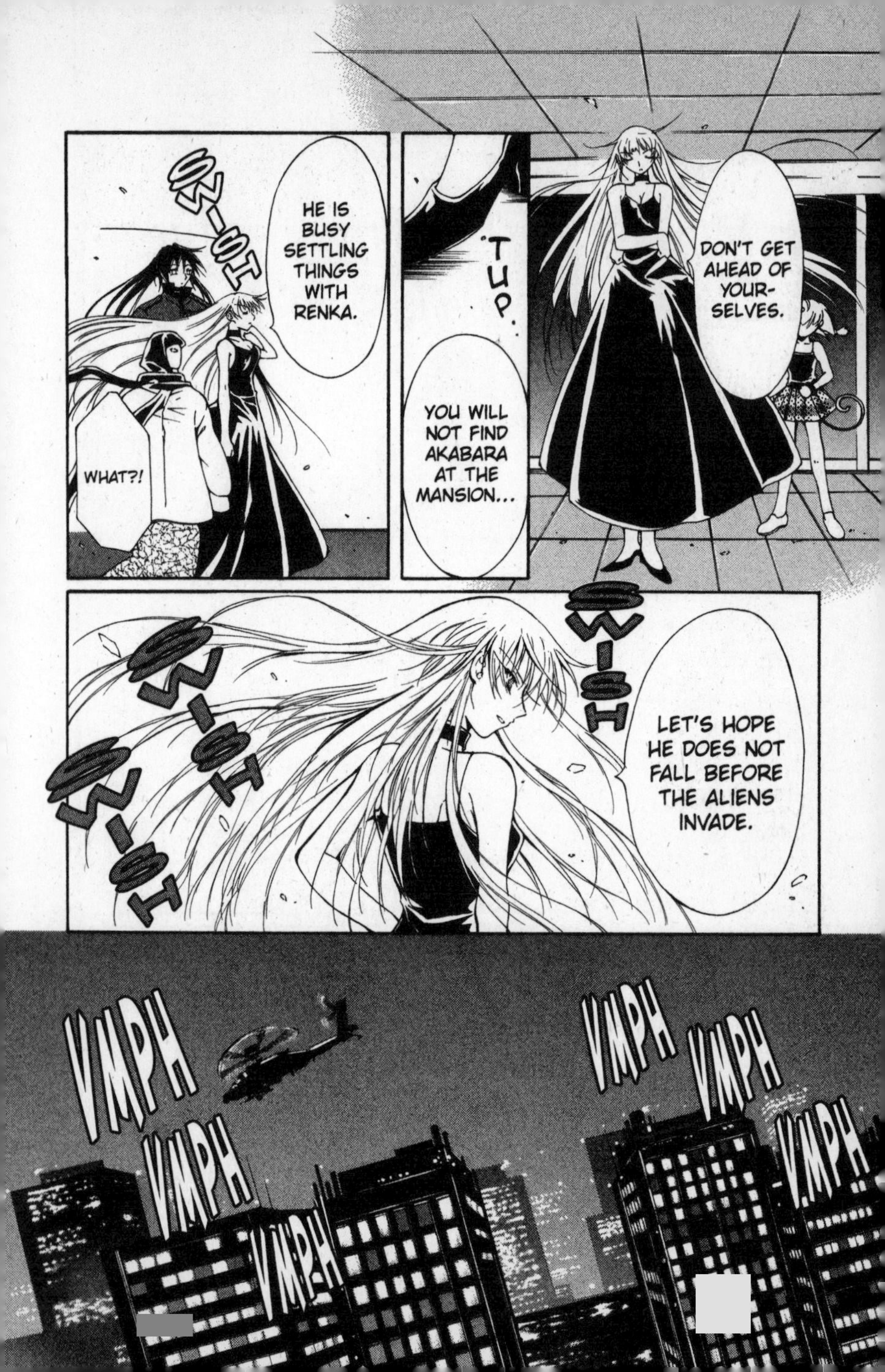
DON'T GET AHEAD OF YOUR-SELVES.
TUP
YOU WILL NOT FIND AKABARA AT THE MANSION...
SWISH
HE IS BUSY SETTLING THINGS WITH RENKA.
WHAT?!
SWISH
LET'S HOPE HE DOES NOT FALL BEFORE THE ALIENS INVADE.
SWISH
SWISH
VMPH
VMPH
VMPH
VMPH
VMPH
VMPH

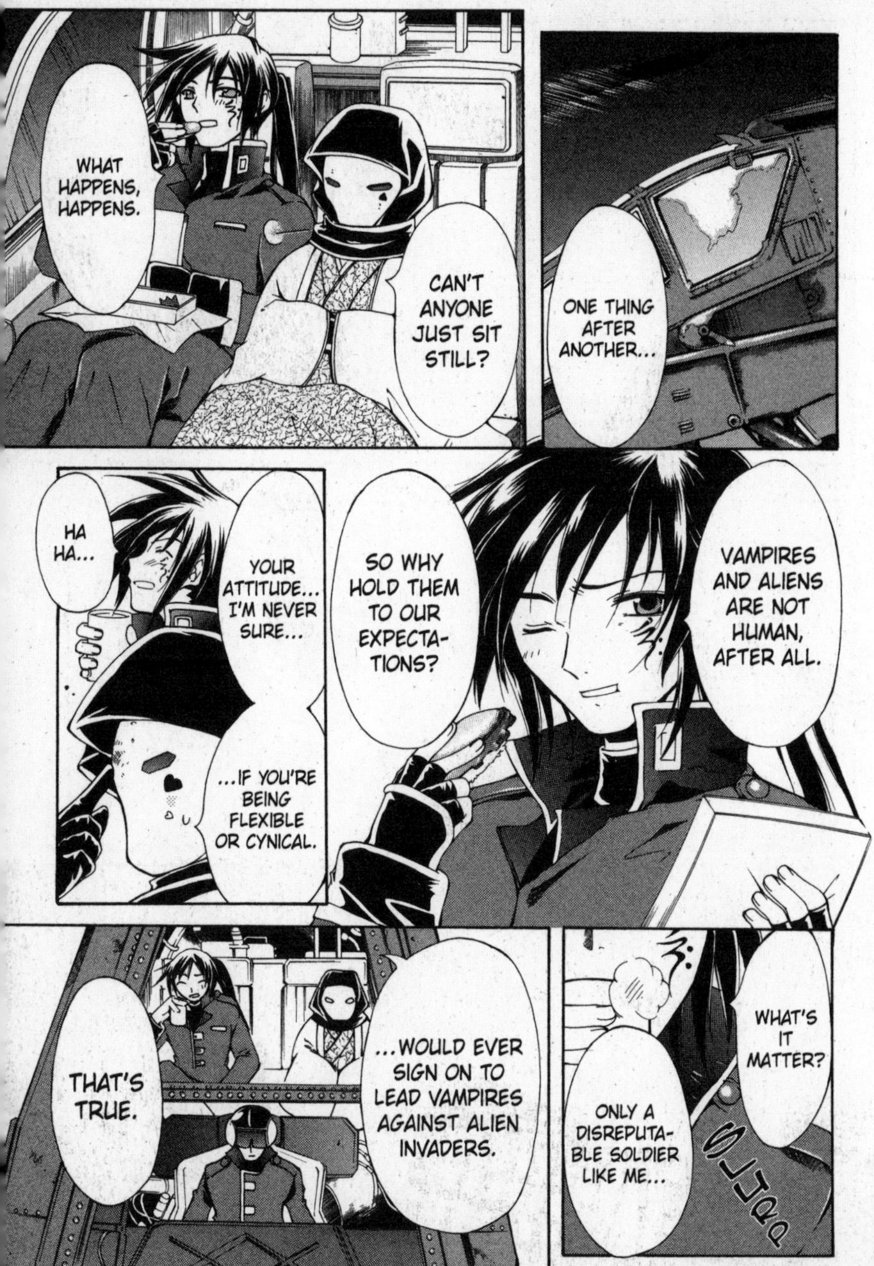
ONE THING AFTER ANOTHER...
CAN'T ANYONE JUST SIT STILL?
WHAT HAPPENS, HAPPENS.
VAMPIRES AND ALIENS ARE NOT HUMAN, AFTER ALL.
SO WHY HOLD THEM TO OUR EXPECTATIONS?
YOUR ATTITUDE... I'M NEVER SURE...
...IF YOU'RE BEING FLEXIBLE OR CYNICAL.
HA HA...
WHAT'S IT MATTER?
ONLY A DISREPUTABLE SOLDIER LIKE ME...
...WOULD EVER SIGN ON TO LEAD VAMPIRES AGAINST ALIEN INVADERS.
THAT'S TRUE.

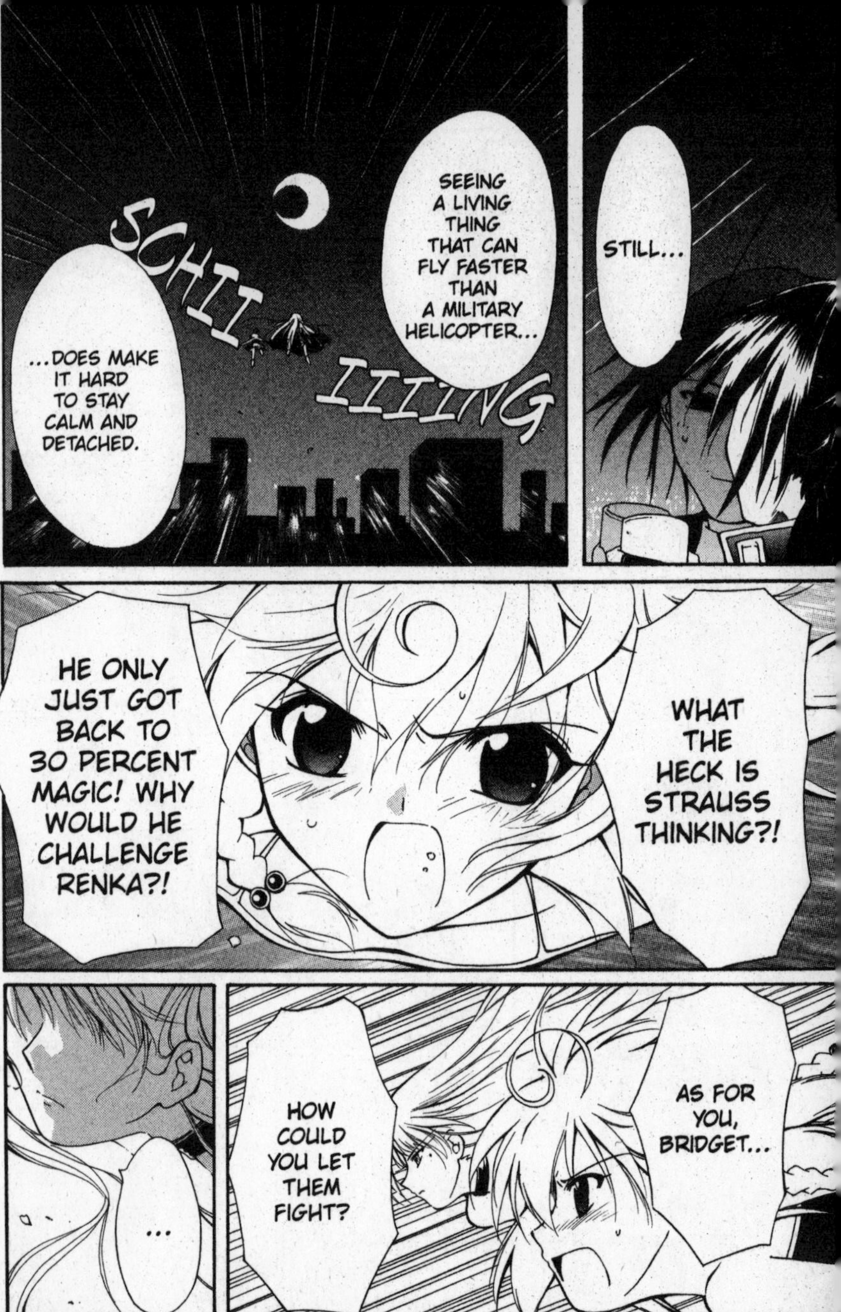
STILL...
SEEING A LIVING THING THAT CAN FLY FASTER THAN A MILITARY HELICOPTER...
SCHIIIIIIING
...DOES MAKE IT HARD TO STAY CALM AND DETACHED.
WHAT THE HECK IS STRAUSS THINKING?!
HE ONLY JUST GOT BACK TO 30 PERCENT MAGIC! WHY WOULD HE CHALLENGE RENKA?!
AS FOR YOU, BRIDGET...
HOW COULD YOU LET THEM FIGHT?
...

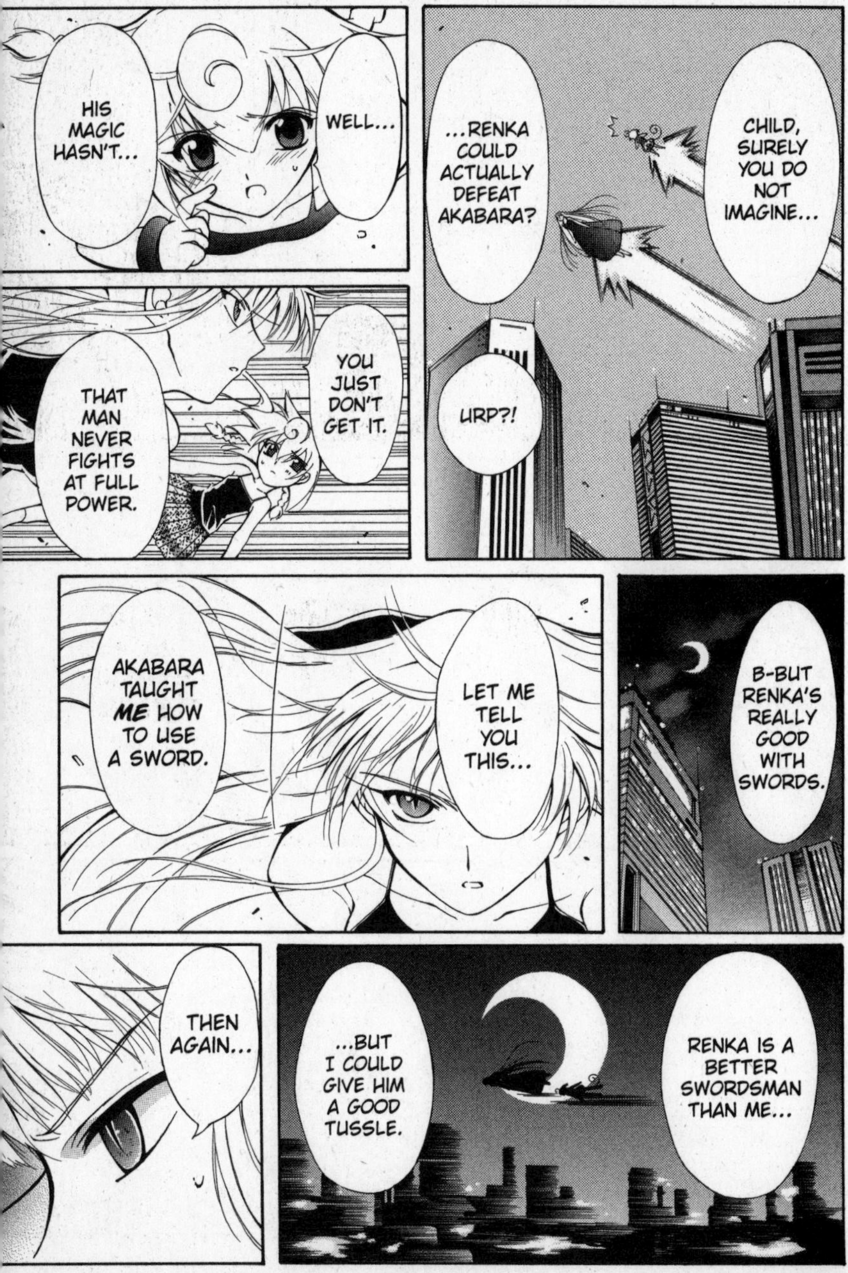
CHILD, SURELY YOU DO NOT IMAGINE...
...RENKA COULD ACTUALLY DEFEAT AKABARA?
URP?!
WELL...
HIS MAGIC HASN'T...
YOU JUST DON'T GET IT.
THAT MAN NEVER FIGHTS AT FULL POWER.
B-BUT RENKA'S REALLY GOOD WITH SWORDS.
LET ME TELL YOU THIS...
AKABARA TAUGHT *ME* HOW TO USE A SWORD.
RENKA IS A BETTER SWORDSMAN THAN ME...
...BUT I COULD GIVE HIM A GOOD TUSSLE.
THEN AGAIN...

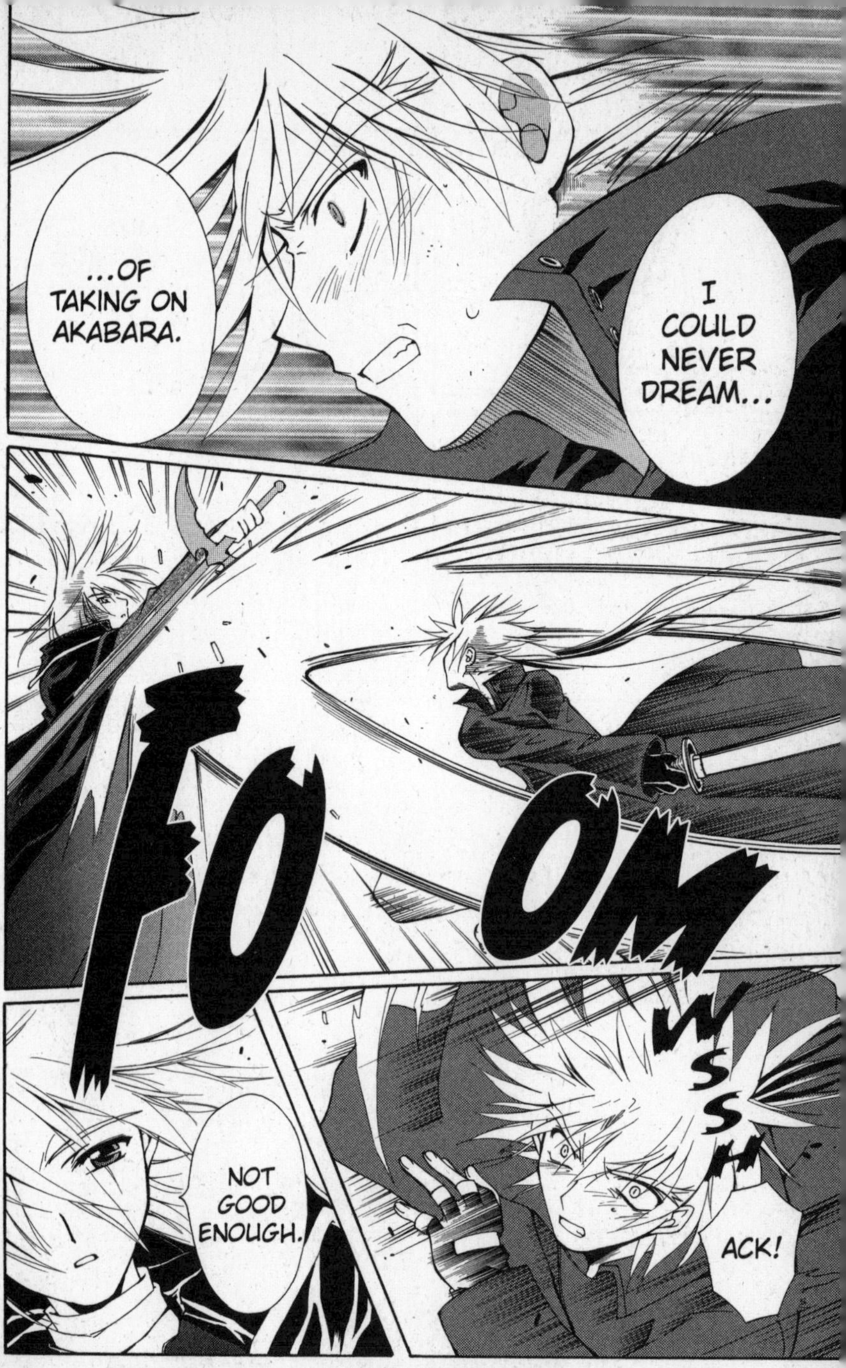
I COULD NEVER DREAM...
...OF TAKING ON AKABARA.
FOOM
WSSH
ACK!
NOT GOOD ENOUGH.

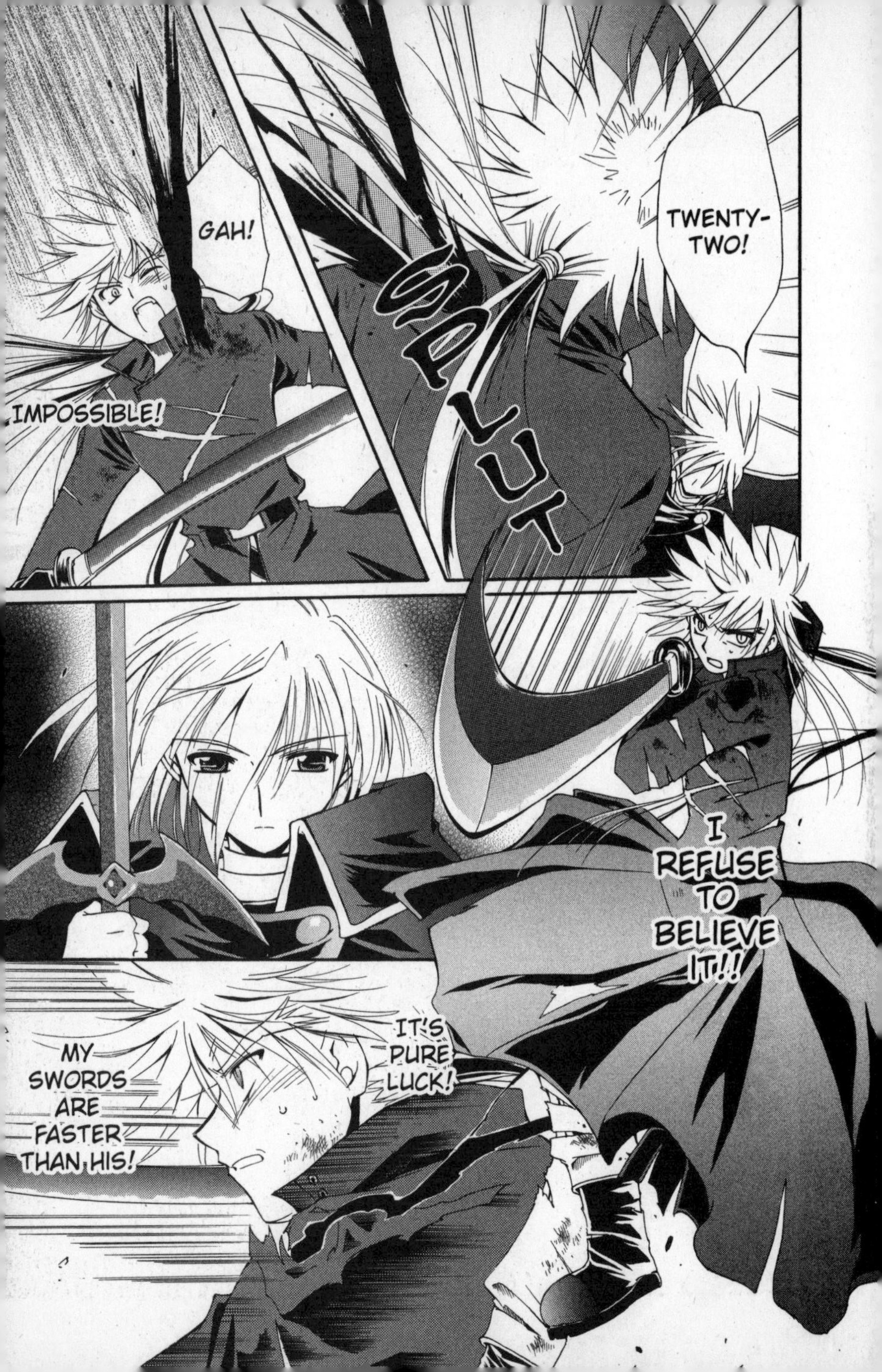
TWENTY-TWO!
SPLUT
GAH!
IMPOSSIBLE!
I REFUSE TO BELIEVE IT!!
IT'S PURE LUCK!
MY SWORDS ARE FASTER THAN HIS!

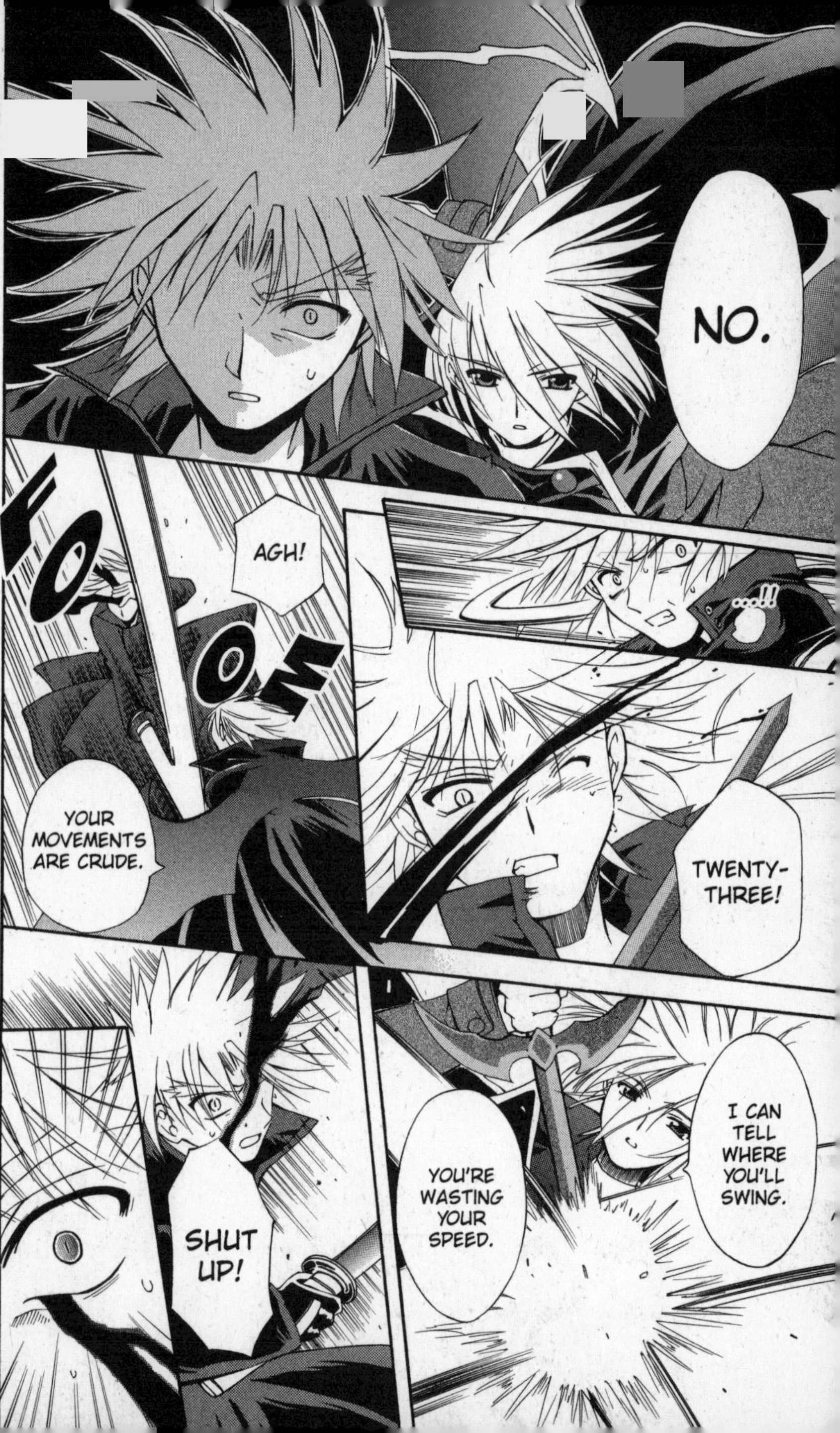
NO.
TWENTY-THREE!
AGH!
YOUR MOVEMENTS ARE CRUDE.
I CAN TELL WHERE YOU'LL SWING.
YOU'RE WASTING YOUR SPEED.
SHUT UP!

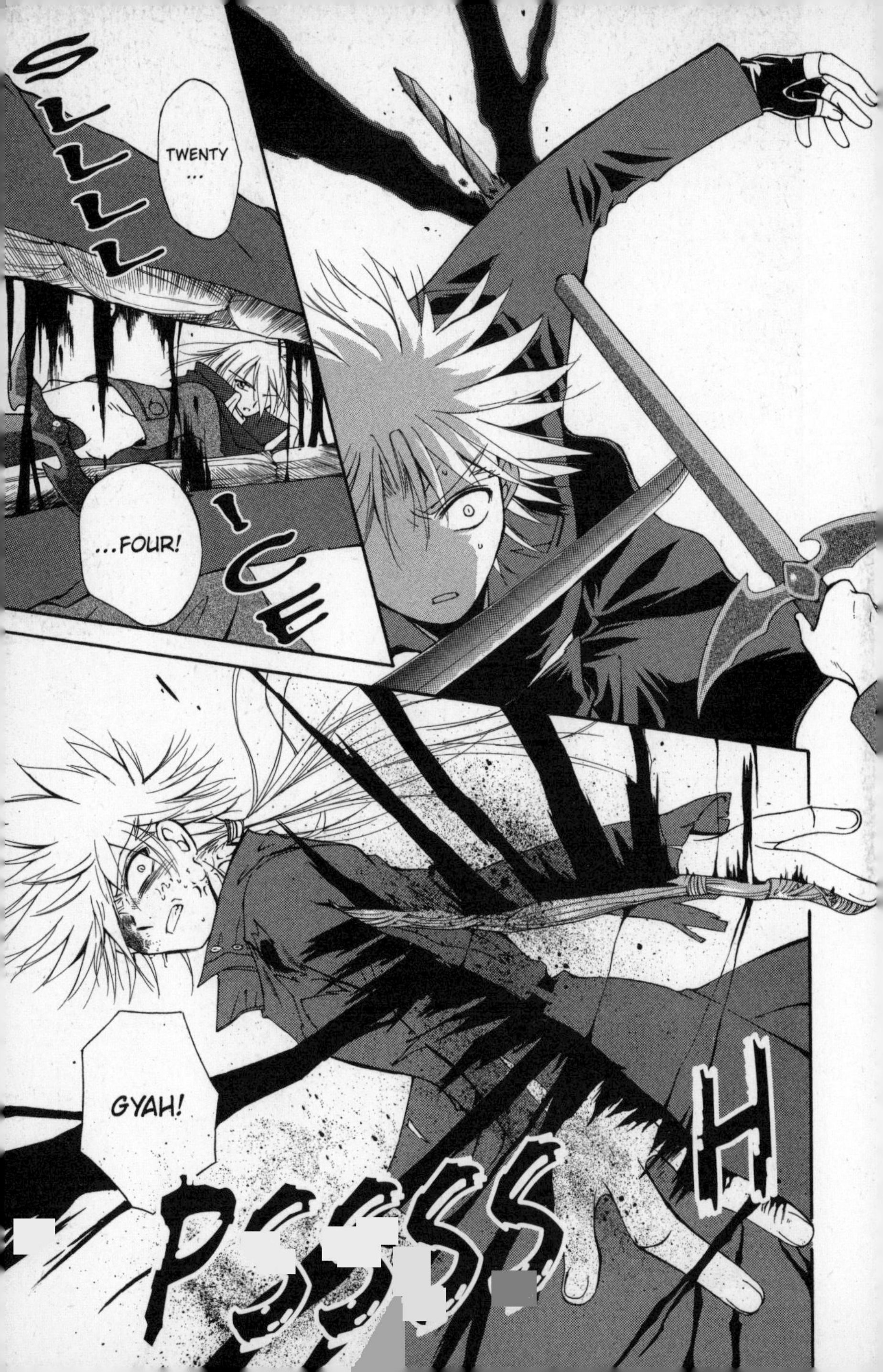
TWENTY ...
SLLLLICE
...FOUR!
GYAH!
PSSSSH

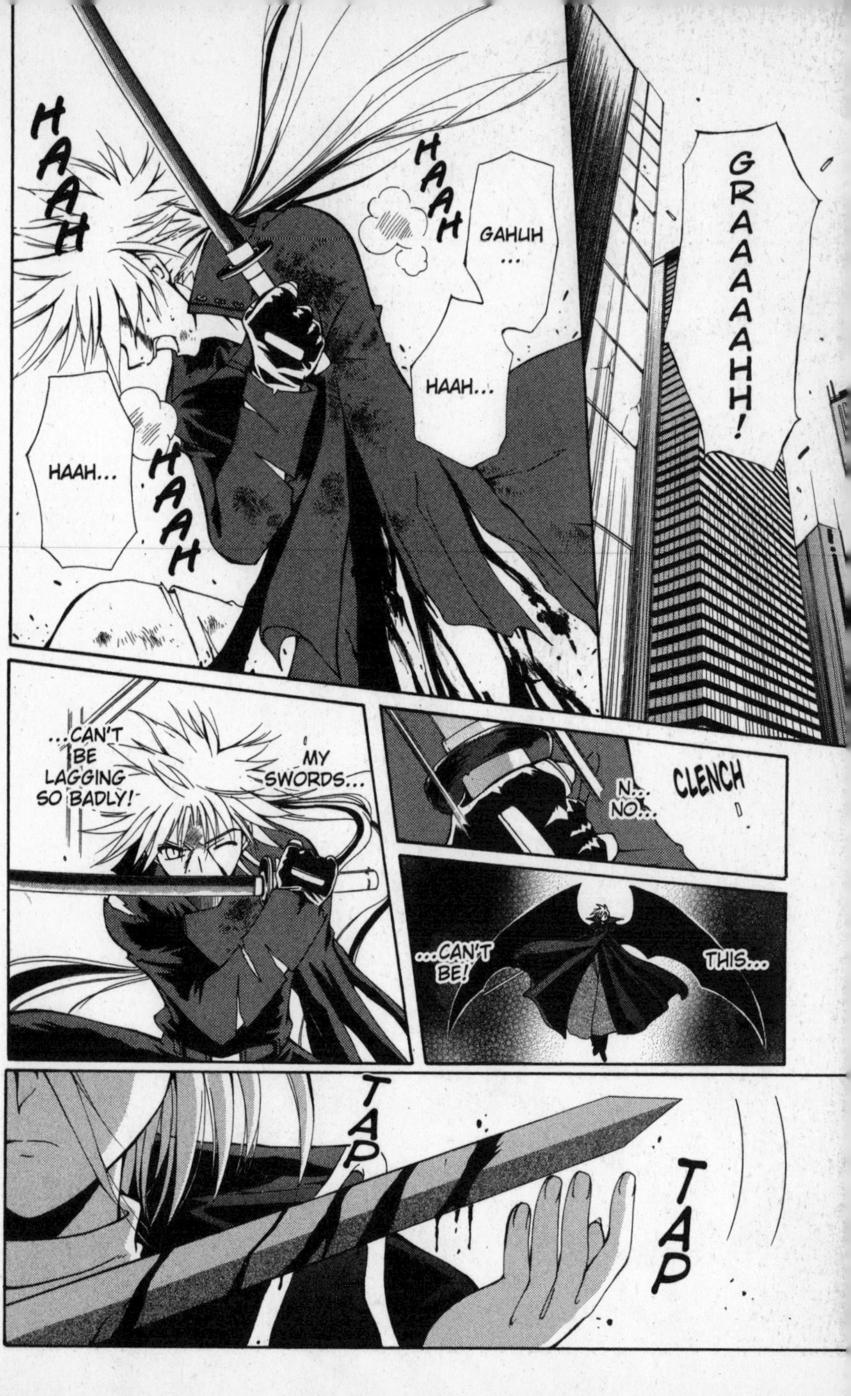
GRAAAAAAHH!
HAAH
GAHUH...
HAAH...
HAAH
HAAH...
HAAH
CLENCH
N... NO...
THIS...
...CAN'T BE!
MY SWORDS...
...CAN'T BE LAGGING SO BADLY!
TAP
TAP

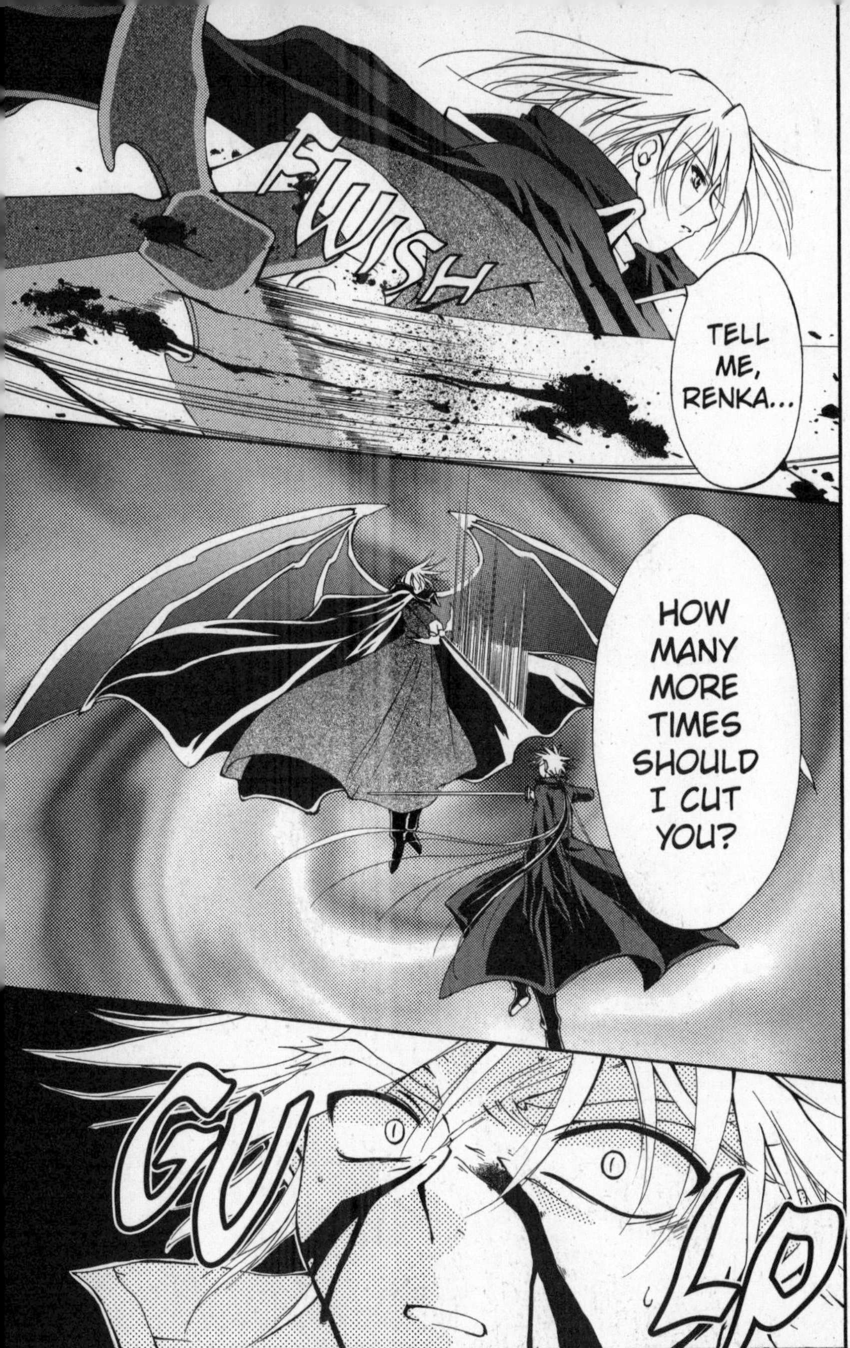
TELL ME, RENKA...
FWISH
HOW MANY MORE TIMES SHOULD I CUT YOU?
GULP

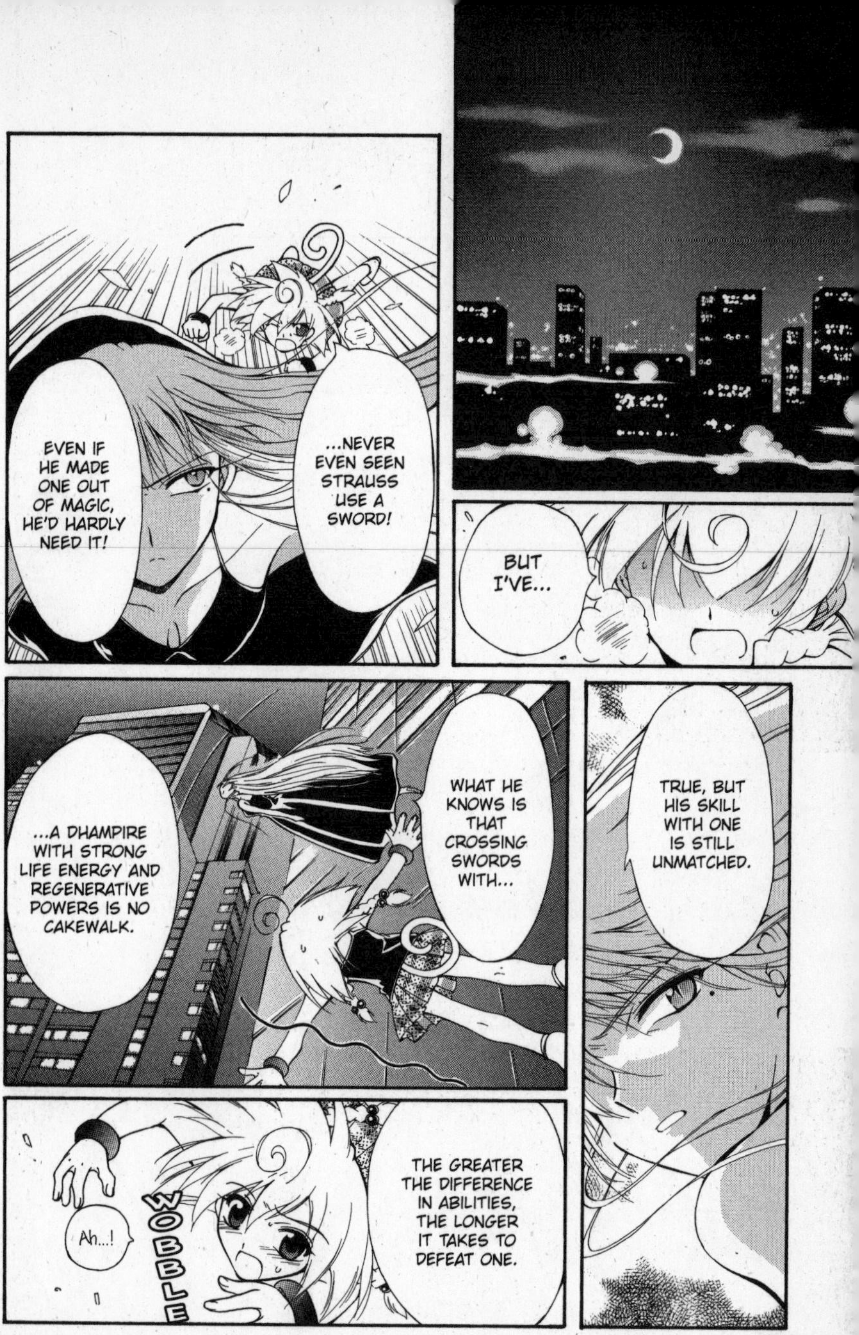
BUT I'VE...
...NEVER EVEN SEEN STRAUSS USE A SWORD!
EVEN IF HE MADE ONE OUT OF MAGIC, HE'D HARDLY NEED IT!
TRUE, BUT HIS SKILL WITH ONE IS STILL UNMATCHED.
WHAT HE KNOWS IS THAT CROSSING SWORDS WITH...
...A DHAMPIRE WITH STRONG LIFE ENERGY AND REGENERATIVE POWERS IS NO CAKEWALK.
THE GREATER THE DIFFERENCE IN ABILITIES, THE LONGER IT TAKES TO DEFEAT ONE.
WOBBLE
Ah...!

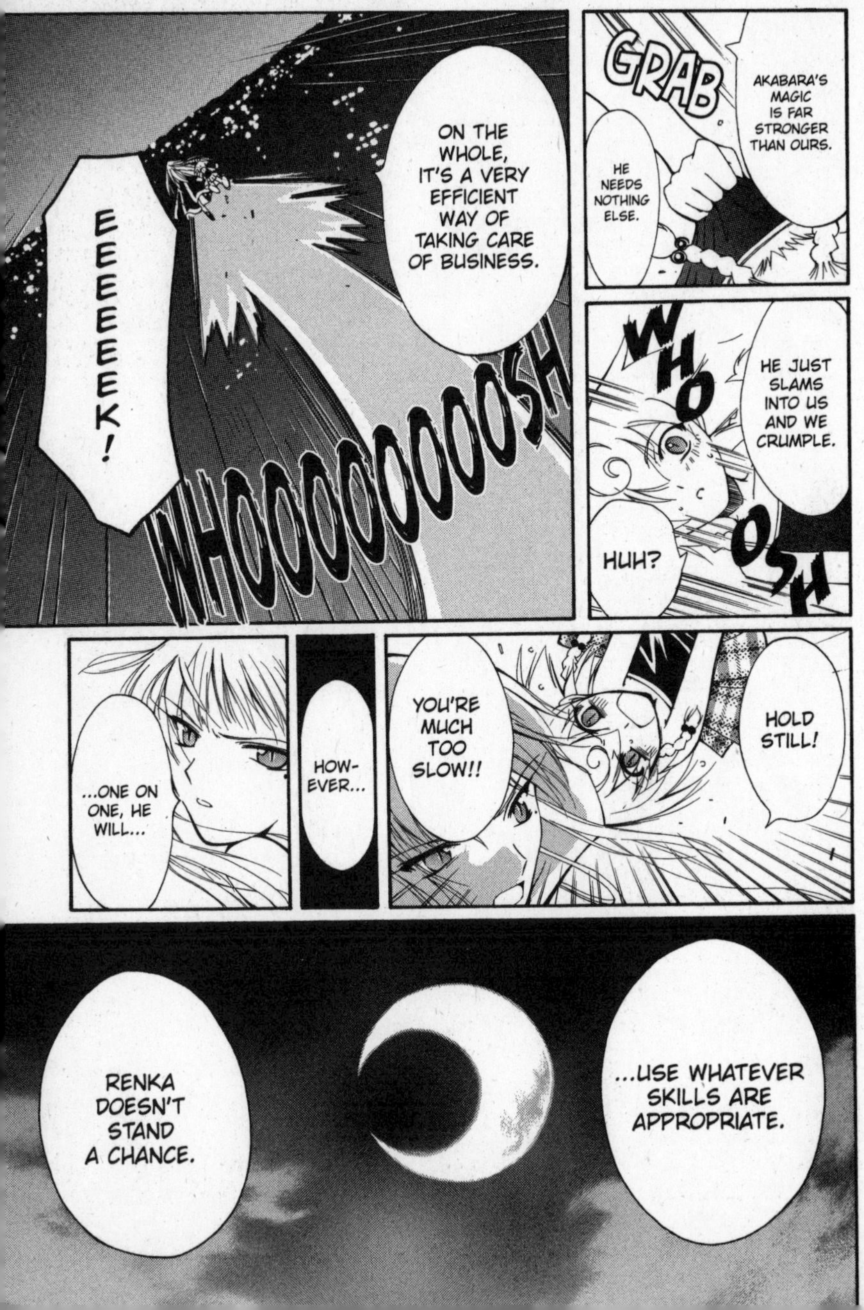
GRAB
AKABARA'S MAGIC IS FAR STRONGER THAN OURS.
HE NEEDS NOTHING ELSE.
WHOOOSH
HE JUST SLAMS INTO US AND WE CRUMPLE.
HUH?
ON THE WHOLE, IT'S A VERY EFFICIENT WAY OF TAKING CARE OF BUSINESS.
EEEEEEEK!
WHOOOOOOOOOSH
HOLD STILL!
YOU'RE MUCH TOO SLOW!!
HOW-EVER...
...ONE ON ONE, HE WILL...
...USE WHATEVER SKILLS ARE APPROPRIATE.
RENKA DOESN'T STAND A CHANCE.

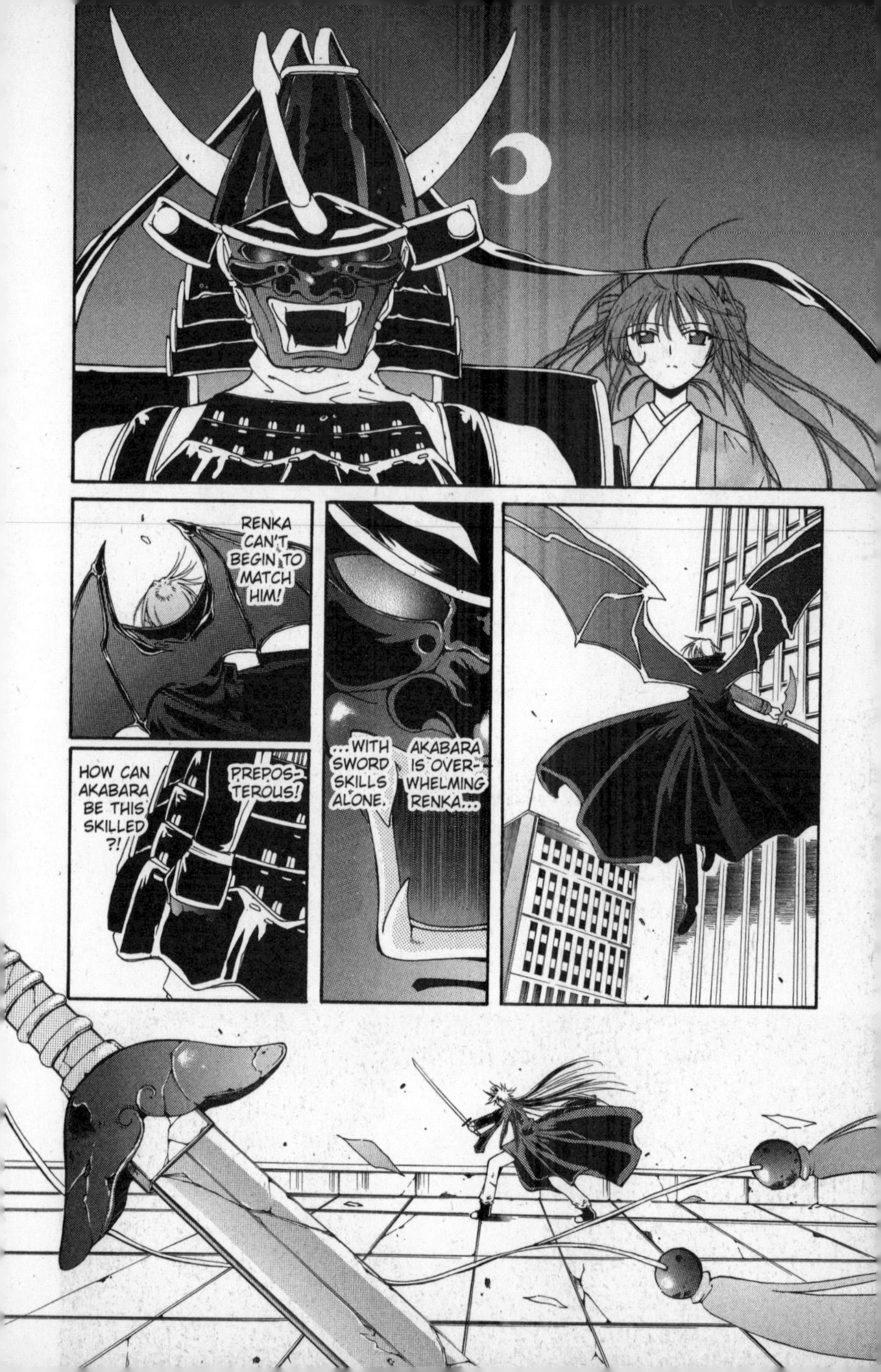
AKABARA IS OVER-WHELMING RENKA...
...WITH SWORD SKILLS ALONE.
RENKA CAN'T BEGIN TO MATCH HIM!
PREPOSTEROUS!
HOW CAN AKABARA BE THIS SKILLED?!

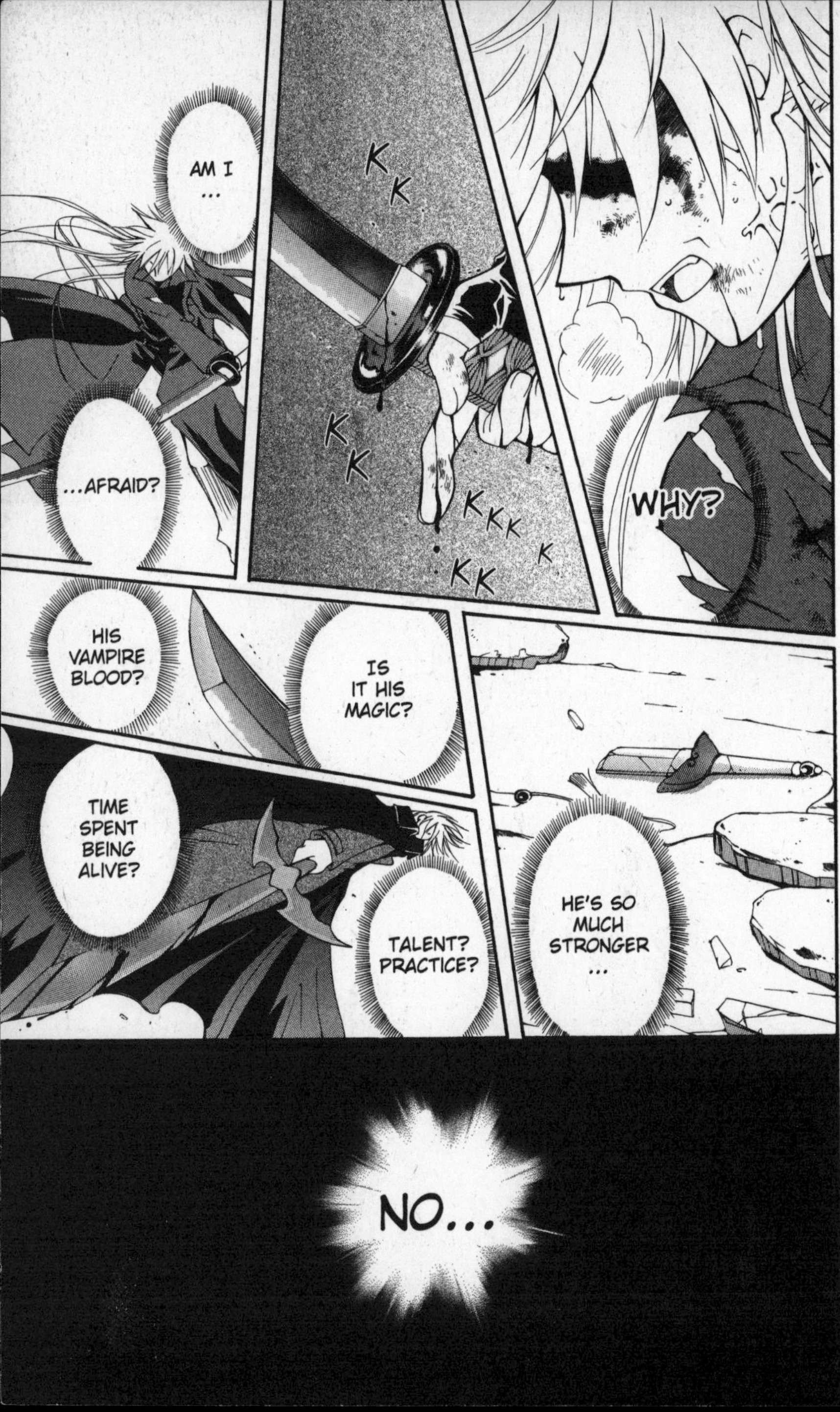
WHY?
KK
KK
KKKK
KK
AM I ...
...AFRAID?
HE'S SO MUCH STRONGER ...
IS IT HIS MAGIC?
HIS VAMPIRE BLOOD?
TALENT? PRACTICE?
TIME SPENT BEING ALIVE?
NO...

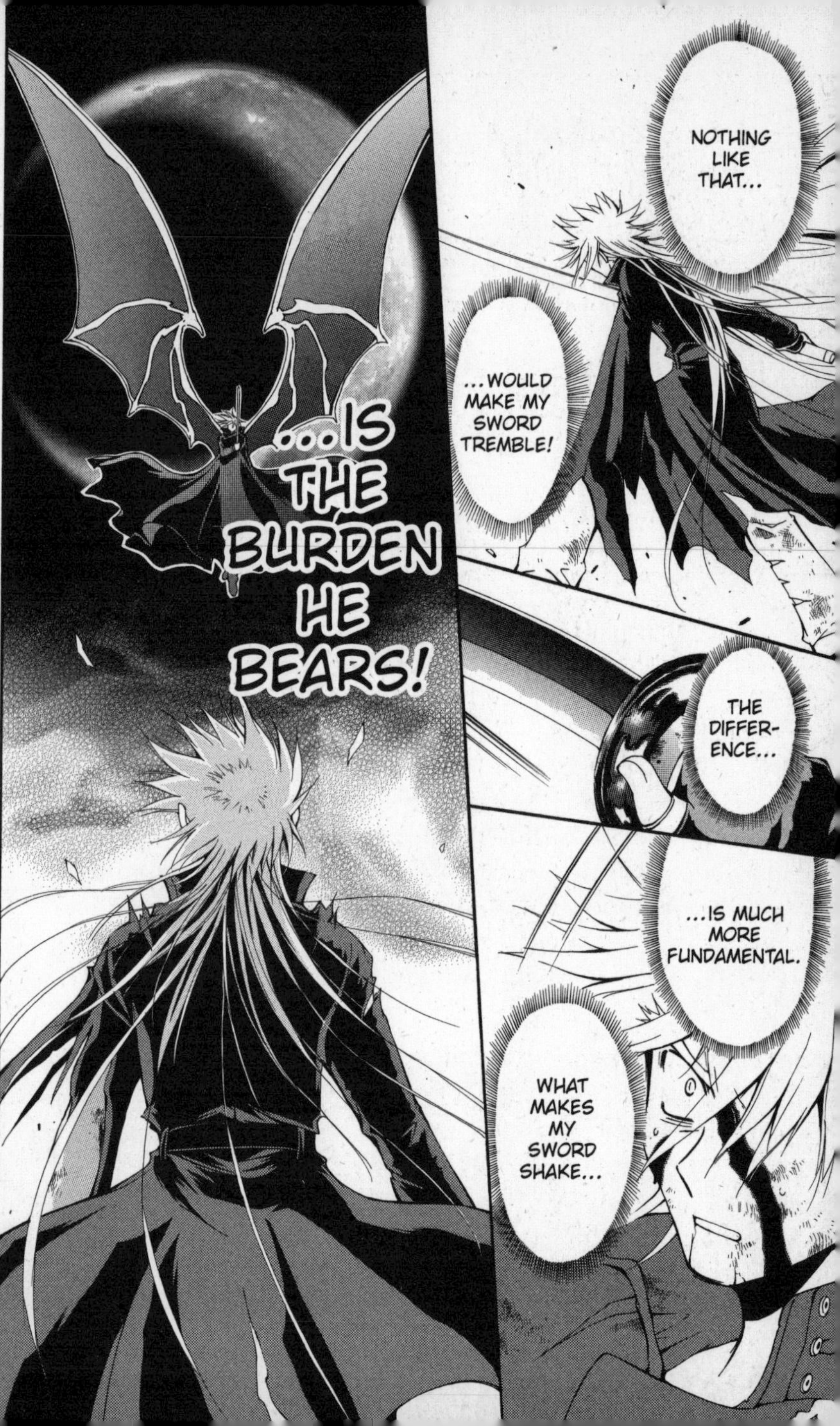
NOTHING LIKE THAT...
...WOULD MAKE MY SWORD TREMBLE!
THE DIFFER-ENCE...
...IS MUCH MORE FUNDAMENTAL.
WHAT MAKES MY SWORD SHAKE...
...IS THE BURDEN HE BEARS!

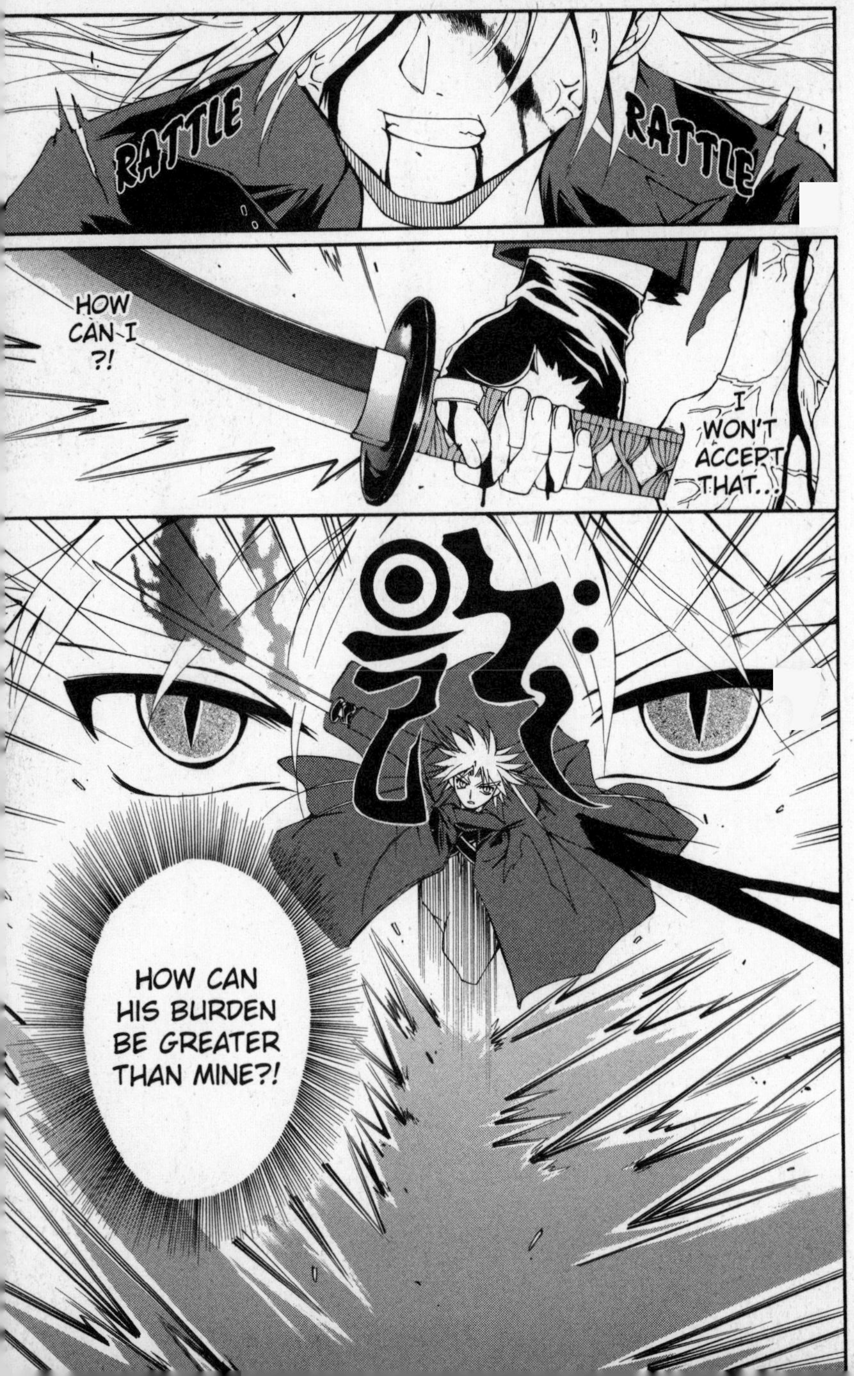
RATTLE
RATTLE
I WON'T ACCEPT THAT...
HOW CAN I ?!
HOW CAN HIS BURDEN BE GREATER THAN MINE?!

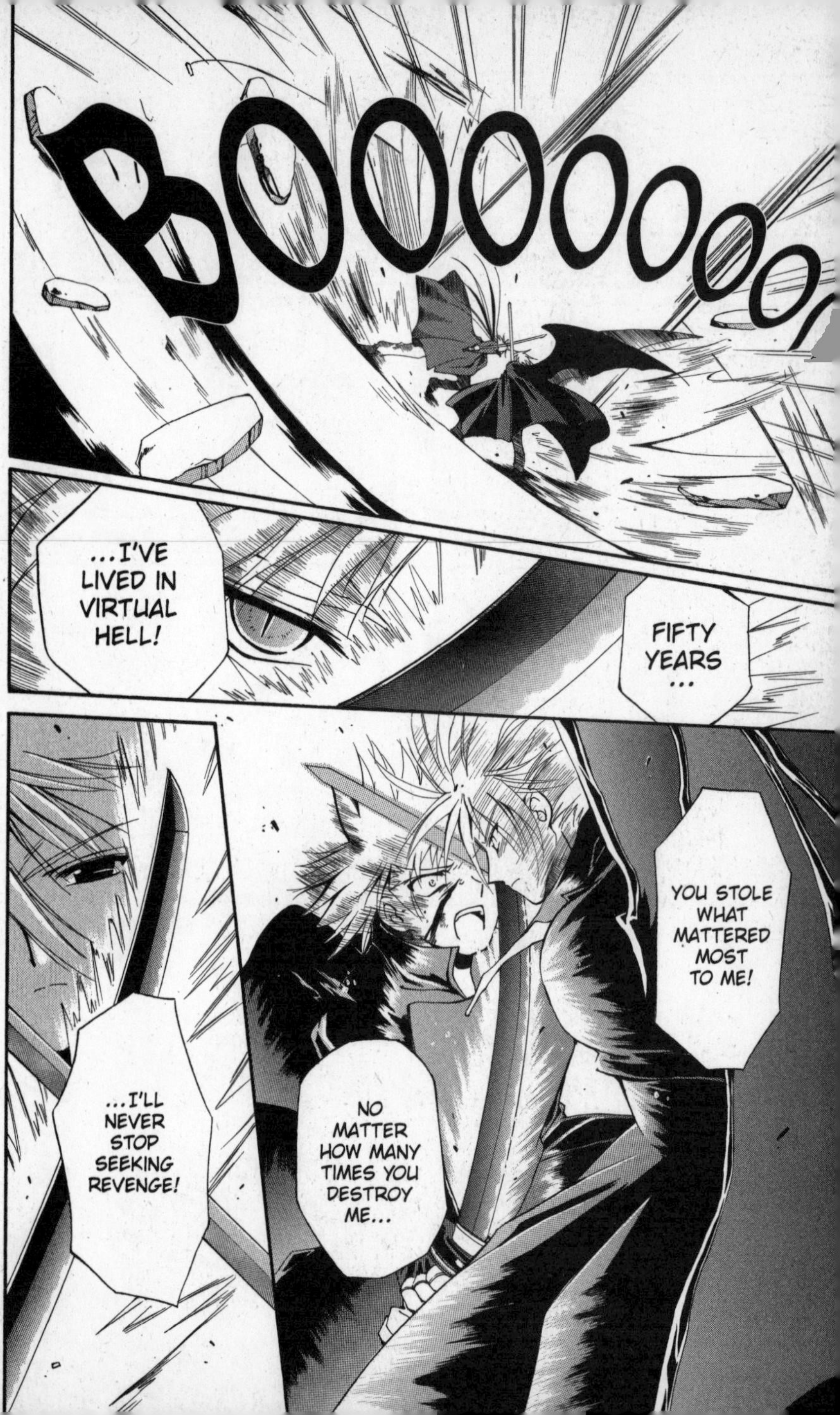
BOOOOOOO
FIFTY YEARS...
...I'VE LIVED IN VIRTUAL HELL!
YOU STOLE WHAT MATTERED MOST TO ME!
NO MATTER HOW MANY TIMES YOU DESTROY ME...
...I'LL NEVER STOP SEEKING REVENGE!

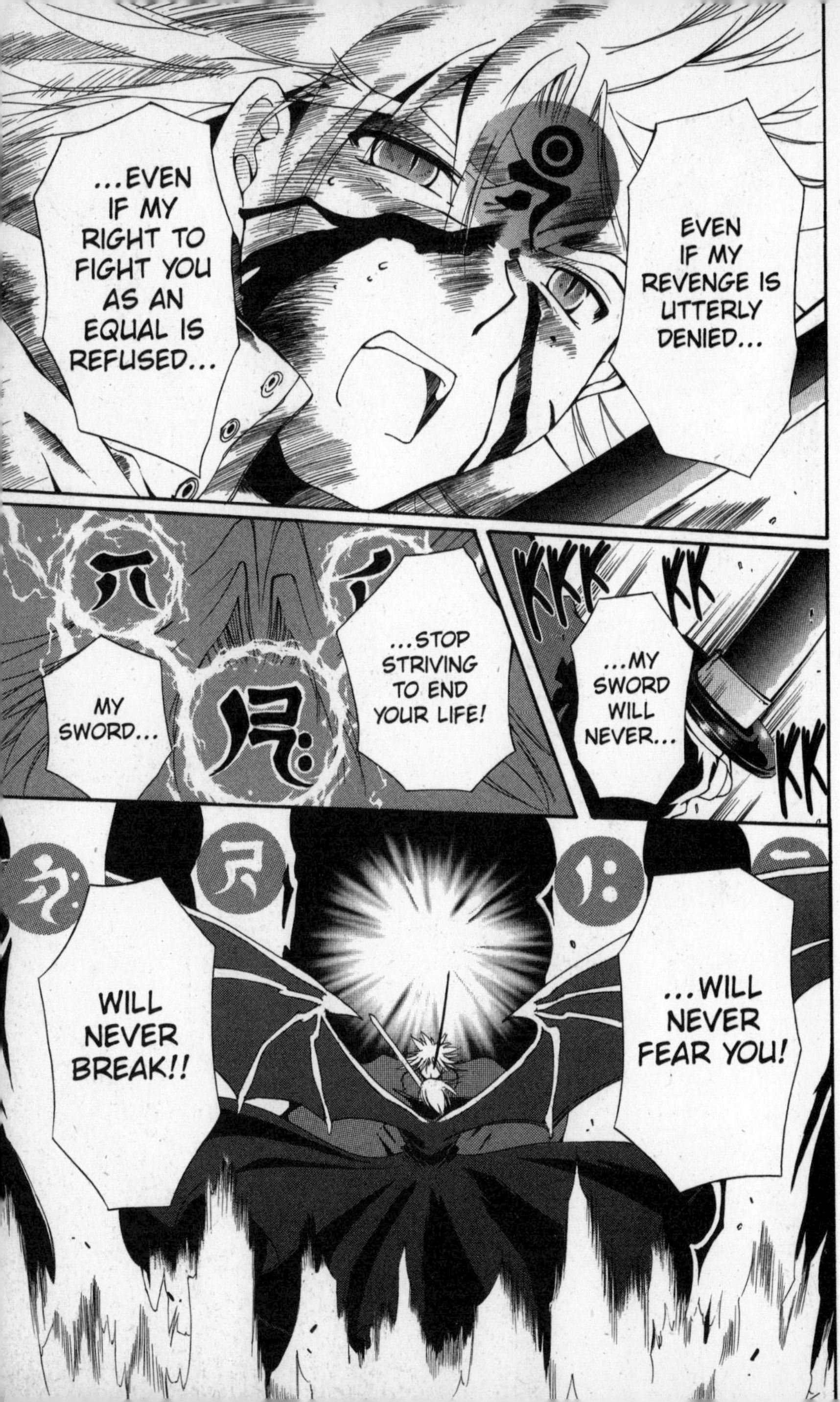
EVEN IF MY REVENGE IS UTTERLY DENIED...
...EVEN IF MY RIGHT TO FIGHT YOU AS AN EQUAL IS REFUSED...
KKK KK
...MY SWORD WILL NEVER...
KK
...STOP STRIVING TO END YOUR LIFE!
MY SWORD...
...WILL NEVER FEAR YOU!
WILL NEVER BREAK!!

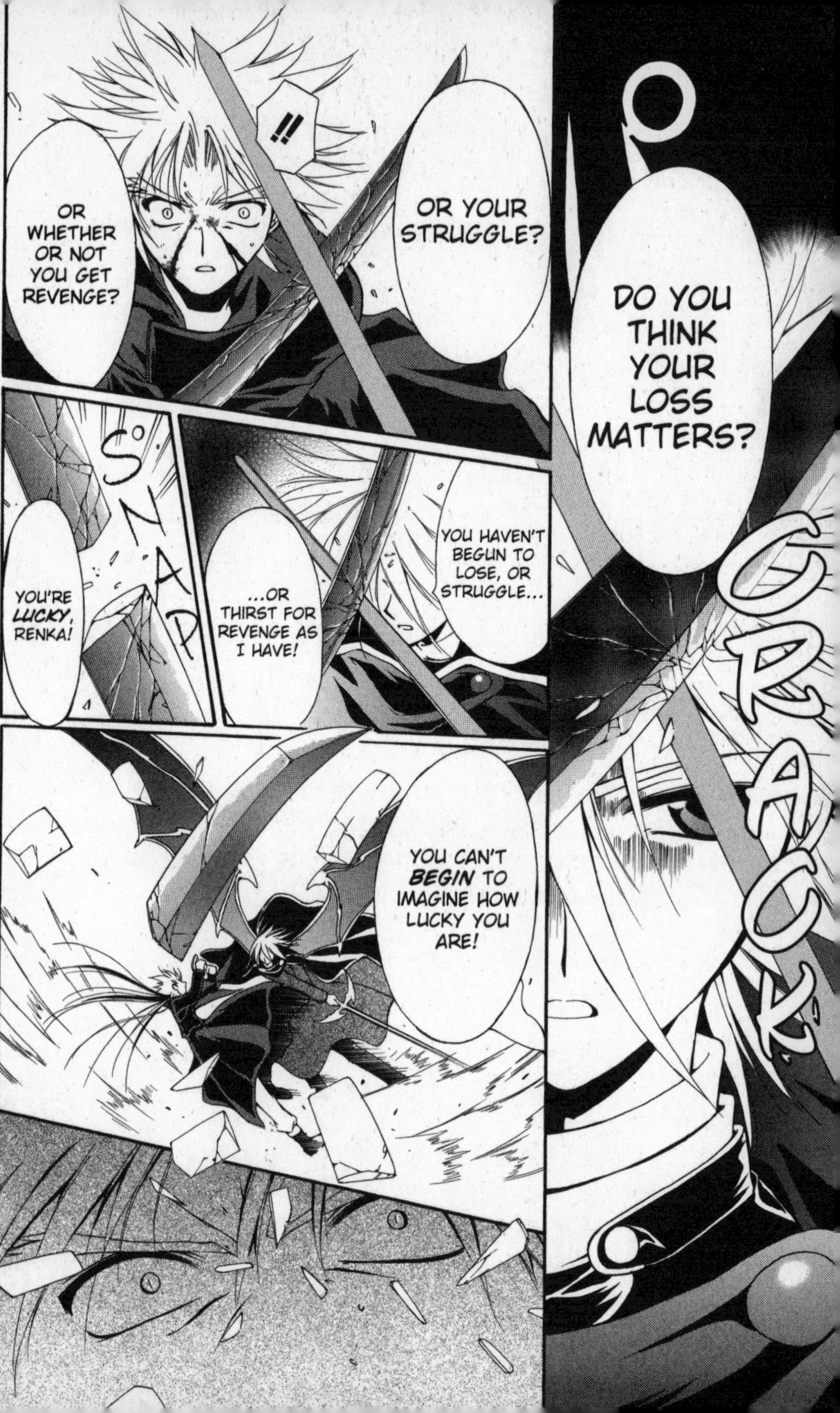
DO YOU THINK YOUR LOSS MATTERS?
CRACK
OR YOUR STRUGGLE?
!!
OR WHETHER OR NOT YOU GET REVENGE?
YOU HAVEN'T BEGUN TO LOSE, OR STRUGGLE...
...OR THIRST FOR REVENGE AS I HAVE!
SNAP
YOU'RE *LUCKY*, RENKA!
YOU CAN'T *BEGIN* TO IMAGINE HOW LUCKY YOU ARE!

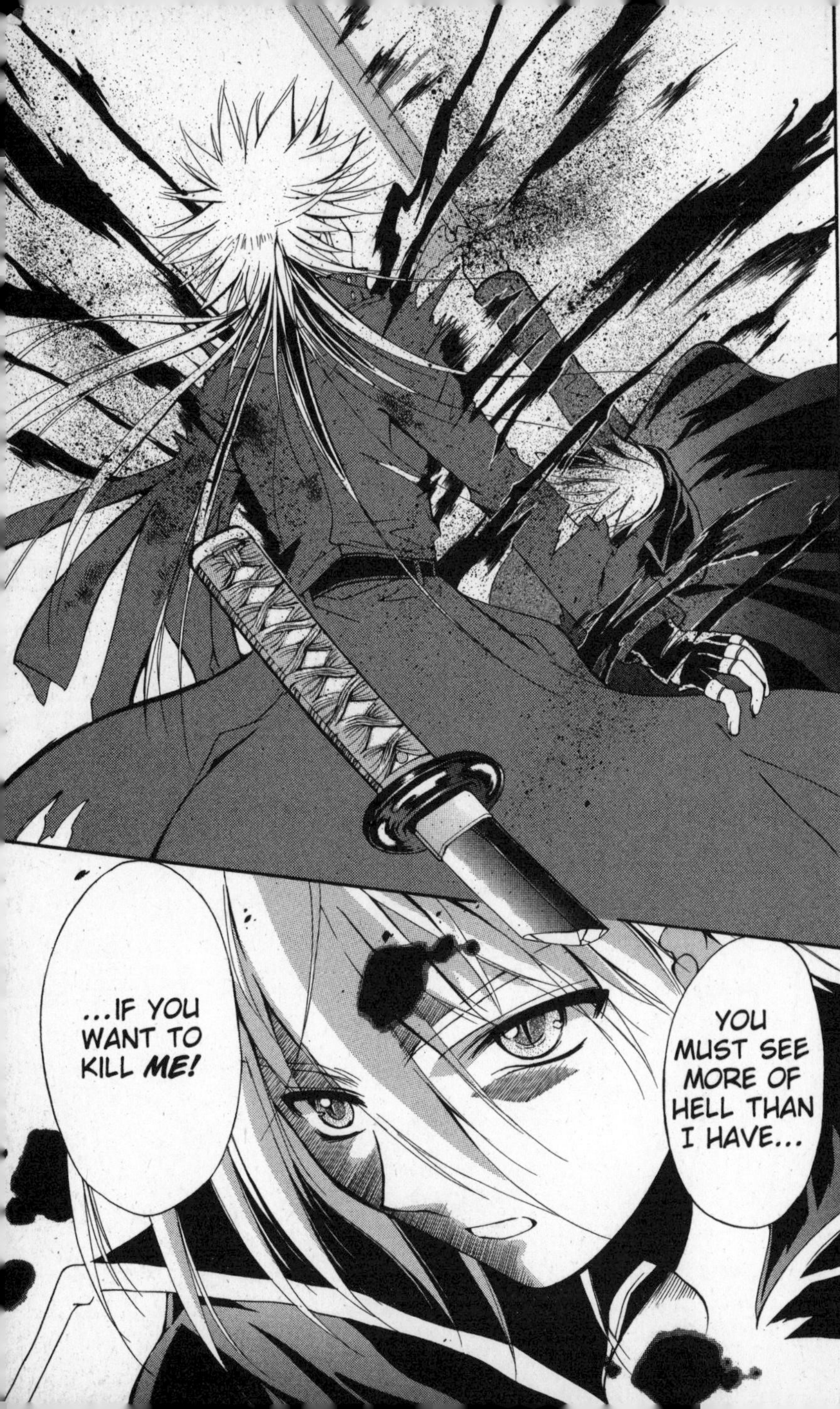
YOU MUST SEE MORE OF HELL THAN I HAVE...
...IF YOU WANT TO KILL *ME!*

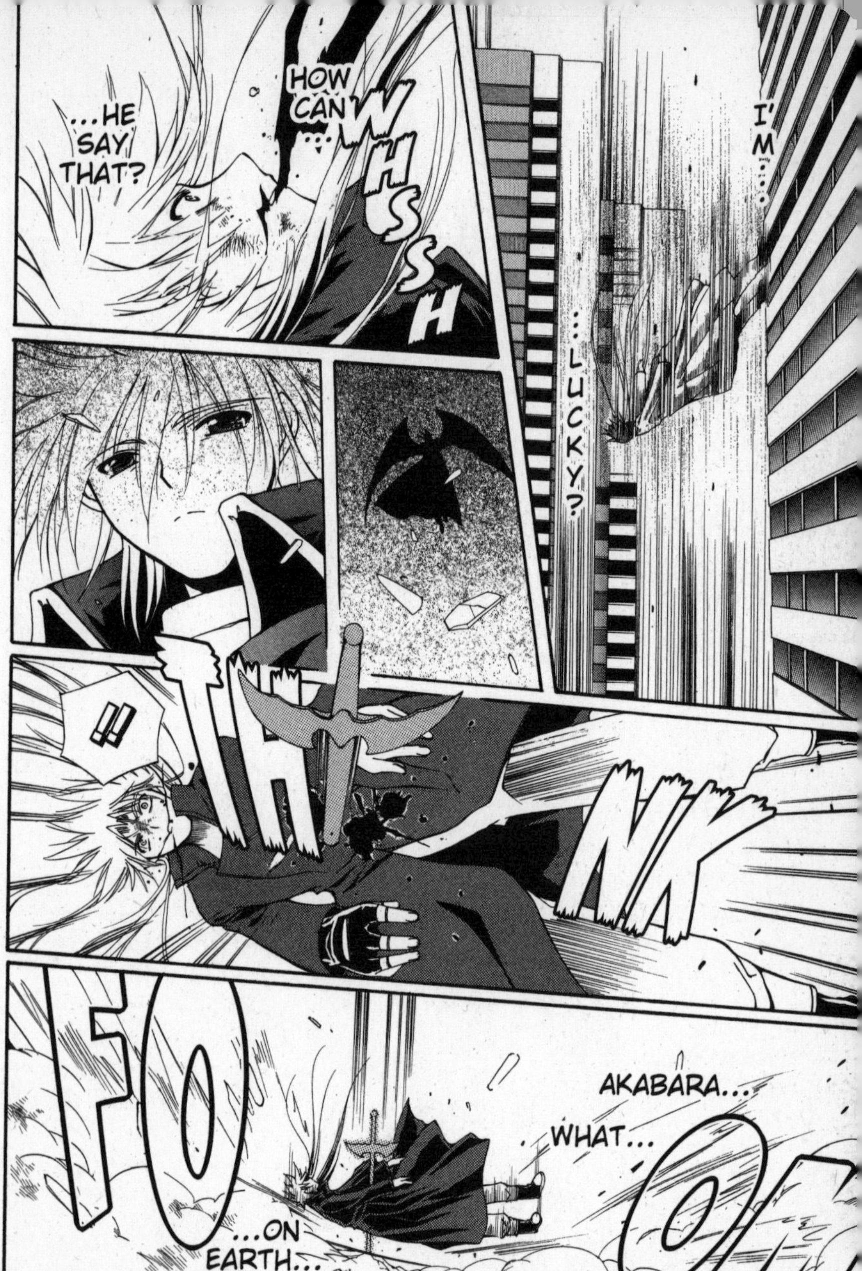
I'M...
...LUCKY?
HOW CAN...
...HE SAY THAT?
WHSSH
THNK
!!
FOOM
AKABARA...
WHAT...
...ON EARTH...

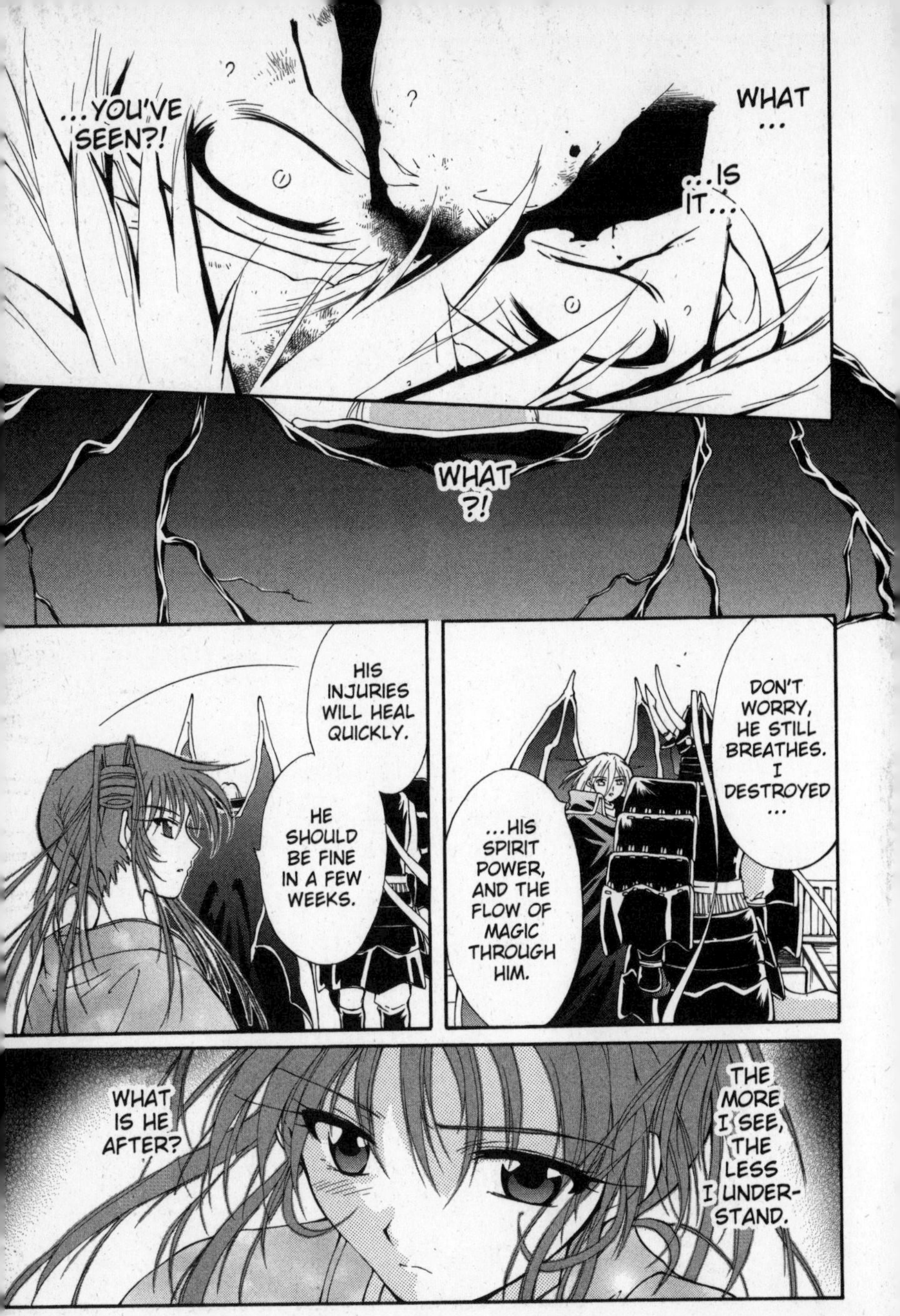
WHAT ...
...IS IT...
...YOU'VE SEEN?!
WHAT?!
DON'T WORRY, HE STILL BREATHES. I DESTROYED ...
...HIS SPIRIT POWER, AND THE FLOW OF MAGIC THROUGH HIM.
HIS INJURIES WILL HEAL QUICKLY.
HE SHOULD BE FINE IN A FEW WEEKS.
THE MORE I SEE, THE LESS I UNDER-STAND.
WHAT IS HE AFTER?

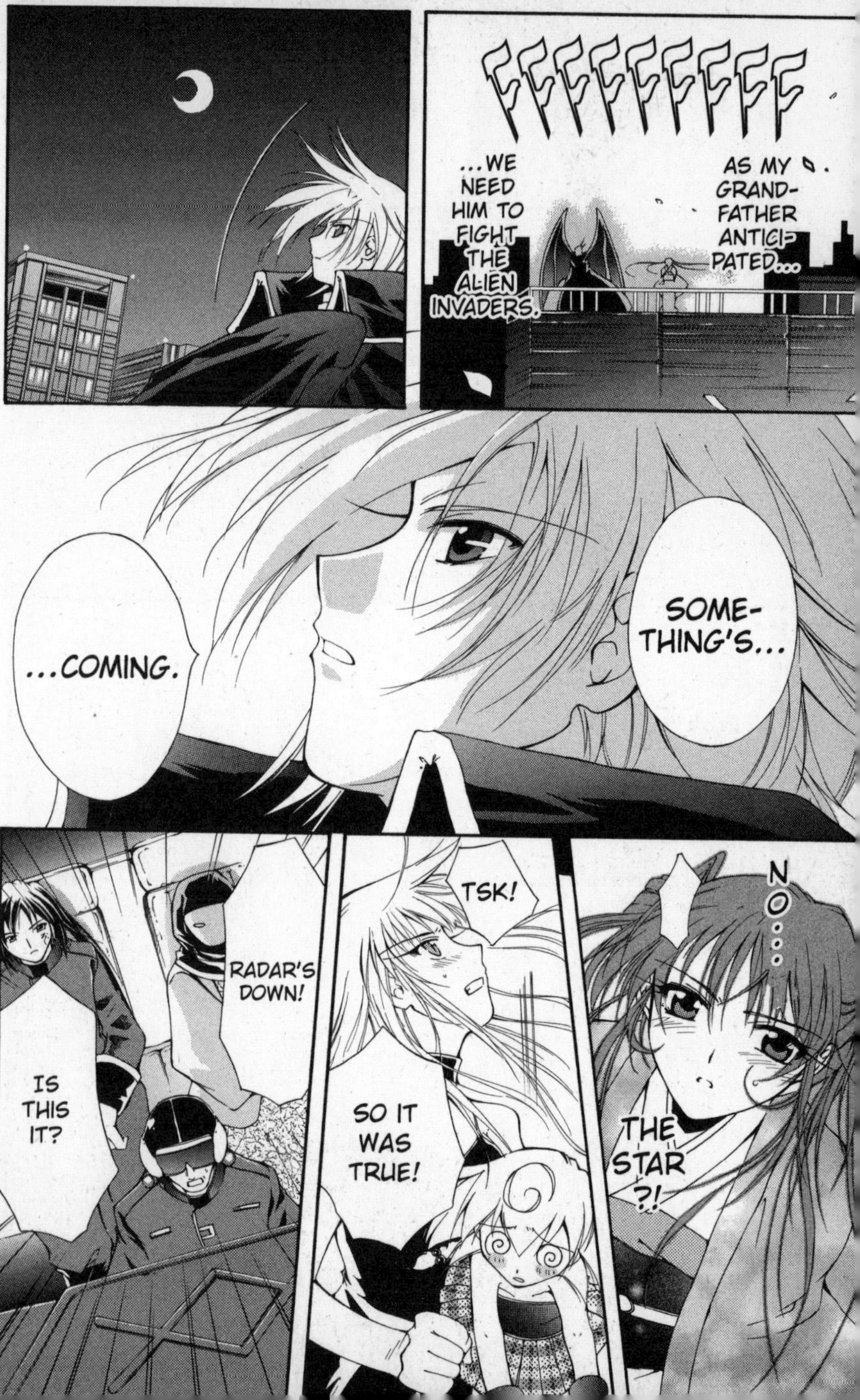
FFFFFFFFFFFF
AS MY GRAND-FATHER ANTICI-PATED...
...WE NEED HIM TO FIGHT THE ALIEN INVADERS.
SOME-THING'S...
...COMING.
NO...
THE STAR?!
TSK!
SO IT WAS TRUE!
RADAR'S DOWN!
IS THIS IT?

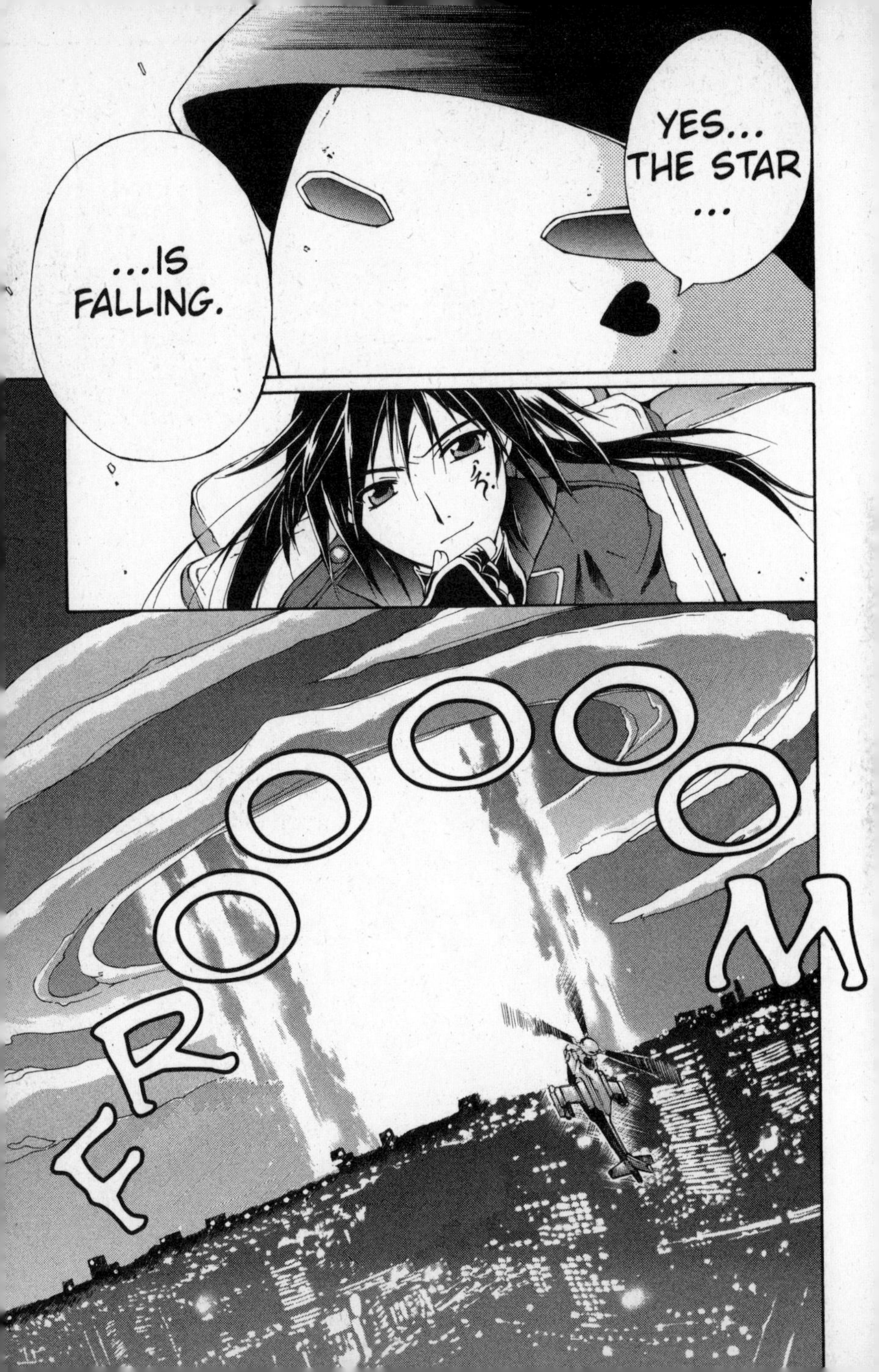
YES... THE STAR ...
...IS FALLING.
FROOOOOM

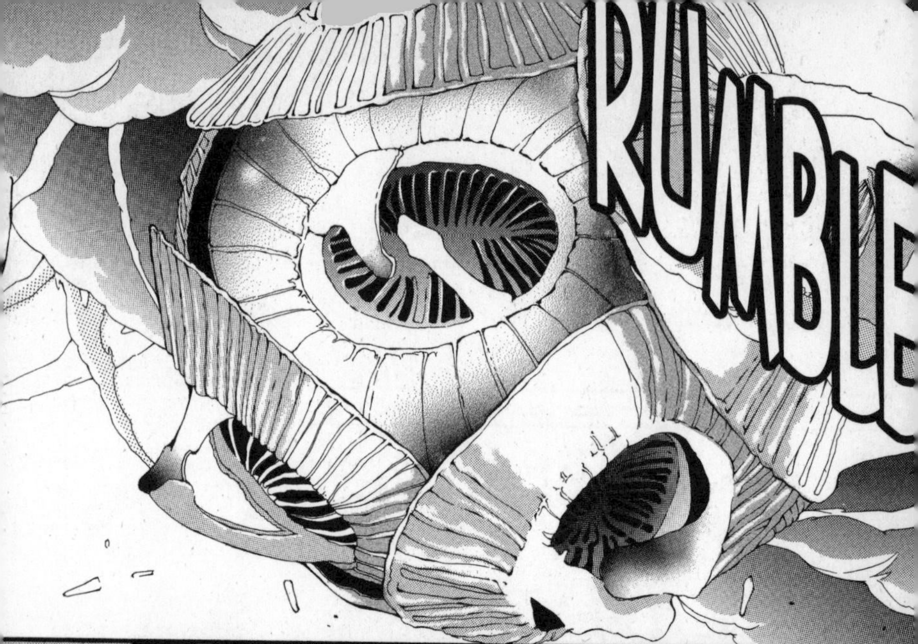
RUMBLE
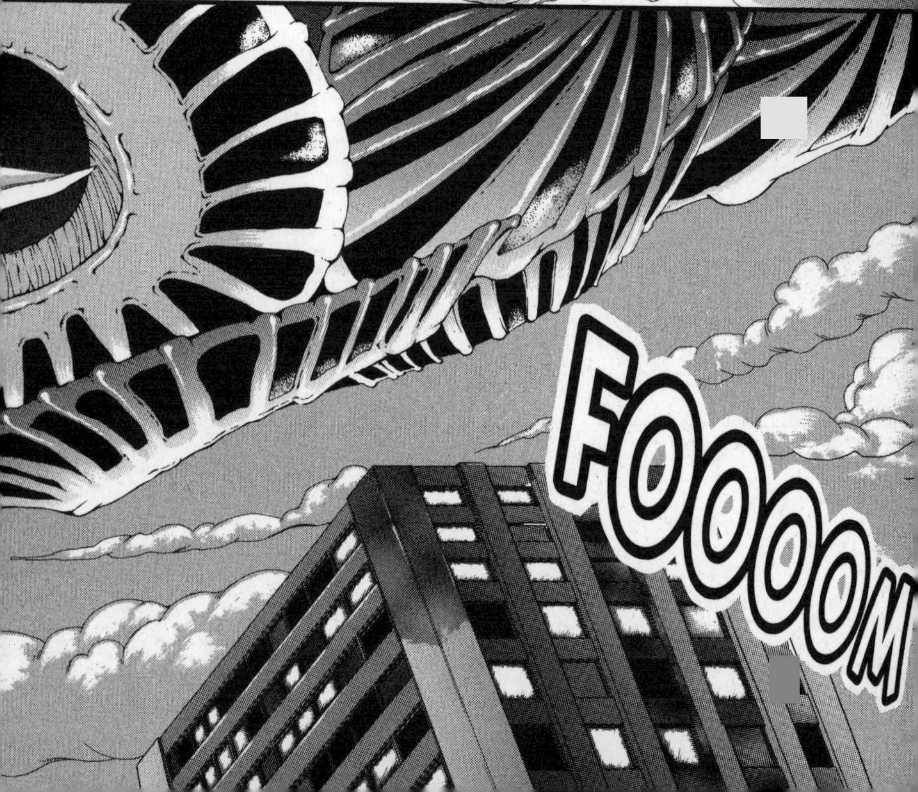
FOOOOOM

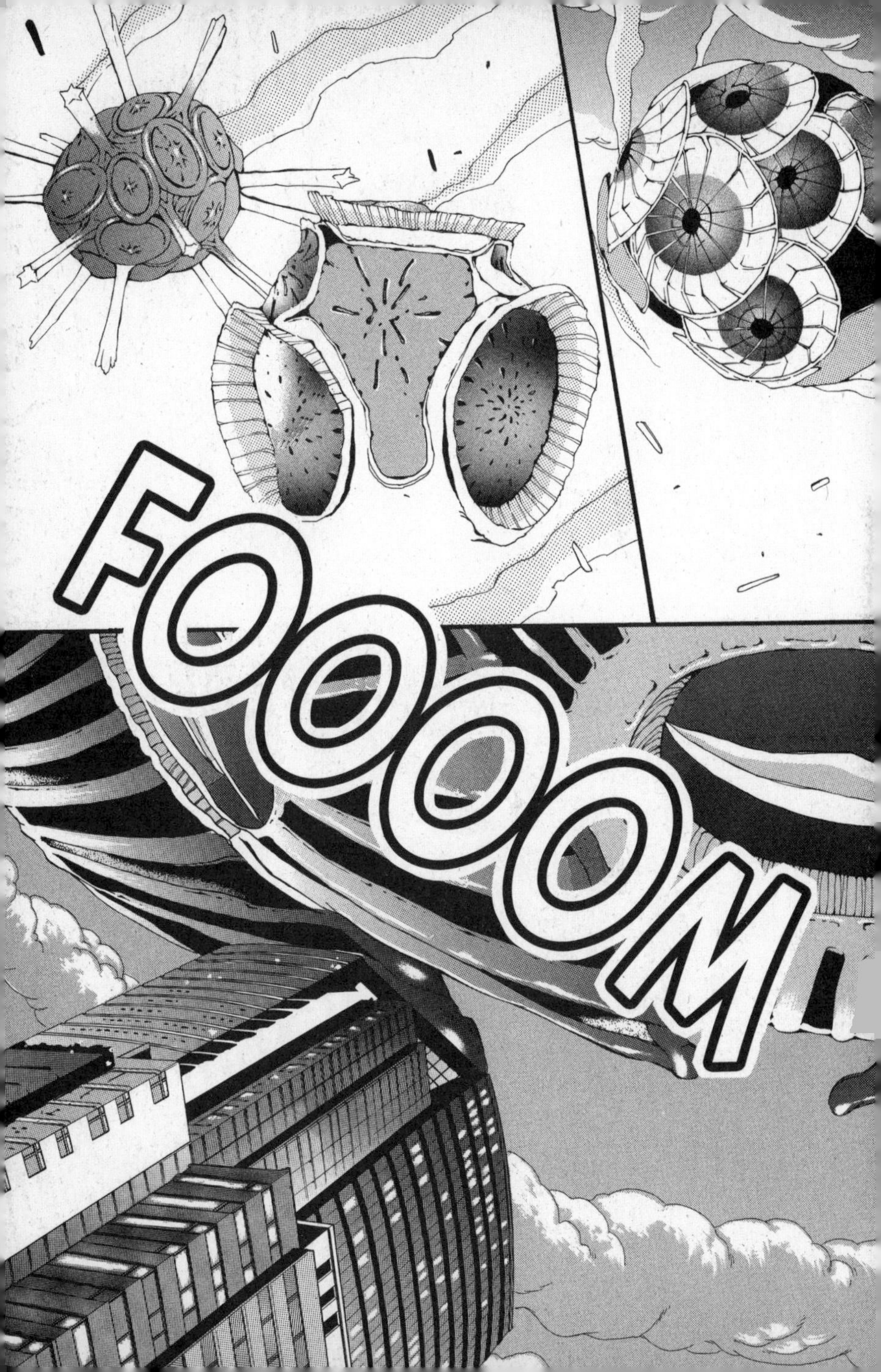
FOOOOOM

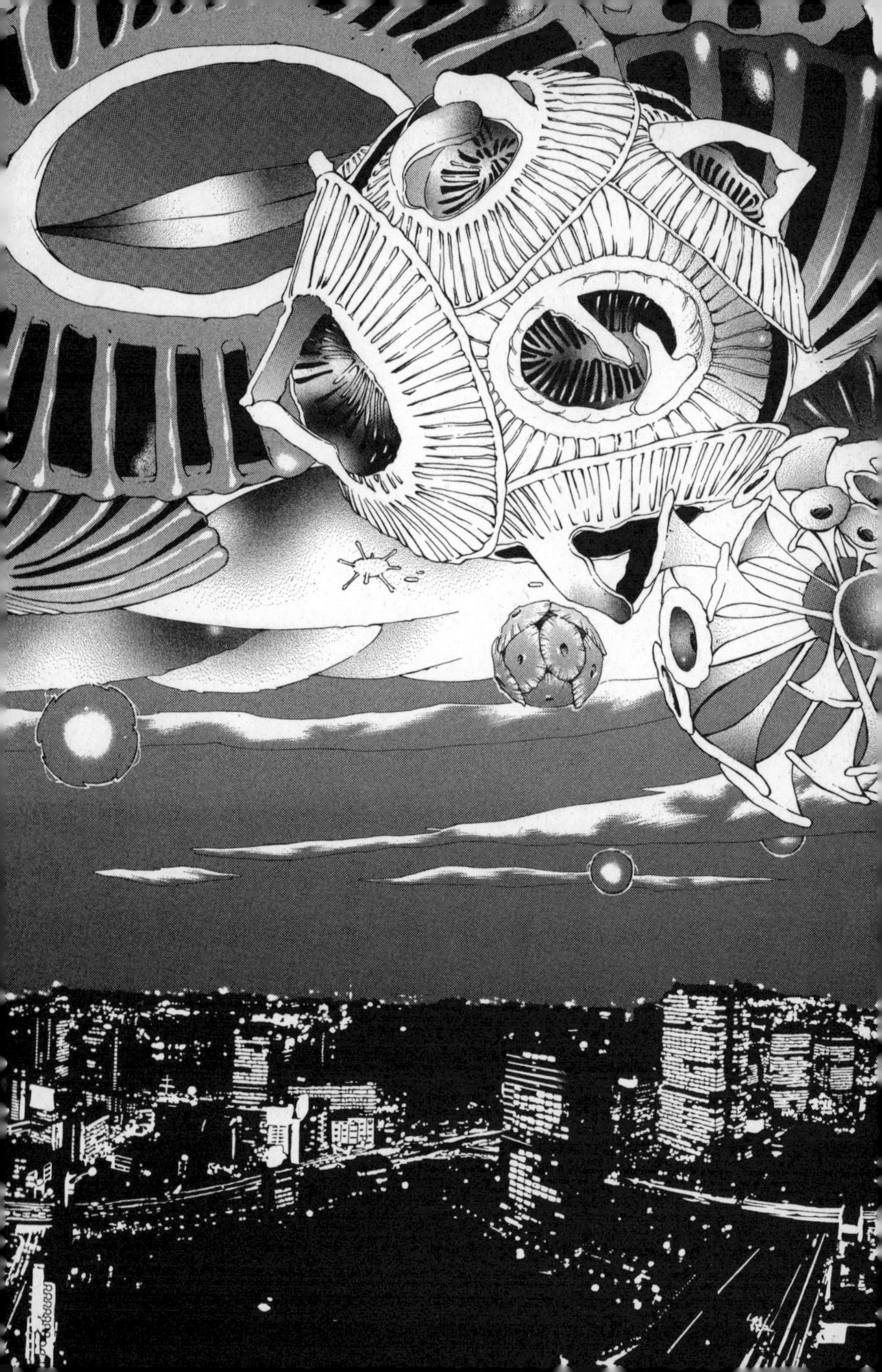

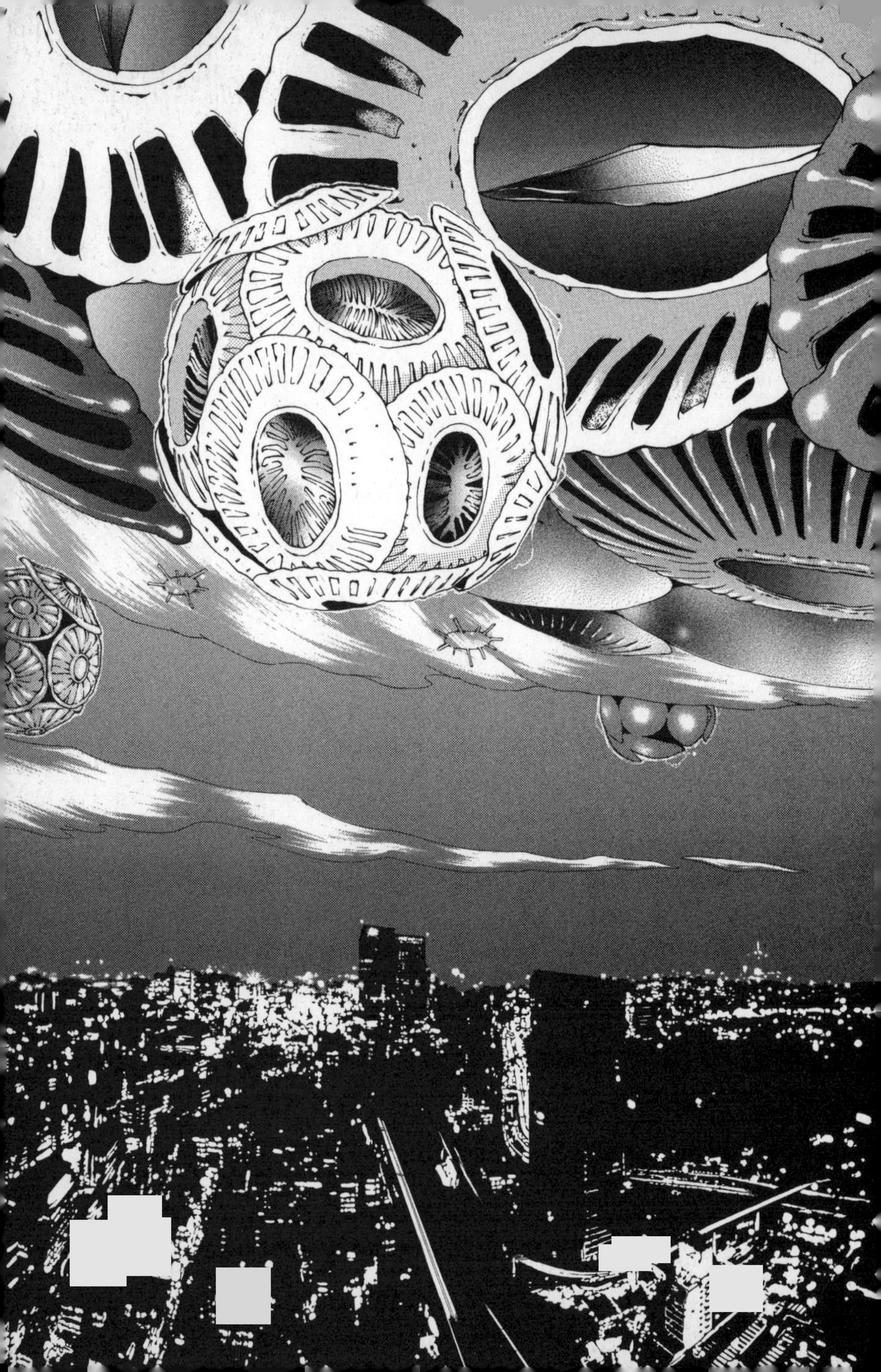

THE RECORD OF A

FALLEN VAMPIRE

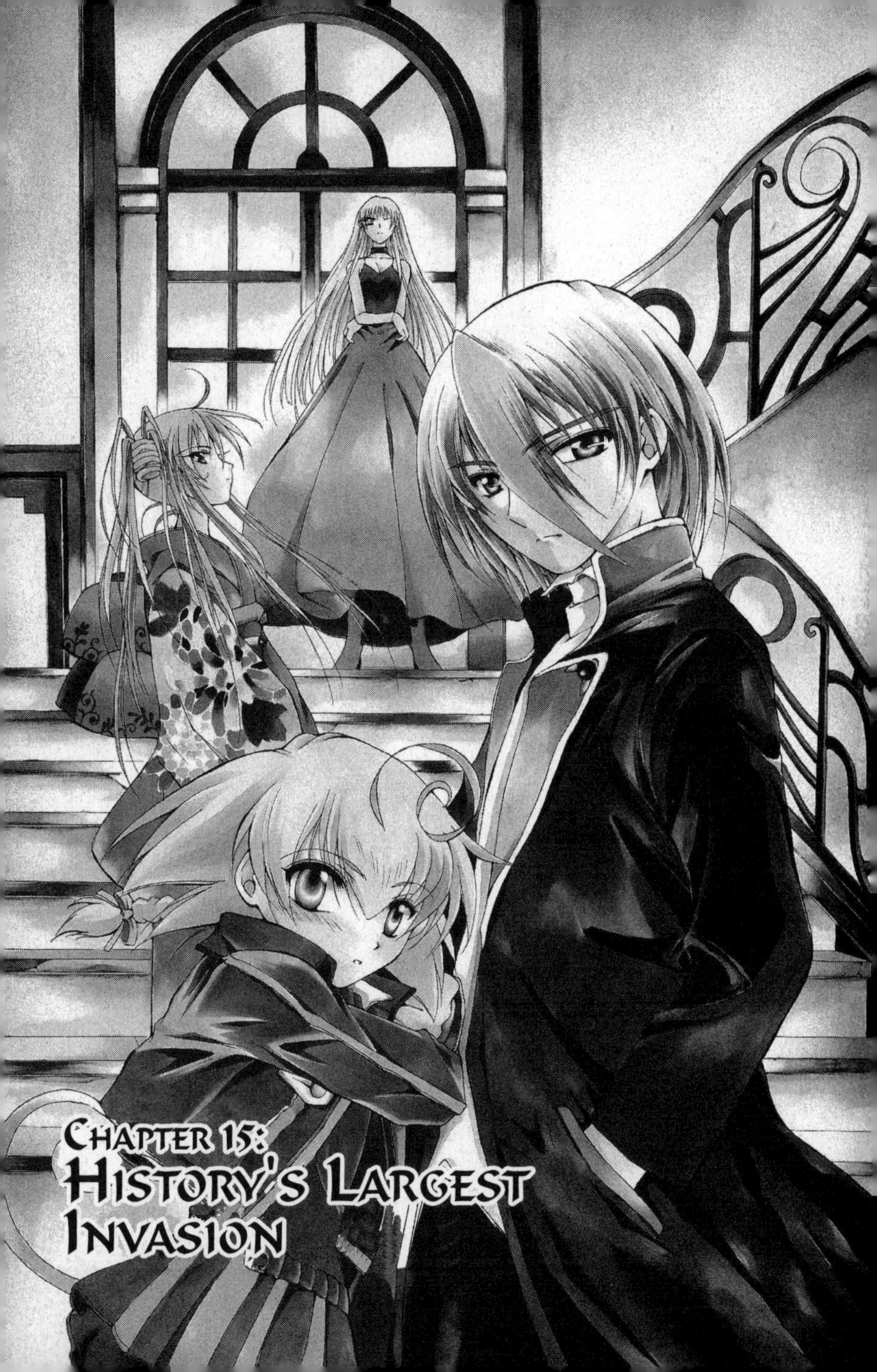
Chapter 15:
History's Largest Invasion

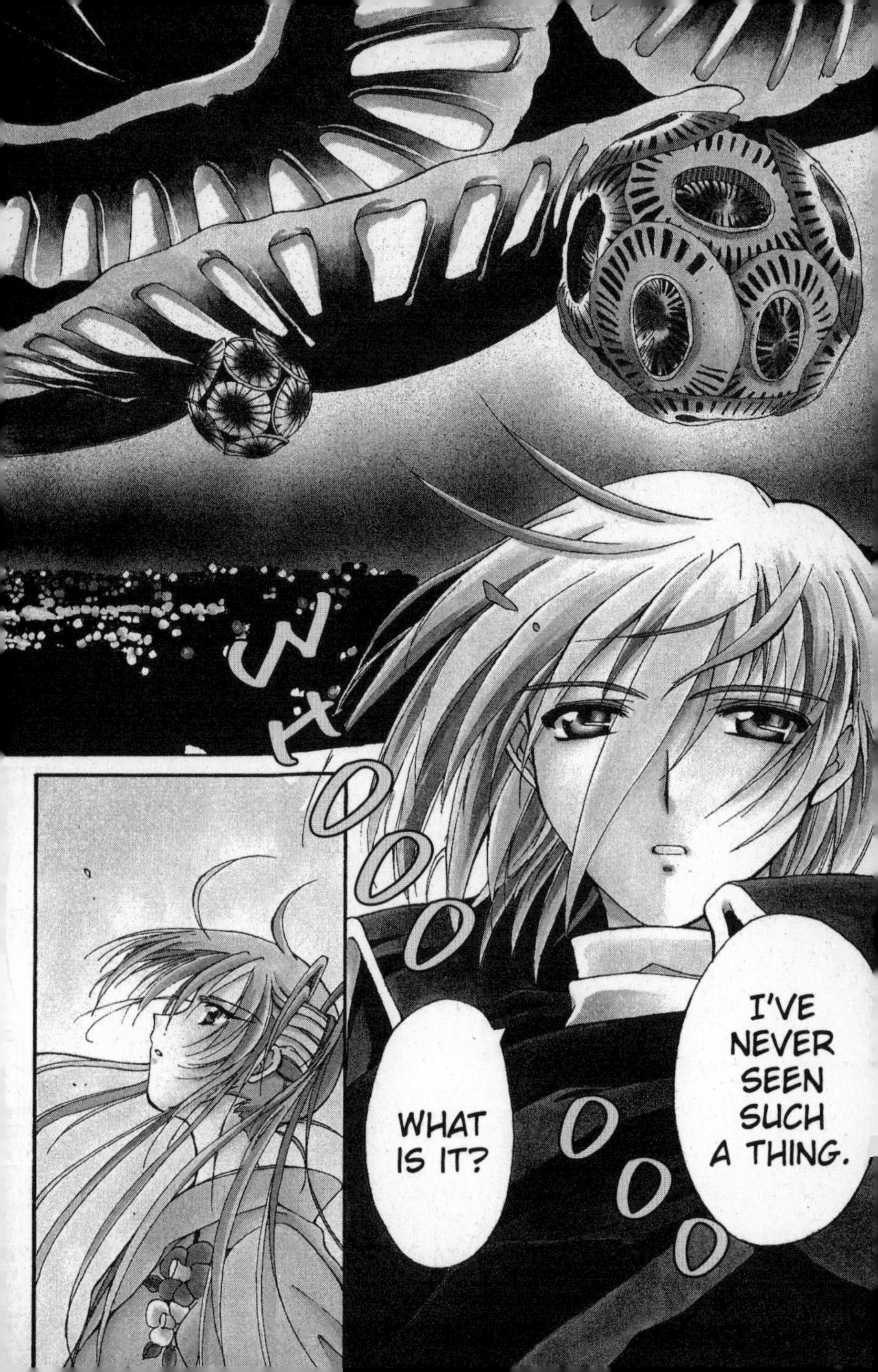
I'VE NEVER SEEN SUCH A THING.
WHAT IS IT?

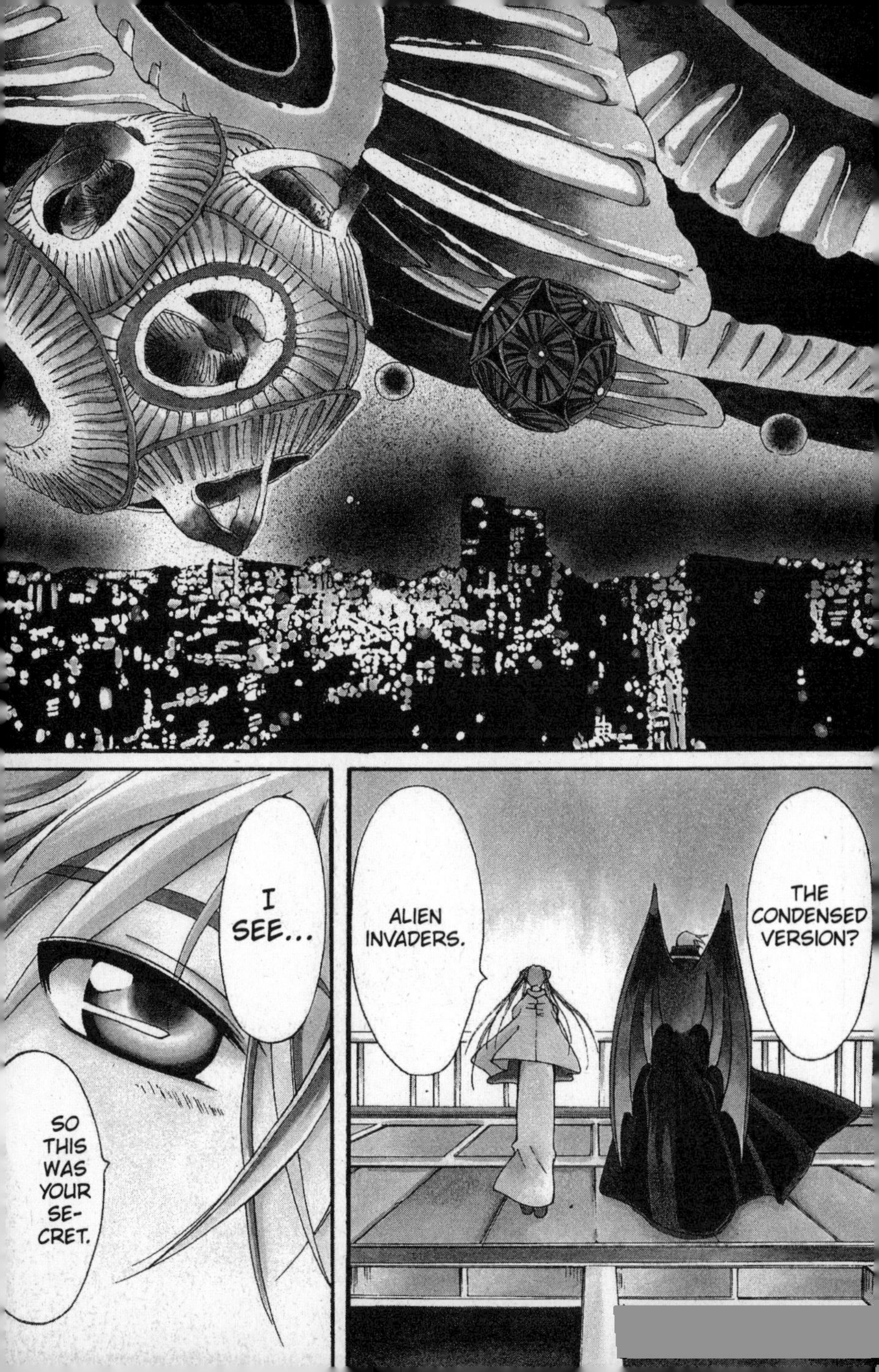
THE CONDENSED VERSION?
ALIEN INVADERS.
I SEE...
SO THIS WAS YOUR SE-CRET.

THE RECORD OF A

FALLEN VAMPIRE

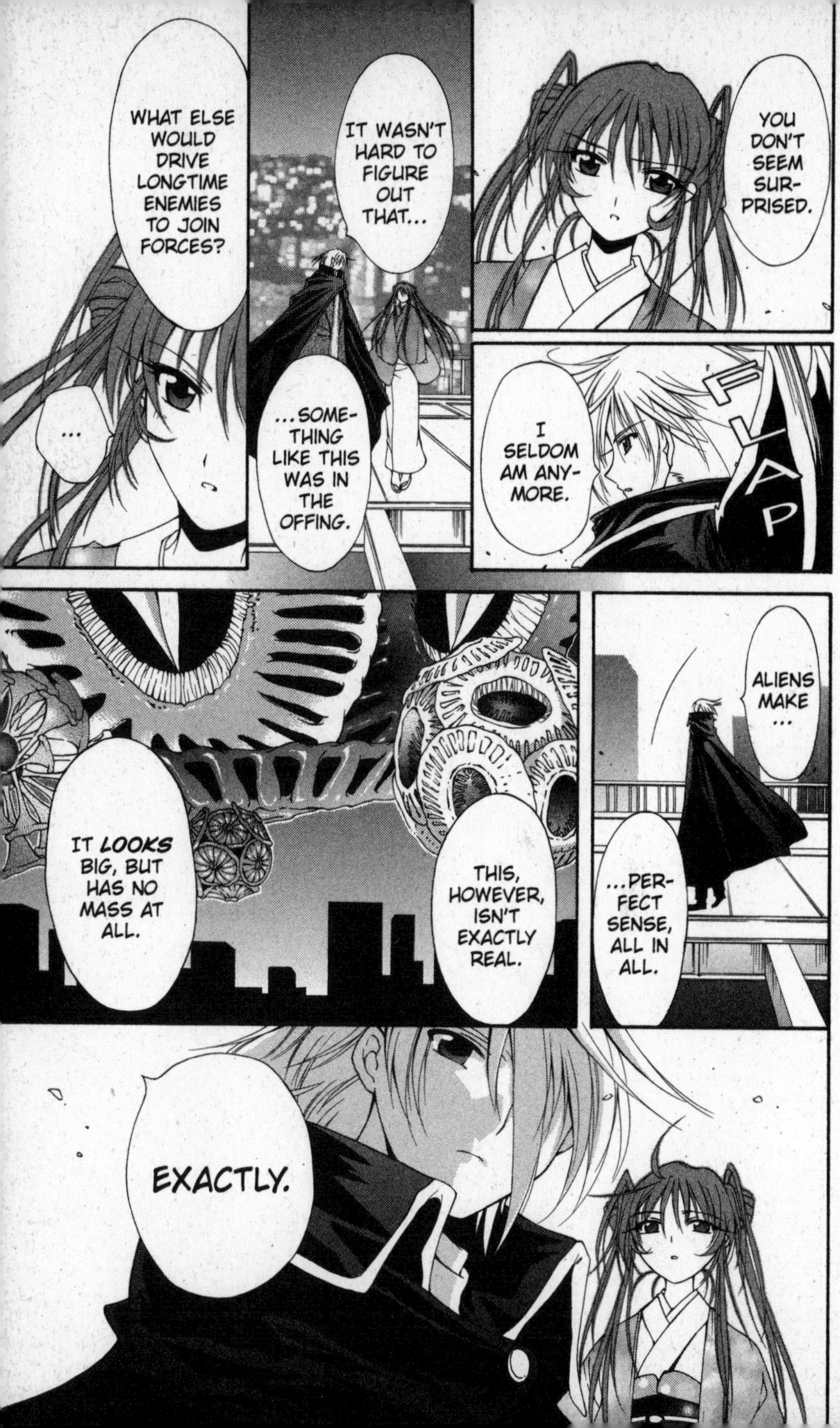
YOU DON'T SEEM SURPRISED.
I SELDOM AM ANYMORE.
FLAP
IT WASN'T HARD TO FIGURE OUT THAT...
...SOMETHING LIKE THIS WAS IN THE OFFING.
WHAT ELSE WOULD DRIVE LONGTIME ENEMIES TO JOIN FORCES?
...
ALIENS MAKE...
...PERFECT SENSE, ALL IN ALL.
THIS, HOWEVER, ISN'T EXACTLY REAL.
IT *LOOKS* BIG, BUT HAS NO MASS AT ALL.
EXACTLY.

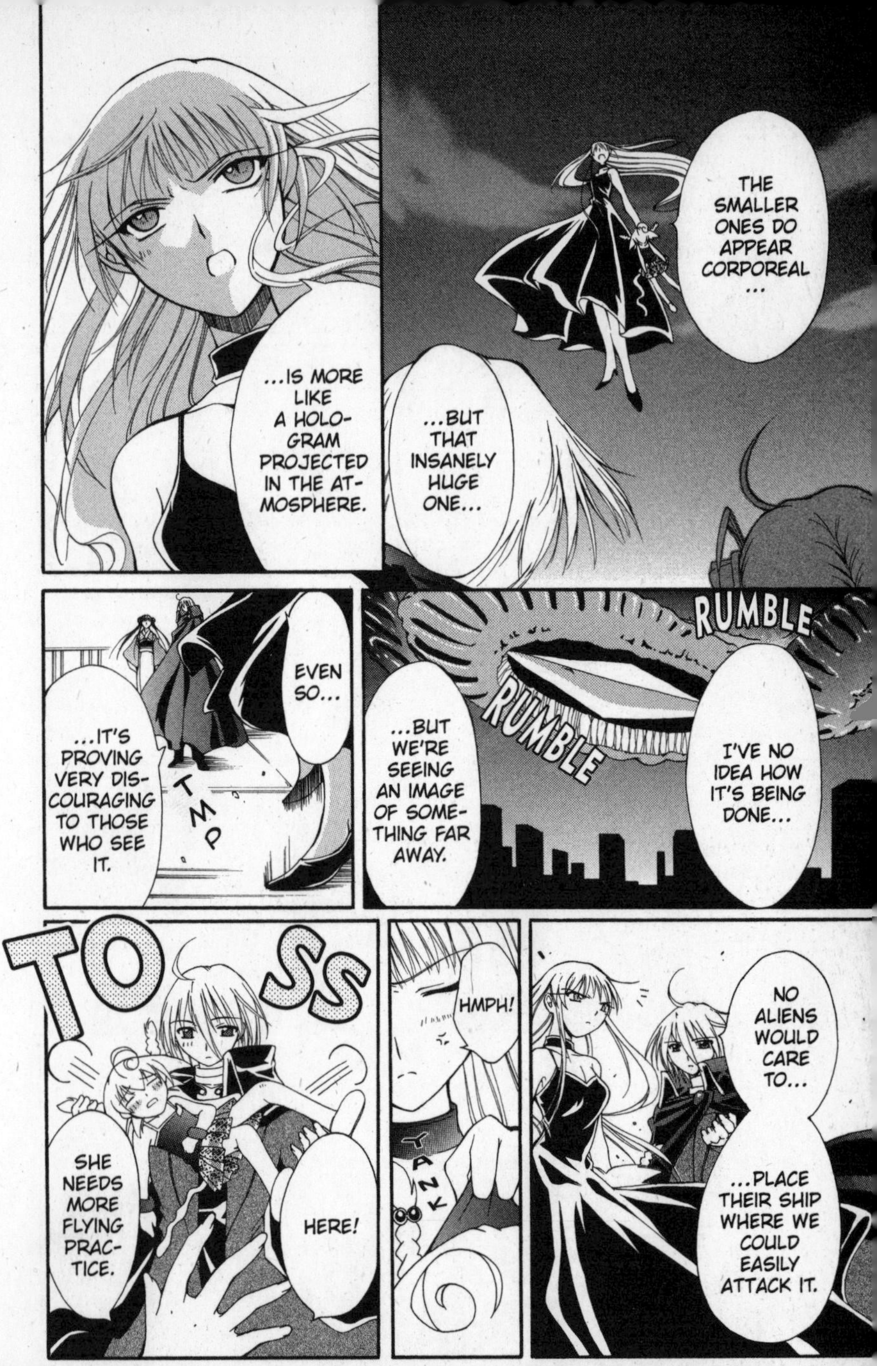
THE SMALLER ONES DO APPEAR CORPOREAL ...
...BUT THAT INSANELY HUGE ONE...
...IS MORE LIKE A HOLOGRAM PROJECTED IN THE ATMOSPHERE.
RUMBLE
RUMBLE
I'VE NO IDEA HOW IT'S BEING DONE...
...BUT WE'RE SEEING AN IMAGE OF SOMETHING FAR AWAY.
EVEN SO...
TMP
...IT'S PROVING VERY DISCOURAGING TO THOSE WHO SEE IT.
NO ALIENS WOULD CARE TO...
...PLACE THEIR SHIP WHERE WE COULD EASILY ATTACK IT.
HMPH!
YANK
TOSS
HERE!
SHE NEEDS MORE FLYING PRACTICE.

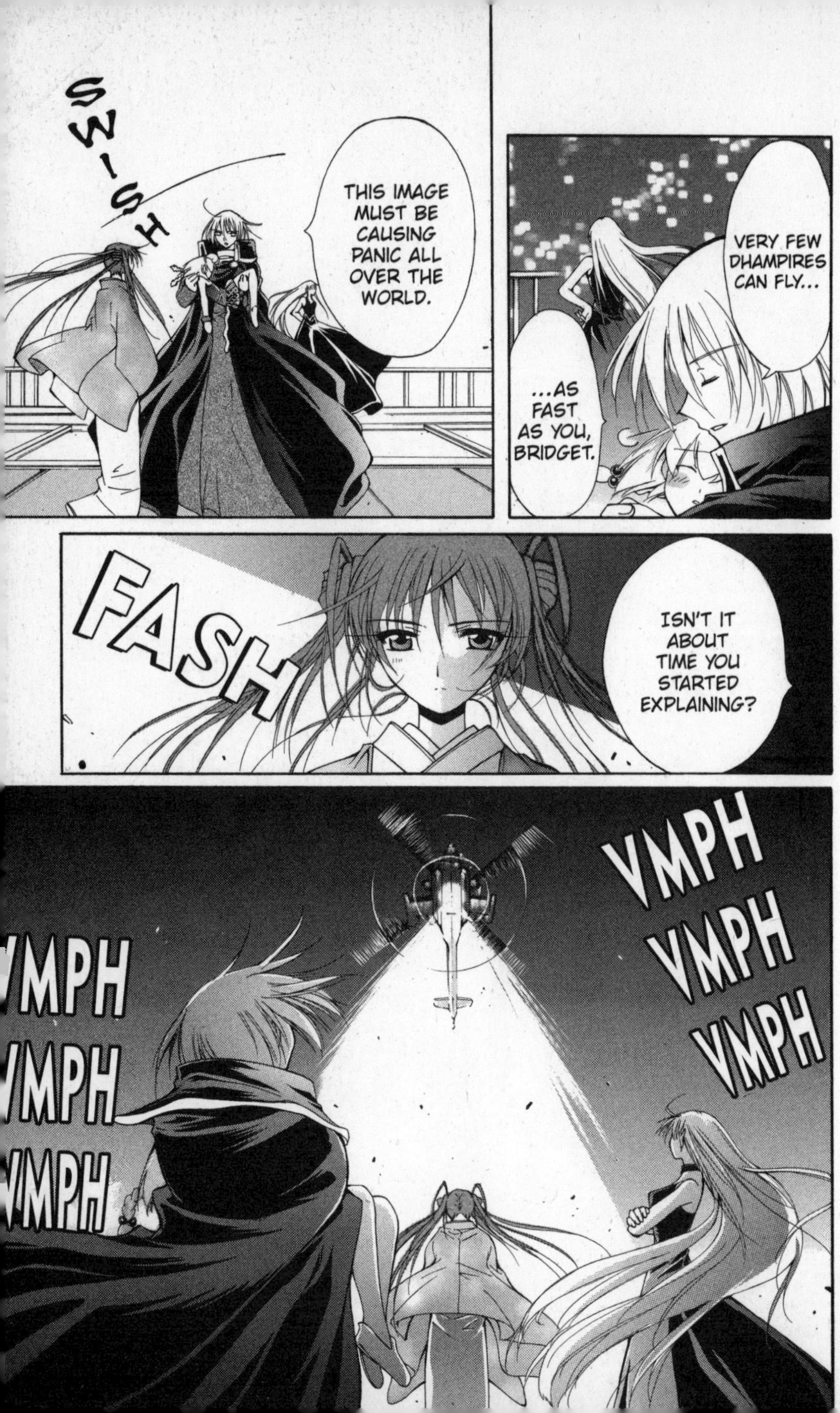
VERY FEW DHAMPIRES CAN FLY...
...AS FAST AS YOU, BRIDGET.
SWISH
THIS IMAGE MUST BE CAUSING PANIC ALL OVER THE WORLD.
ISN'T IT ABOUT TIME YOU STARTED EXPLAINING?
FASH
VMPH VMPH VMPH
VMPH VMPH VMPH

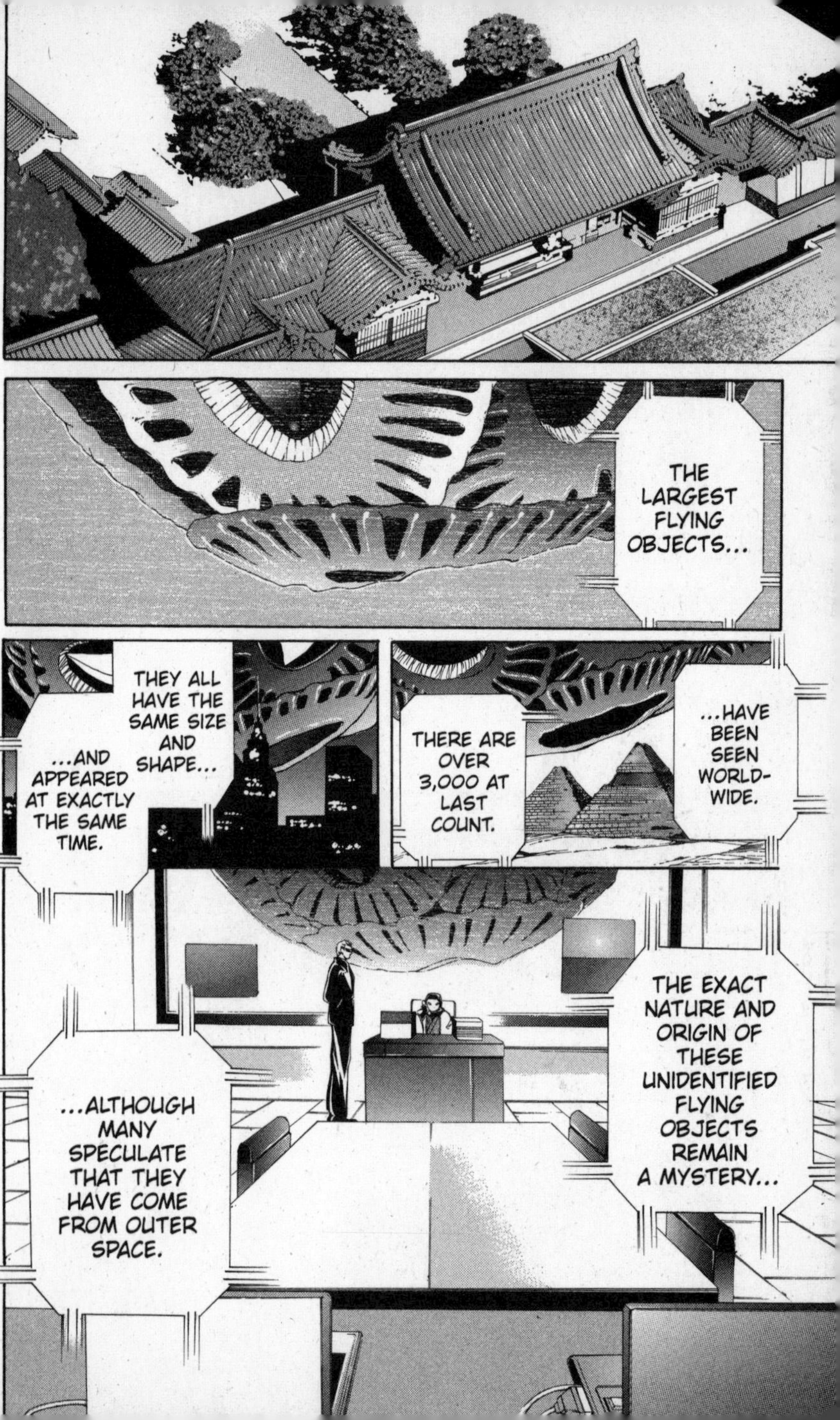
THE LARGEST FLYING OBJECTS...
...HAVE BEEN SEEN WORLD-WIDE.
THERE ARE OVER 3,000 AT LAST COUNT.
THEY ALL HAVE THE SAME SIZE AND SHAPE...
...AND APPEARED AT EXACTLY THE SAME TIME.
THE EXACT NATURE AND ORIGIN OF THESE UNIDENTIFIED FLYING OBJECTS REMAIN A MYSTERY...
...ALTHOUGH MANY SPECULATE THAT THEY HAVE COME FROM OUTER SPACE.

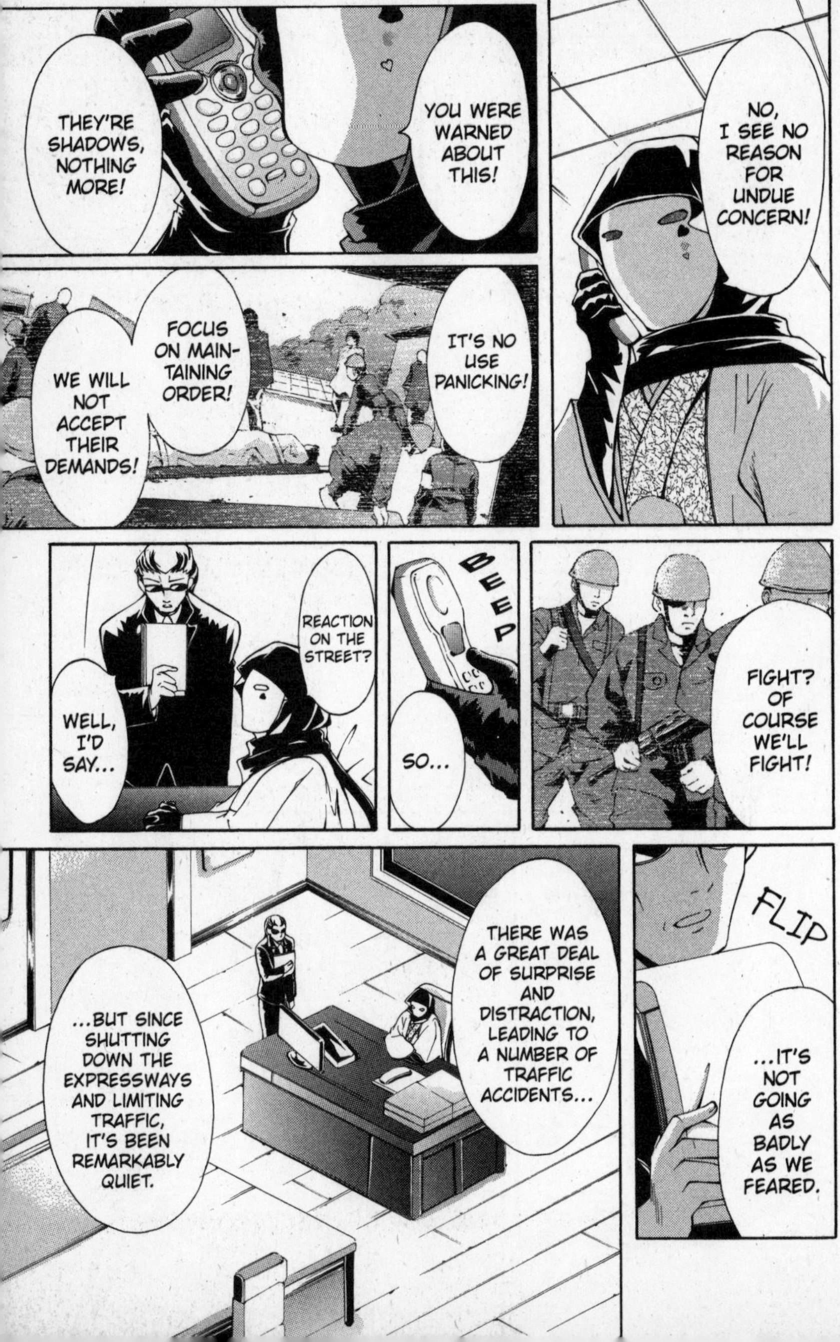
NO, I SEE NO REASON FOR UNDUE CONCERN!
YOU WERE WARNED ABOUT THIS!
THEY'RE SHADOWS, NOTHING MORE!
IT'S NO USE PANICKING!
FOCUS ON MAIN-TAINING ORDER!
WE WILL NOT ACCEPT THEIR DEMANDS!
FIGHT? OF COURSE WE'LL FIGHT!
BEEP
SO...
REACTION ON THE STREET?
WELL, I'D SAY...
FLIP
...IT'S NOT GOING AS BADLY AS WE FEARED.
THERE WAS A GREAT DEAL OF SURPRISE AND DISTRACTION, LEADING TO A NUMBER OF TRAFFIC ACCIDENTS...
...BUT SINCE SHUTTING DOWN THE EXPRESSWAYS AND LIMITING TRAFFIC, IT'S BEEN REMARKABLY QUIET.

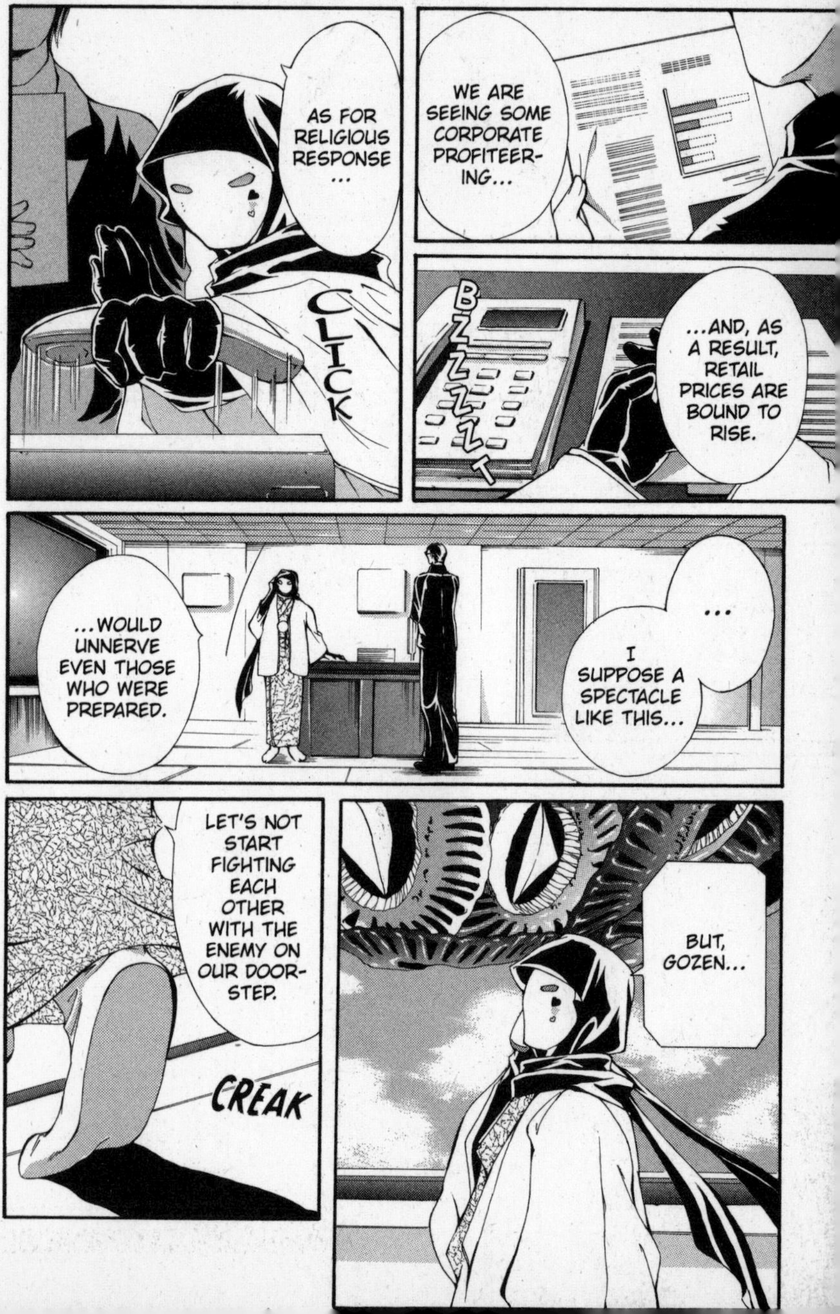
WE ARE SEEING SOME CORPORATE PROFITEER-ING...
BZZZZT
...AND, AS A RESULT, RETAIL PRICES ARE BOUND TO RISE.
AS FOR RELIGIOUS RESPONSE ...
CLICK
...
I SUPPOSE A SPECTACLE LIKE THIS...
...WOULD UNNERVE EVEN THOSE WHO WERE PREPARED.
BUT, GOZEN...
LET'S NOT START FIGHTING EACH OTHER WITH THE ENEMY ON OUR DOOR-STEP.
CREAK

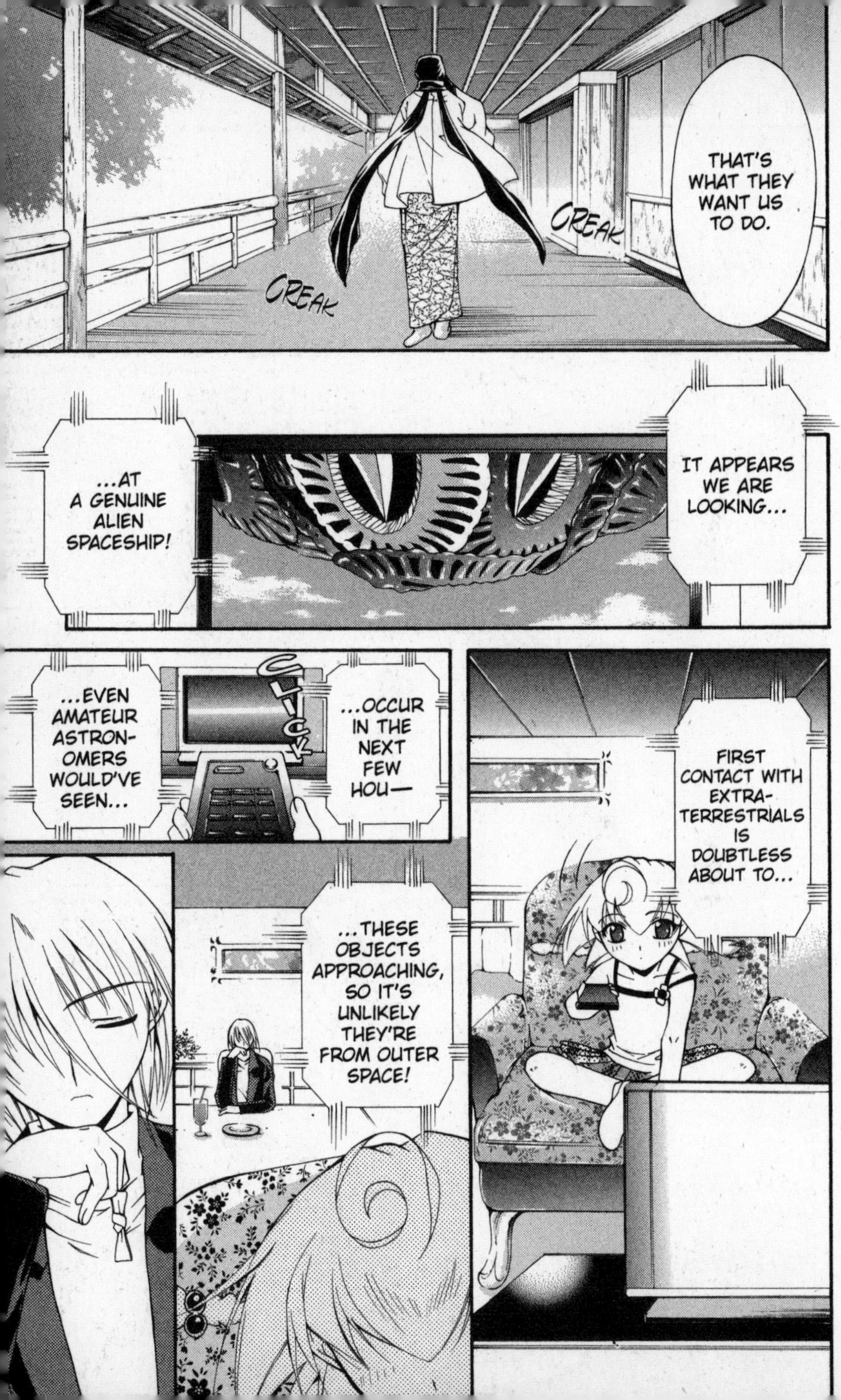
THAT'S WHAT THEY WANT US TO DO.
CREAK
CREAK
IT APPEARS WE ARE LOOKING...
...AT A GENUINE ALIEN SPACESHIP!
FIRST CONTACT WITH EXTRA-TERRESTRIALS IS DOUBTLESS ABOUT TO...
...OCCUR IN THE NEXT FEW HOU—
CLICK
...EVEN AMATEUR ASTRON-OMERS WOULD'VE SEEN...
...THESE OBJECTS APPROACHING, SO IT'S UNLIKELY THEY'RE FROM OUTER SPACE!

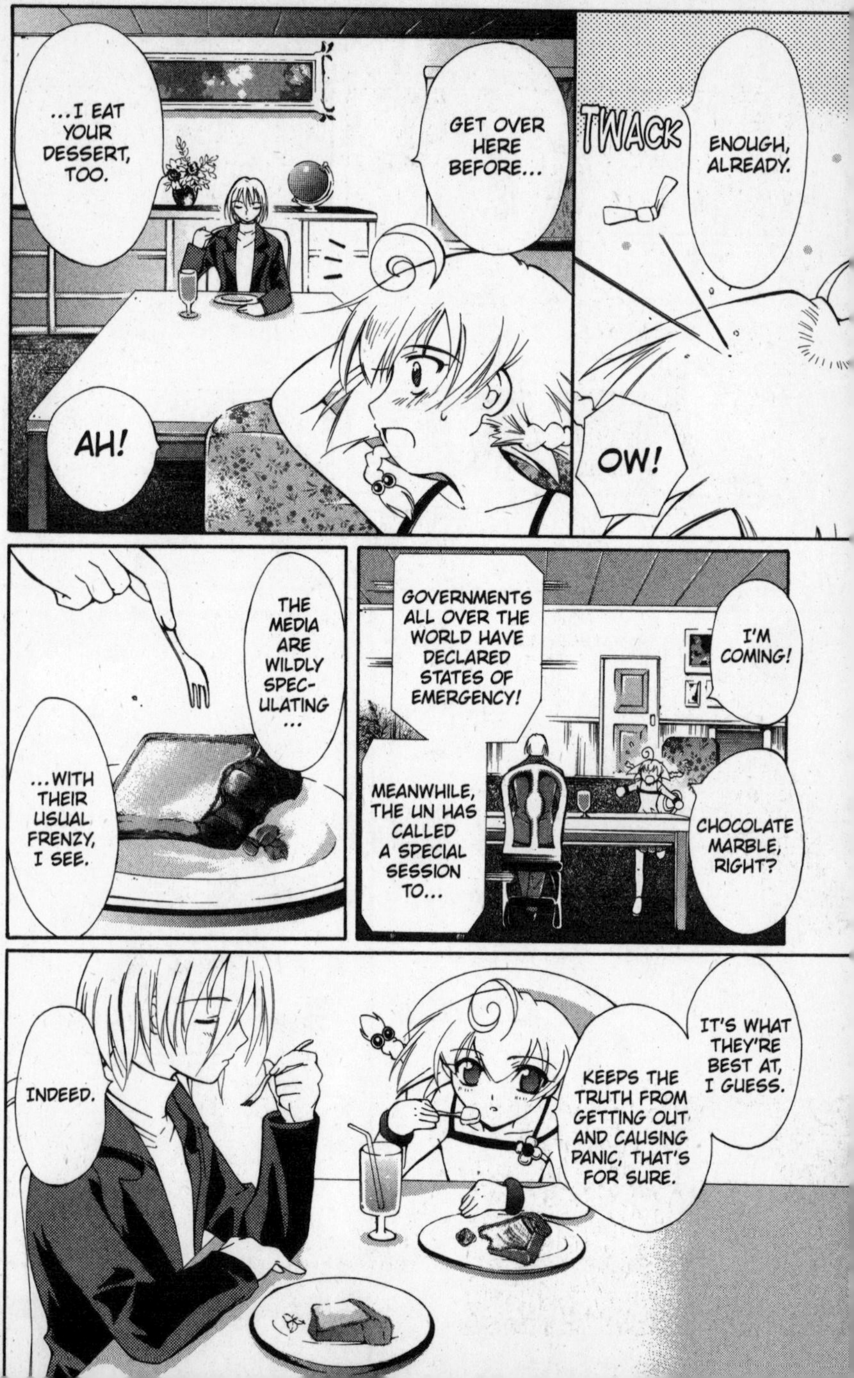
TWACK
ENOUGH, ALREADY.
OW!
GET OVER HERE BEFORE...
...I EAT YOUR DESSERT, TOO.
AH!
I'M COMING!
GOVERNMENTS ALL OVER THE WORLD HAVE DECLARED STATES OF EMERGENCY!
CHOCOLATE MARBLE, RIGHT?
MEANWHILE, THE UN HAS CALLED A SPECIAL SESSION TO...
THE MEDIA ARE WILDLY SPEC-ULATING...
...WITH THEIR USUAL FRENZY, I SEE.
IT'S WHAT THEY'RE BEST AT, I GUESS.
KEEPS THE TRUTH FROM GETTING OUT AND CAUSING PANIC, THAT'S FOR SURE.
INDEED.

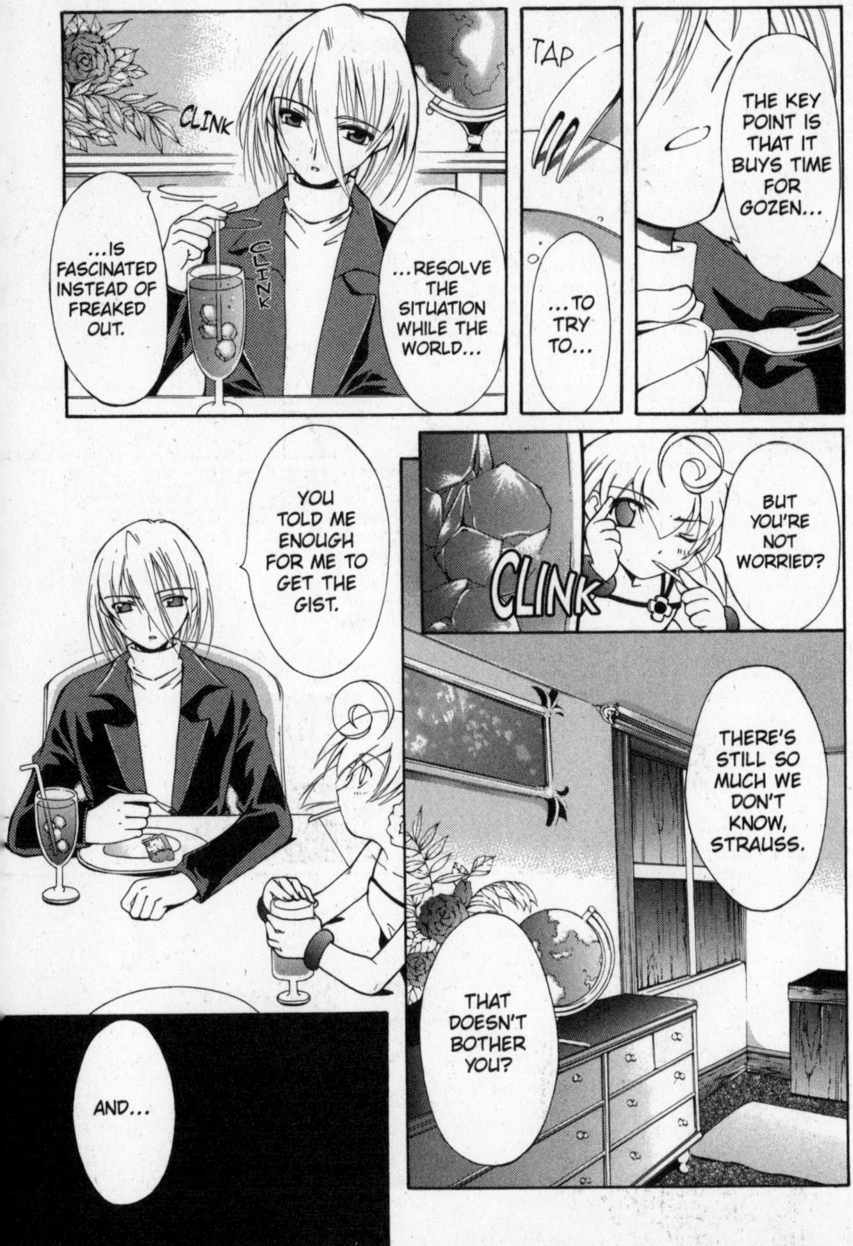
THE KEY POINT IS THAT IT BUYS TIME FOR GOZEN...
TAP
...TO TRY TO...
...RESOLVE THE SITUATION WHILE THE WORLD...
CLINK
CLINK
...IS FASCINATED INSTEAD OF FREAKED OUT.
BUT YOU'RE NOT WORRIED?
CLINK
YOU TOLD ME ENOUGH FOR ME TO GET THE GIST.
THERE'S STILL SO MUCH WE DON'T KNOW, STRAUSS.
THAT DOESN'T BOTHER YOU?
AND...

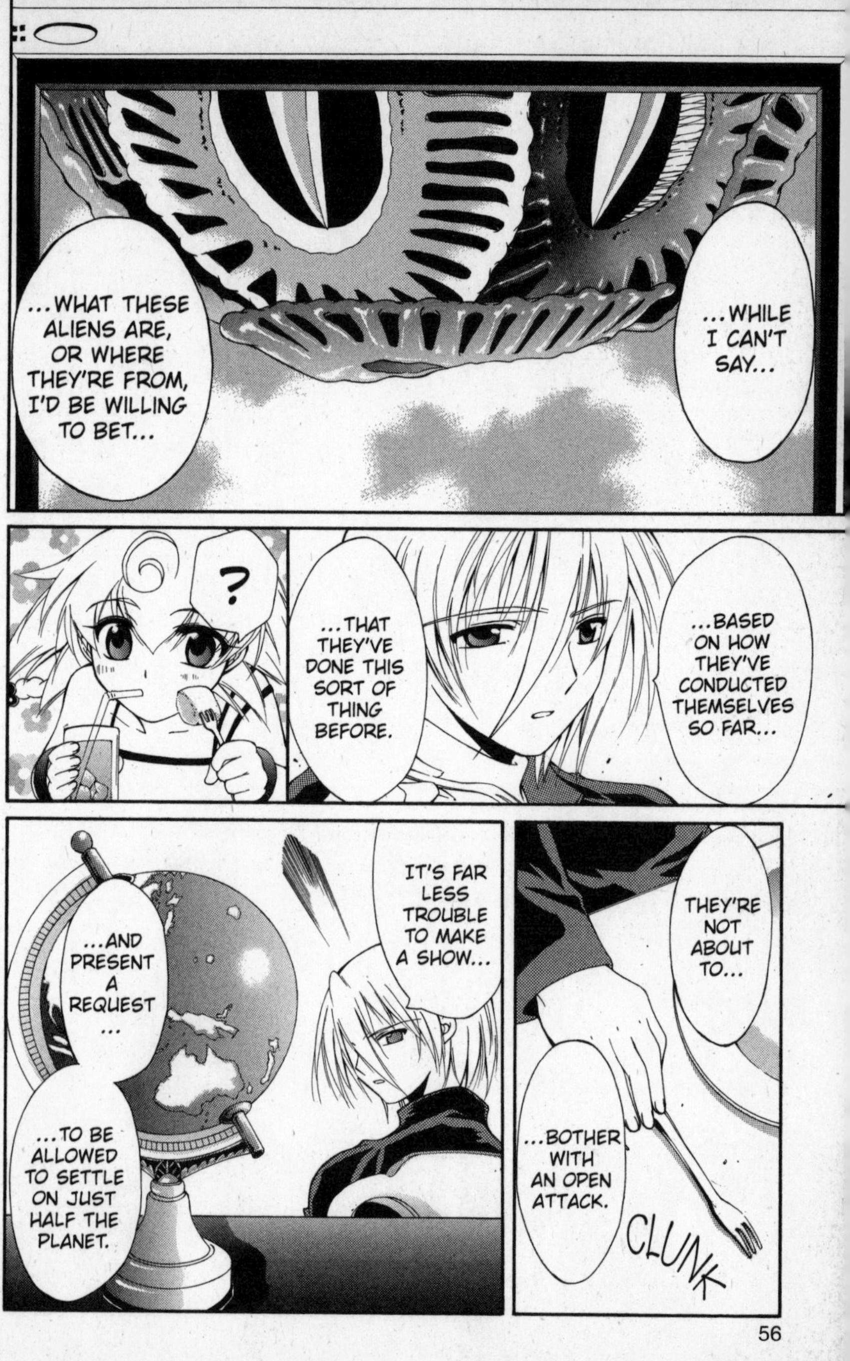
...WHILE I CAN'T SAY...
...WHAT THESE ALIENS ARE, OR WHERE THEY'RE FROM, I'D BE WILLING TO BET...
...BASED ON HOW THEY'VE CONDUCTED THEMSELVES SO FAR...
...THAT THEY'VE DONE THIS SORT OF THING BEFORE.
?
THEY'RE NOT ABOUT TO...
...BOTHER WITH AN OPEN ATTACK.
CLUNK
IT'S FAR LESS TROUBLE TO MAKE A SHOW...
...AND PRESENT A REQUEST...
...TO BE ALLOWED TO SETTLE ON JUST HALF THE PLANET.

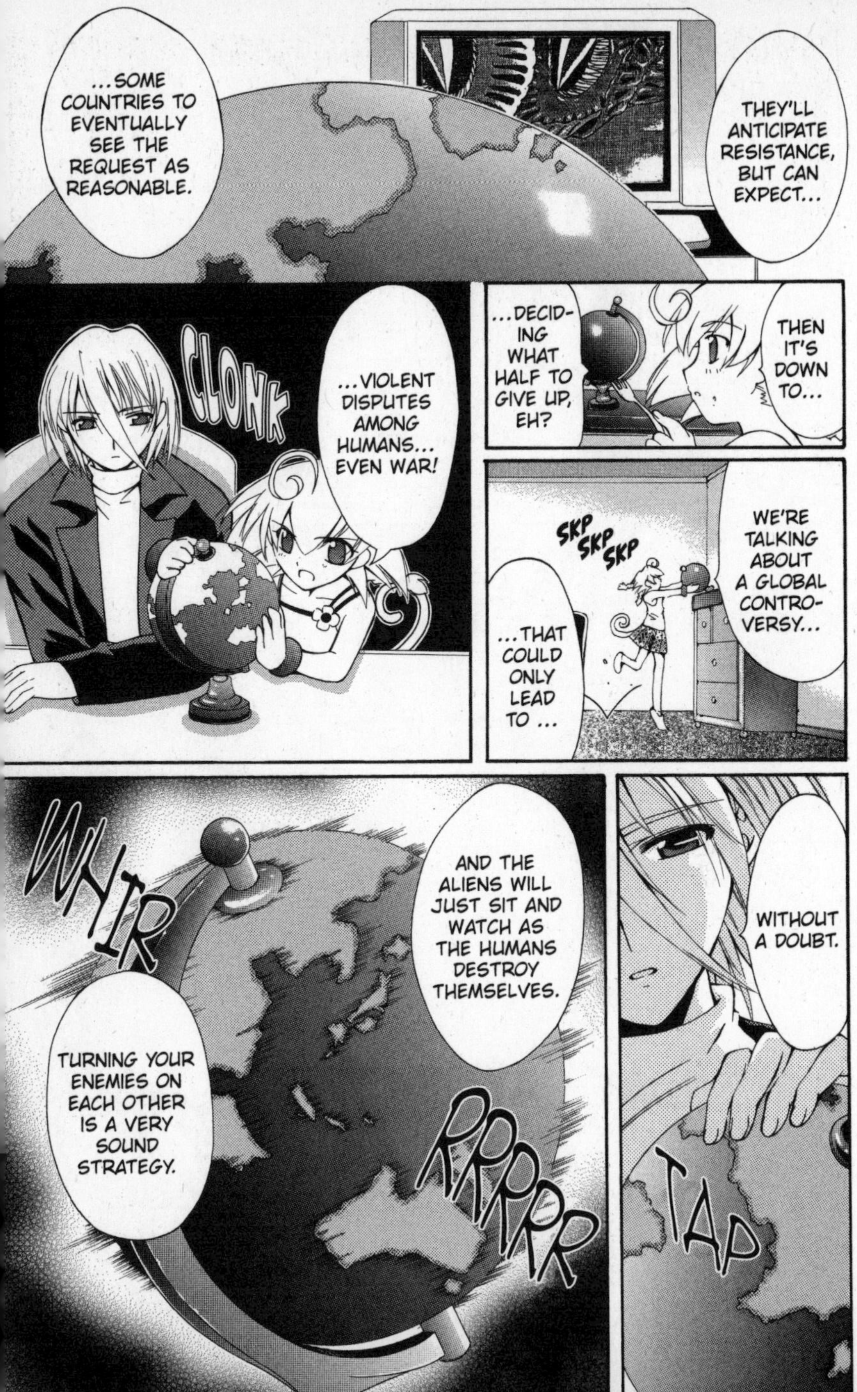
THEY'LL ANTICIPATE RESISTANCE, BUT CAN EXPECT...
...SOME COUNTRIES TO EVENTUALLY SEE THE REQUEST AS REASONABLE.
THEN IT'S DOWN TO...
...DECID-ING WHAT HALF TO GIVE UP, EH?
WE'RE TALKING ABOUT A GLOBAL CONTRO-VERSY...
SKP SKP SKP
...THAT COULD ONLY LEAD TO ...
...VIOLENT DISPUTES AMONG HUMANS... EVEN WAR!
CLONK
WITHOUT A DOUBT.
TAP
AND THE ALIENS WILL JUST SIT AND WATCH AS THE HUMANS DESTROY THEMSELVES.
WHIR
TURNING YOUR ENEMIES ON EACH OTHER IS A VERY SOUND STRATEGY.
RRRRR

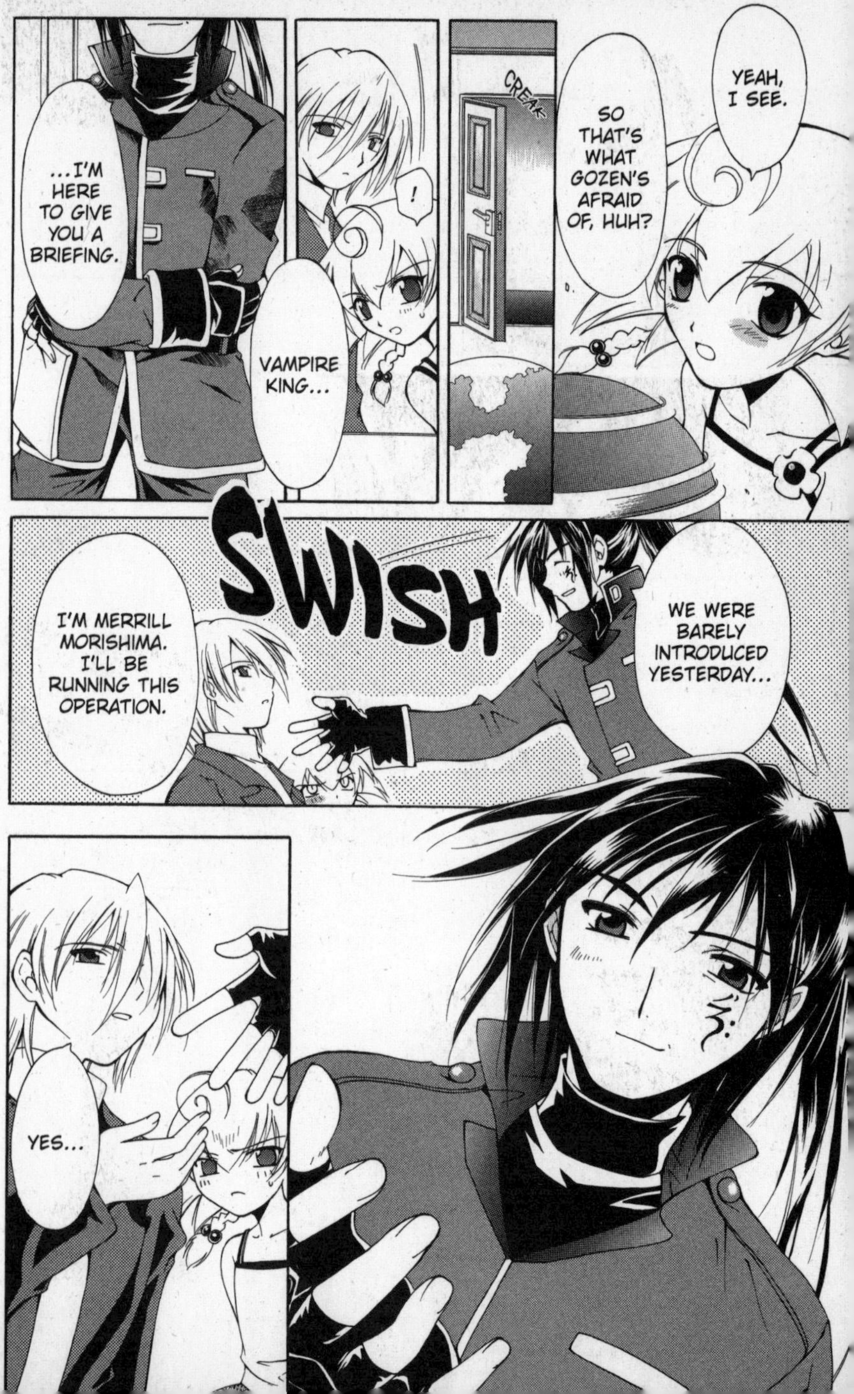
YEAH, I SEE.
SO THAT'S WHAT GOZEN'S AFRAID OF, HUH?
CREAK
!
VAMPIRE KING...
...I'M HERE TO GIVE YOU A BRIEFING.
SWISH
WE WERE BARELY INTRODUCED YESTERDAY...
I'M MERRILL MORISHIMA. I'LL BE RUNNING THIS OPERATION.
YES...

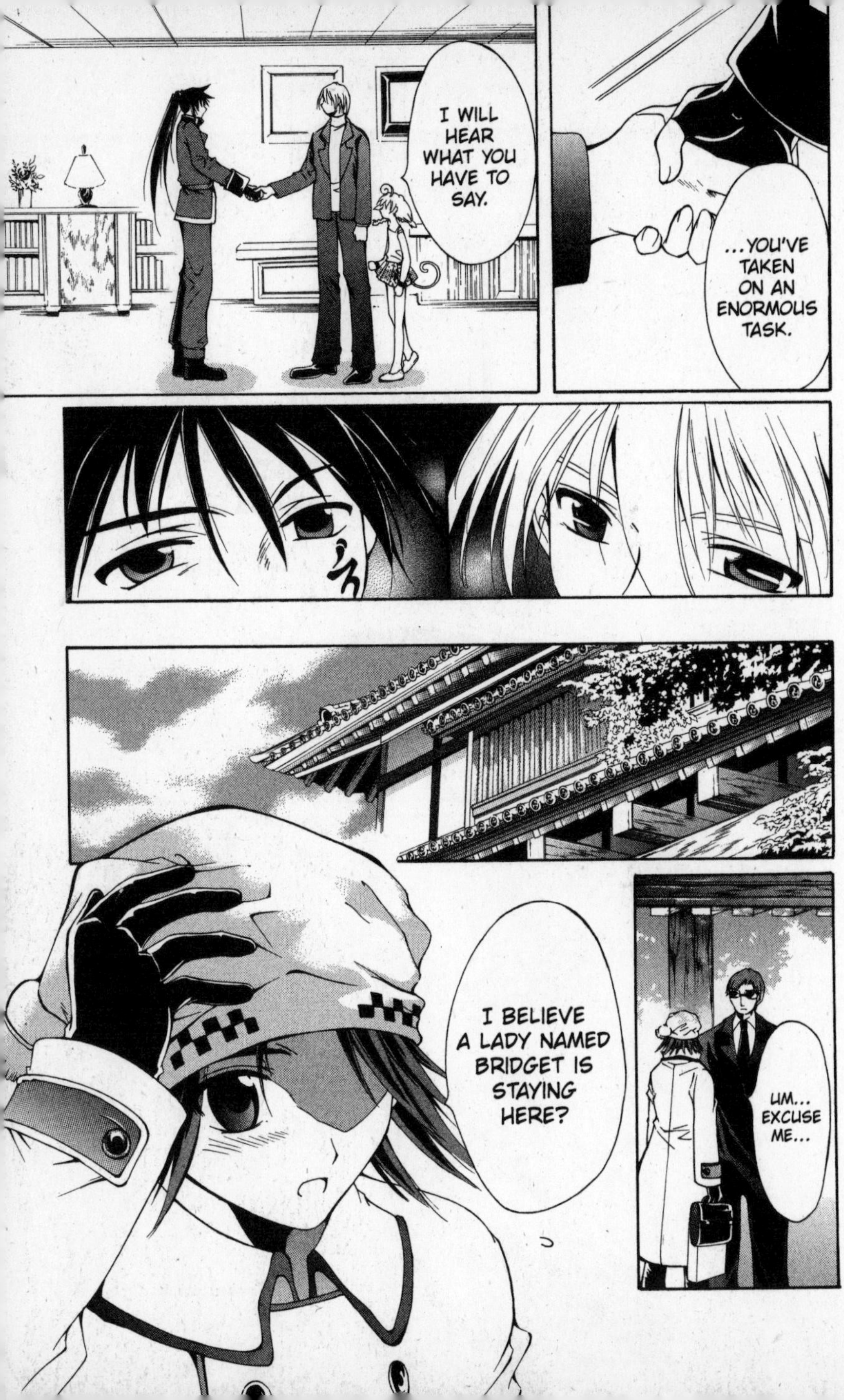
...YOU'VE TAKEN ON AN ENORMOUS TASK.
I WILL HEAR WHAT YOU HAVE TO SAY.
UM... EXCUSE ME...
I BELIEVE A LADY NAMED BRIDGET IS STAYING HERE?

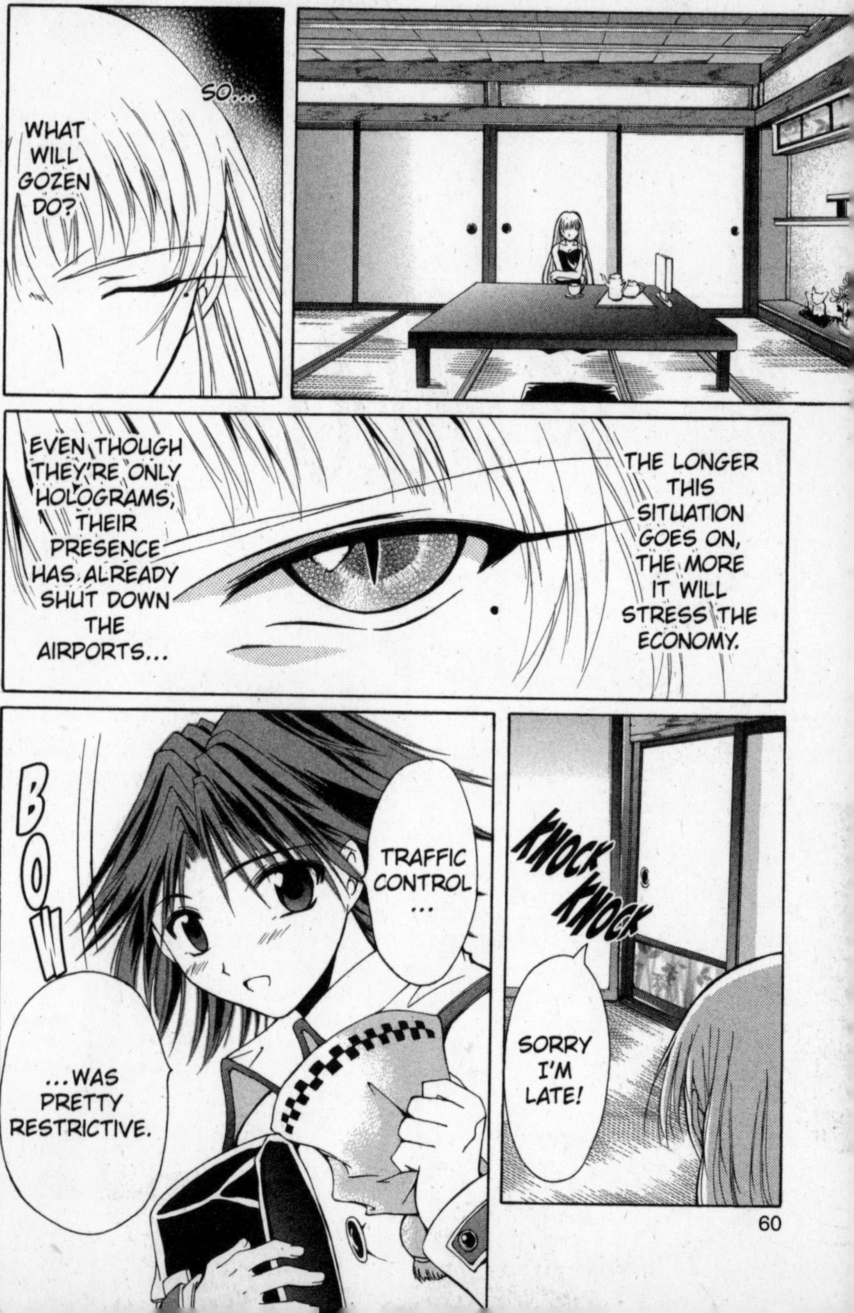
SO...
WHAT WILL GOZEN DO?
THE LONGER THIS SITUATION GOES ON, THE MORE IT WILL STRESS THE ECONOMY.
EVEN THOUGH THEY'RE ONLY HOLOGRAMS, THEIR PRESENCE HAS ALREADY SHUT DOWN THE AIRPORTS...
KNOCK KNOCK
SORRY I'M LATE!
TRAFFIC CONTROL ...
BOW
...WAS PRETTY RESTRICTIVE.

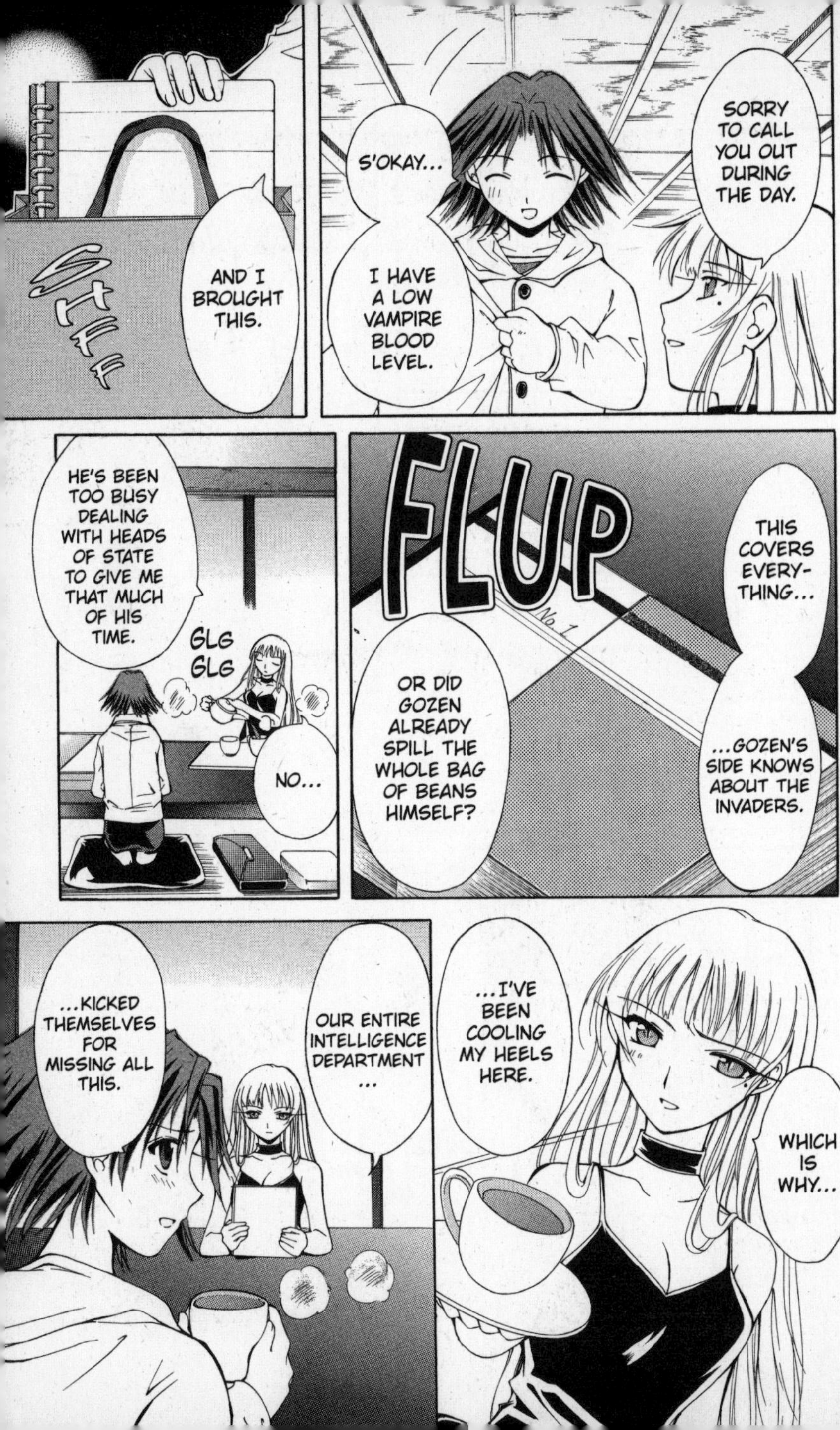
SORRY TO CALL YOU OUT DURING THE DAY.
S'OKAY...
I HAVE A LOW VAMPIRE BLOOD LEVEL.
AND I BROUGHT THIS.
SHFF
FLUP
No. 1
THIS COVERS EVERY-THING...
...GOZEN'S SIDE KNOWS ABOUT THE INVADERS.
OR DID GOZEN ALREADY SPILL THE WHOLE BAG OF BEANS HIMSELF?
GLG GLG
NO...
HE'S BEEN TOO BUSY DEALING WITH HEADS OF STATE TO GIVE ME THAT MUCH OF HIS TIME.
WHICH IS WHY...
...I'VE BEEN COOLING MY HEELS HERE.
OUR ENTIRE INTELLIGENCE DEPARTMENT ...
...KICKED THEMSELVES FOR MISSING ALL THIS.

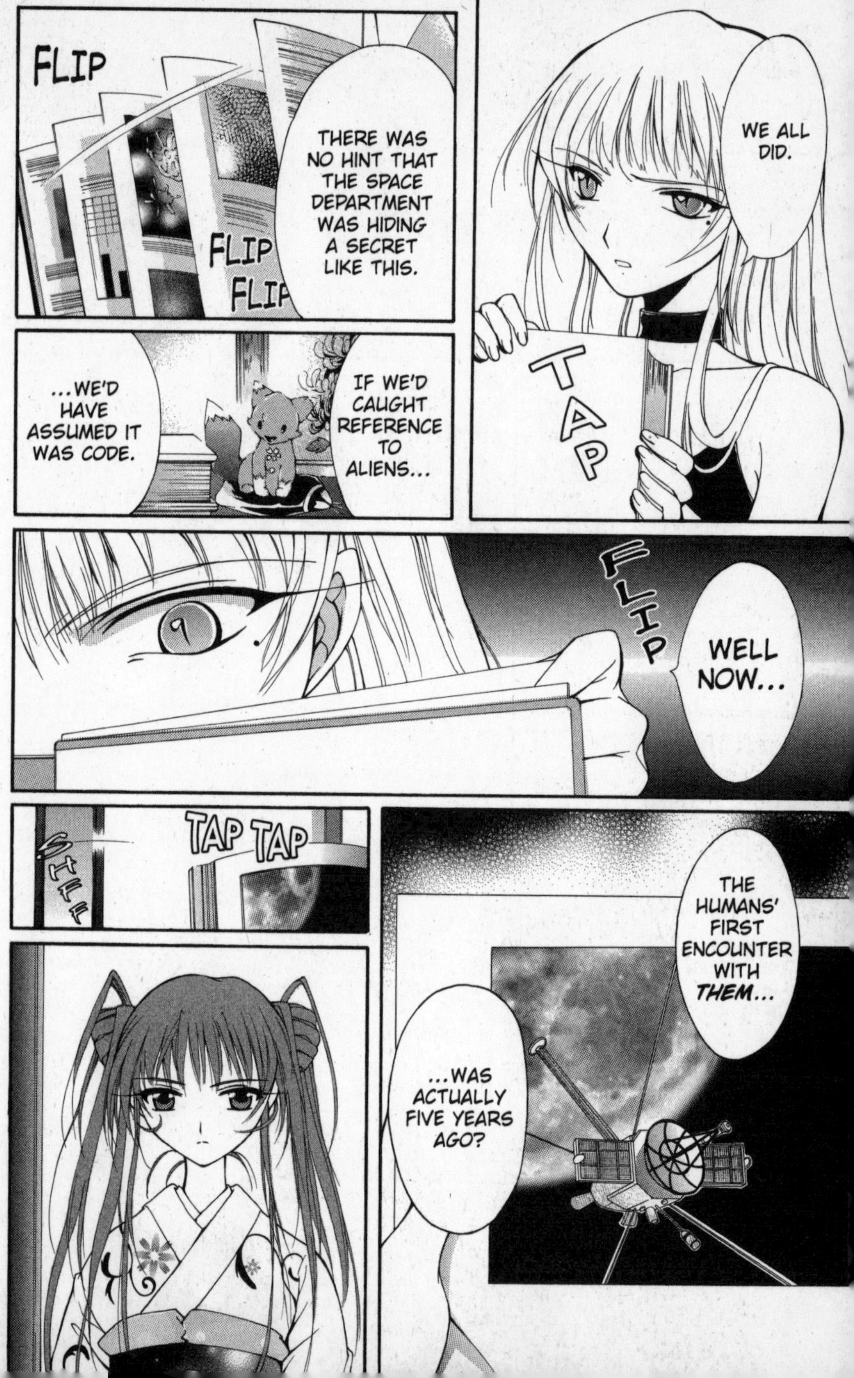
WE ALL DID.
TAP
FLIP
THERE WAS NO HINT THAT THE SPACE DEPARTMENT WAS HIDING A SECRET LIKE THIS.
FLIP
FLIP
IF WE'D CAUGHT REFERENCE TO ALIENS...
...WE'D HAVE ASSUMED IT WAS CODE.
FLIP
WELL NOW...
THE HUMANS' FIRST ENCOUNTER WITH *THEM*...
...WAS ACTUALLY FIVE YEARS AGO?
TAP TAP
SHFF

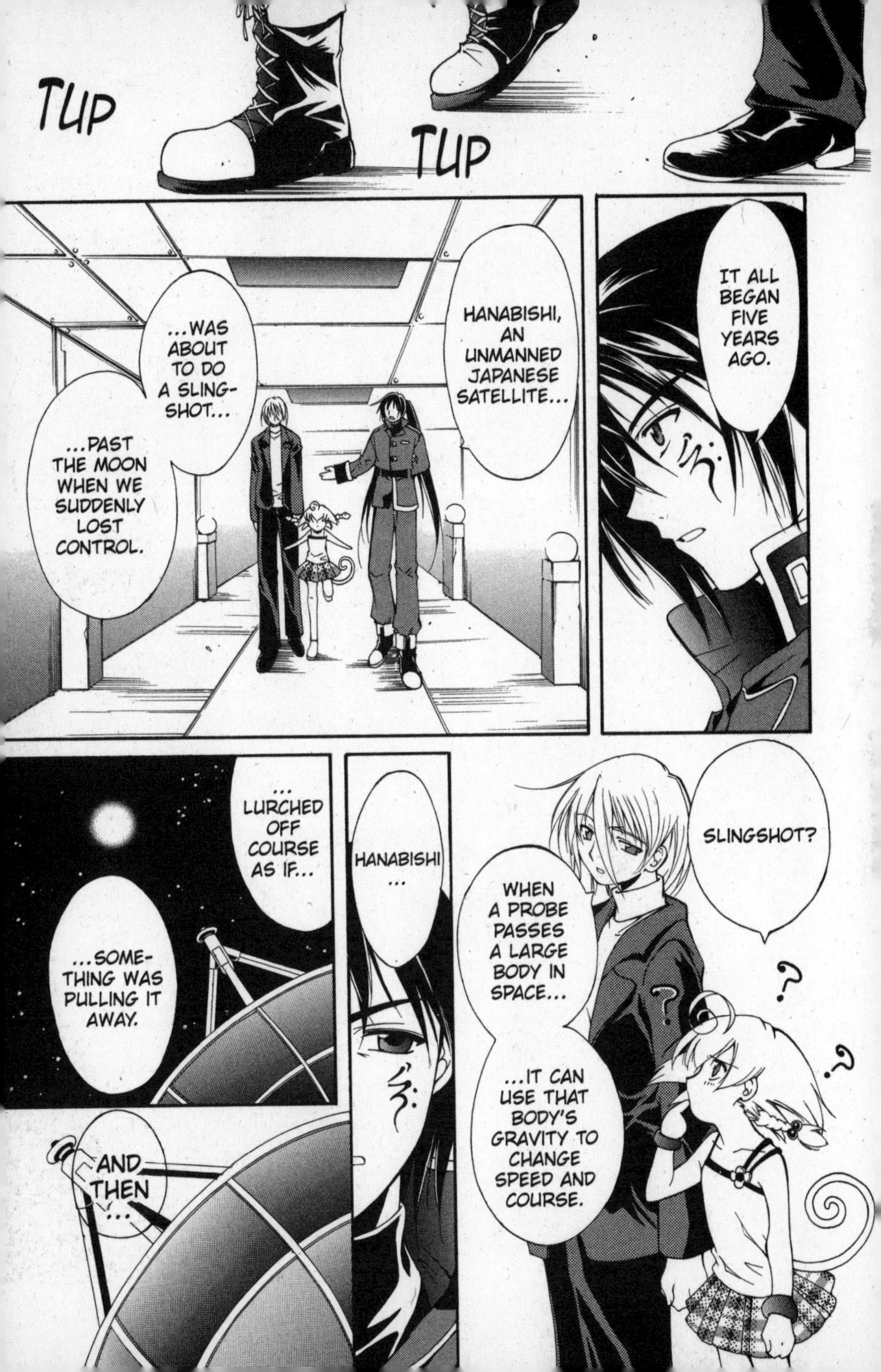
TUP
TUP
IT ALL BEGAN FIVE YEARS AGO.
HANABISHI, AN UNMANNED JAPANESE SATELLITE...
...WAS ABOUT TO DO A SLING-SHOT...
...PAST THE MOON WHEN WE SUDDENLY LOST CONTROL.
SLINGSHOT?
WHEN A PROBE PASSES A LARGE BODY IN SPACE...
...IT CAN USE THAT BODY'S GRAVITY TO CHANGE SPEED AND COURSE.
HANABISHI...
...LURCHED OFF COURSE AS IF...
...SOME-THING WAS PULLING IT AWAY.
AND THEN...

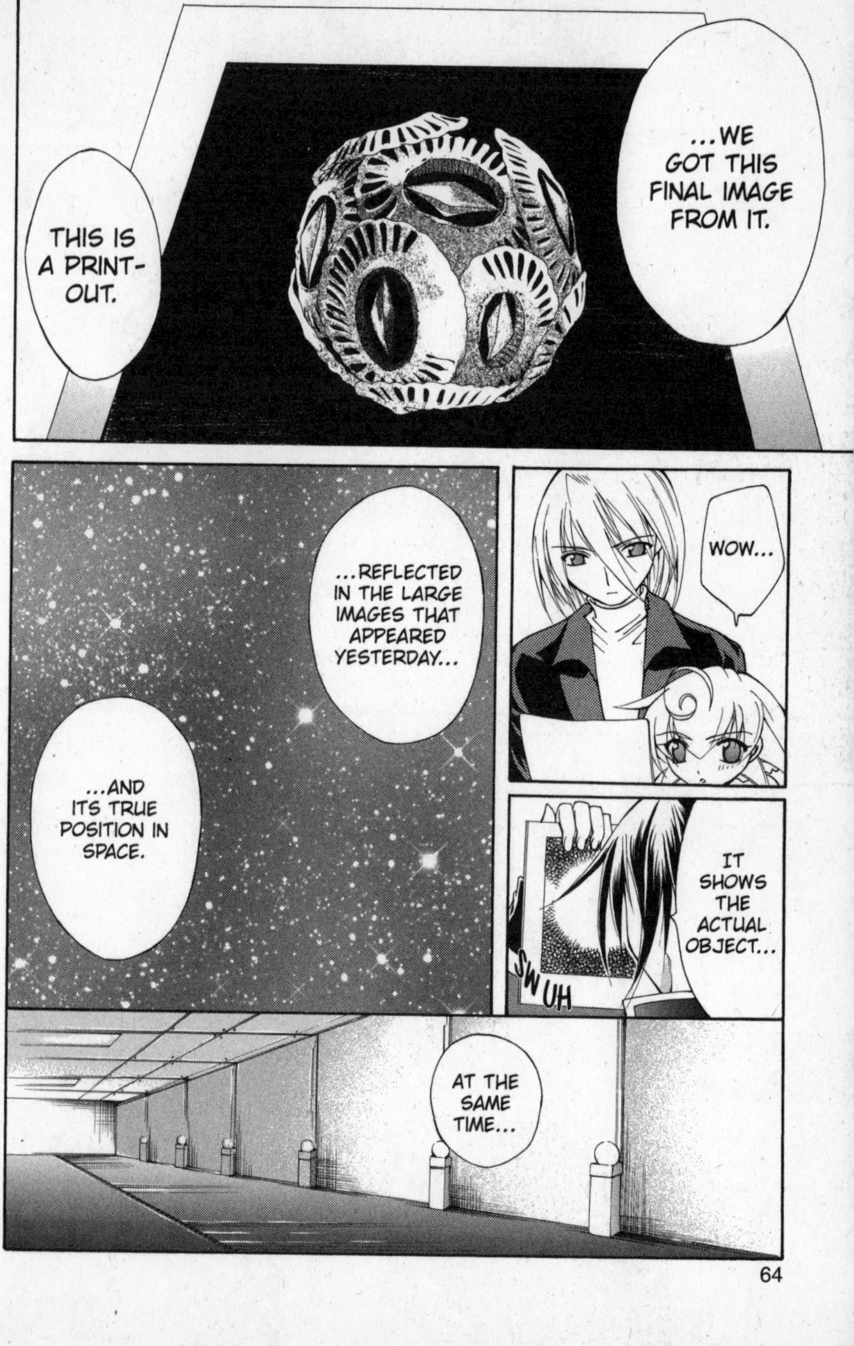
...WE GOT THIS FINAL IMAGE FROM IT.
THIS IS A PRINT-OUT.
WOW...
IT SHOWS THE ACTUAL OBJECT...
SWUH
...REFLECTED IN THE LARGE IMAGES THAT APPEARED YESTERDAY...
...AND ITS TRUE POSITION IN SPACE.
AT THE SAME TIME...

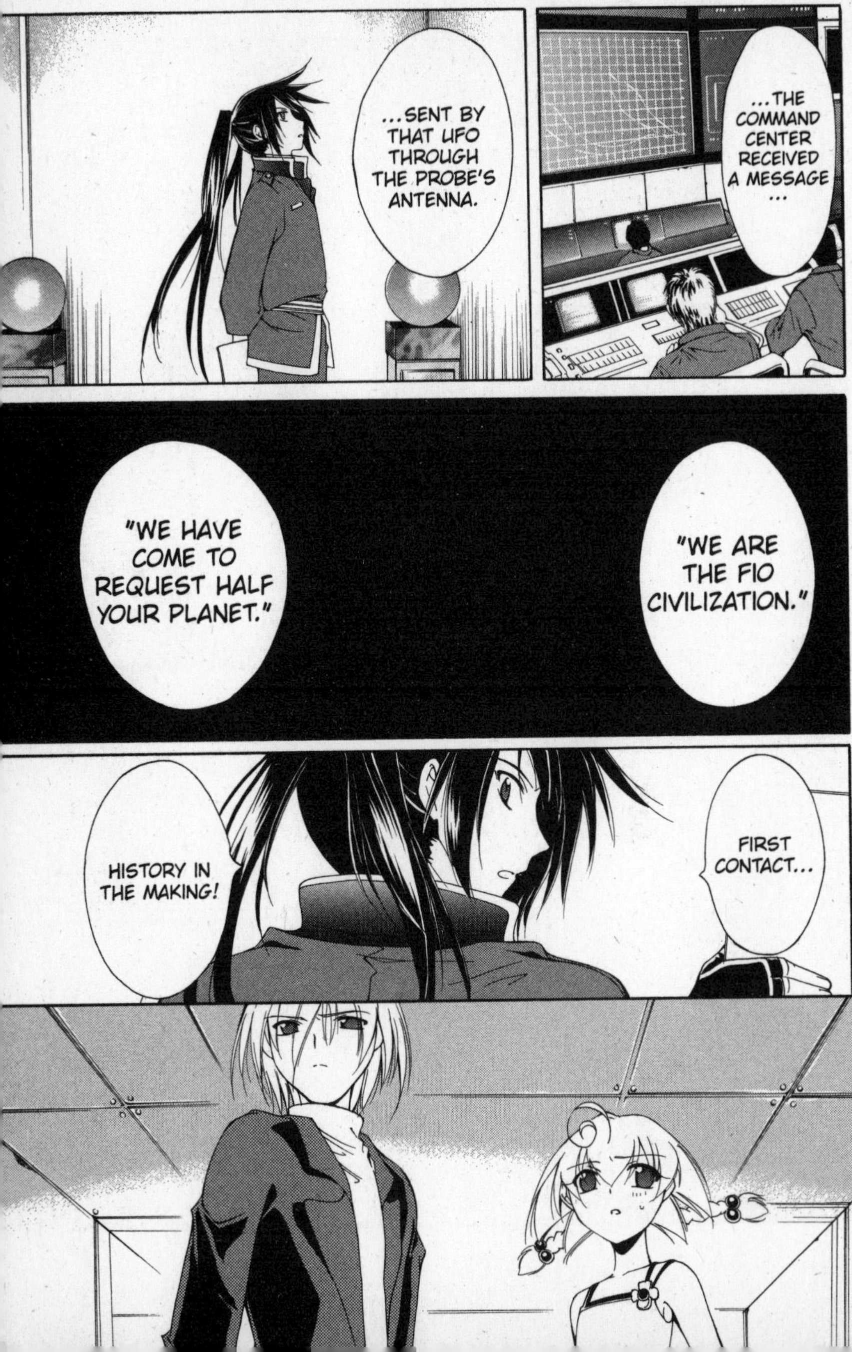
...THE COMMAND CENTER RECEIVED A MESSAGE ...
...SENT BY THAT UFO THROUGH THE PROBE'S ANTENNA.
"WE ARE THE FIO CIVILIZATION."
"WE HAVE COME TO REQUEST HALF YOUR PLANET."
FIRST CONTACT...
HISTORY IN THE MAKING!

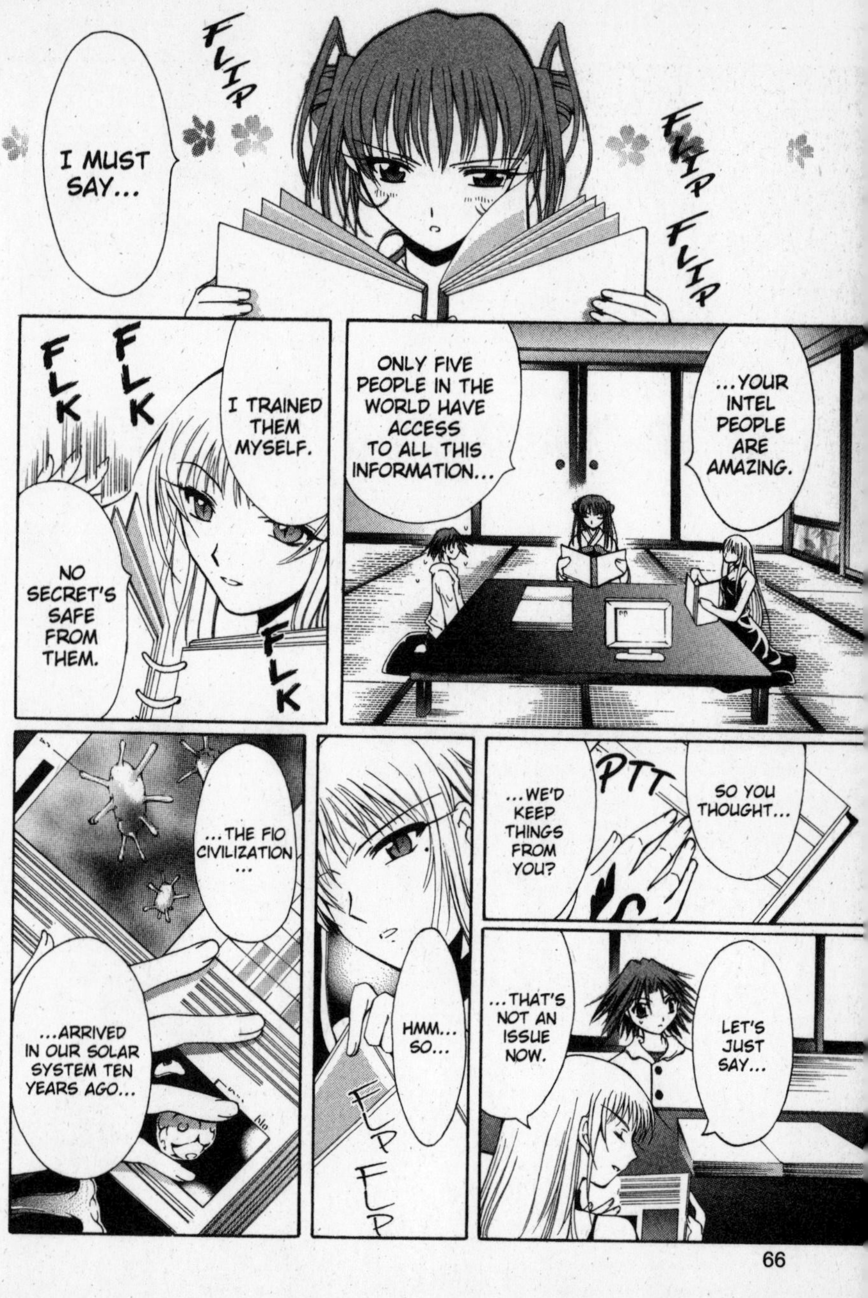
FLIP FLIP
FLIP
I MUST SAY...
...YOUR INTEL PEOPLE ARE AMAZING.
ONLY FIVE PEOPLE IN THE WORLD HAVE ACCESS TO ALL THIS INFORMATION...
I TRAINED THEM MYSELF.
FLK FLK
NO SECRET'S SAFE FROM THEM.
FLK
SO YOU THOUGHT...
PTT
...WE'D KEEP THINGS FROM YOU?
LET'S JUST SAY...
...THAT'S NOT AN ISSUE NOW.
HMM... SO...
FLP FLP
...THE FIO CIVILIZATION...
...ARRIVED IN OUR SOLAR SYSTEM TEN YEARS AGO...

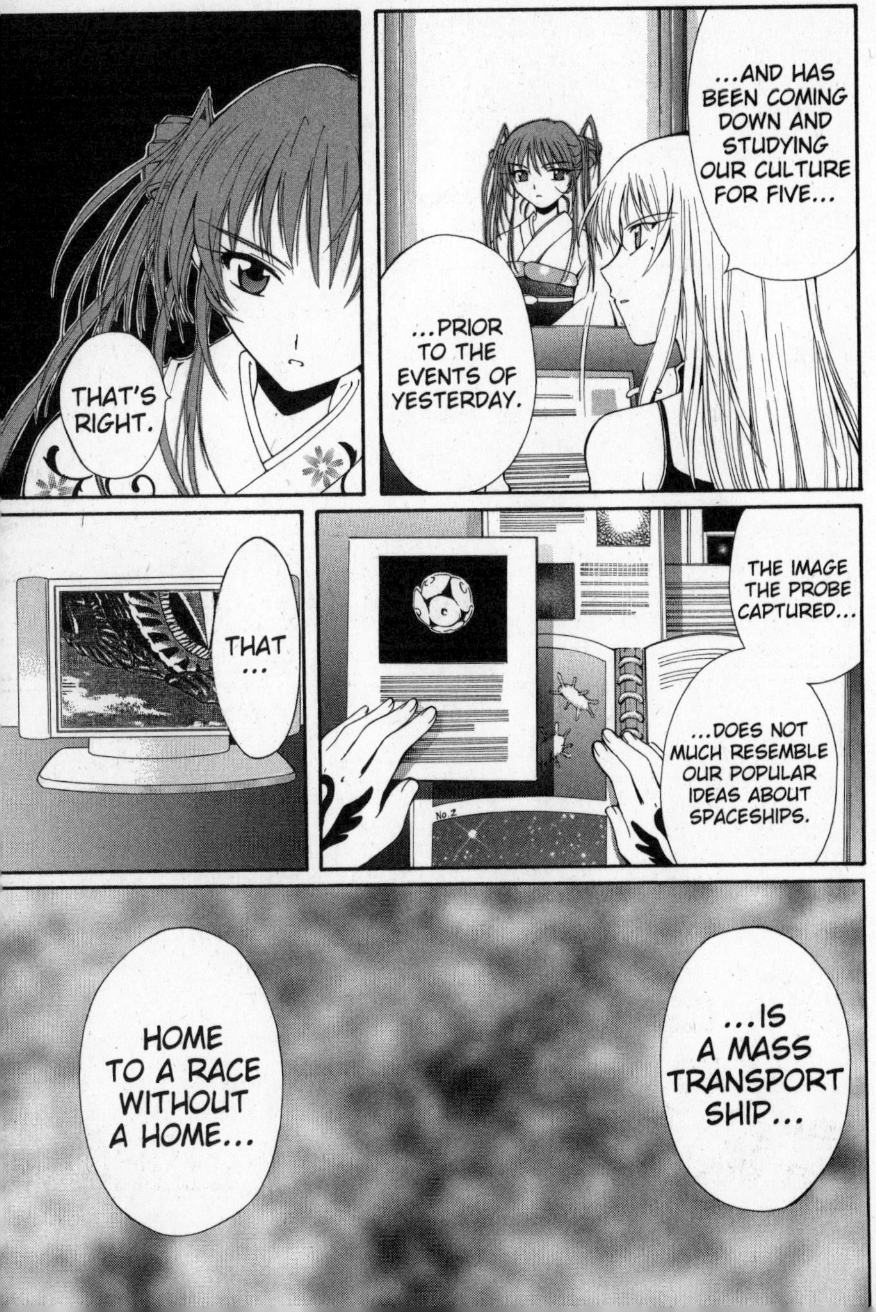
...AND HAS BEEN COMING DOWN AND STUDYING OUR CULTURE FOR FIVE...
...PRIOR TO THE EVENTS OF YESTERDAY.
THAT'S RIGHT.
THE IMAGE THE PROBE CAPTURED...
...DOES NOT MUCH RESEMBLE OUR POPULAR IDEAS ABOUT SPACESHIPS.
No.2
THAT ...
...IS A MASS TRANSPORT SHIP...
HOME TO A RACE WITHOUT A HOME...

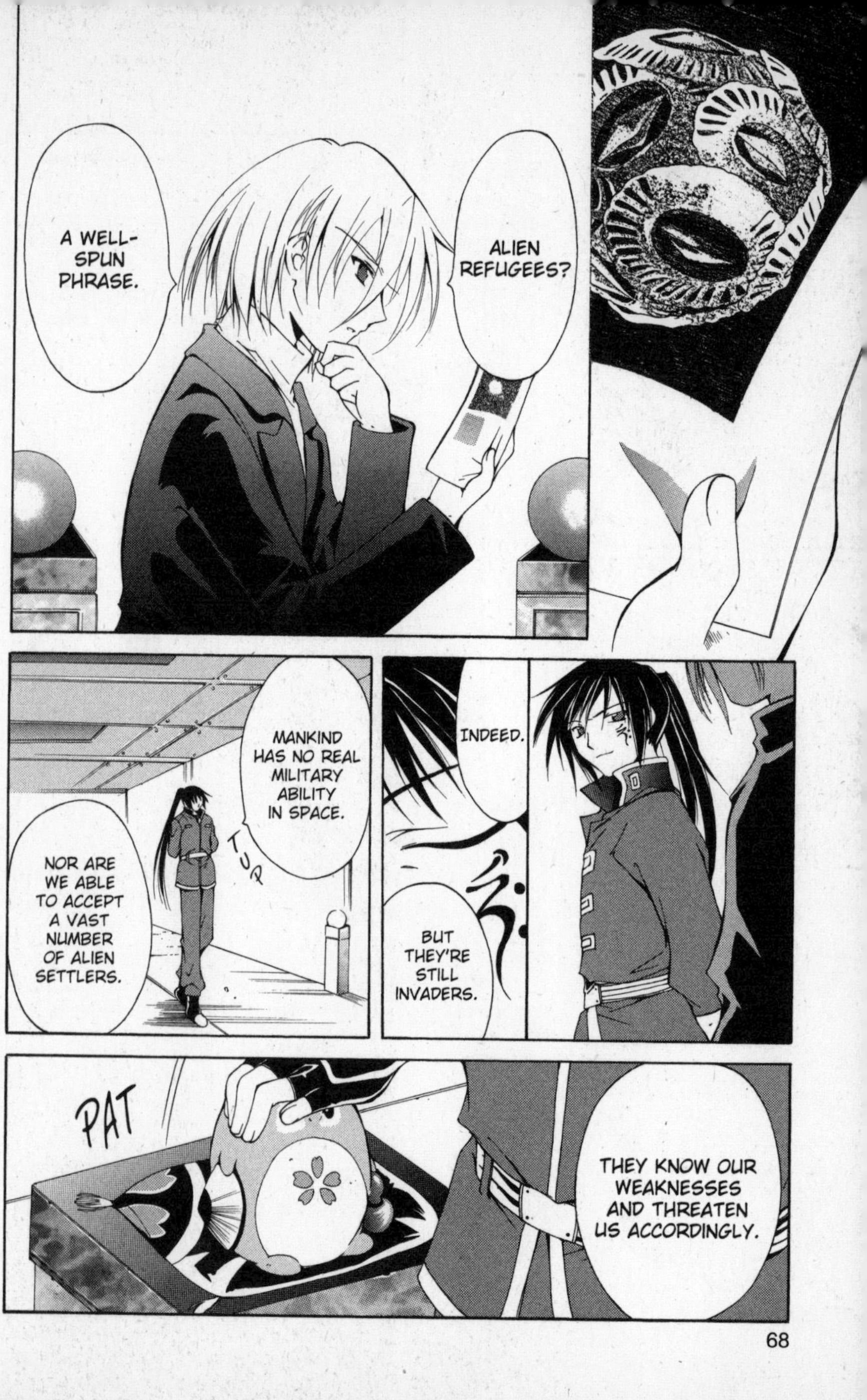
ALIEN REFUGEES?
A WELL-SPUN PHRASE.
INDEED.
BUT THEY'RE STILL INVADERS.
MANKIND HAS NO REAL MILITARY ABILITY IN SPACE.
TUP
NOR ARE WE ABLE TO ACCEPT A VAST NUMBER OF ALIEN SETTLERS.
THEY KNOW OUR WEAKNESSES AND THREATEN US ACCORDINGLY.
PAT

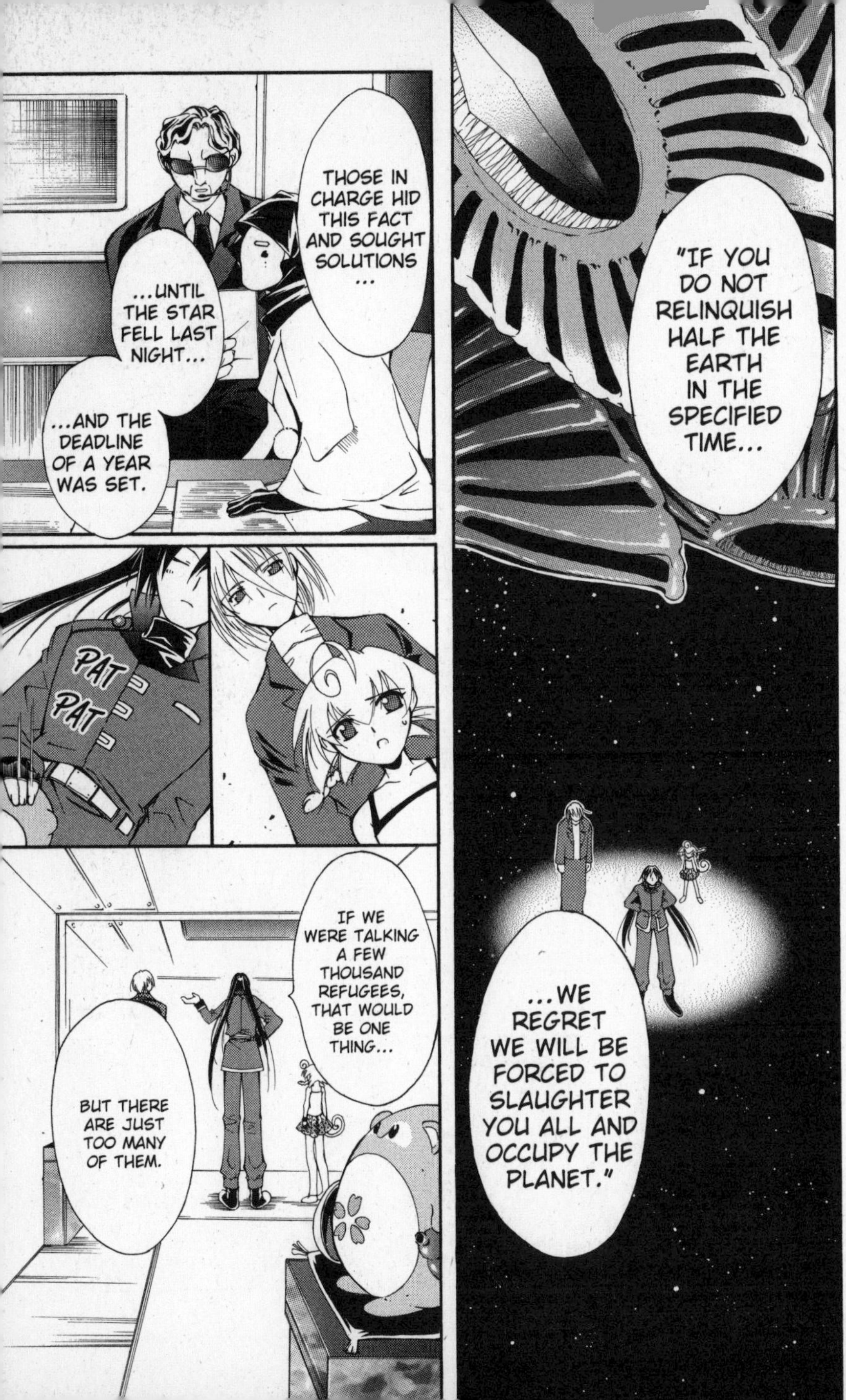
"IF YOU DO NOT RELINQUISH HALF THE EARTH IN THE SPECIFIED TIME...
...WE REGRET WE WILL BE FORCED TO SLAUGHTER YOU ALL AND OCCUPY THE PLANET."
THOSE IN CHARGE HID THIS FACT AND SOUGHT SOLUTIONS...
...UNTIL THE STAR FELL LAST NIGHT...
...AND THE DEADLINE OF A YEAR WAS SET.
PAT PAT
IF WE WERE TALKING A FEW THOUSAND REFUGEES, THAT WOULD BE ONE THING...
BUT THERE ARE JUST TOO MANY OF THEM.

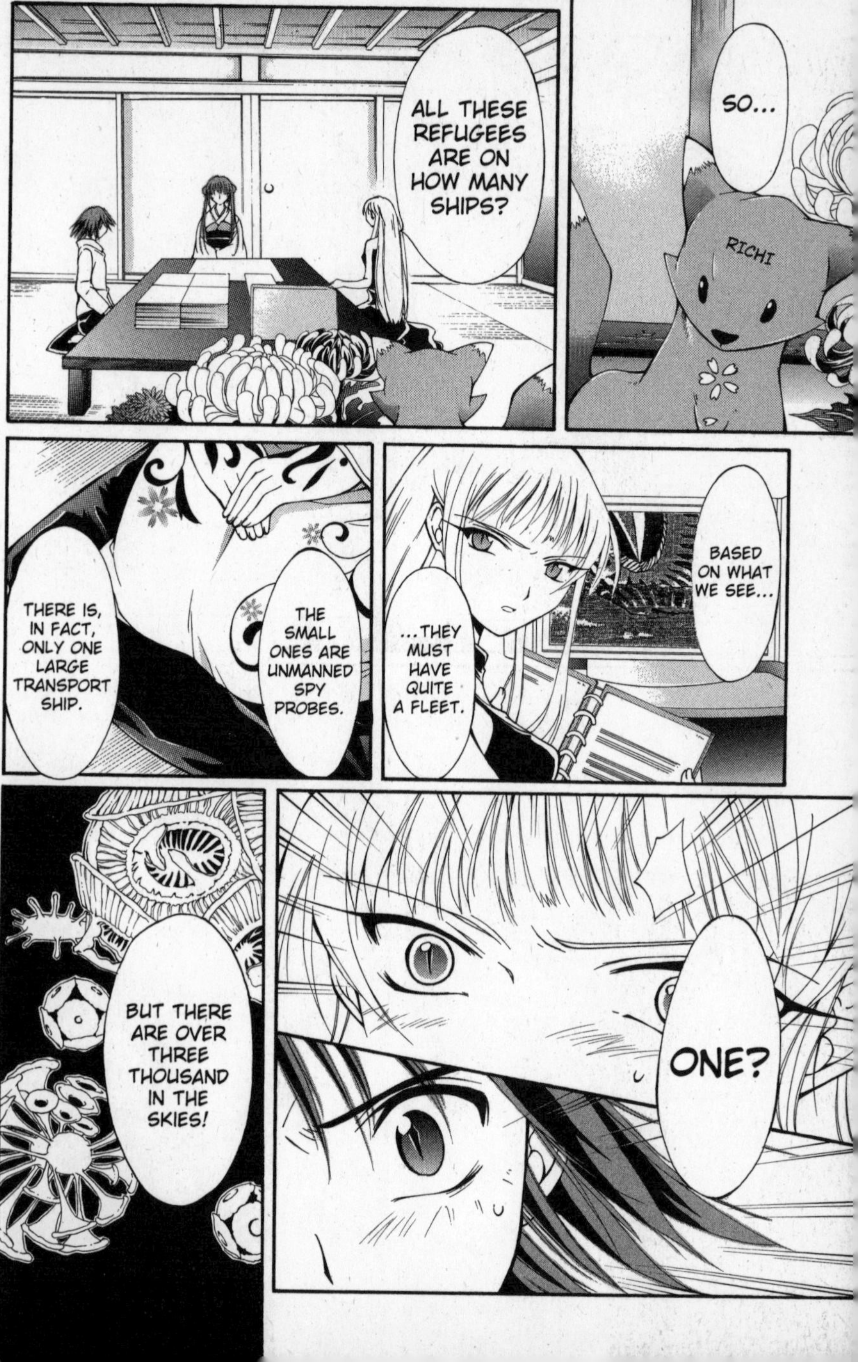
SO...
RICHI
ALL THESE REFUGEES ARE ON HOW MANY SHIPS?
BASED ON WHAT WE SEE...
...THEY MUST HAVE QUITE A FLEET.
THE SMALL ONES ARE UNMANNED SPY PROBES.
THERE IS, IN FACT, ONLY ONE LARGE TRANSPORT SHIP.
ONE?
BUT THERE ARE OVER THREE THOUSAND IN THE SKIES!

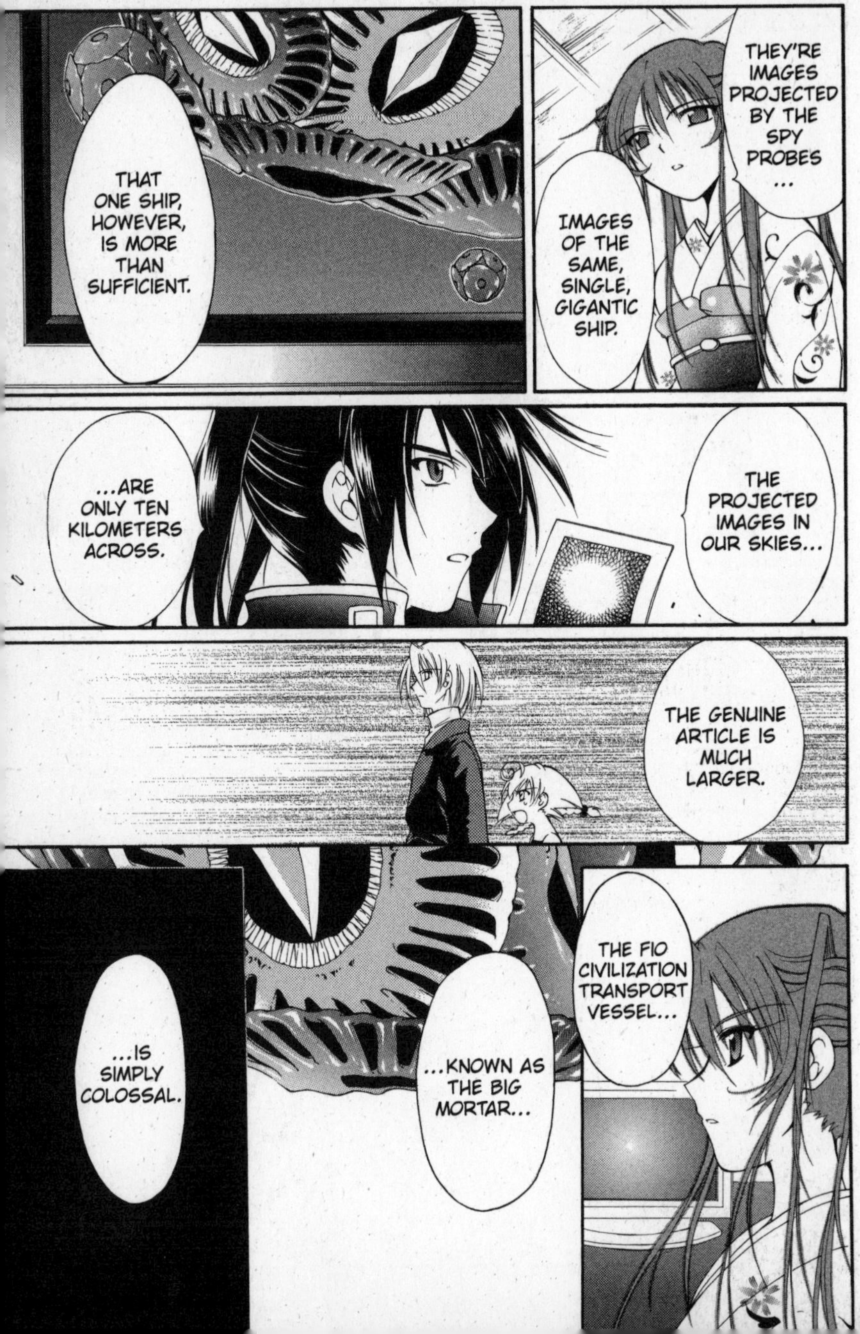
THEY'RE IMAGES PROJECTED BY THE SPY PROBES...
IMAGES OF THE SAME, SINGLE, GIGANTIC SHIP.
THAT ONE SHIP, HOWEVER, IS MORE THAN SUFFICIENT.
THE PROJECTED IMAGES IN OUR SKIES...
...ARE ONLY TEN KILOMETERS ACROSS.
THE GENUINE ARTICLE IS MUCH LARGER.
THE FIO CIVILIZATION TRANSPORT VESSEL...
...KNOWN AS THE BIG MORTAR...
...IS SIMPLY COLOSSAL.

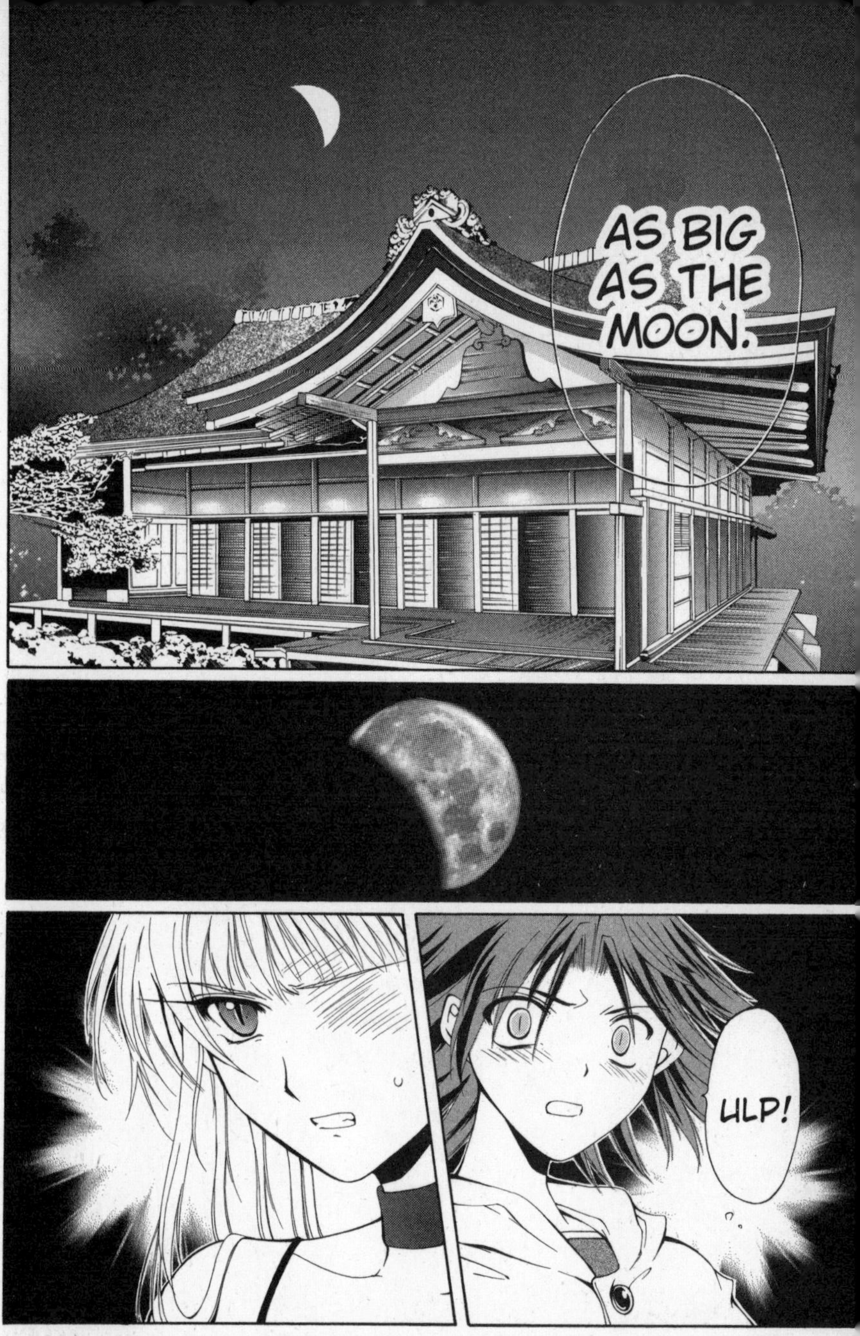
AS BIG AS THE MOON.
ULP!

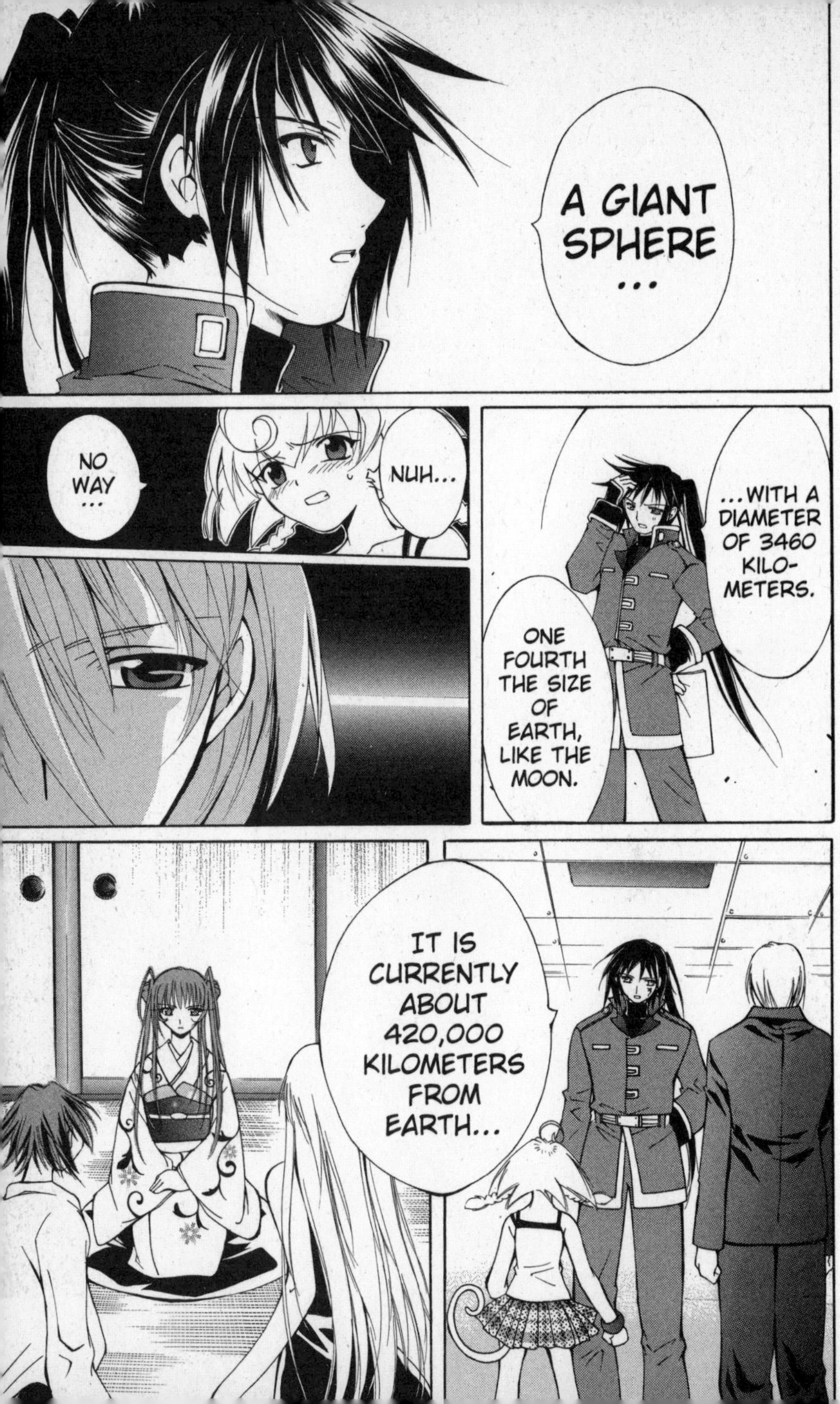
A GIANT SPHERE ...
...WITH A DIAMETER OF 3460 KILO- METERS.
ONE FOURTH THE SIZE OF EARTH, LIKE THE MOON.
NUH...
NO WAY ...
IT IS CURRENTLY ABOUT 420,000 KILOMETERS FROM EARTH...

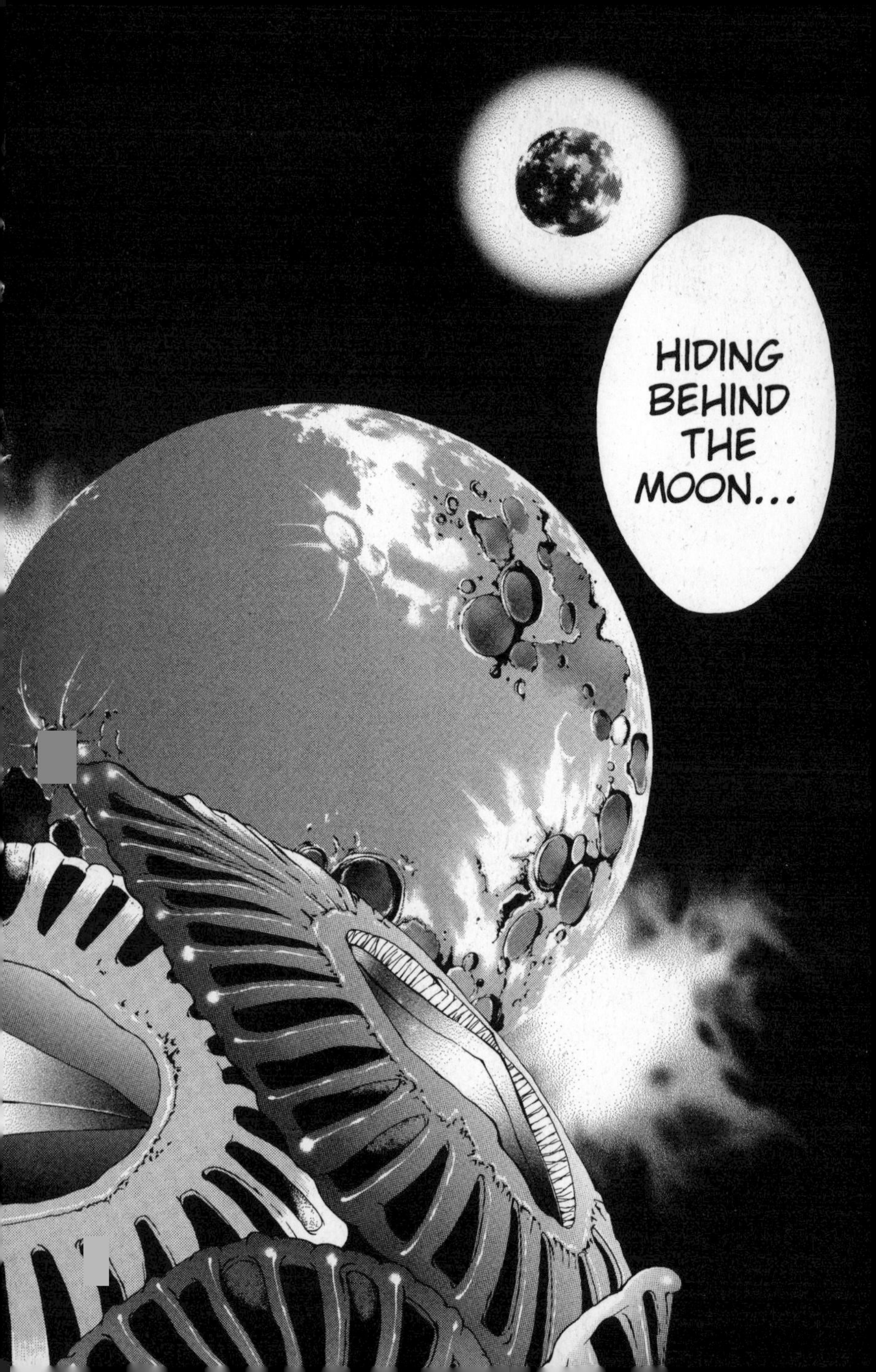
HIDING BEHIND THE MOON...

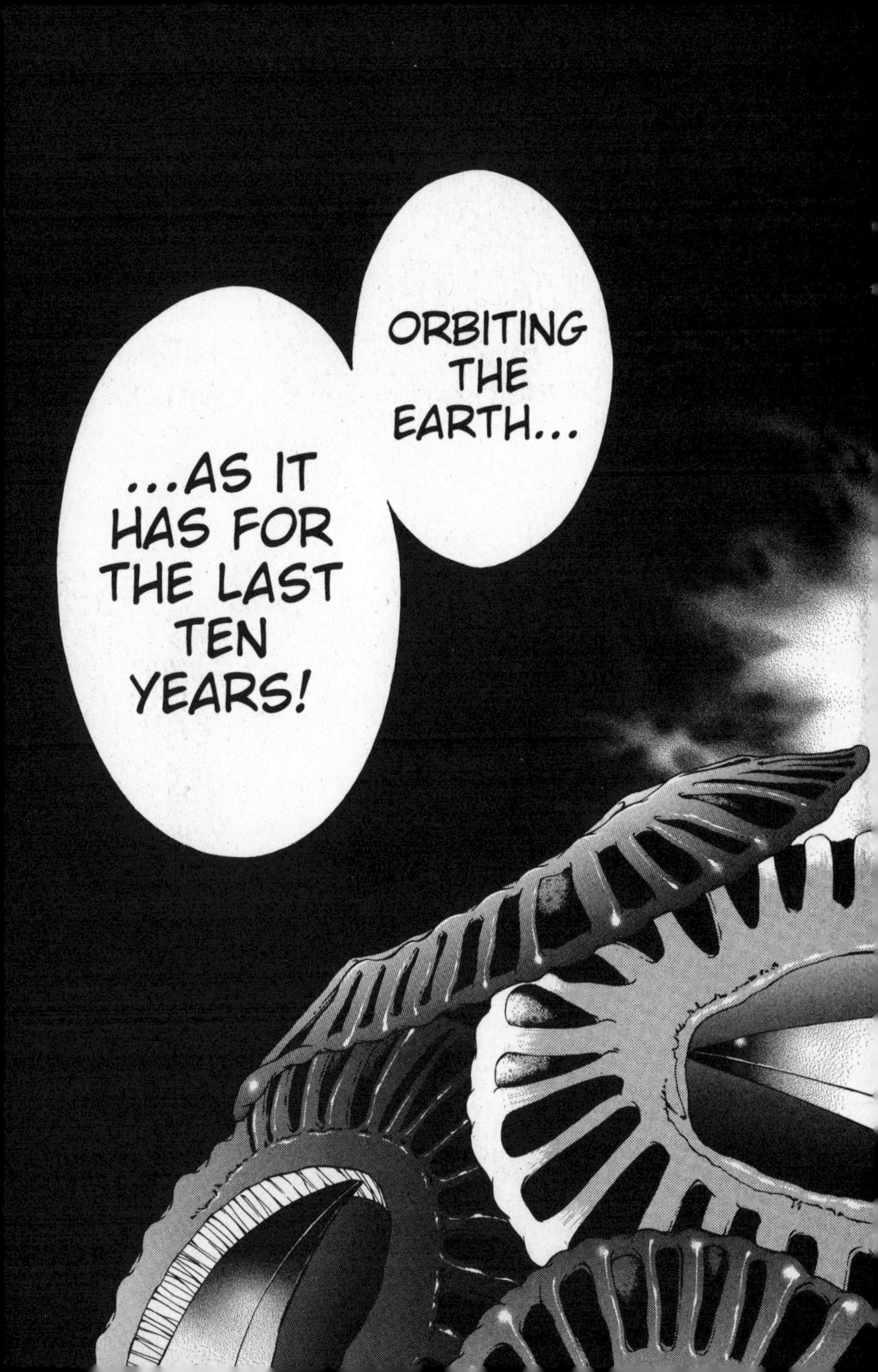
ORBITING THE EARTH...
...AS IT HAS FOR THE LAST TEN YEARS!

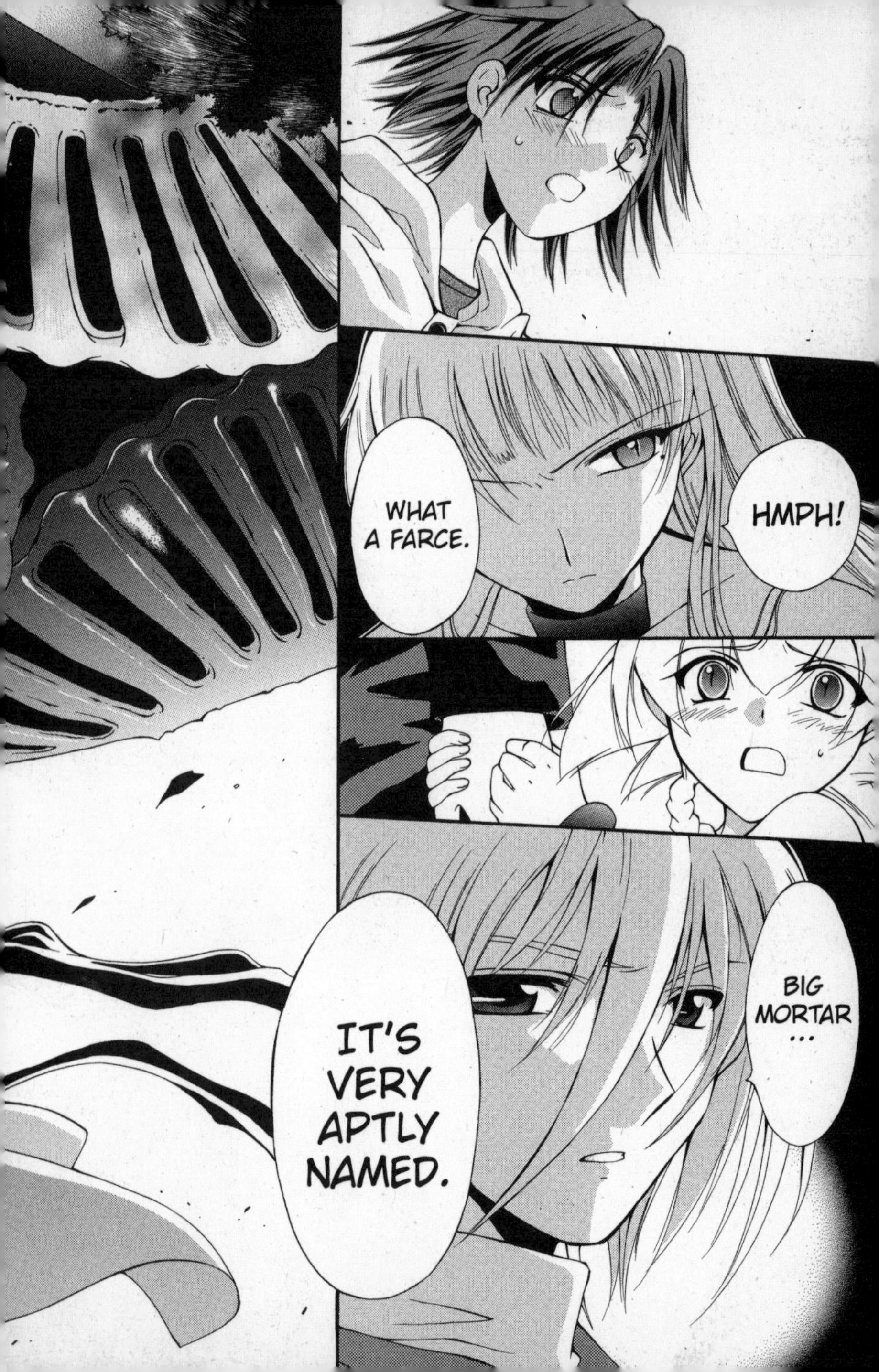
HMPH!
WHAT A FARCE.
BIG MORTAR ...
IT'S VERY APTLY NAMED.

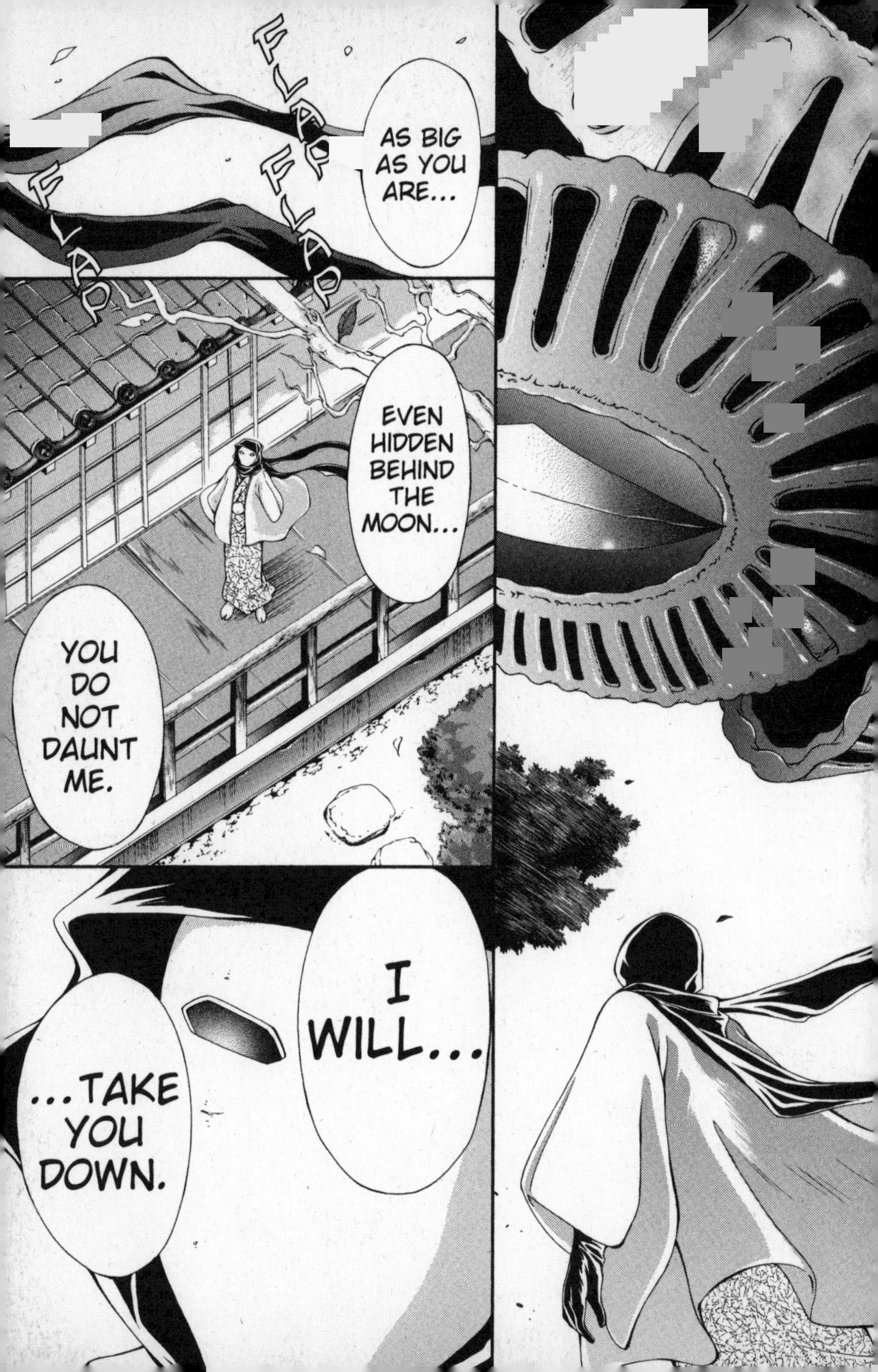
FLAP
FLAP
FLAP
AS BIG AS YOU ARE...
EVEN HIDDEN BEHIND THE MOON...
YOU DO NOT DAUNT ME.
I WILL...
...TAKE YOU DOWN.

THE RECORD OF A
FALLEN VAMPIRE

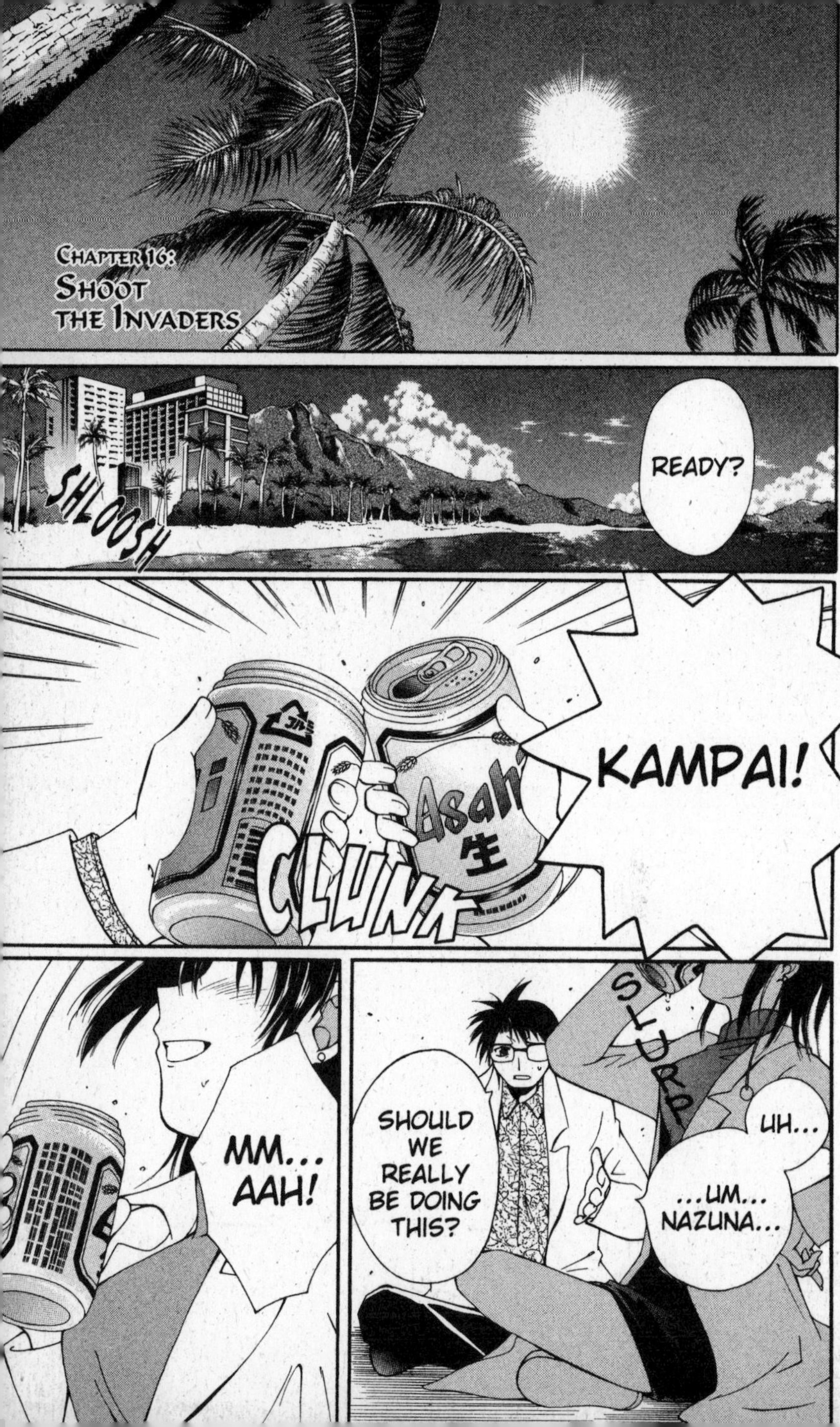
Chapter 16:
Shoot the Invaders
READY?
SHLOOSH
KAMPAI!
Asahi 生
CLUNK
SLURP
UH...
...UM... NAZUNA...
SHOULD WE REALLY BE DOING THIS?
MM... AAH!

Chapter 16: Shoot the Invaders

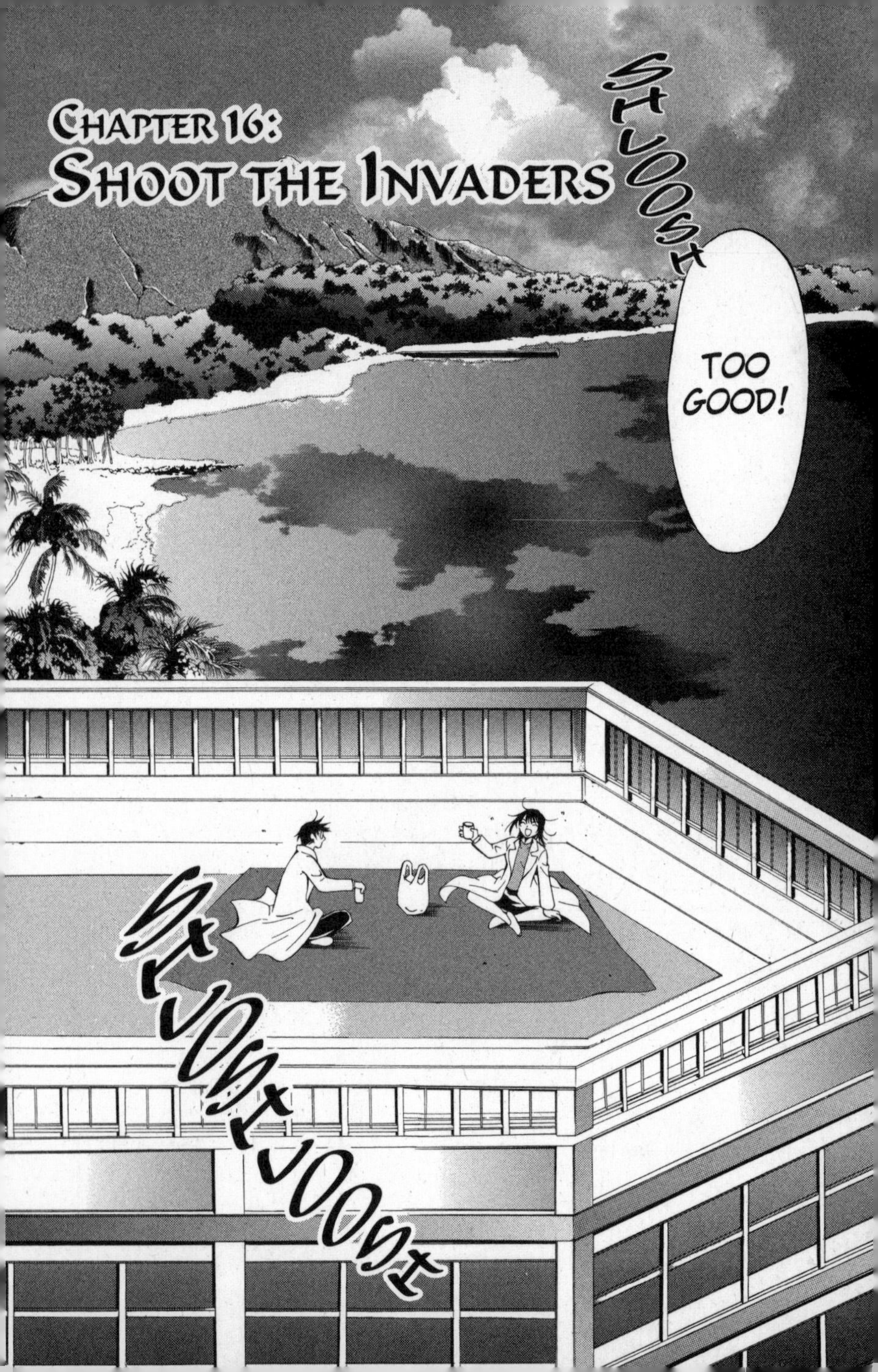

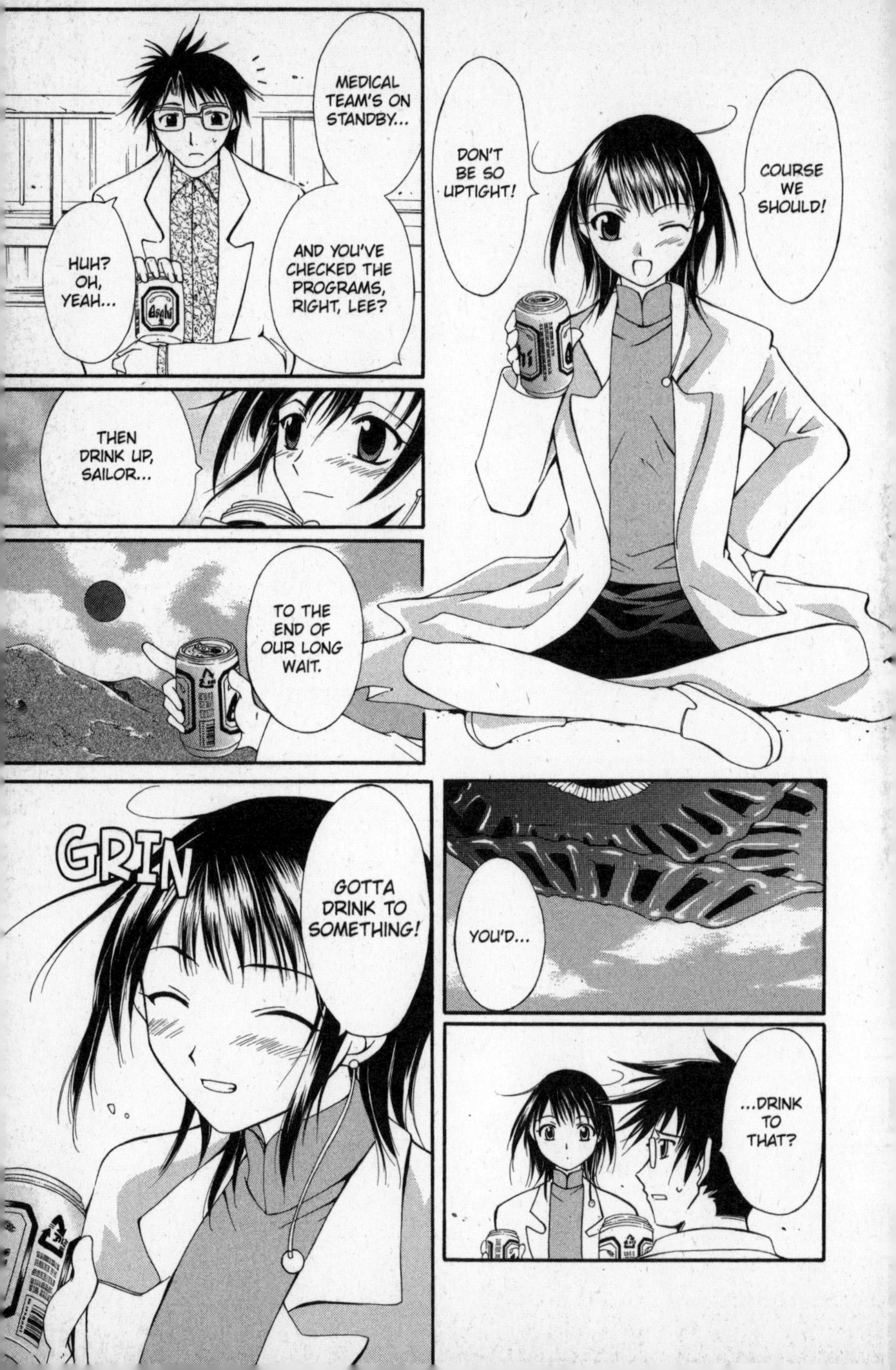
COURSE WE SHOULD!
DON'T BE SO UPTIGHT!
MEDICAL TEAM'S ON STANDBY...
AND YOU'VE CHECKED THE PROGRAMS, RIGHT, LEE?
HUH? OH, YEAH...
THEN DRINK UP, SAILOR...
TO THE END OF OUR LONG WAIT.
YOU'D...
...DRINK TO THAT?
GRIN
GOTTA DRINK TO SOMETHING!

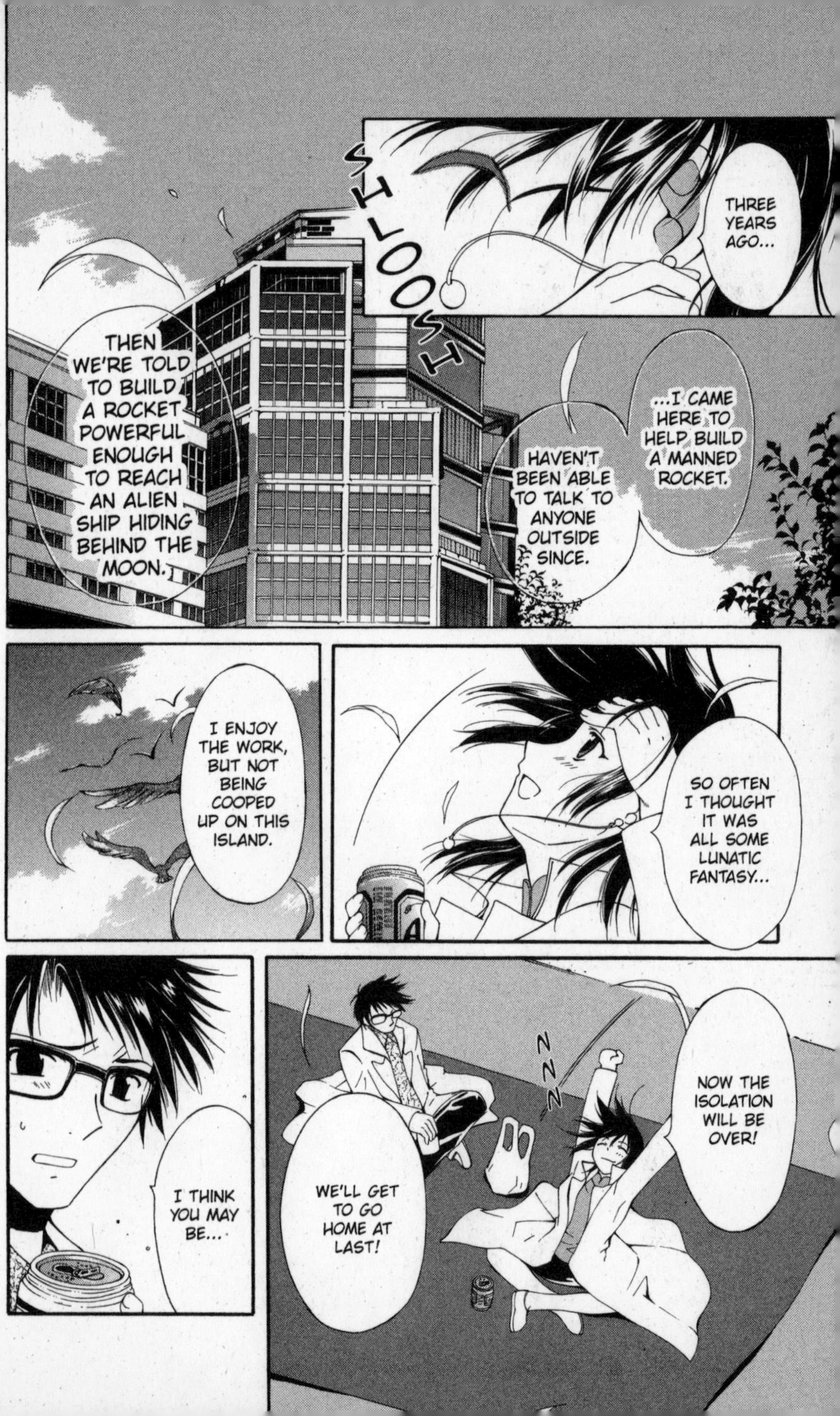
THREE YEARS AGO...
SHLOOSH
...I CAME HERE TO HELP BUILD A MANNED ROCKET.
HAVEN'T BEEN ABLE TO TALK TO ANYONE OUTSIDE SINCE.
THEN WE'RE TOLD TO BUILD A ROCKET POWERFUL ENOUGH TO REACH AN ALIEN SHIP HIDING BEHIND THE MOON.
SO OFTEN I THOUGHT IT WAS ALL SOME LUNATIC FANTASY...
I ENJOY THE WORK, BUT NOT BEING COOPED UP ON THIS ISLAND.
NOW THE ISOLATION WILL BE OVER!
NNN
WE'LL GET TO GO HOME AT LAST!
I THINK YOU MAY BE...

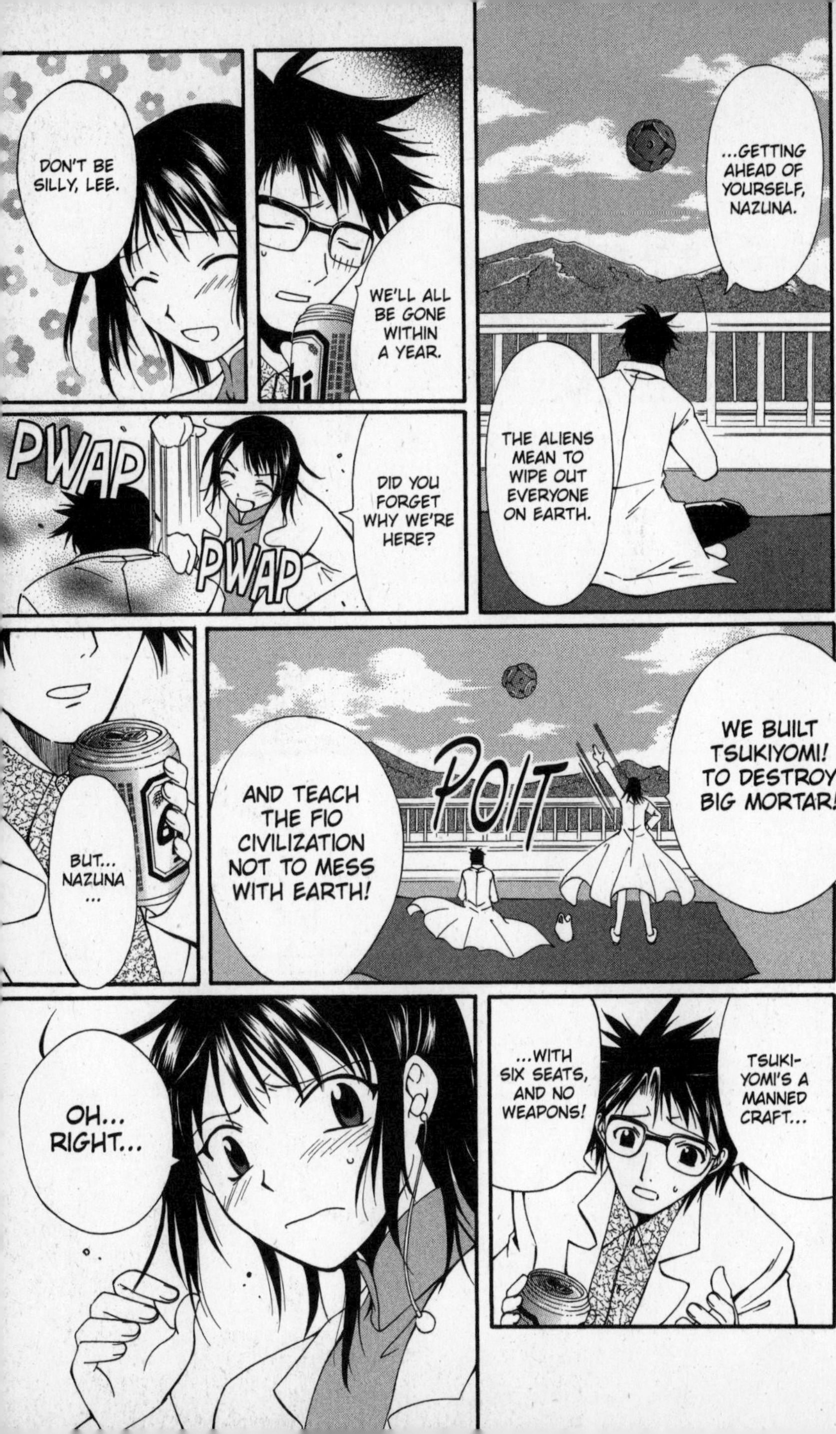
...GETTING AHEAD OF YOURSELF, NAZUNA.
THE ALIENS MEAN TO WIPE OUT EVERYONE ON EARTH.
WE'LL ALL BE GONE WITHIN A YEAR.
DON'T BE SILLY, LEE.
DID YOU FORGET WHY WE'RE HERE?
PWAP
PWAP
WE BUILT TSUKIYOMI! TO DESTROY BIG MORTAR!
POIT
AND TEACH THE FIO CIVILIZATION NOT TO MESS WITH EARTH!
BUT... NAZUNA ...
TSUKI-YOMI'S A MANNED CRAFT...
...WITH SIX SEATS, AND NO WEAPONS!
OH... RIGHT...

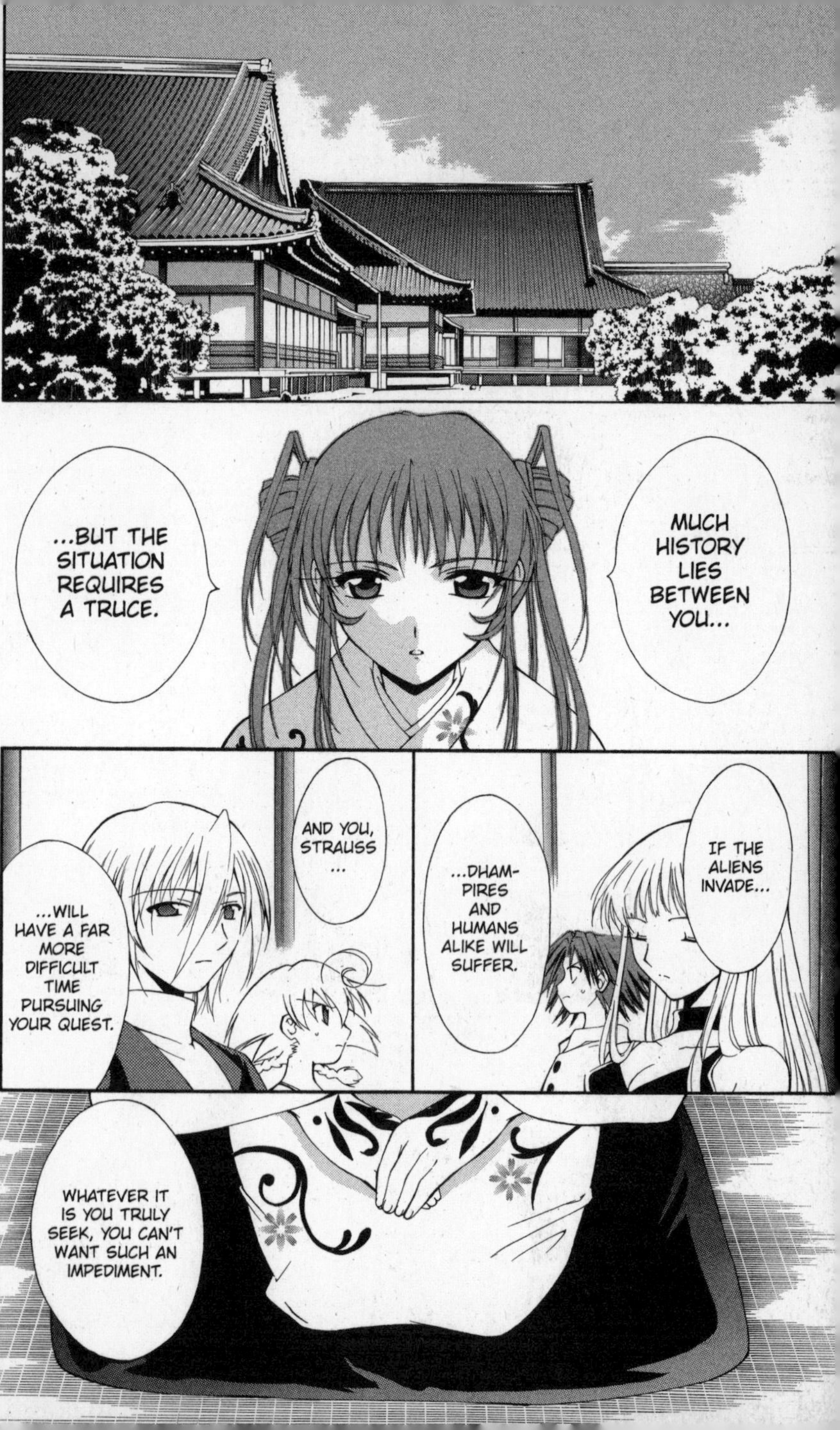
MUCH HISTORY LIES BETWEEN YOU...
...BUT THE SITUATION REQUIRES A TRUCE.
IF THE ALIENS INVADE...
...DHAMPIRES AND HUMANS ALIKE WILL SUFFER.
AND YOU, STRAUSS ...
...WILL HAVE A FAR MORE DIFFICULT TIME PURSUING YOUR QUEST.
WHATEVER IT IS YOU TRULY SEEK, YOU CAN'T WANT SUCH AN IMPEDIMENT.

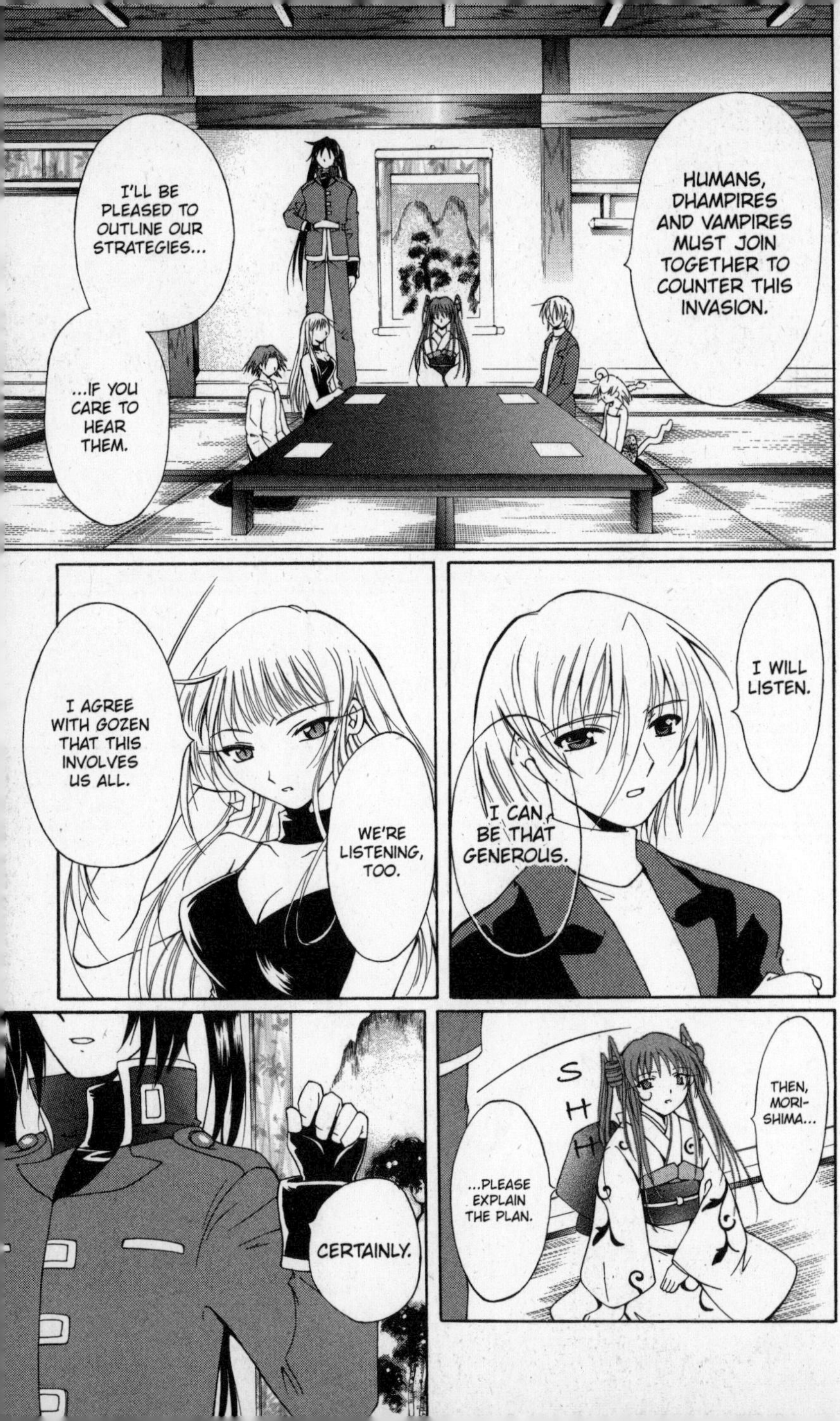
HUMANS, DHAMPIRES AND VAMPIRES MUST JOIN TOGETHER TO COUNTER THIS INVASION.
I'LL BE PLEASED TO OUTLINE OUR STRATEGIES...
...IF YOU CARE TO HEAR THEM.
I WILL LISTEN.
I CAN BE THAT GENEROUS.
I AGREE WITH GOZEN THAT THIS INVOLVES US ALL.
WE'RE LISTENING, TOO.
THEN, MORI-SHIMA...
SHH
...PLEASE EXPLAIN THE PLAN.
CERTAINLY.

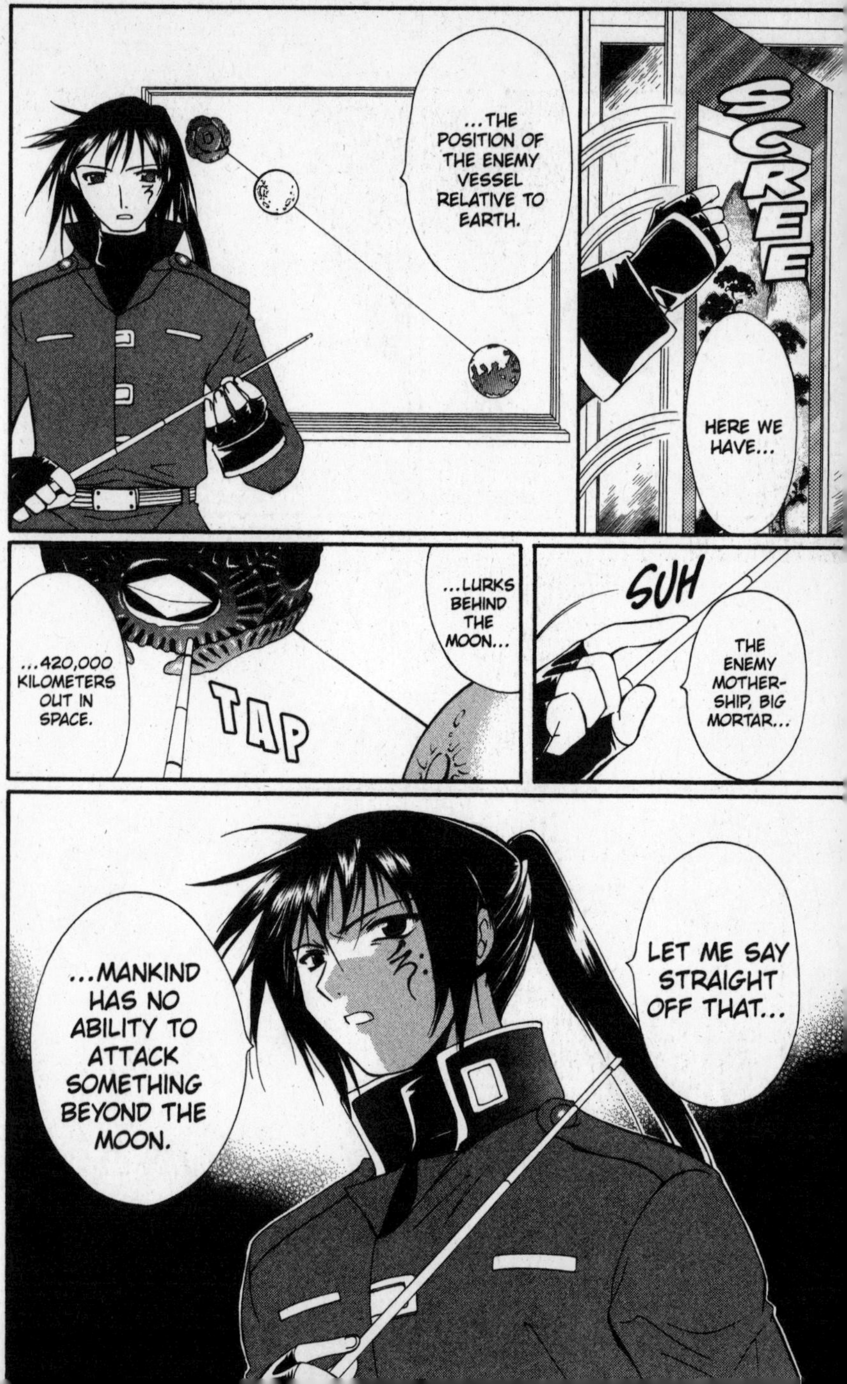
SCREE
HERE WE HAVE...
...THE POSITION OF THE ENEMY VESSEL RELATIVE TO EARTH.
SUH
THE ENEMY MOTHERSHIP, BIG MORTAR...
...LURKS BEHIND THE MOON...
TAP
...420,000 KILOMETERS OUT IN SPACE.
LET ME SAY STRAIGHT OFF THAT...
...MANKIND HAS NO ABILITY TO ATTACK SOMETHING BEYOND THE MOON.

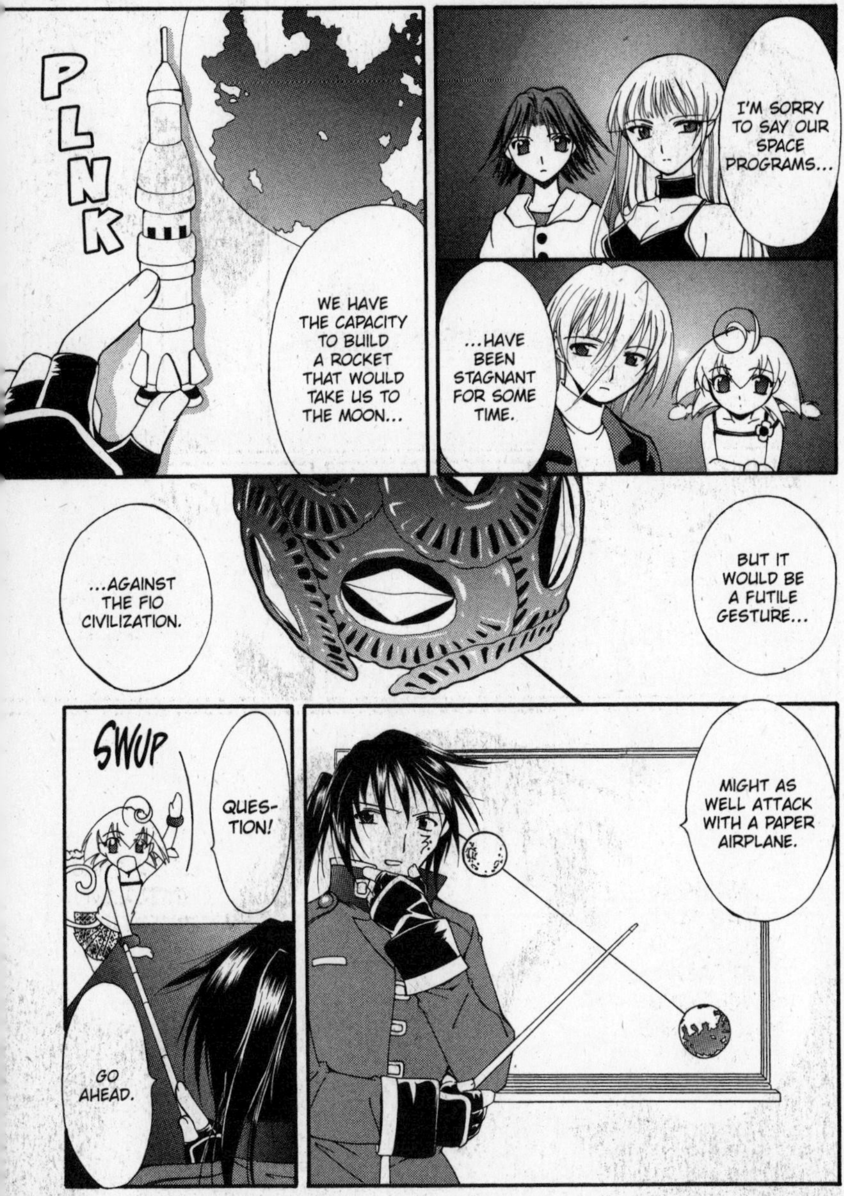
I'M SORRY TO SAY OUR SPACE PROGRAMS...
...HAVE BEEN STAGNANT FOR SOME TIME.
PLNK
WE HAVE THE CAPACITY TO BUILD A ROCKET THAT WOULD TAKE US TO THE MOON...
BUT IT WOULD BE A FUTILE GESTURE...
...AGAINST THE FIO CIVILIZATION.
MIGHT AS WELL ATTACK WITH A PAPER AIRPLANE.
SWUP
QUES-TION!
GO AHEAD.

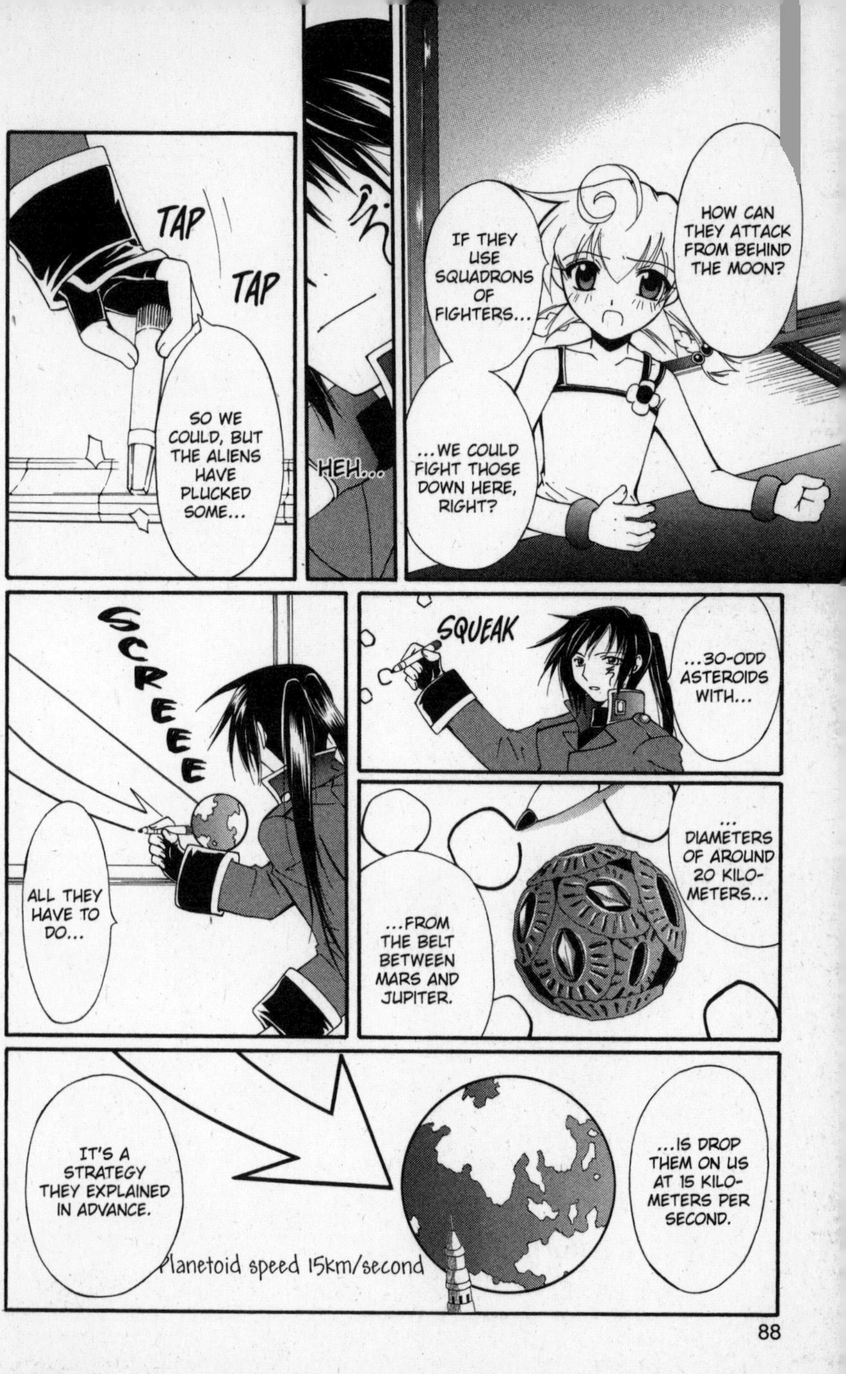
HOW CAN THEY ATTACK FROM BEHIND THE MOON?
IF THEY USE SQUADRONS OF FIGHTERS...
...WE COULD FIGHT THOSE DOWN HERE, RIGHT?
HEH...
TAP
TAP
SO WE COULD, BUT THE ALIENS HAVE PLUCKED SOME...
SQUEAK
...30-ODD ASTEROIDS WITH...
...DIAMETERS OF AROUND 20 KILOMETERS...
...FROM THE BELT BETWEEN MARS AND JUPITER.
SCREEEE
ALL THEY HAVE TO DO...
...IS DROP THEM ON US AT 15 KILOMETERS PER SECOND.
IT'S A STRATEGY THEY EXPLAINED IN ADVANCE.
Planetoid speed 15km/second

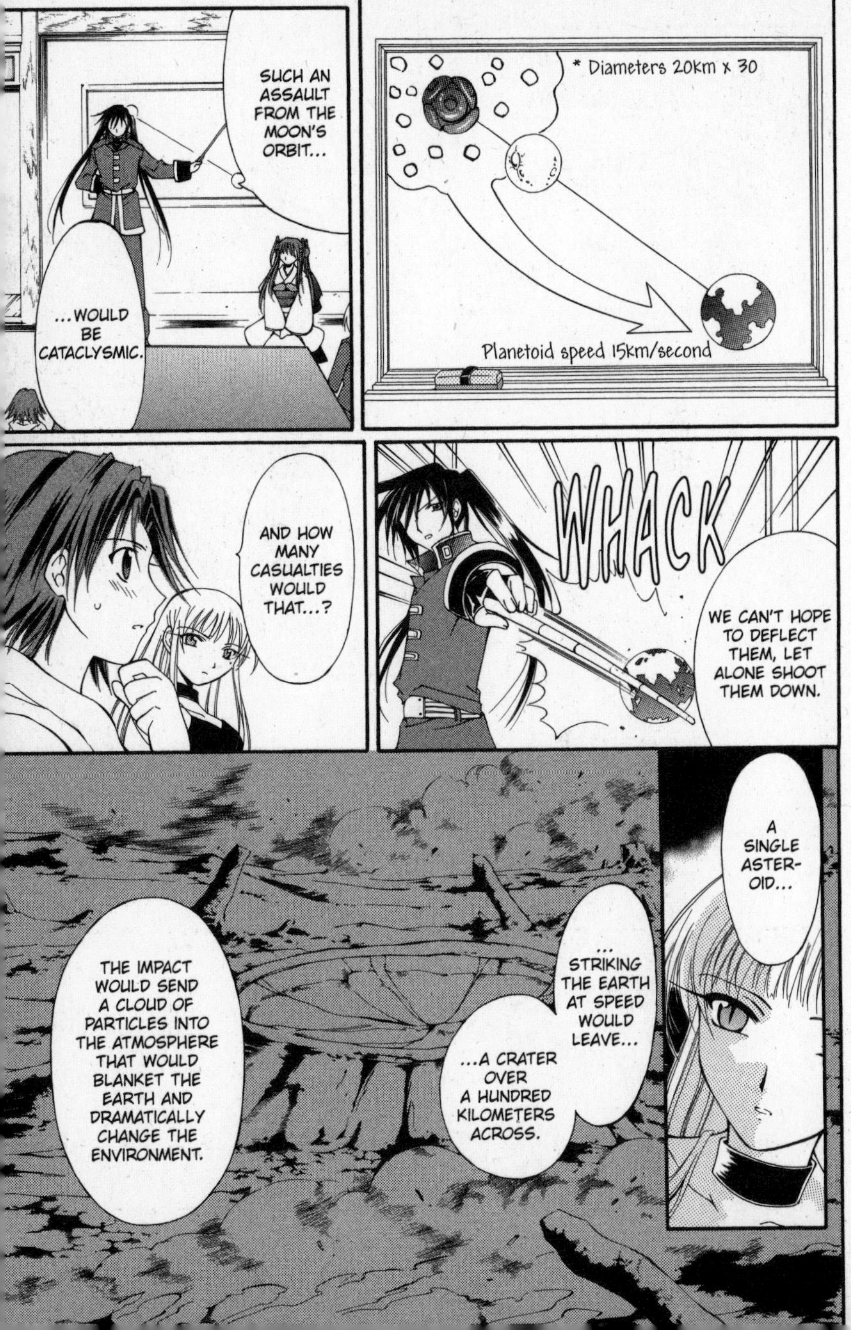
* Diameters 20km x 30
Planetoid speed 15km/second
SUCH AN ASSAULT FROM THE MOON'S ORBIT...
...WOULD BE CATACLYSMIC.
WHACK
WE CAN'T HOPE TO DEFLECT THEM, LET ALONE SHOOT THEM DOWN.
AND HOW MANY CASUALTIES WOULD THAT...?
A SINGLE ASTER-OID...
...STRIKING THE EARTH AT SPEED WOULD LEAVE...
...A CRATER OVER A HUNDRED KILOMETERS ACROSS.
THE IMPACT WOULD SEND A CLOUD OF PARTICLES INTO THE ATMOSPHERE THAT WOULD BLANKET THE EARTH AND DRAMATICALLY CHANGE THE ENVIRONMENT.

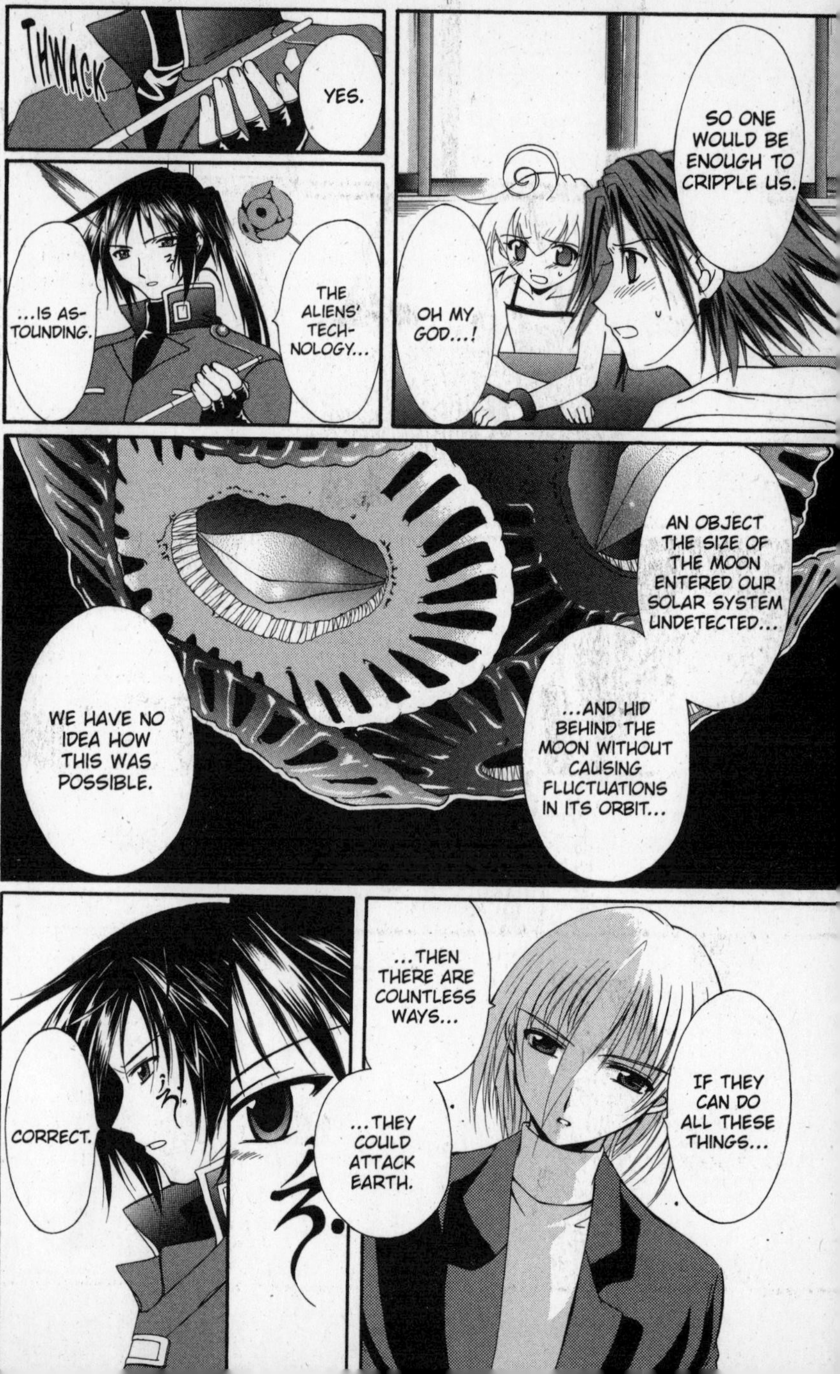
SO ONE WOULD BE ENOUGH TO CRIPPLE US.
OH MY GOD...!
THWACK
YES.
THE ALIENS' TECHNOLOGY...
...IS ASTOUNDING.
AN OBJECT THE SIZE OF THE MOON ENTERED OUR SOLAR SYSTEM UNDETECTED...
...AND HID BEHIND THE MOON WITHOUT CAUSING FLUCTUATIONS IN ITS ORBIT...
WE HAVE NO IDEA HOW THIS WAS POSSIBLE.
IF THEY CAN DO ALL THESE THINGS...
...THEN THERE ARE COUNTLESS WAYS...
...THEY COULD ATTACK EARTH.
CORRECT.

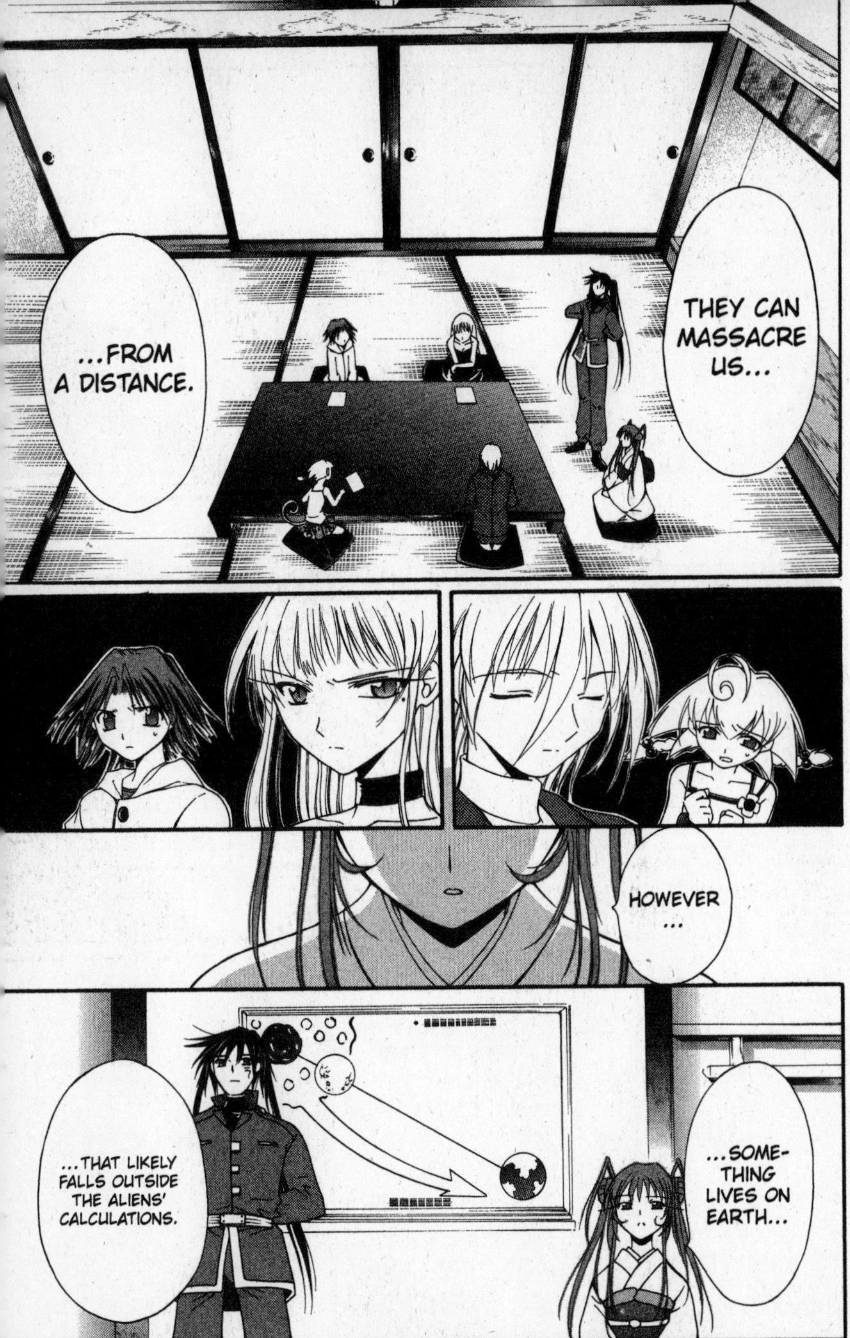
THEY CAN MASSACRE US...
...FROM A DISTANCE.
HOWEVER ...
...SOME-THING LIVES ON EARTH...
...THAT LIKELY FALLS OUTSIDE THE ALIENS' CALCULATIONS.

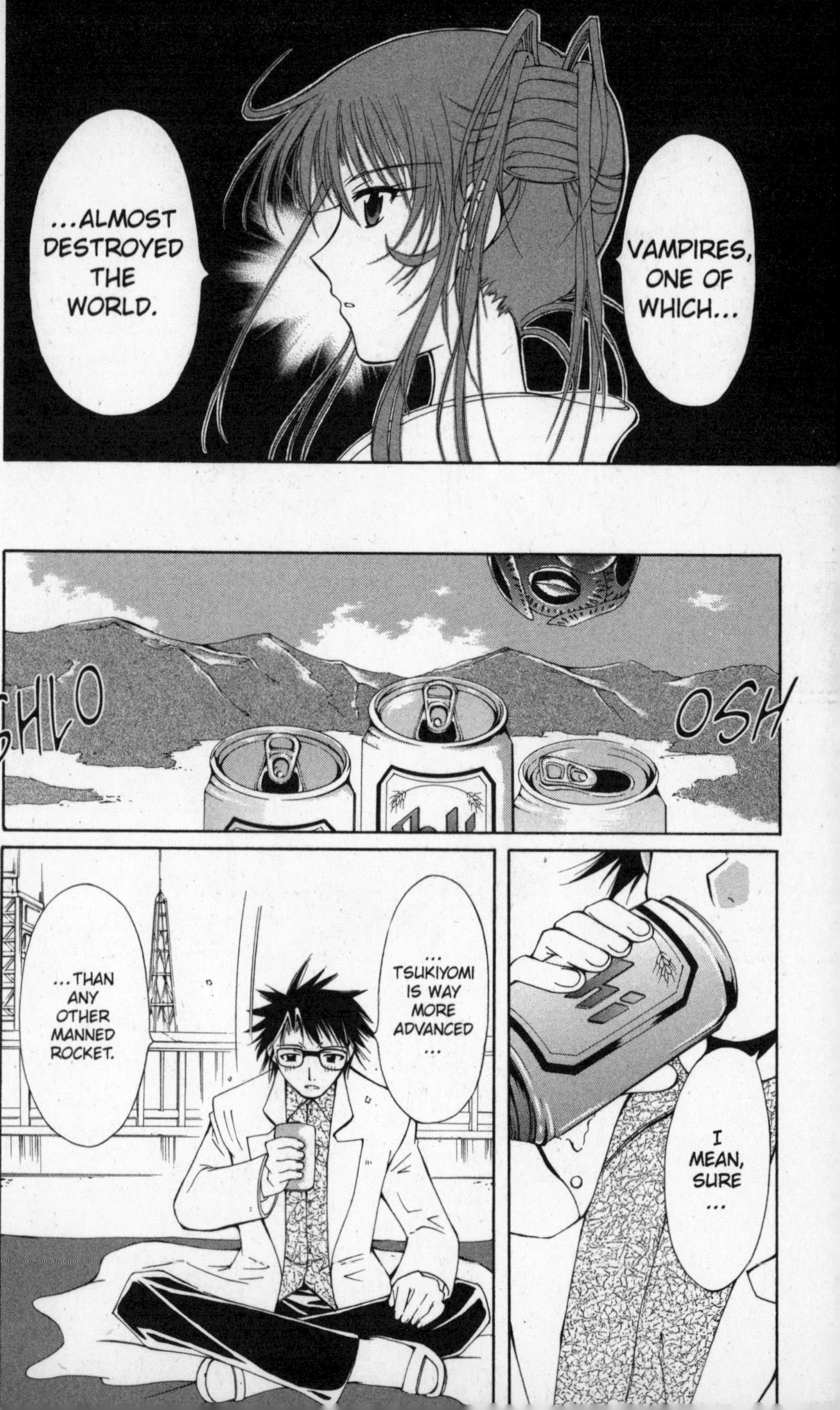
VAMPIRES, ONE OF WHICH...
...ALMOST DESTROYED THE WORLD.
SHLO
OSH
I MEAN, SURE ...
... TSUKIYOMI IS WAY MORE ADVANCED ...
...THAN ANY OTHER MANNED ROCKET.

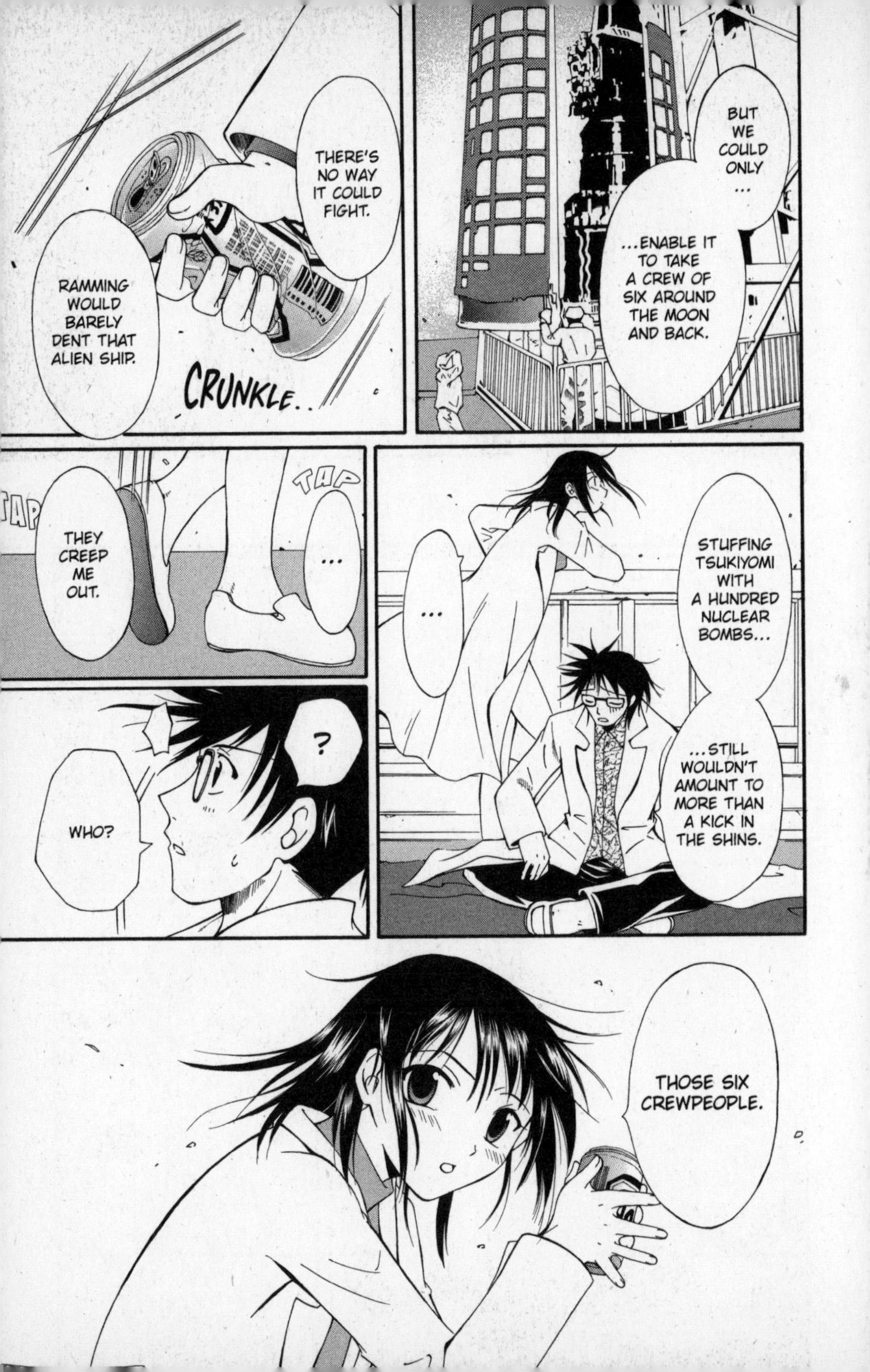
BUT WE COULD ONLY ...
...ENABLE IT TO TAKE A CREW OF SIX AROUND THE MOON AND BACK.
THERE'S NO WAY IT COULD FIGHT.
RAMMING WOULD BARELY DENT THAT ALIEN SHIP.
CRUNKLE..
STUFFING TSUKIYOMI WITH A HUNDRED NUCLEAR BOMBS...
...STILL WOULDN'T AMOUNT TO MORE THAN A KICK IN THE SHINS.
...
TAP
...
THEY CREEP ME OUT.
TAP
?
WHO?
THOSE SIX CREWPEOPLE.

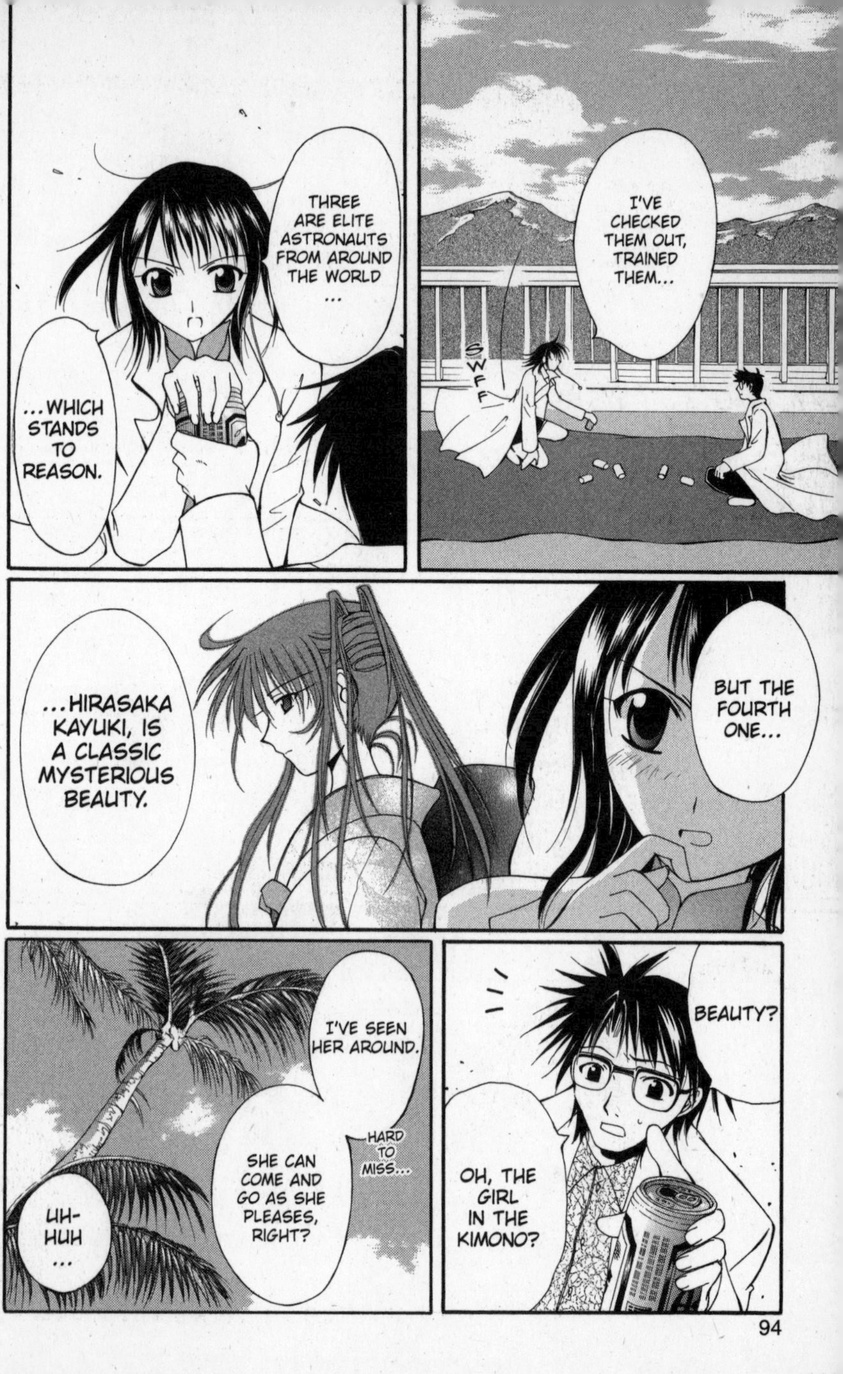
I'VE CHECKED THEM OUT, TRAINED THEM...
SWFF
THREE ARE ELITE ASTRONAUTS FROM AROUND THE WORLD ...
...WHICH STANDS TO REASON.
BUT THE FOURTH ONE...
...HIRASAKA KAYUKI, IS A CLASSIC MYSTERIOUS BEAUTY.
BEAUTY?
OH, THE GIRL IN THE KIMONO?
I'VE SEEN HER AROUND.
HARD TO MISS...
SHE CAN COME AND GO AS SHE PLEASES, RIGHT?
UH-HUH ...

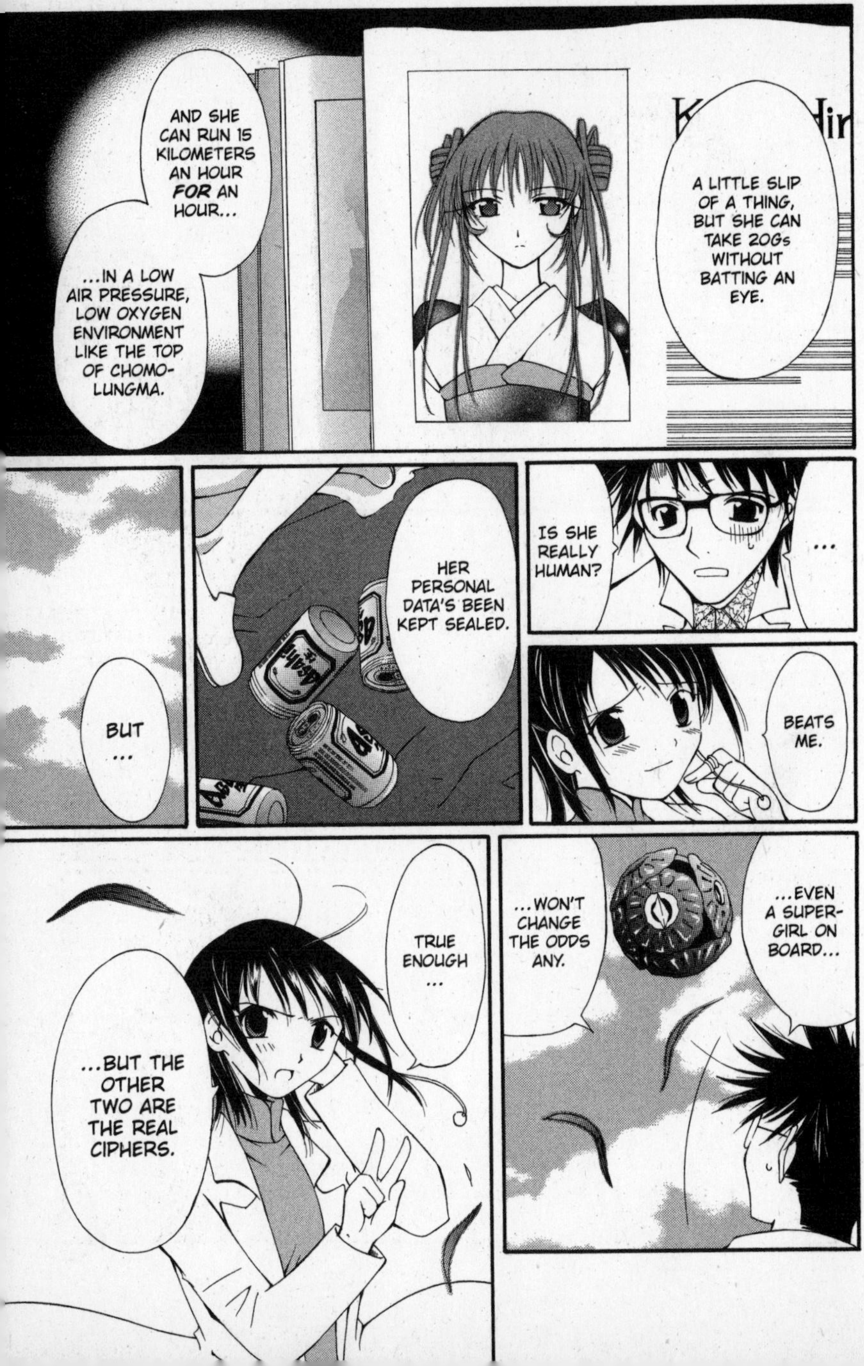
A LITTLE SLIP OF A THING, BUT SHE CAN TAKE 20Gs WITHOUT BATTING AN EYE.
AND SHE CAN RUN 15 KILOMETERS AN HOUR *FOR* AN HOUR...
...IN A LOW AIR PRESSURE, LOW OXYGEN ENVIRONMENT LIKE THE TOP OF CHOMO-LUNGMA.
...
IS SHE REALLY HUMAN?
BEATS ME.
HER PERSONAL DATA'S BEEN KEPT SEALED.
BUT ...
...EVEN A SUPER-GIRL ON BOARD...
...WON'T CHANGE THE ODDS ANY.
TRUE ENOUGH ...
...BUT THE OTHER TWO ARE THE REAL CIPHERS.

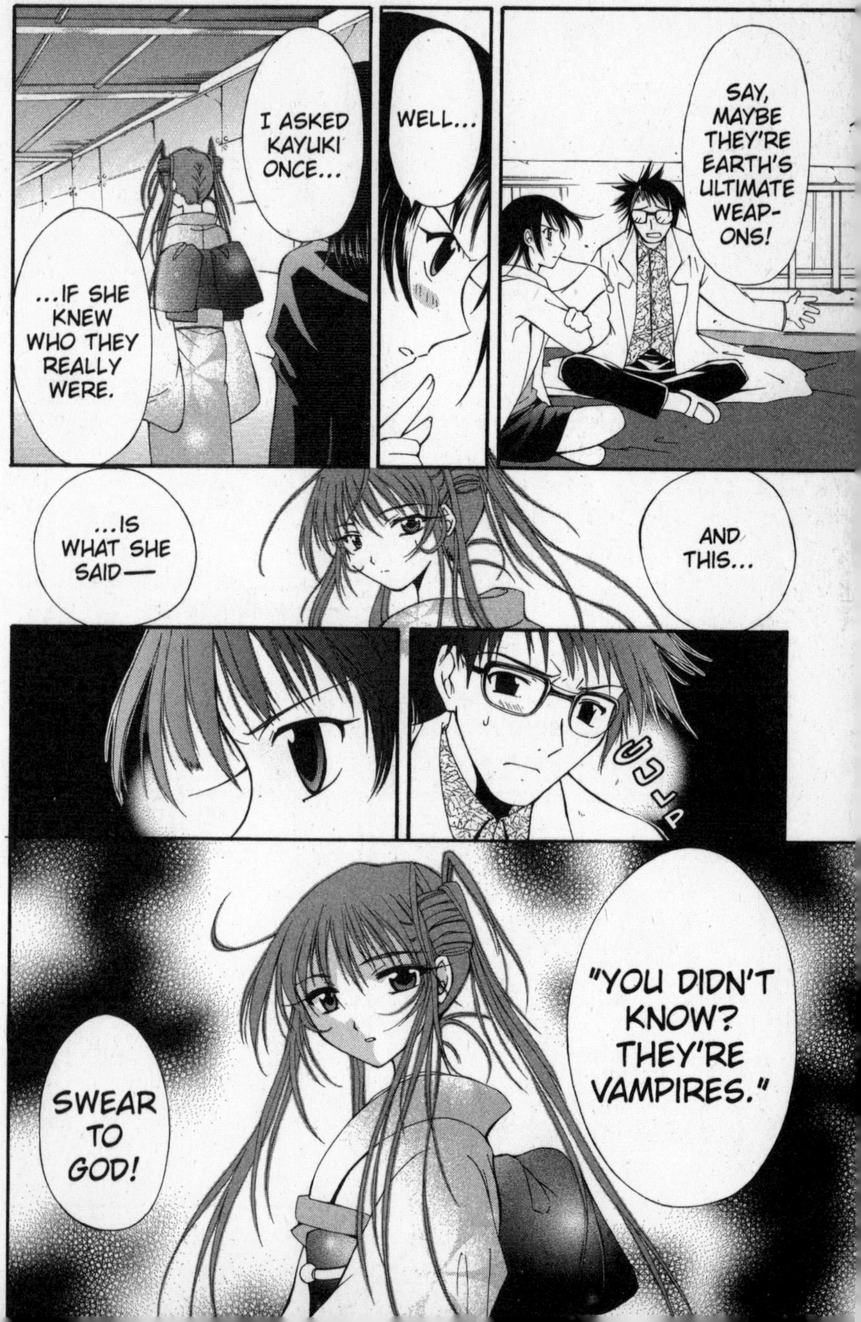
SAY, MAYBE THEY'RE EARTH'S ULTIMATE WEAP-ONS!
WELL...
I ASKED KAYUKI ONCE...
...IF SHE KNEW WHO THEY REALLY WERE.
AND THIS...
...IS WHAT SHE SAID—
GULP
"YOU DIDN'T KNOW? THEY'RE VAMPIRES."
SWEAR TO GOD!

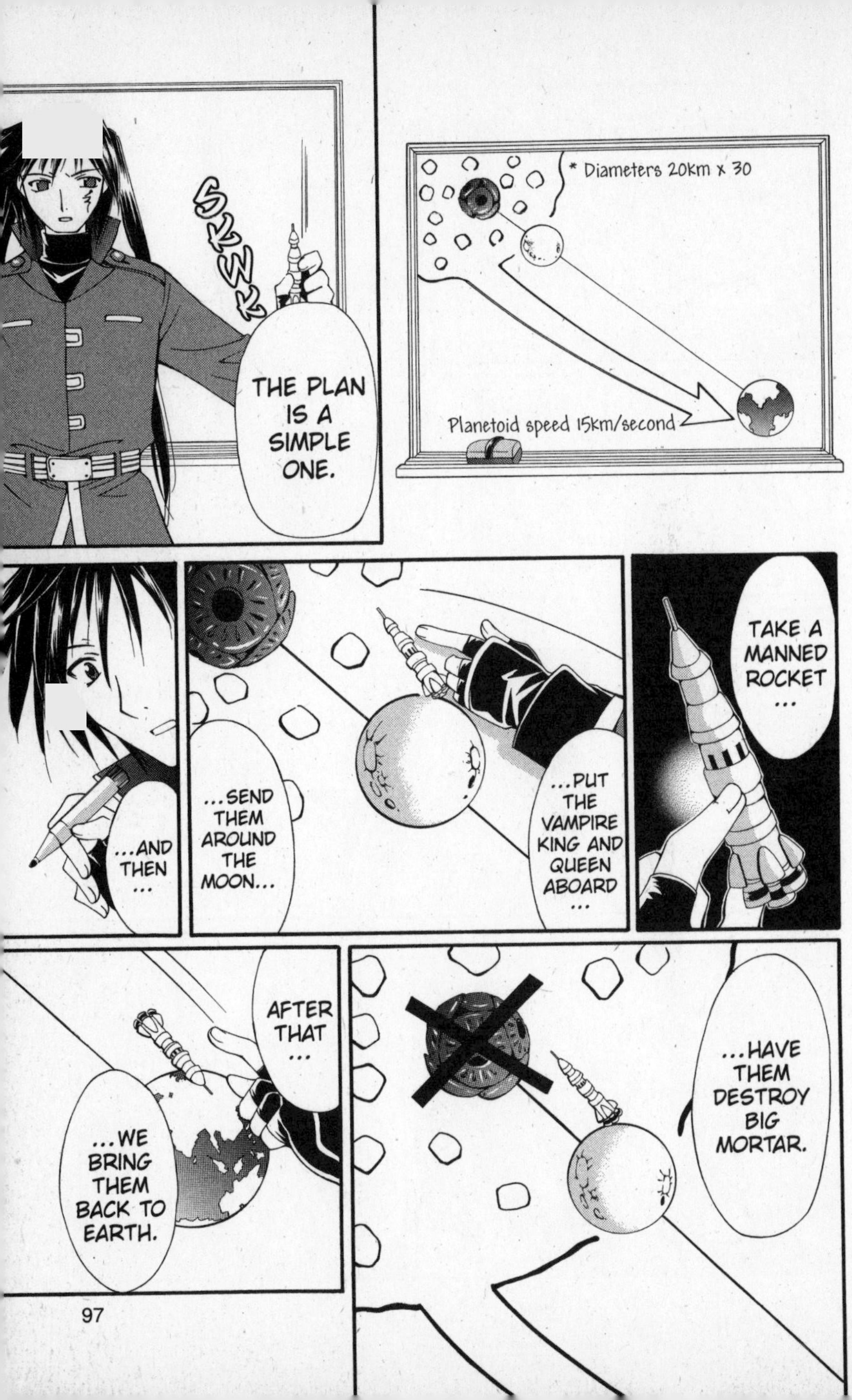
* Diameters 20km x 30
Planetoid speed 15km/second
SKWK
THE PLAN IS A SIMPLE ONE.
TAKE A MANNED ROCKET...
...PUT THE VAMPIRE KING AND QUEEN ABOARD...
...SEND THEM AROUND THE MOON...
...AND THEN...
...HAVE THEM DESTROY BIG MORTAR.
AFTER THAT...
...WE BRING THEM BACK TO EARTH.

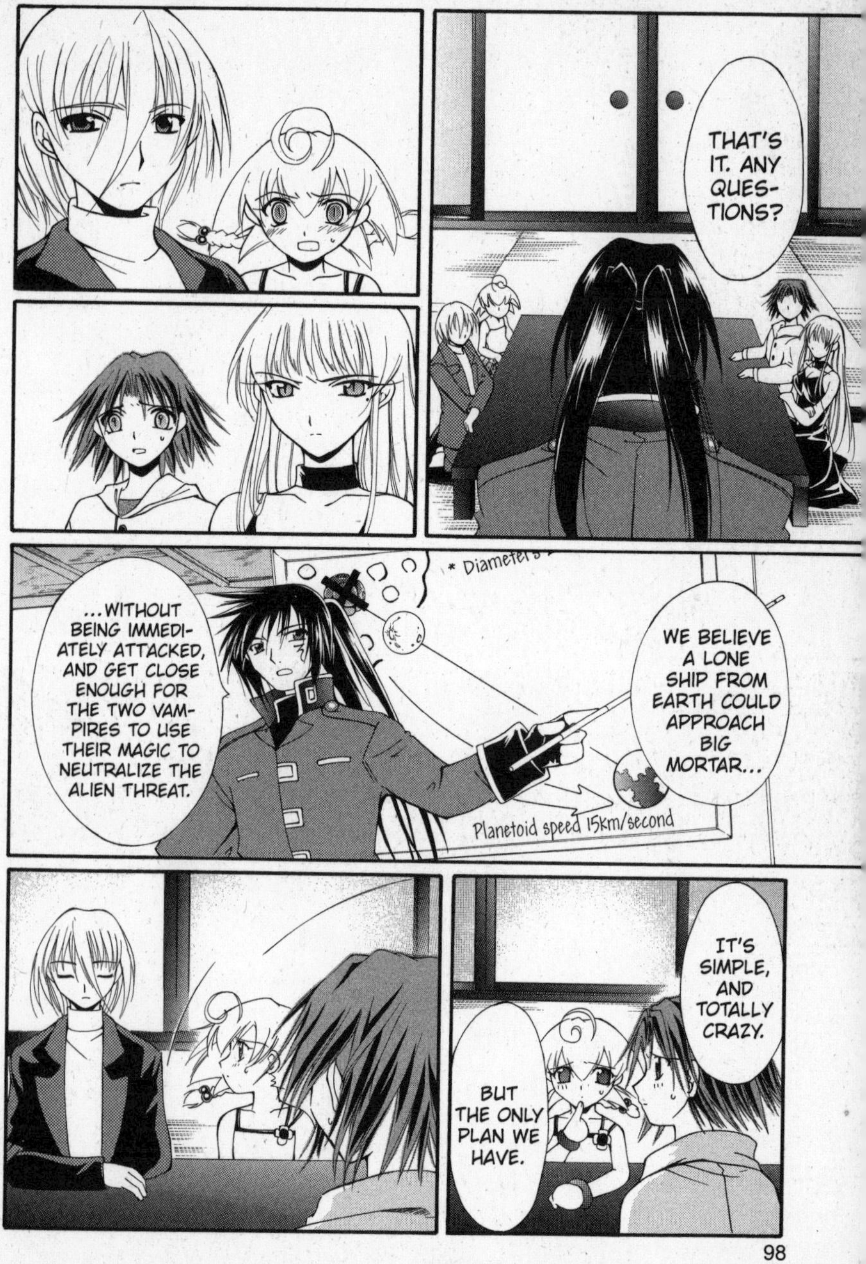
THAT'S IT. ANY QUES-TIONS?
WE BELIEVE A LONE SHIP FROM EARTH COULD APPROACH BIG MORTAR...
...WITHOUT BEING IMMEDI-ATELY ATTACKED, AND GET CLOSE ENOUGH FOR THE TWO VAM-PIRES TO USE THEIR MAGIC TO NEUTRALIZE THE ALIEN THREAT.
Planetoid speed 15km/second
IT'S SIMPLE, AND TOTALLY CRAZY.
BUT THE ONLY PLAN WE HAVE.

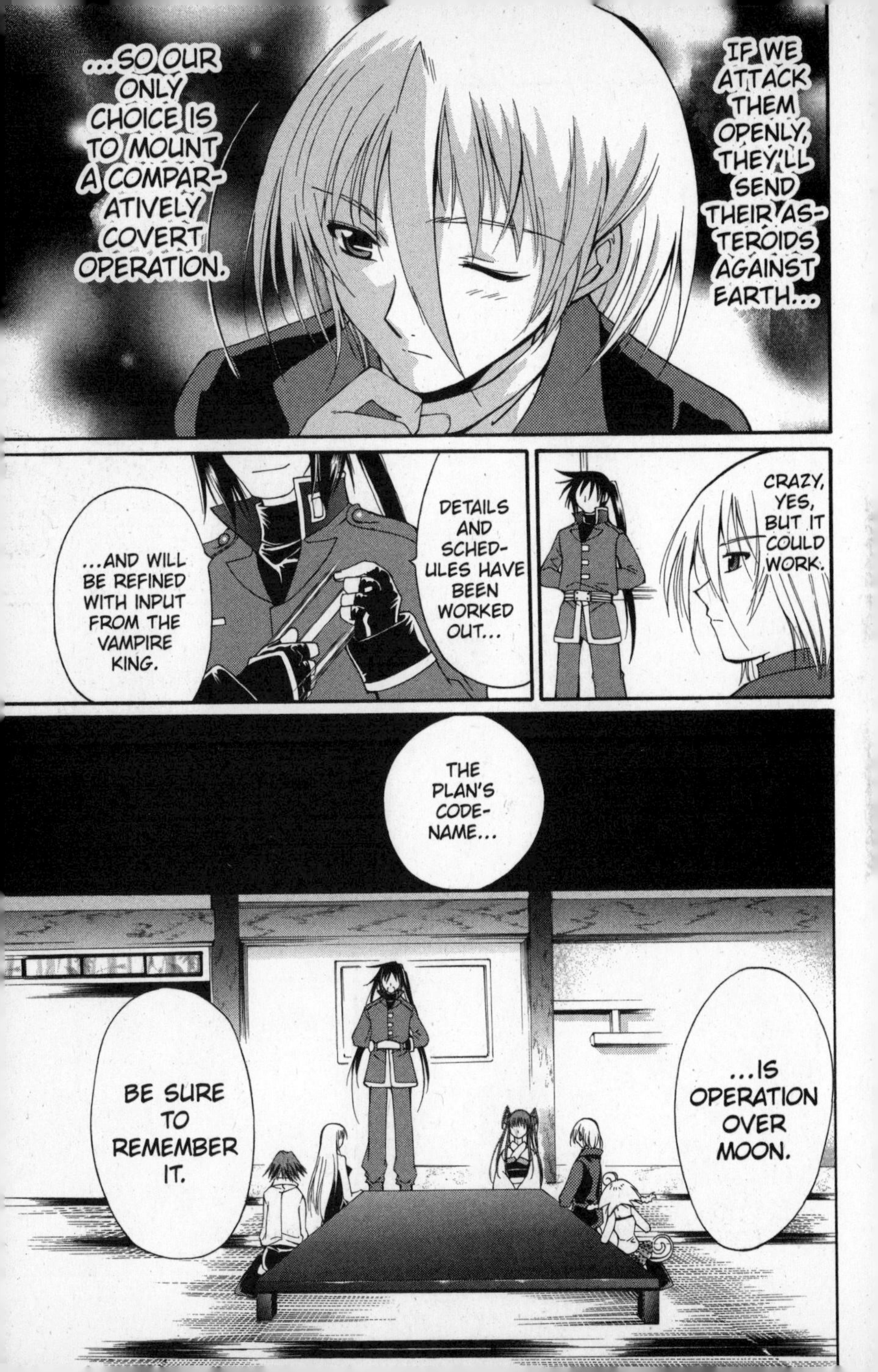
IF WE ATTACK THEM OPENLY, THEY'LL SEND THEIR ASTEROIDS AGAINST EARTH...
...SO OUR ONLY CHOICE IS TO MOUNT A COMPARATIVELY COVERT OPERATION.
CRAZY, YES, BUT IT COULD WORK.
DETAILS AND SCHEDULES HAVE BEEN WORKED OUT...
...AND WILL BE REFINED WITH INPUT FROM THE VAMPIRE KING.
THE PLAN'S CODE-NAME...
...IS OPERATION OVER MOON.
BE SURE TO REMEMBER IT.

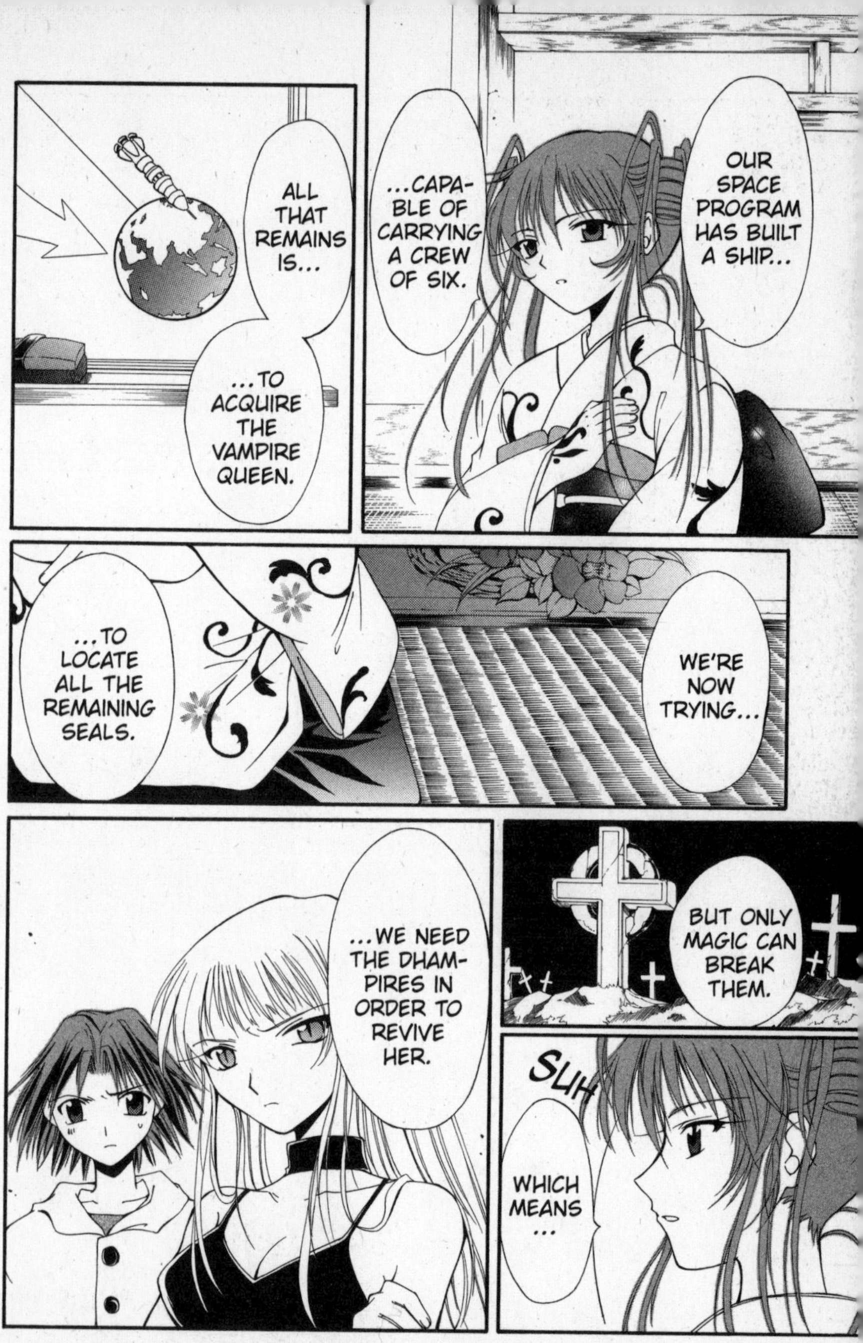
OUR SPACE PROGRAM HAS BUILT A SHIP...
...CAPA-BLE OF CARRYING A CREW OF SIX.
ALL THAT REMAINS IS...
...TO ACQUIRE THE VAMPIRE QUEEN.
WE'RE NOW TRYING...
...TO LOCATE ALL THE REMAINING SEALS.
BUT ONLY MAGIC CAN BREAK THEM.
SUH
WHICH MEANS...
...WE NEED THE DHAM-PIRES IN ORDER TO REVIVE HER.

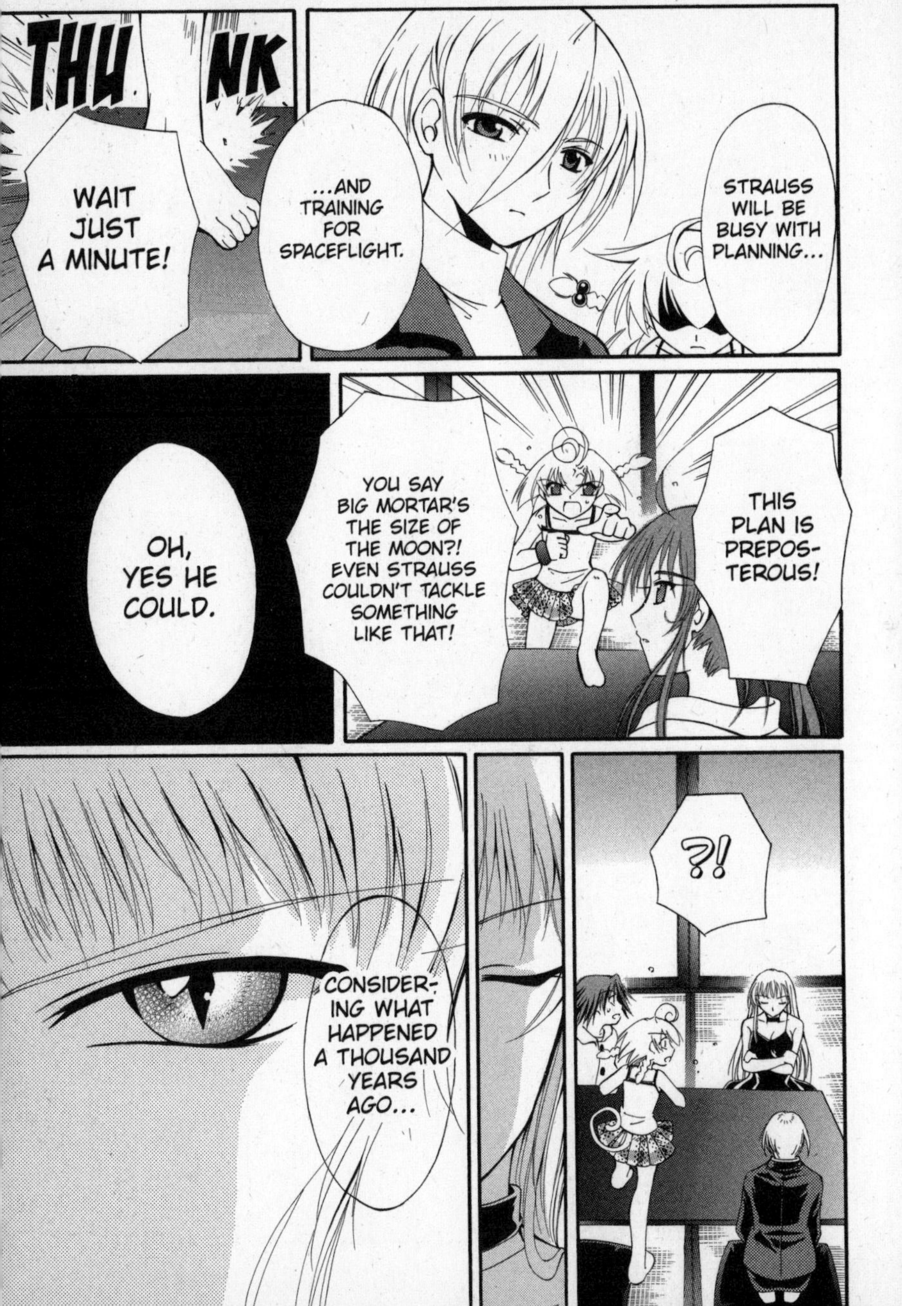
STRAUSS WILL BE BUSY WITH PLANNING...
...AND TRAINING FOR SPACEFLIGHT.
THU NK
WAIT JUST A MINUTE!
THIS PLAN IS PREPOS-TEROUS!
YOU SAY BIG MORTAR'S THE SIZE OF THE MOON?! EVEN STRAUSS COULDN'T TACKLE SOMETHING LIKE THAT!
OH, YES HE COULD.
?!
CONSIDER-ING WHAT HAPPENED A THOUSAND YEARS AGO...

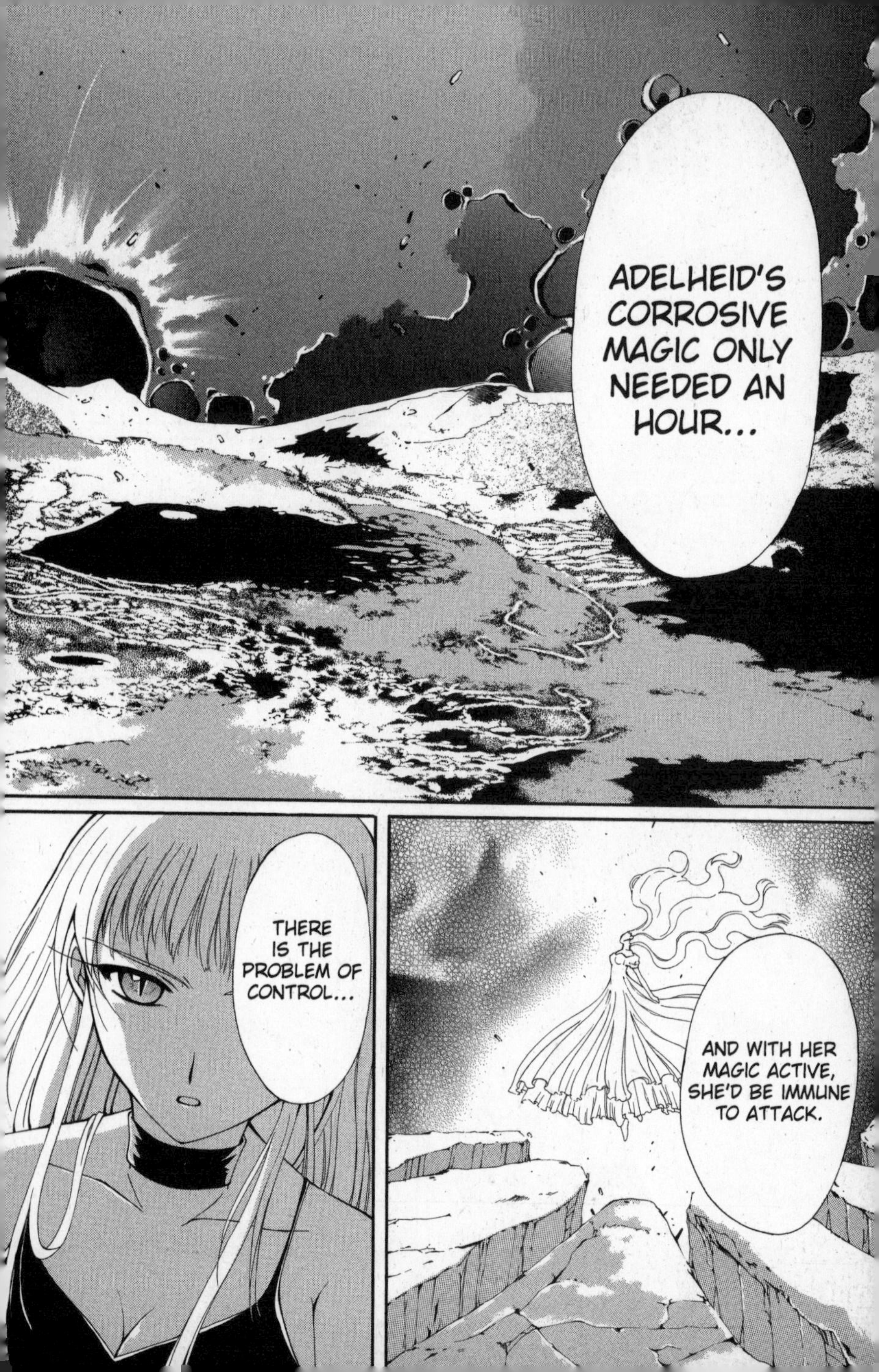
ADELHEID'S CORROSIVE MAGIC ONLY NEEDED AN HOUR...
AND WITH HER MAGIC ACTIVE, SHE'D BE IMMUNE TO ATTACK.
THERE IS THE PROBLEM OF CONTROL...

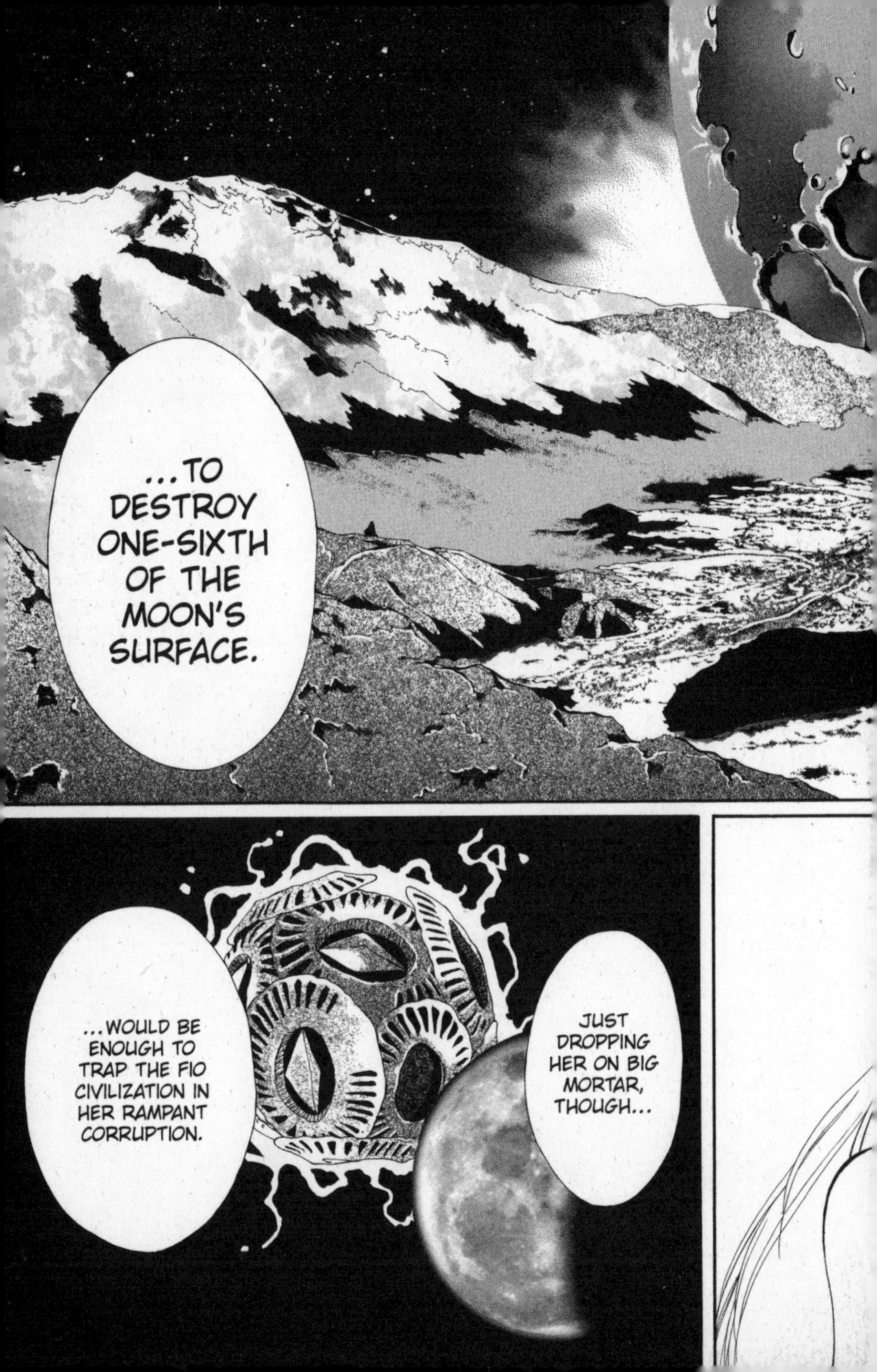
...TO DESTROY ONE-SIXTH OF THE MOON'S SURFACE.
JUST DROPPING HER ON BIG MORTAR, THOUGH...
...WOULD BE ENOUGH TO TRAP THE FIO CIVILIZATION IN HER RAMPANT CORRUPTION.

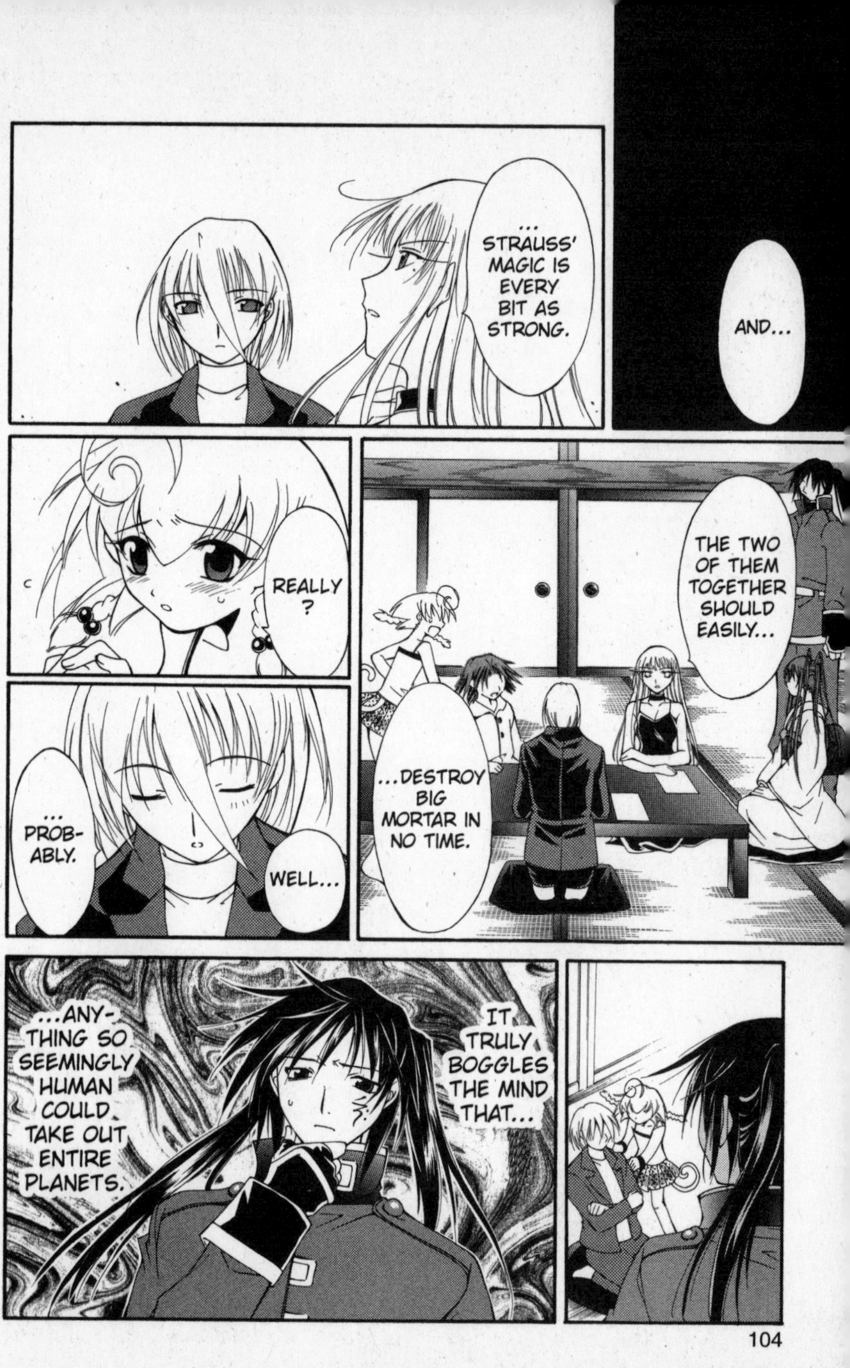
AND...
... STRAUSS' MAGIC IS EVERY BIT AS STRONG.
THE TWO OF THEM TOGETHER SHOULD EASILY...
...DESTROY BIG MORTAR IN NO TIME.
REALLY?
WELL...
... PROBABLY.
IT TRULY BOGGLES THE MIND THAT...
...ANYTHING SO SEEMINGLY HUMAN COULD TAKE OUT ENTIRE PLANETS.

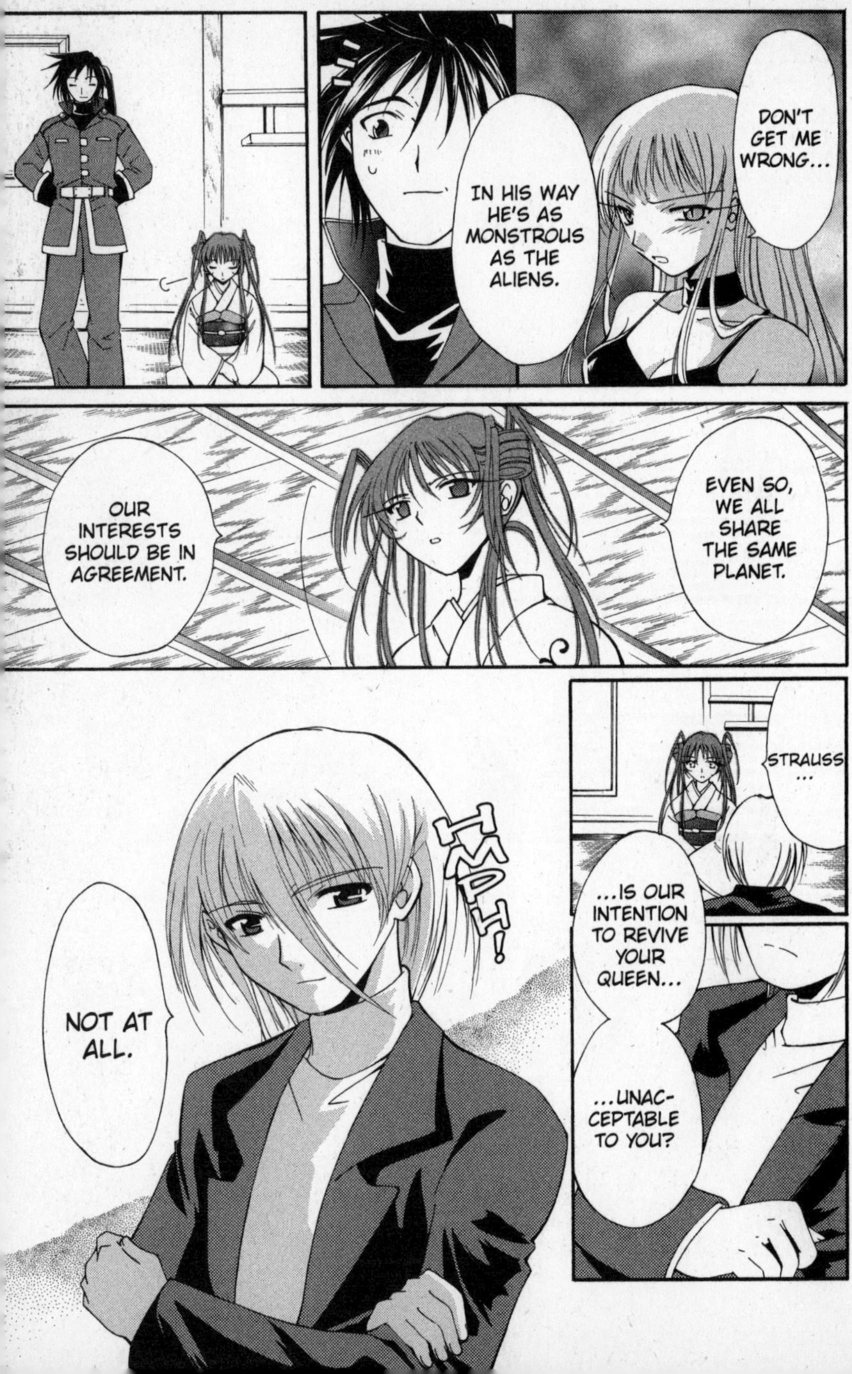
DON'T GET ME WRONG...
IN HIS WAY HE'S AS MONSTROUS AS THE ALIENS.
EVEN SO, WE ALL SHARE THE SAME PLANET.
OUR INTERESTS SHOULD BE IN AGREEMENT.
STRAUSS...
...IS OUR INTENTION TO REVIVE YOUR QUEEN...
...UNAC-CEPTABLE TO YOU?
HMPH!
NOT AT ALL.

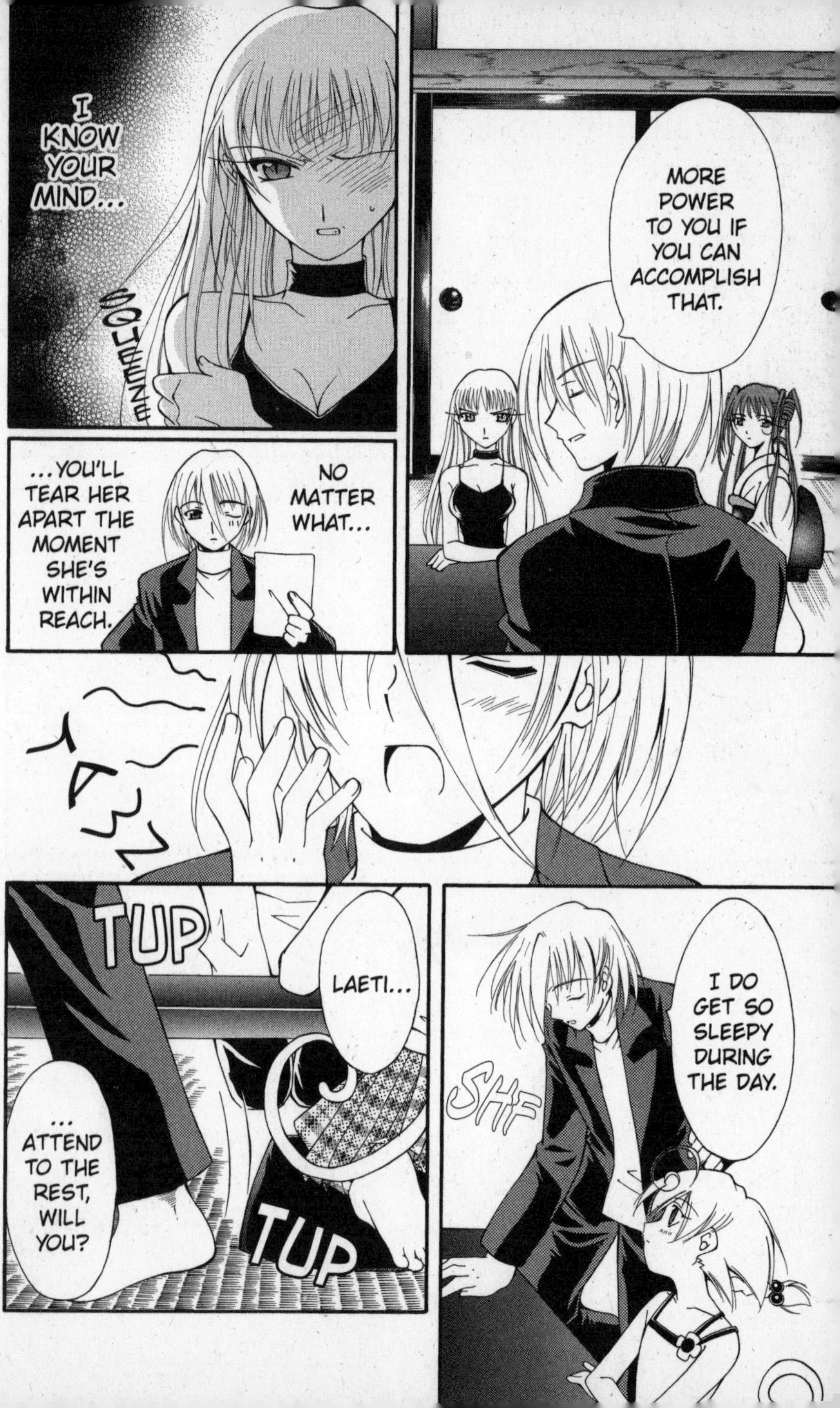
MORE POWER TO YOU IF YOU CAN ACCOMPLISH THAT.
I KNOW YOUR MIND...
SQUEEZE
NO MATTER WHAT...
...YOU'LL TEAR HER APART THE MOMENT SHE'S WITHIN REACH.
YAWN
I DO GET SO SLEEPY DURING THE DAY.
SHF
TUP
LAETI...
...ATTEND TO THE REST, WILL YOU?
TUP

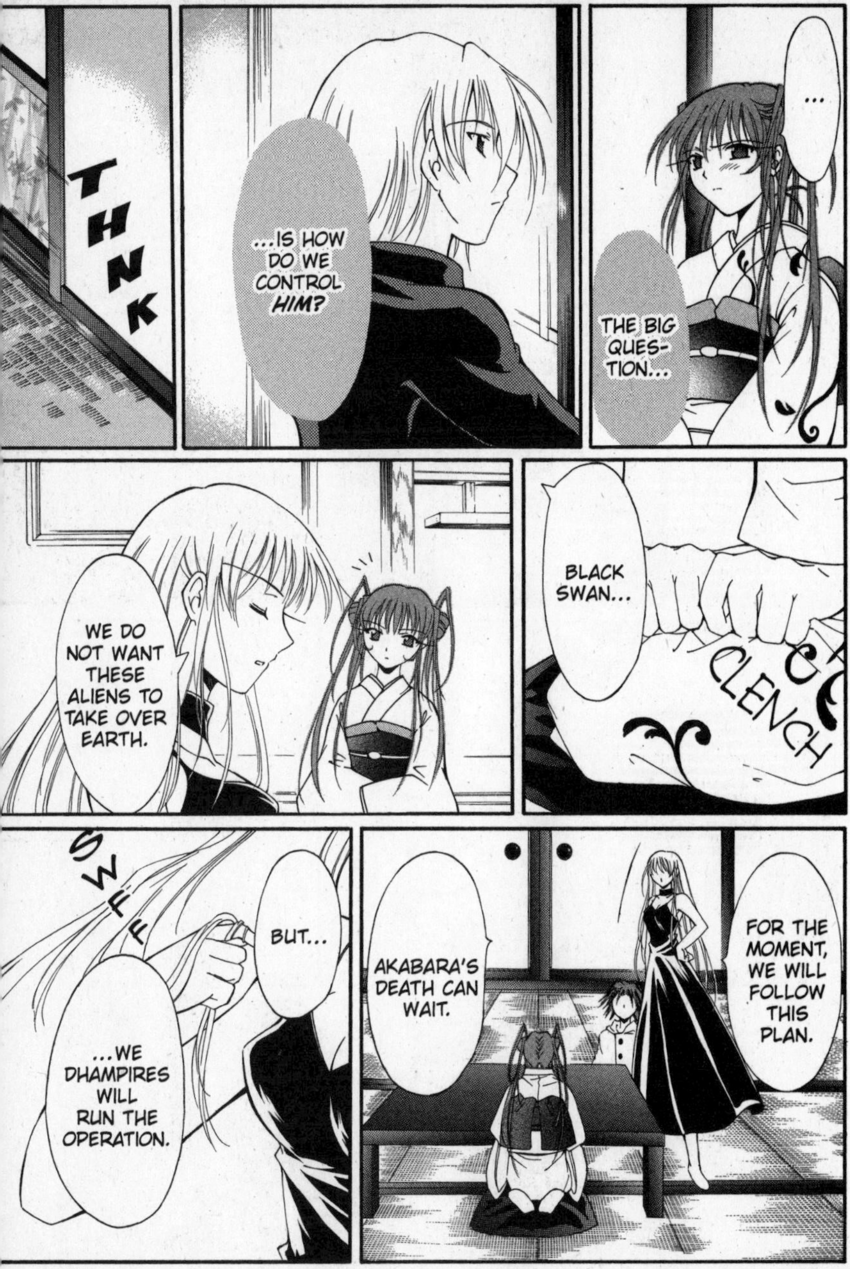
...
THE BIG QUES-TION...
...IS HOW DO WE CONTROL HIM?
THNK
BLACK SWAN...
CLENCH
WE DO NOT WANT THESE ALIENS TO TAKE OVER EARTH.
FOR THE MOMENT, WE WILL FOLLOW THIS PLAN.
AKABARA'S DEATH CAN WAIT.
BUT...
...WE DHAMPIRES WILL RUN THE OPERATION.
SWFF

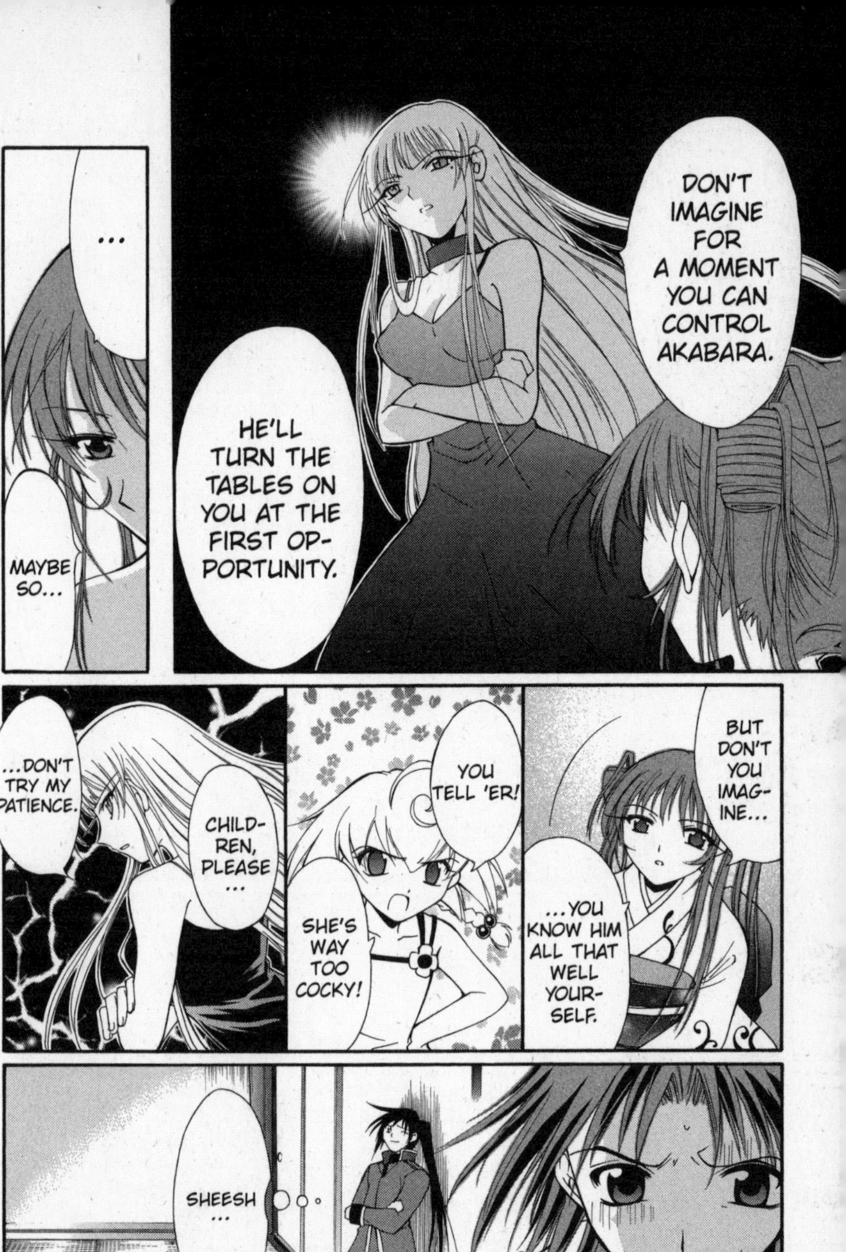
DON'T IMAGINE FOR A MOMENT YOU CAN CONTROL AKABARA.
HE'LL TURN THE TABLES ON YOU AT THE FIRST OP-PORTUNITY.
...
MAYBE SO...
BUT DON'T YOU IMAG-INE...
...YOU KNOW HIM ALL THAT WELL YOUR-SELF.
YOU TELL 'ER!
SHE'S WAY TOO COCKY!
...DON'T TRY MY PATIENCE.
CHILD-REN, PLEASE...
SHEESH...

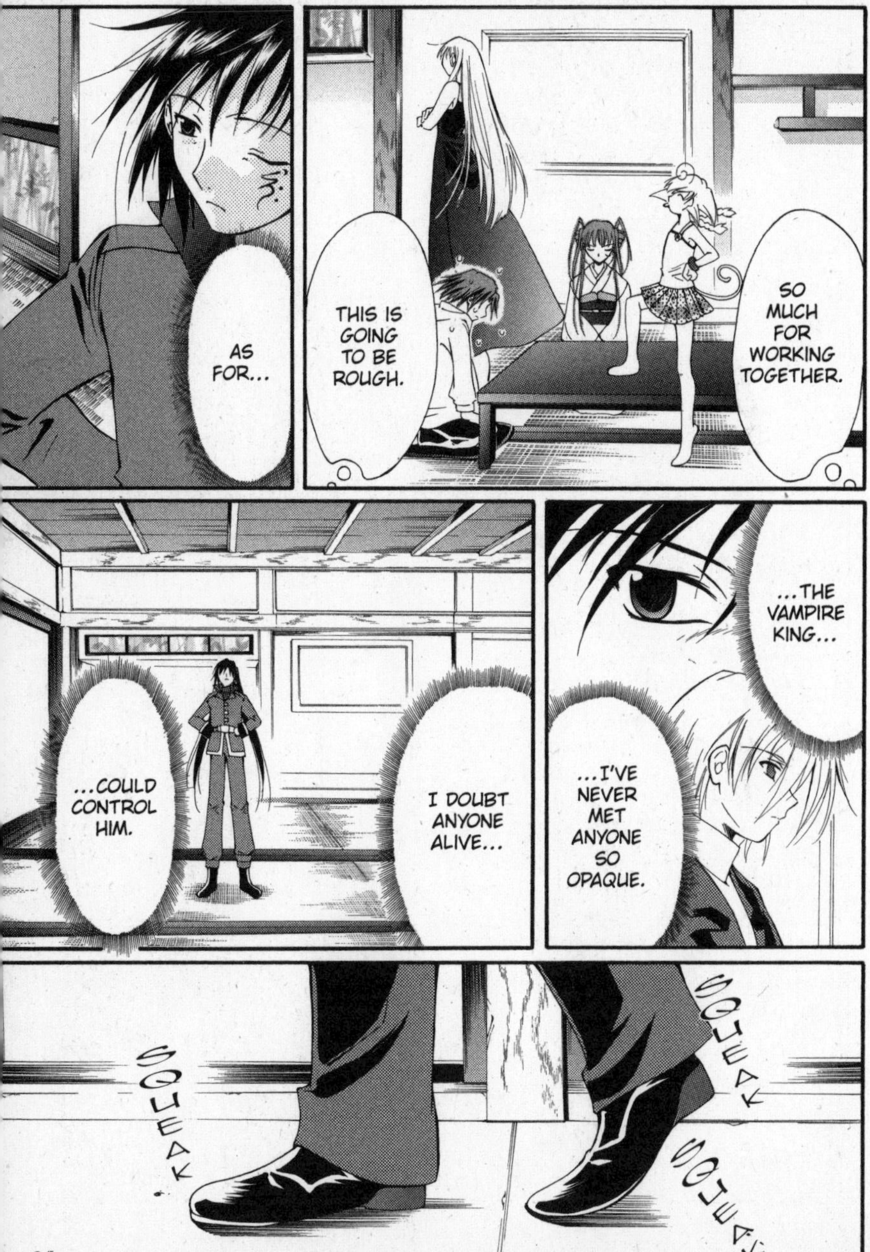
SO MUCH FOR WORKING TOGETHER.
THIS IS GOING TO BE ROUGH.
AS FOR...
...THE VAMPIRE KING...
...I'VE NEVER MET ANYONE SO OPAQUE.
I DOUBT ANYONE ALIVE...
...COULD CONTROL HIM.
SQUEAK
SQUEAK
SQUEAK

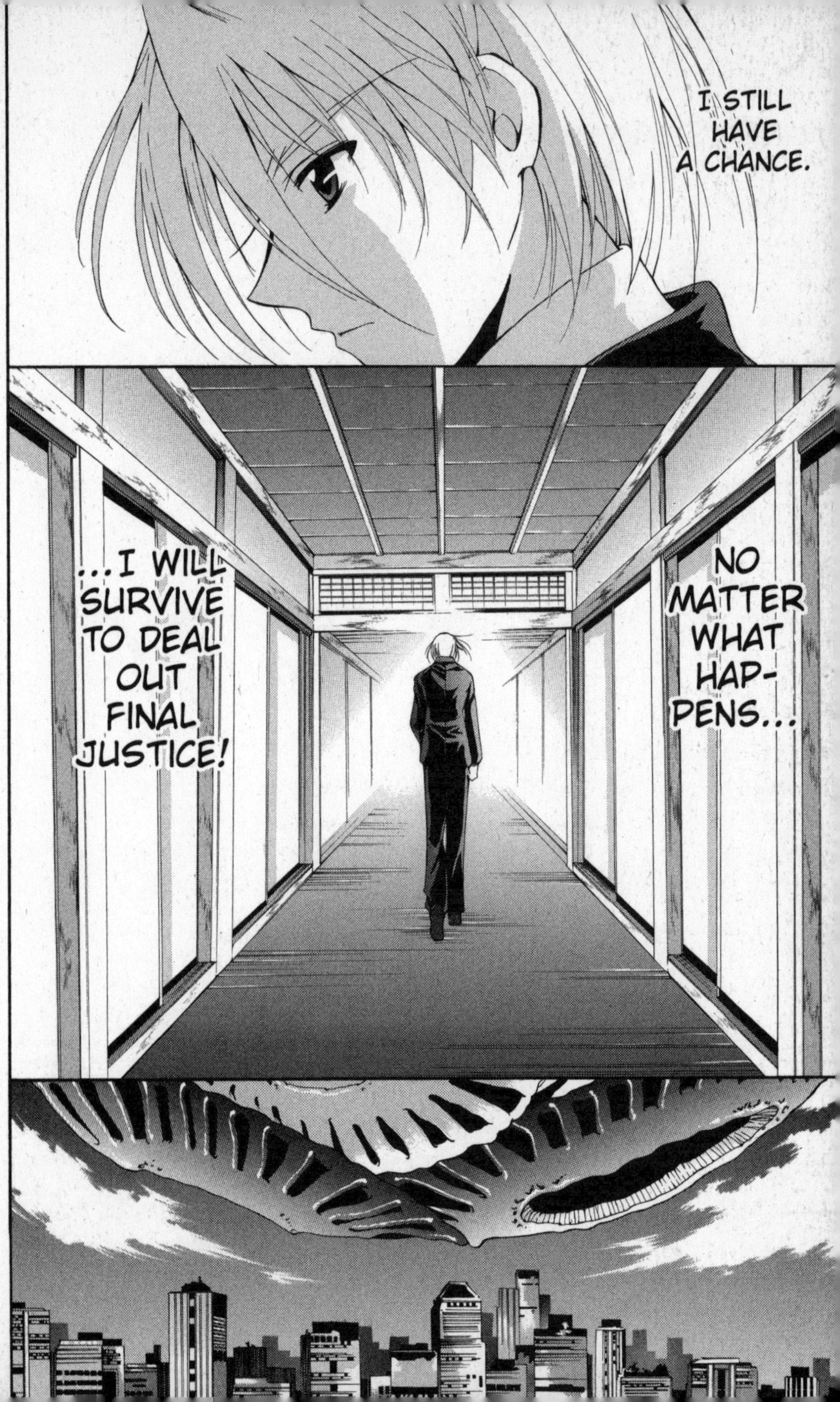
I STILL HAVE A CHANCE.
NO MATTER WHAT HAP-PENS...
...I WILL SURVIVE TO DEAL OUT FINAL JUSTICE!

THE RECORD OF A

FALLEN VAMPIRE

THE RECORD OF A
FALLEN VAMPIRE

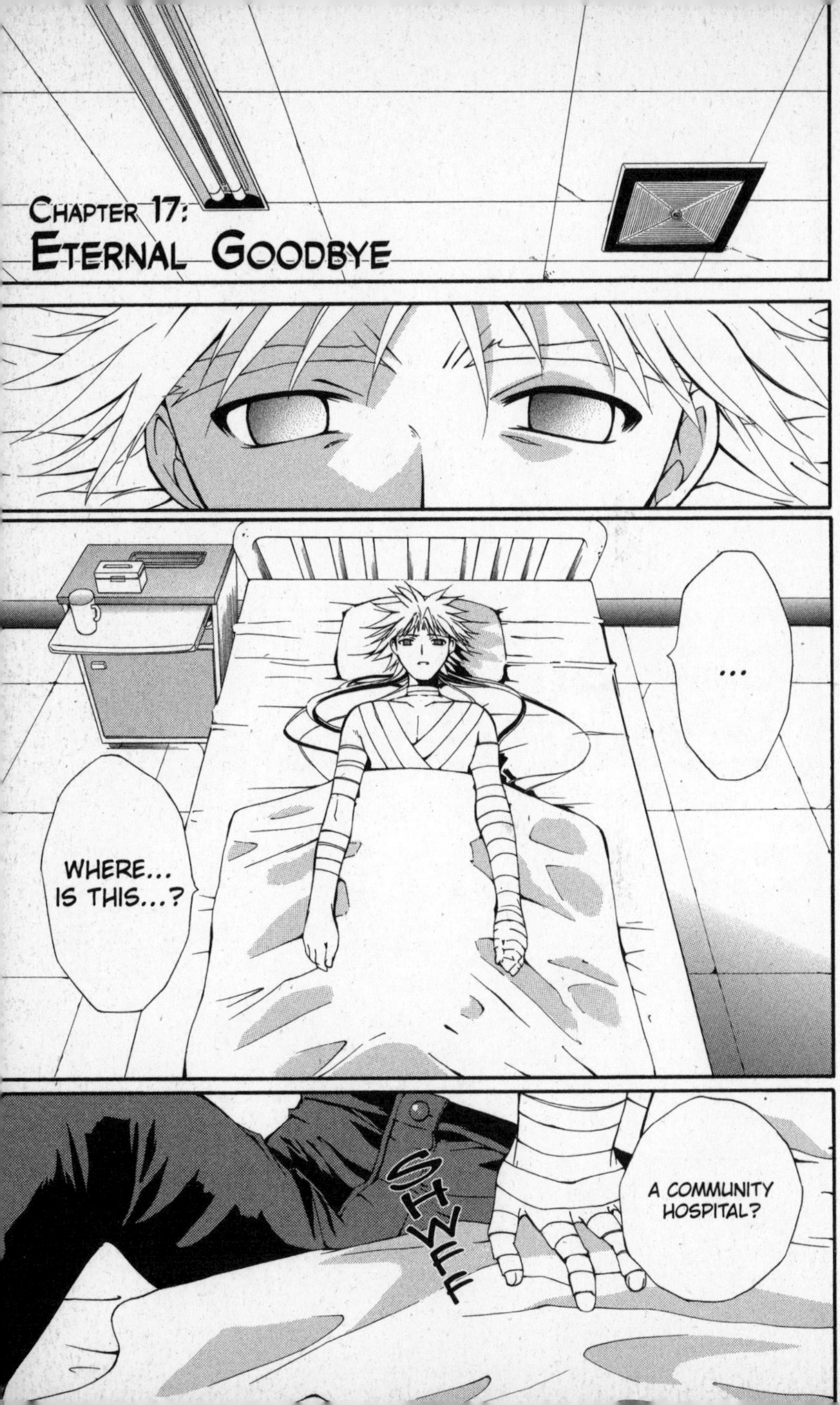
Chapter 17:
Eternal Goodbye
...
WHERE... IS THIS...?
A COMMUNITY HOSPITAL?
SHWFF

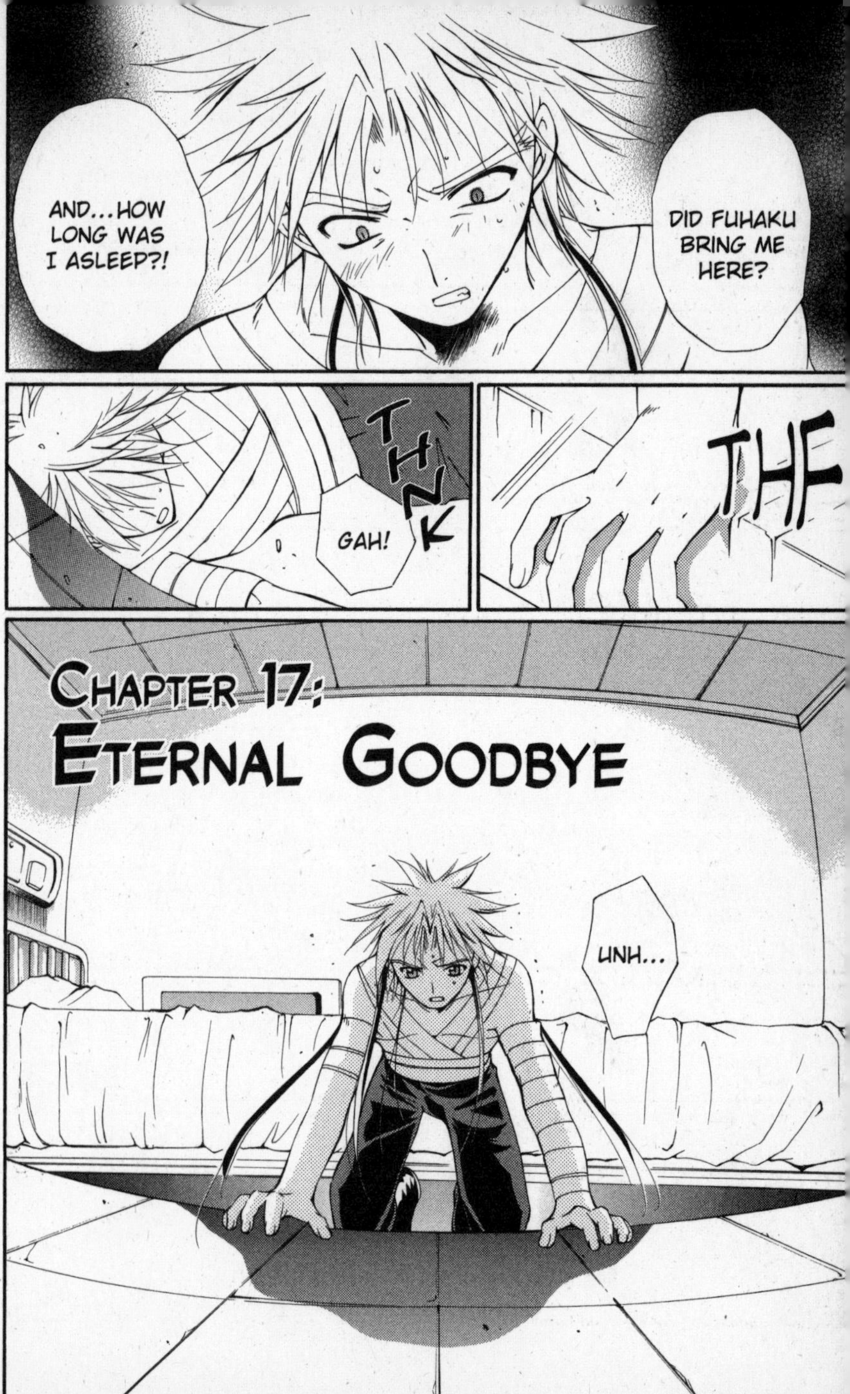
DID FUHAKU BRING ME HERE?
AND...HOW LONG WAS I ASLEEP?!
THF
THNK
GAH!
CHAPTER 17: ETERNAL GOODBYE
UNH...

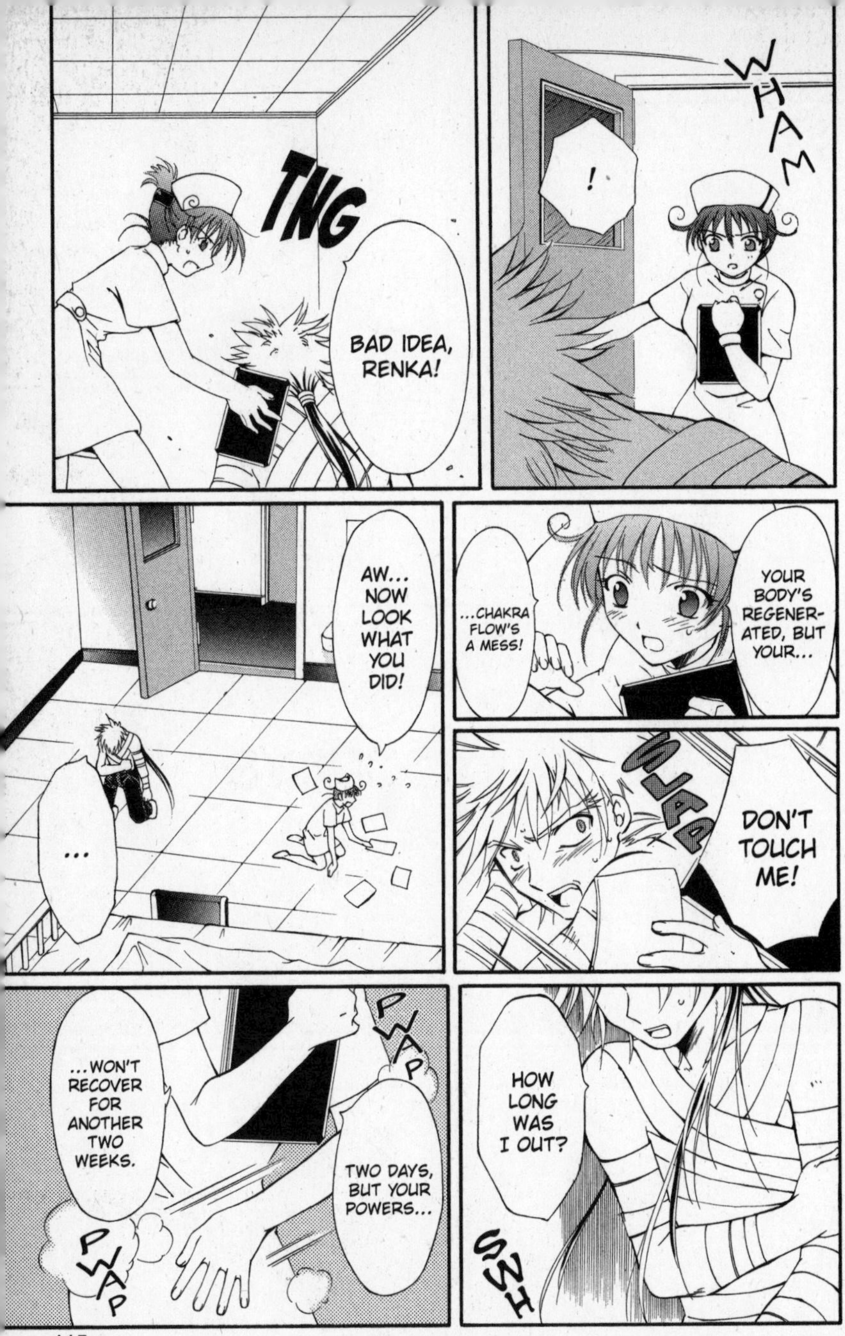
WHAM
!
TNG
BAD IDEA, RENKA!
YOUR BODY'S REGENERATED, BUT YOUR...
...CHAKRA FLOW'S A MESS!
SLAP
DON'T TOUCH ME!
AW... NOW LOOK WHAT YOU DID!
...
HOW LONG WAS I OUT?
...
SWSH
PWAP
TWO DAYS, BUT YOUR POWERS...
...WON'T RECOVER FOR ANOTHER TWO WEEKS.
PWAP

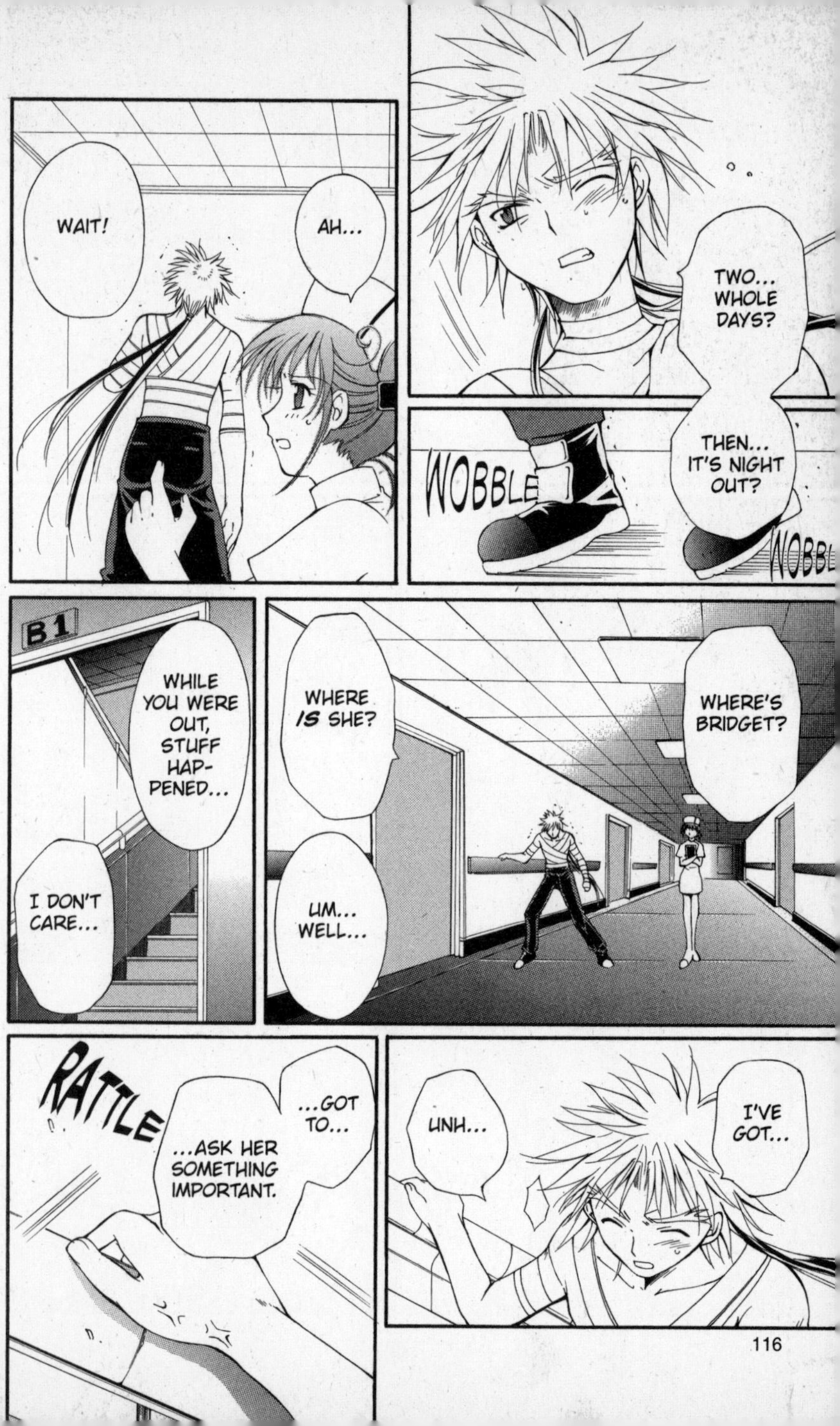
TWO... WHOLE DAYS?
WOBBLE
THEN... IT'S NIGHT OUT?
WOBBL
AH...
WAIT!
WHERE'S BRIDGET?
WHERE *IS* SHE?
UM... WELL...
B1
WHILE YOU WERE OUT, STUFF HAP-PENED...
I DON'T CARE...
I'VE GOT...
UNH...
...GOT TO...
RATTLE
...ASK HER SOMETHING IMPORTANT.

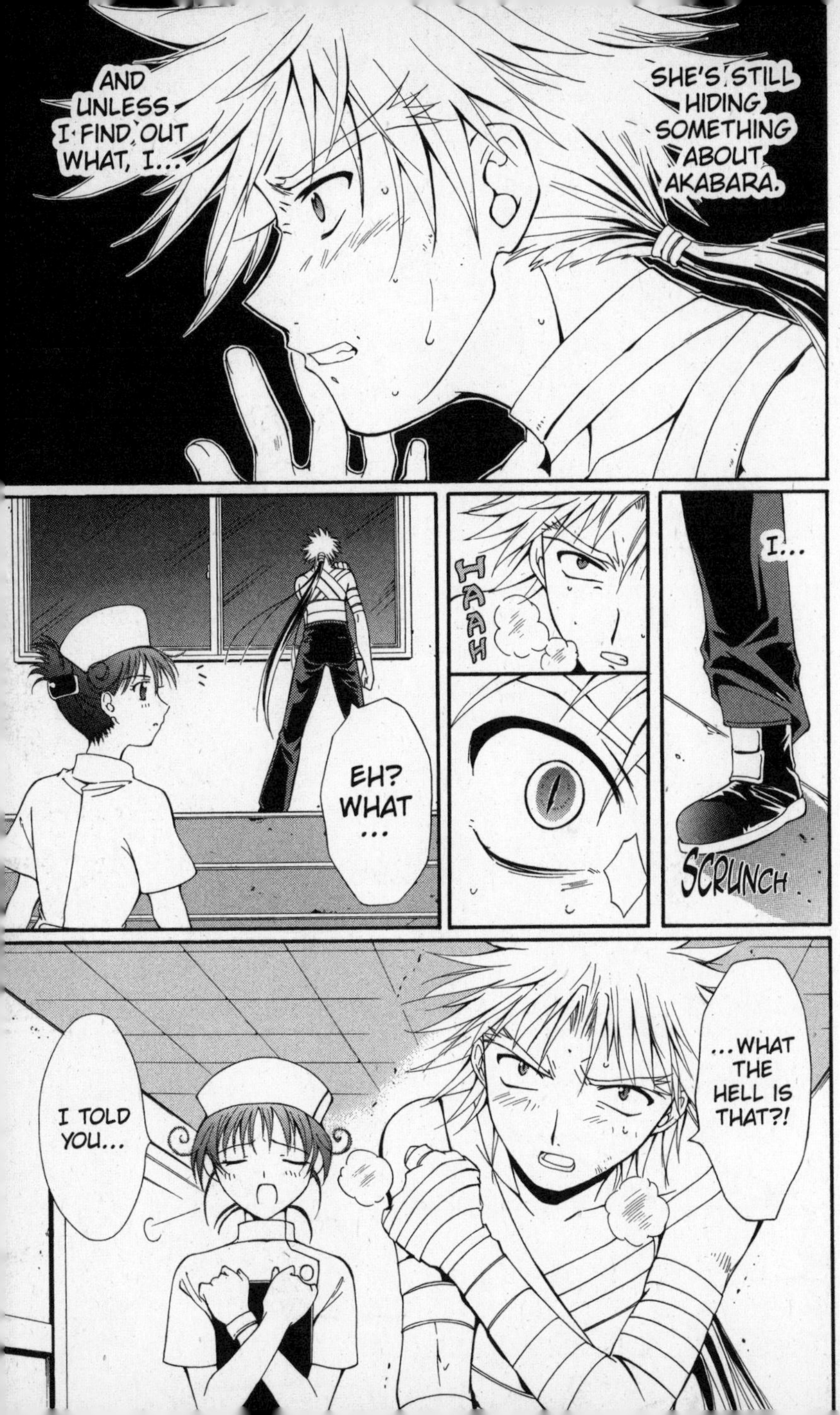
SHE'S STILL HIDING SOMETHING ABOUT AKABARA.
AND UNLESS I FIND OUT WHAT, I...
I...
SCRUNCH
HAAAH
EH? WHAT ...
...WHAT THE HELL IS THAT?!
I TOLD YOU...

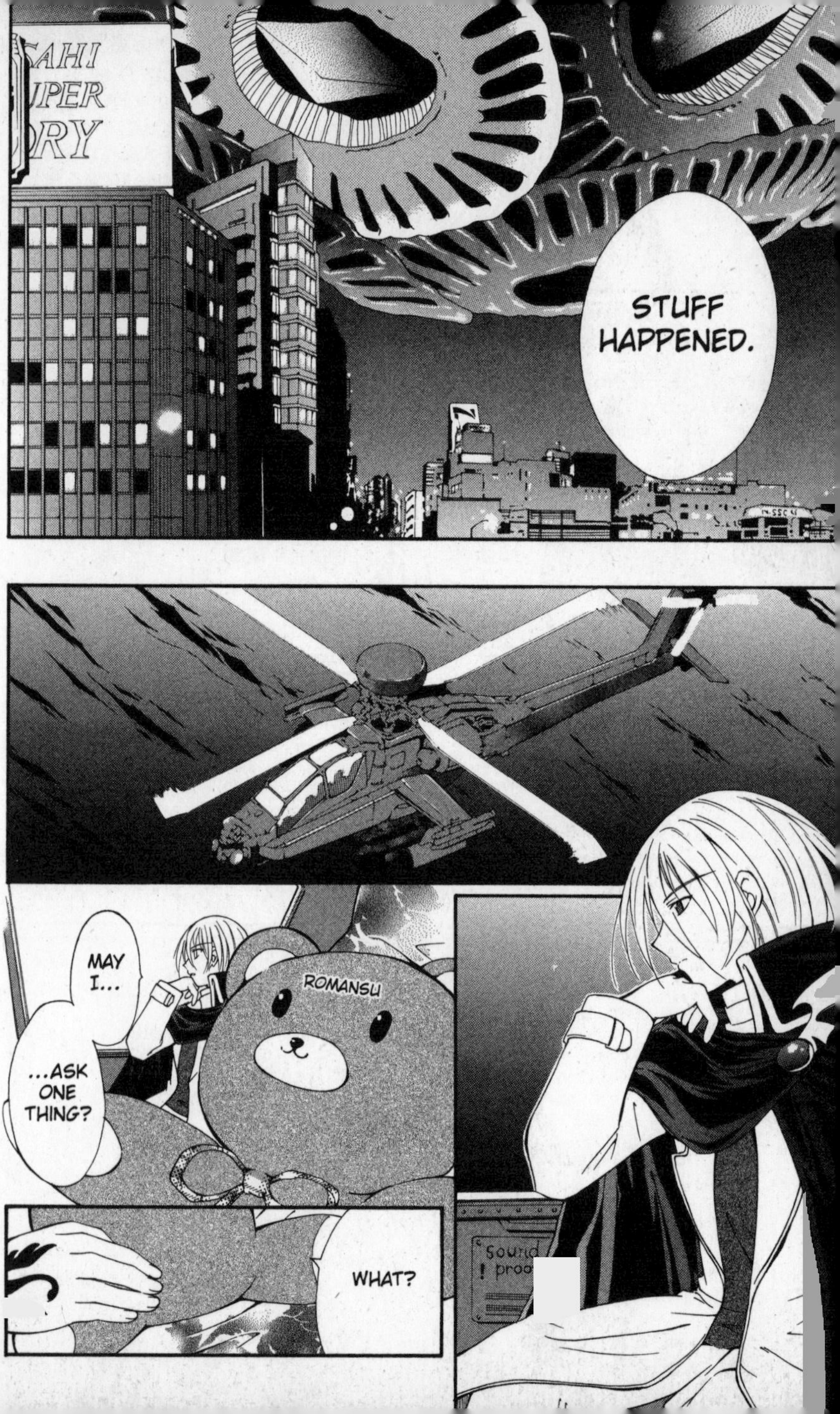
SAHI
UPER
ORY
STUFF HAPPENED.
MAY I...
ROMANSU
...ASK ONE THING?
WHAT?

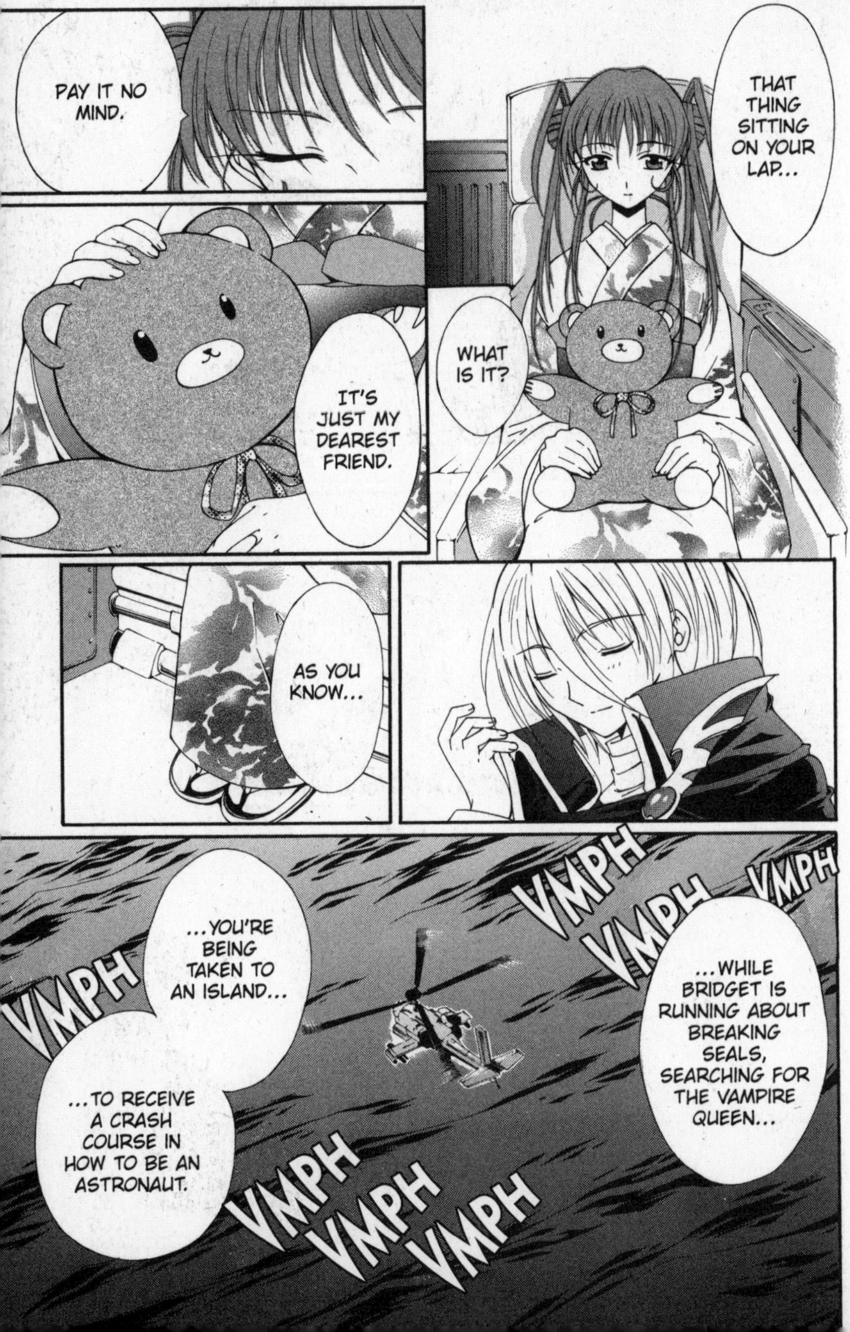
THAT THING SITTING ON YOUR LAP...
WHAT IS IT?
PAY IT NO MIND.
IT'S JUST MY DEAREST FRIEND.
AS YOU KNOW...
VMPH VMPH VMPH
...WHILE BRIDGET IS RUNNING ABOUT BREAKING SEALS, SEARCHING FOR THE VAMPIRE QUEEN...
...YOU'RE BEING TAKEN TO AN ISLAND...
VMPH
...TO RECEIVE A CRASH COURSE IN HOW TO BE AN ASTRONAUT.
VMPH VMPH VMPH

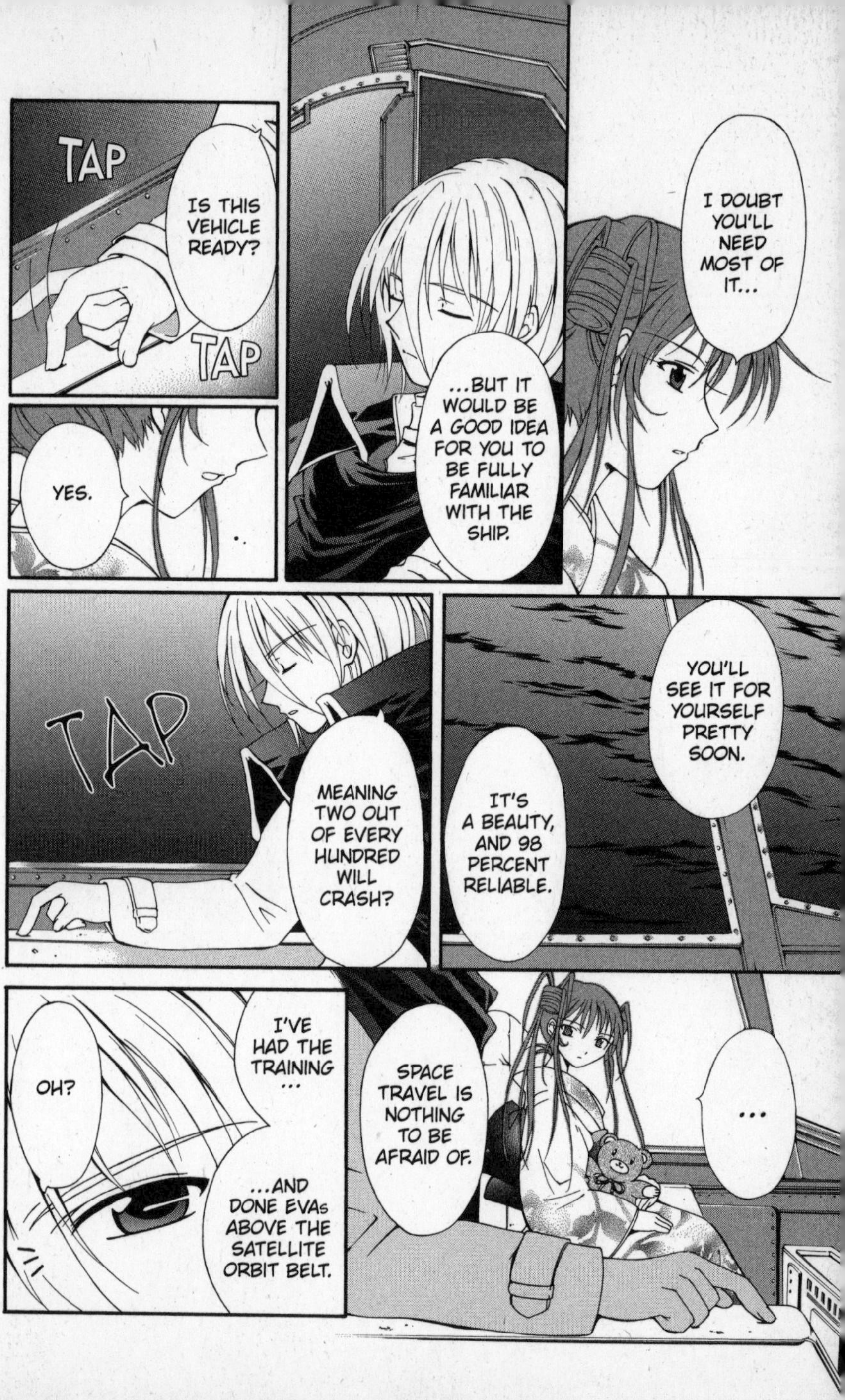
I DOUBT YOU'LL NEED MOST OF IT...
...BUT IT WOULD BE A GOOD IDEA FOR YOU TO BE FULLY FAMILIAR WITH THE SHIP.
TAP
IS THIS VEHICLE READY?
TAP
YES.
YOU'LL SEE IT FOR YOURSELF PRETTY SOON.
IT'S A BEAUTY, AND 98 PERCENT RELIABLE.
MEANING TWO OUT OF EVERY HUNDRED WILL CRASH?
TAP
...
SPACE TRAVEL IS NOTHING TO BE AFRAID OF.
I'VE HAD THE TRAINING...
...AND DONE EVAs ABOVE THE SATELLITE ORBIT BELT.
OH?

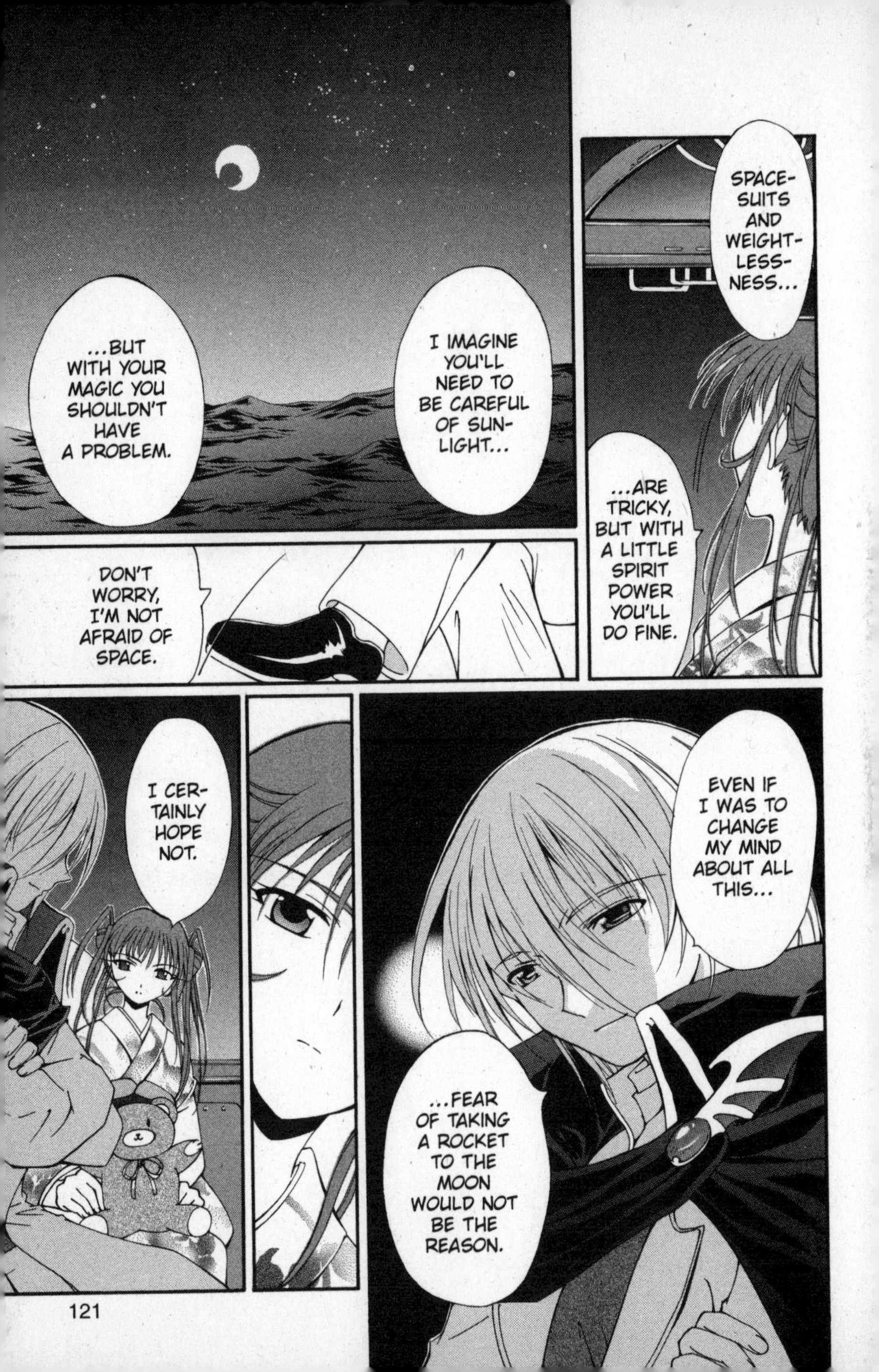
SPACE-SUITS AND WEIGHTLESSNESS...
...ARE TRICKY, BUT WITH A LITTLE SPIRIT POWER YOU'LL DO FINE.
I IMAGINE YOU'LL NEED TO BE CAREFUL OF SUNLIGHT...
...BUT WITH YOUR MAGIC YOU SHOULDN'T HAVE A PROBLEM.
DON'T WORRY, I'M NOT AFRAID OF SPACE.
EVEN IF I WAS TO CHANGE MY MIND ABOUT ALL THIS...
...FEAR OF TAKING A ROCKET TO THE MOON WOULD NOT BE THE REASON.
I CERTAINLY HOPE NOT.

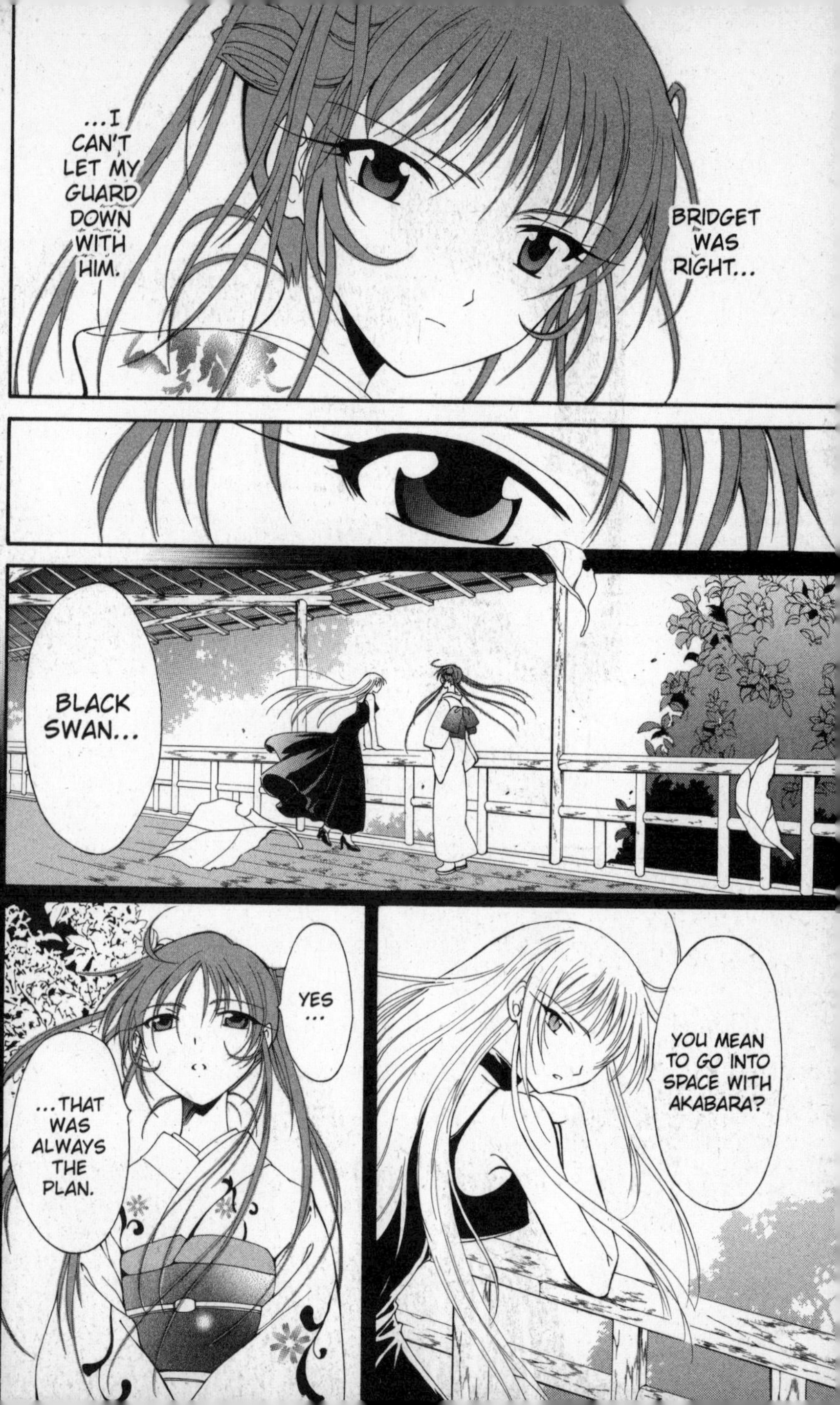
BRIDGET WAS RIGHT...
...I CAN'T LET MY GUARD DOWN WITH HIM.
BLACK SWAN...
YOU MEAN TO GO INTO SPACE WITH AKABARA?
YES...
...THAT WAS ALWAYS THE PLAN.

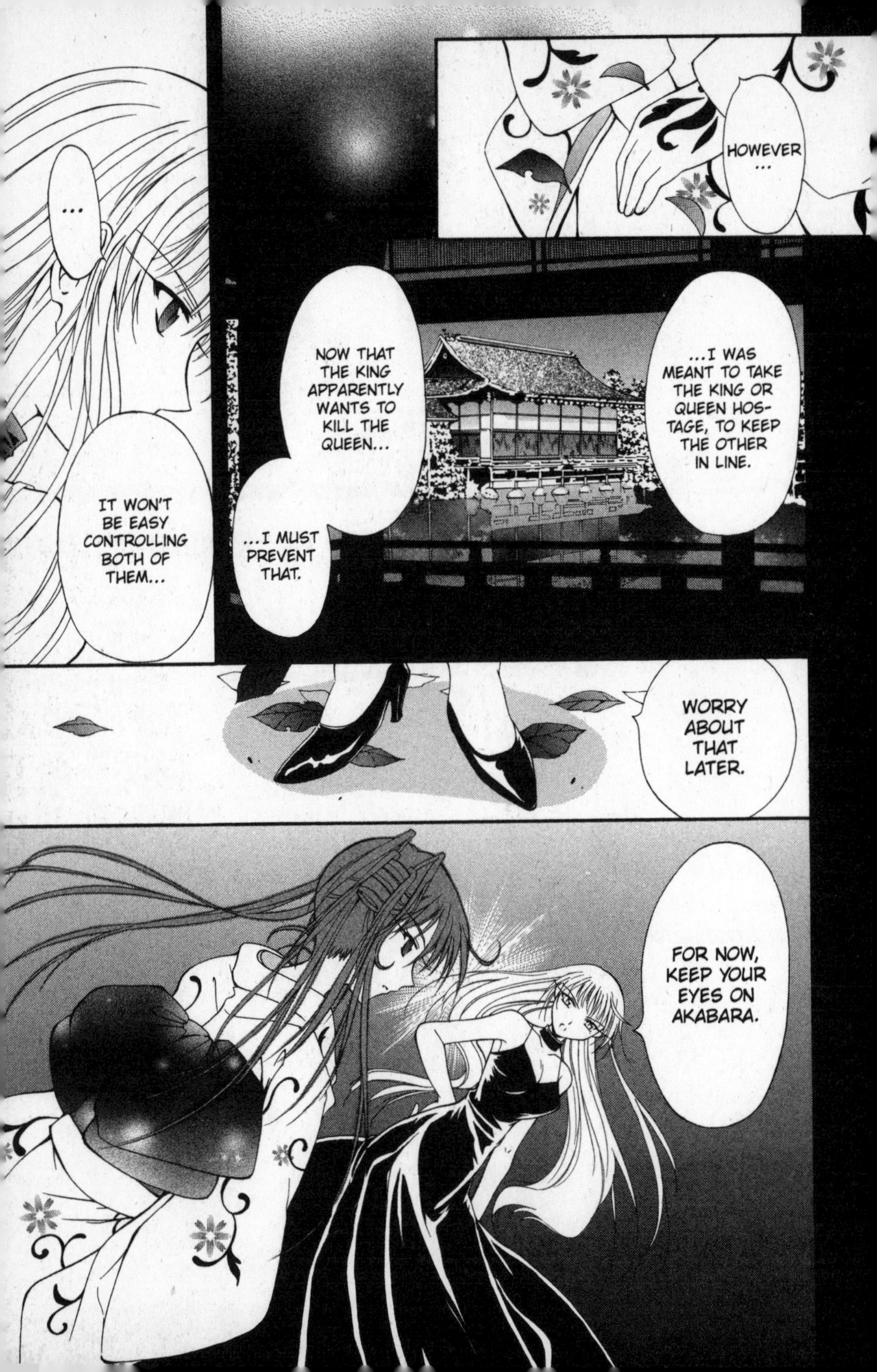
HOWEVER...
...I WAS MEANT TO TAKE THE KING OR QUEEN HOS-TAGE, TO KEEP THE OTHER IN LINE.
NOW THAT THE KING APPARENTLY WANTS TO KILL THE QUEEN...
...I MUST PREVENT THAT.
...
IT WON'T BE EASY CONTROLLING BOTH OF THEM...
WORRY ABOUT THAT LATER.
FOR NOW, KEEP YOUR EYES ON AKABARA.

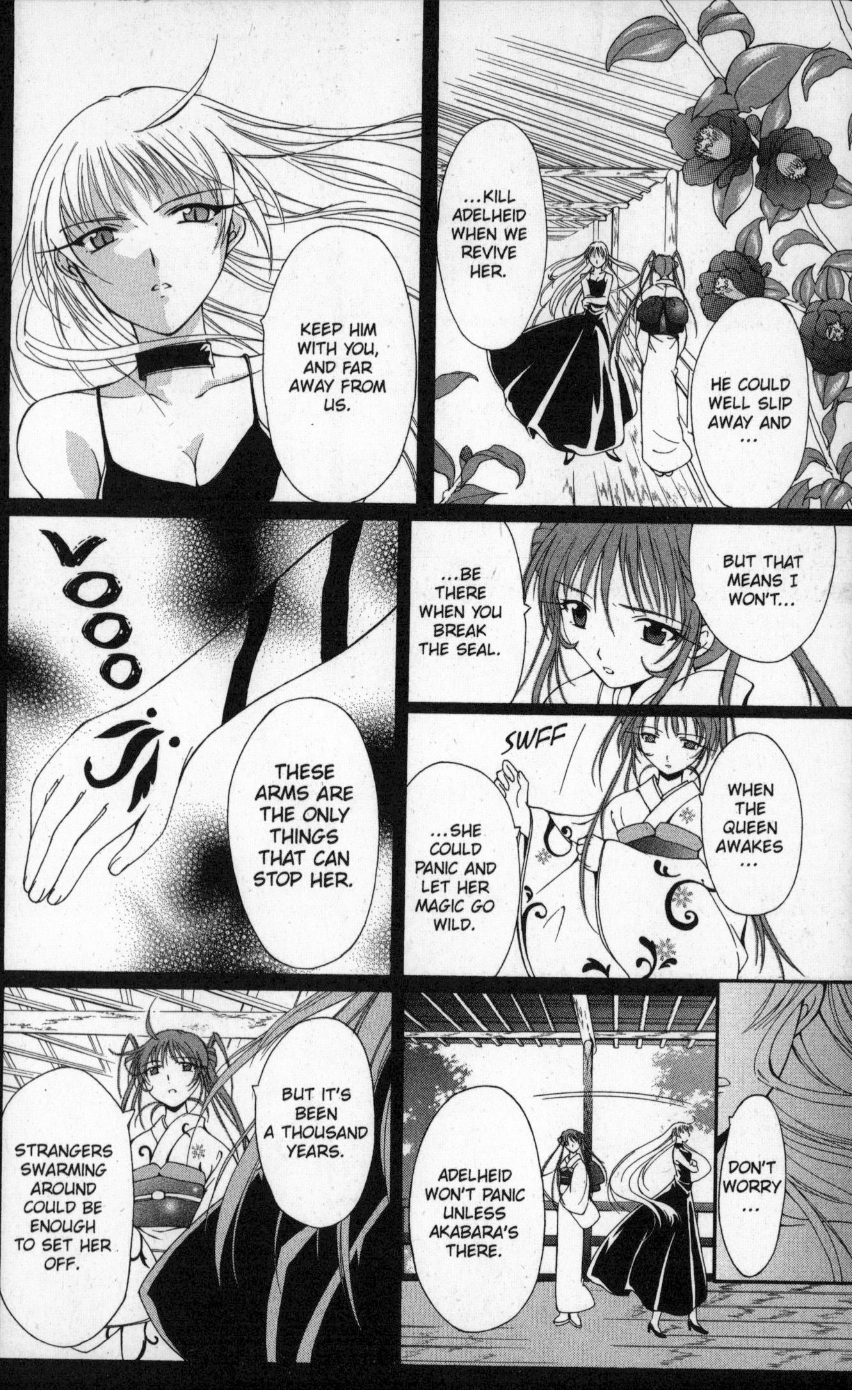
HE COULD WELL SLIP AWAY AND ...
...KILL ADELHEID WHEN WE REVIVE HER.
KEEP HIM WITH YOU, AND FAR AWAY FROM US.
BUT THAT MEANS I WON'T...
...BE THERE WHEN YOU BREAK THE SEAL.
WHEN THE QUEEN AWAKES ...
SWFF
...SHE COULD PANIC AND LET HER MAGIC GO WILD.
VOOO
THESE ARMS ARE THE ONLY THINGS THAT CAN STOP HER.
DON'T WORRY ...
ADELHEID WON'T PANIC UNLESS AKABARA'S THERE.
BUT IT'S BEEN A THOUSAND YEARS.
STRANGERS SWARMING AROUND COULD BE ENOUGH TO SET HER OFF.

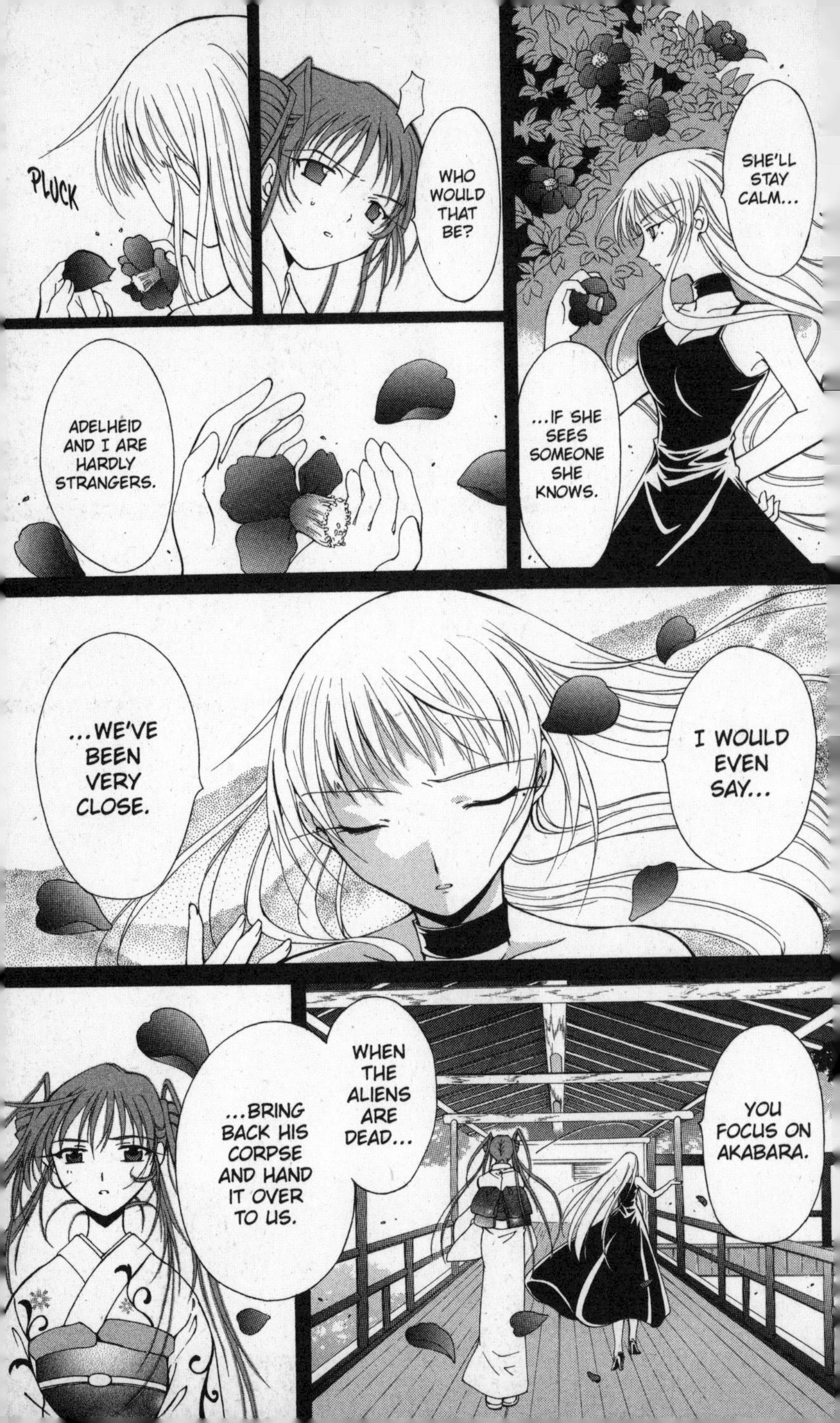
SHE'LL STAY CALM...
...IF SHE SEES SOMEONE SHE KNOWS.
WHO WOULD THAT BE?
PLUCK
ADELHEID AND I ARE HARDLY STRANGERS.
I WOULD EVEN SAY...
...WE'VE BEEN VERY CLOSE.
YOU FOCUS ON AKABARA.
WHEN THE ALIENS ARE DEAD...
...BRING BACK HIS CORPSE AND HAND IT OVER TO US.

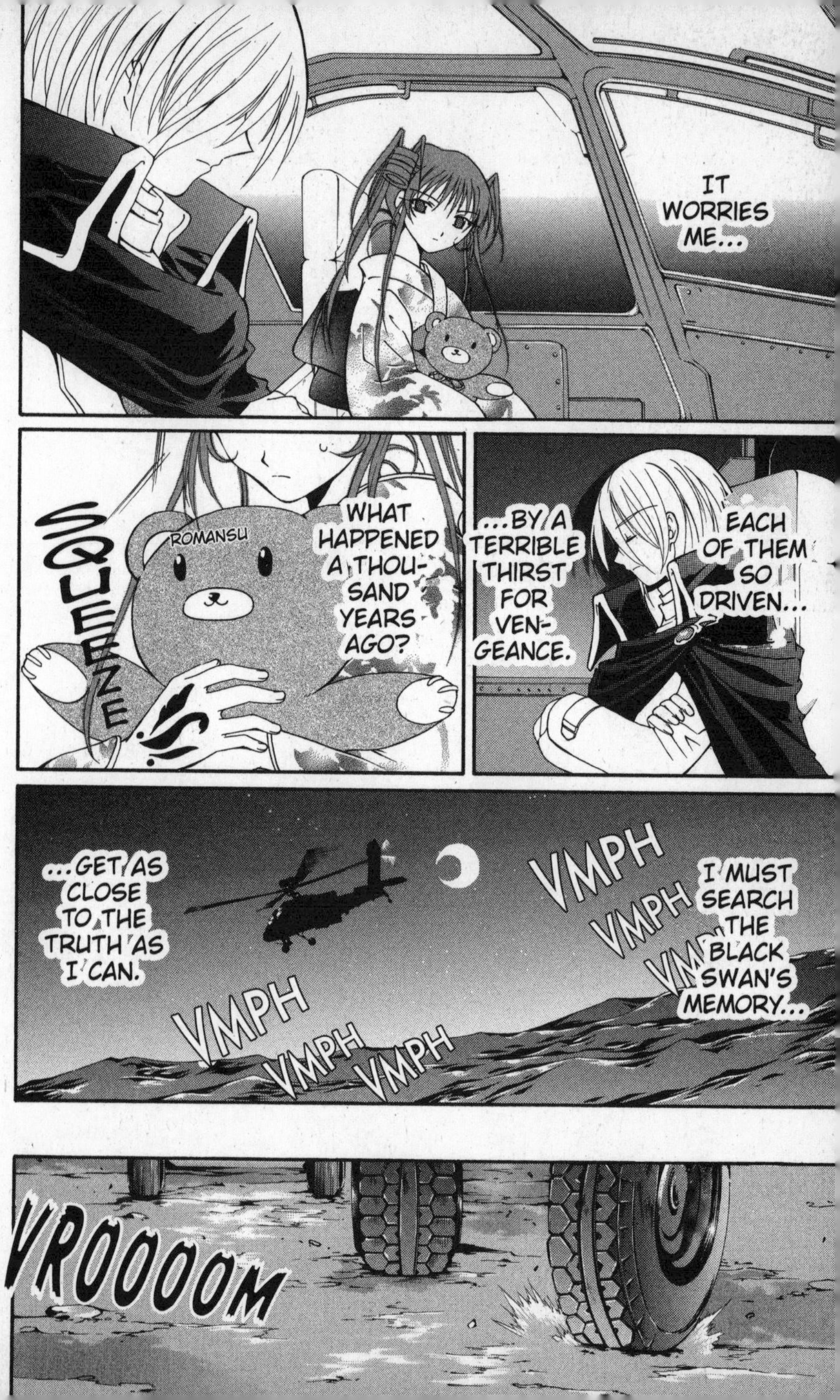
IT WORRIES ME...
EACH OF THEM SO DRIVEN...
...BY A TERRIBLE THIRST FOR VEN-GEANCE.
WHAT HAPPENED A THOU-SAND YEARS AGO?
ROMANSU
SQUEEZE
I MUST SEARCH THE BLACK SWAN'S MEMORY...
VMPH
VMPH
...GET AS CLOSE TO THE TRUTH AS I CAN.
VMPH
VMPH
VMPH
VROOOOM

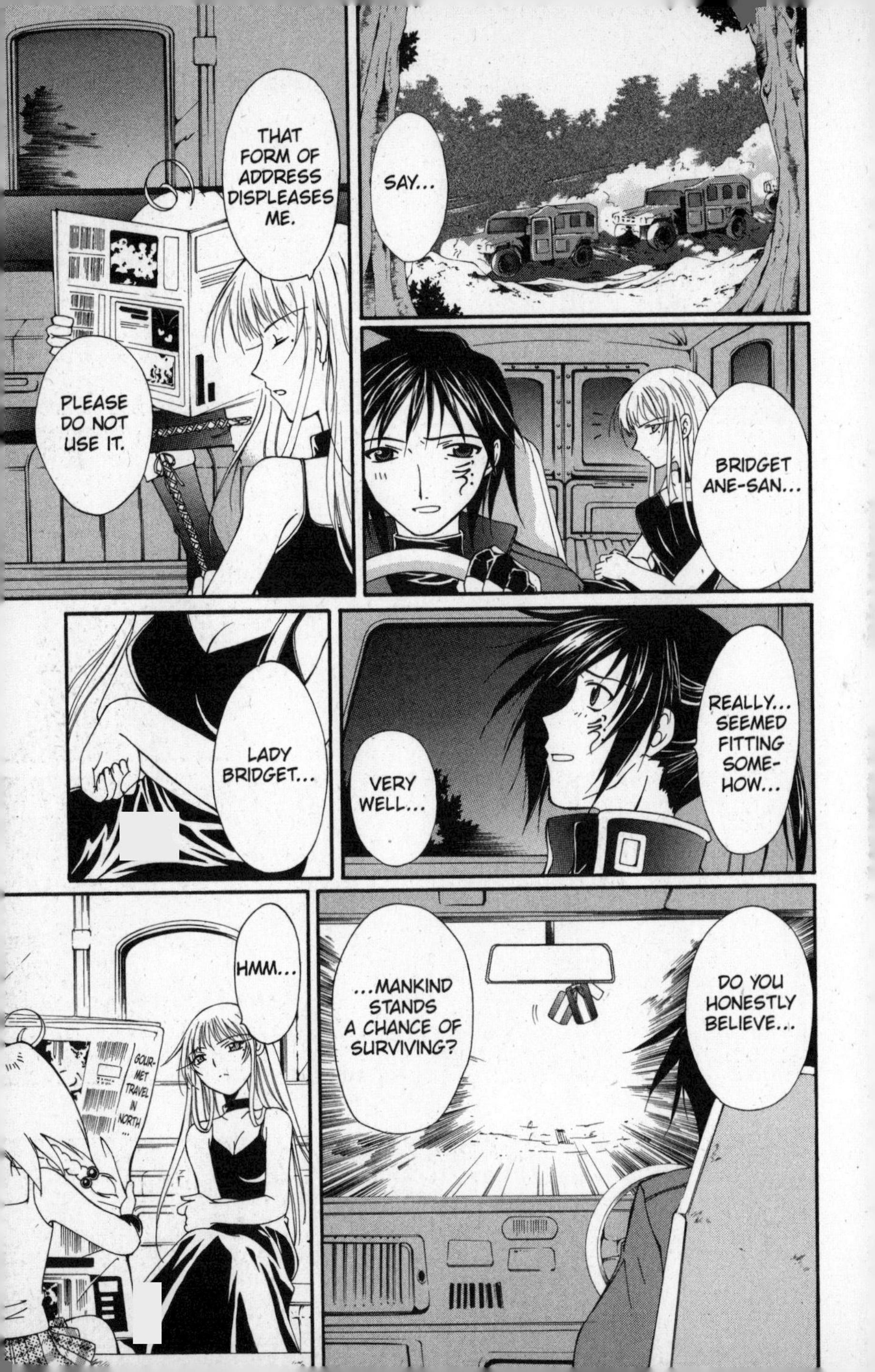
SAY...
BRIDGET ANE-SAN...
THAT FORM OF ADDRESS DISPLEASES ME.
PLEASE DO NOT USE IT.
REALLY... SEEMED FITTING SOME-HOW...
VERY WELL...
LADY BRIDGET...
DO YOU HONESTLY BELIEVE...
...MANKIND STANDS A CHANCE OF SURVIVING?
HMM...
GOURMET TRAVEL IN NORTH ...

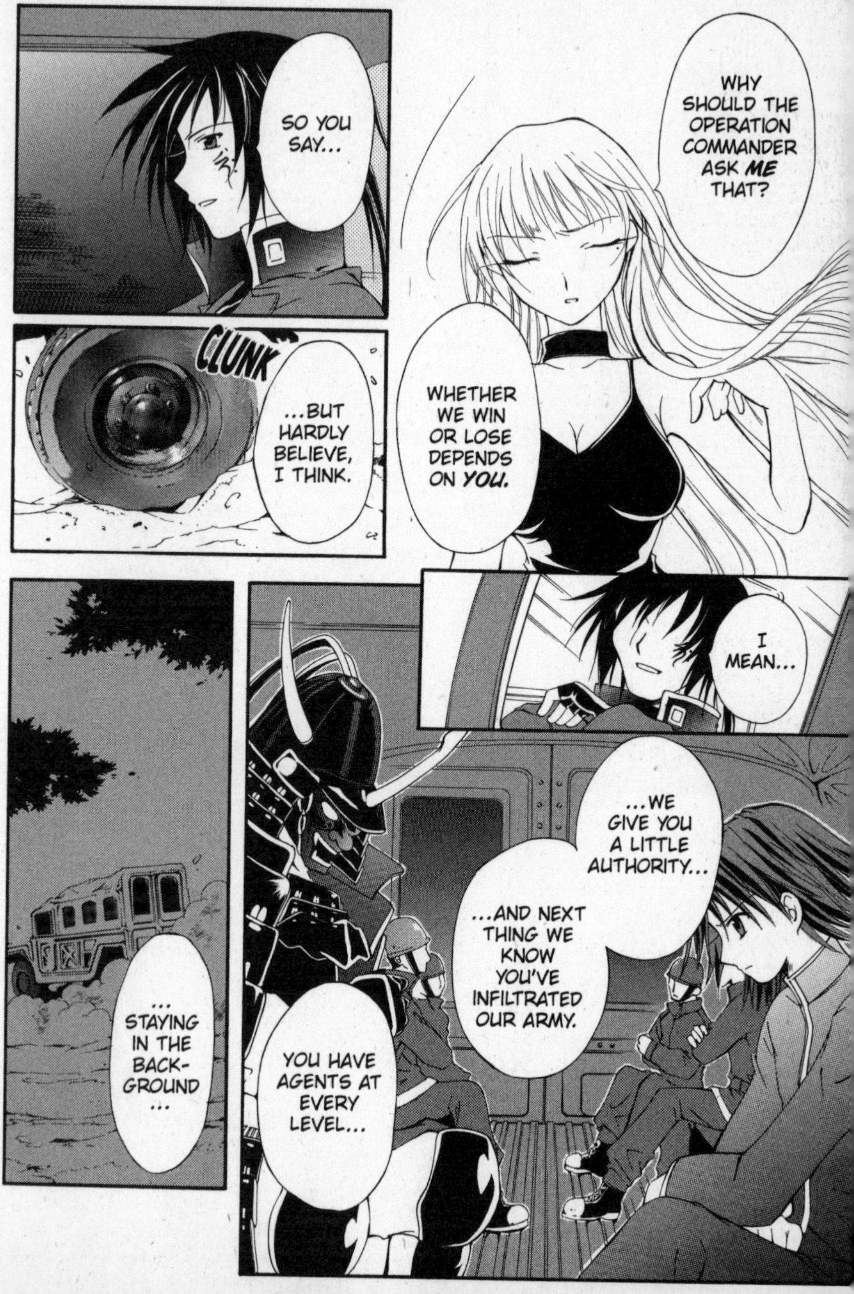
WHY SHOULD THE OPERATION COMMANDER ASK *ME* THAT?
SO YOU SAY...
WHETHER WE WIN OR LOSE DEPENDS ON *YOU.*
CLUNK
...BUT HARDLY BELIEVE, I THINK.
I MEAN...
...WE GIVE YOU A LITTLE AUTHORITY...
...AND NEXT THING WE KNOW YOU'VE INFILTRATED OUR ARMY.
YOU HAVE AGENTS AT EVERY LEVEL...
...STAYING IN THE BACK-GROUND...

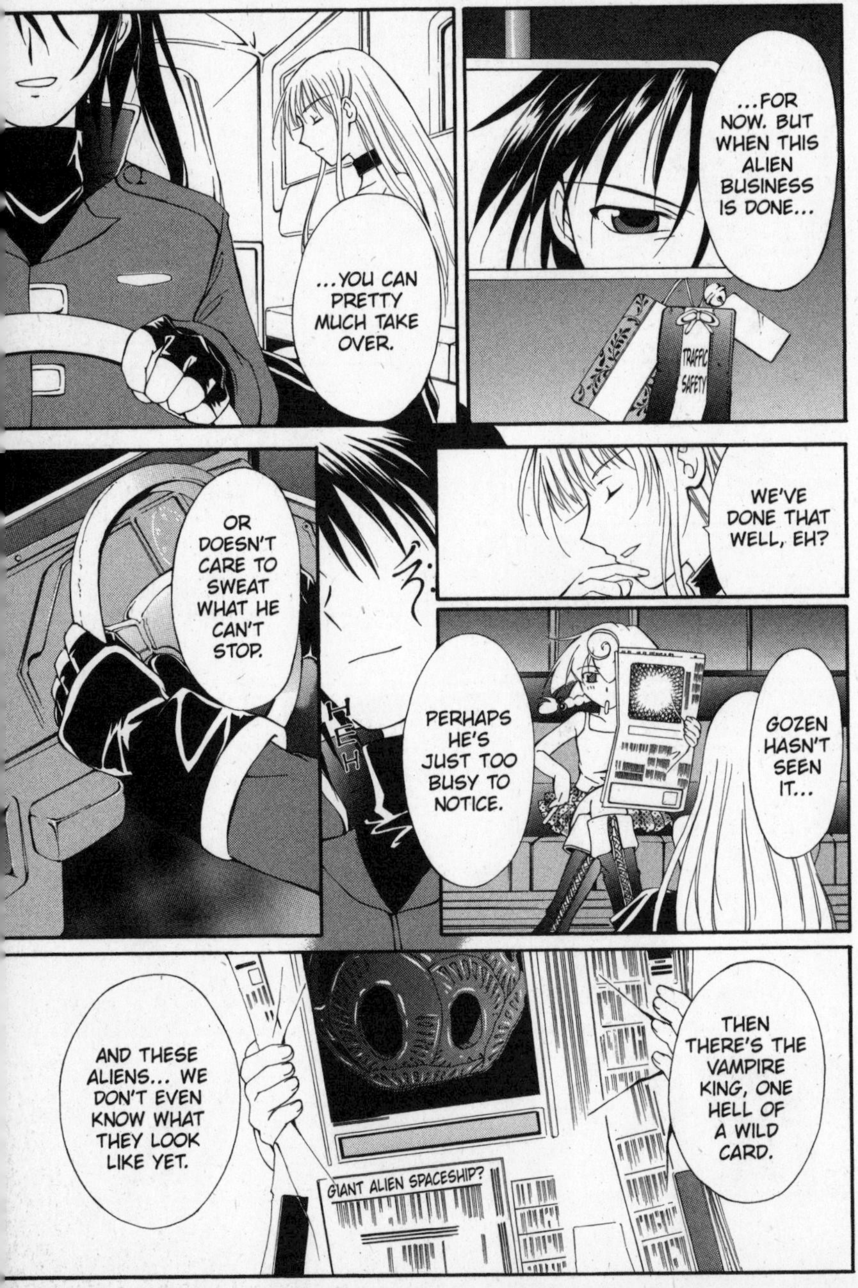
...FOR NOW. BUT WHEN THIS ALIEN BUSINESS IS DONE...
TRAFFIC SAFETY
...YOU CAN PRETTY MUCH TAKE OVER.
WE'VE DONE THAT WELL, EH?
GOZEN HASN'T SEEN IT...
PERHAPS HE'S JUST TOO BUSY TO NOTICE.
HEH
OR DOESN'T CARE TO SWEAT WHAT HE CAN'T STOP.
THEN THERE'S THE VAMPIRE KING, ONE HELL OF A WILD CARD.
AND THESE ALIENS... WE DON'T EVEN KNOW WHAT THEY LOOK LIKE YET.
GIANT ALIEN SPACESHIP?

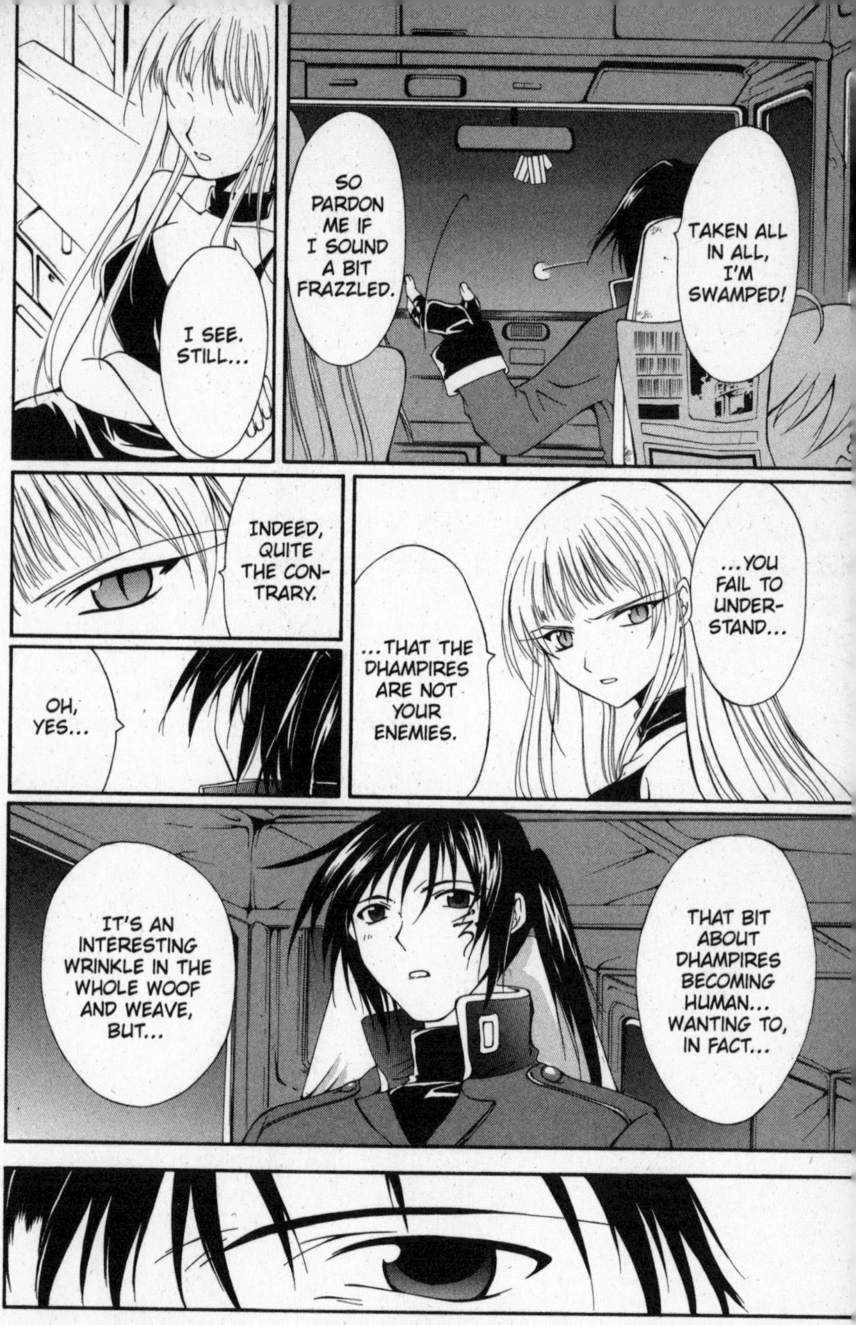
TAKEN ALL IN ALL, I'M SWAMPED!
SO PARDON ME IF I SOUND A BIT FRAZZLED.
I SEE. STILL...
...YOU FAIL TO UNDER-STAND...
...THAT THE DHAMPIRES ARE NOT YOUR ENEMIES.
INDEED, QUITE THE CON-TRARY.
OH, YES...
THAT BIT ABOUT DHAMPIRES BECOMING HUMAN... WANTING TO, IN FACT...
IT'S AN INTERESTING WRINKLE IN THE WHOLE WOOF AND WEAVE, BUT...

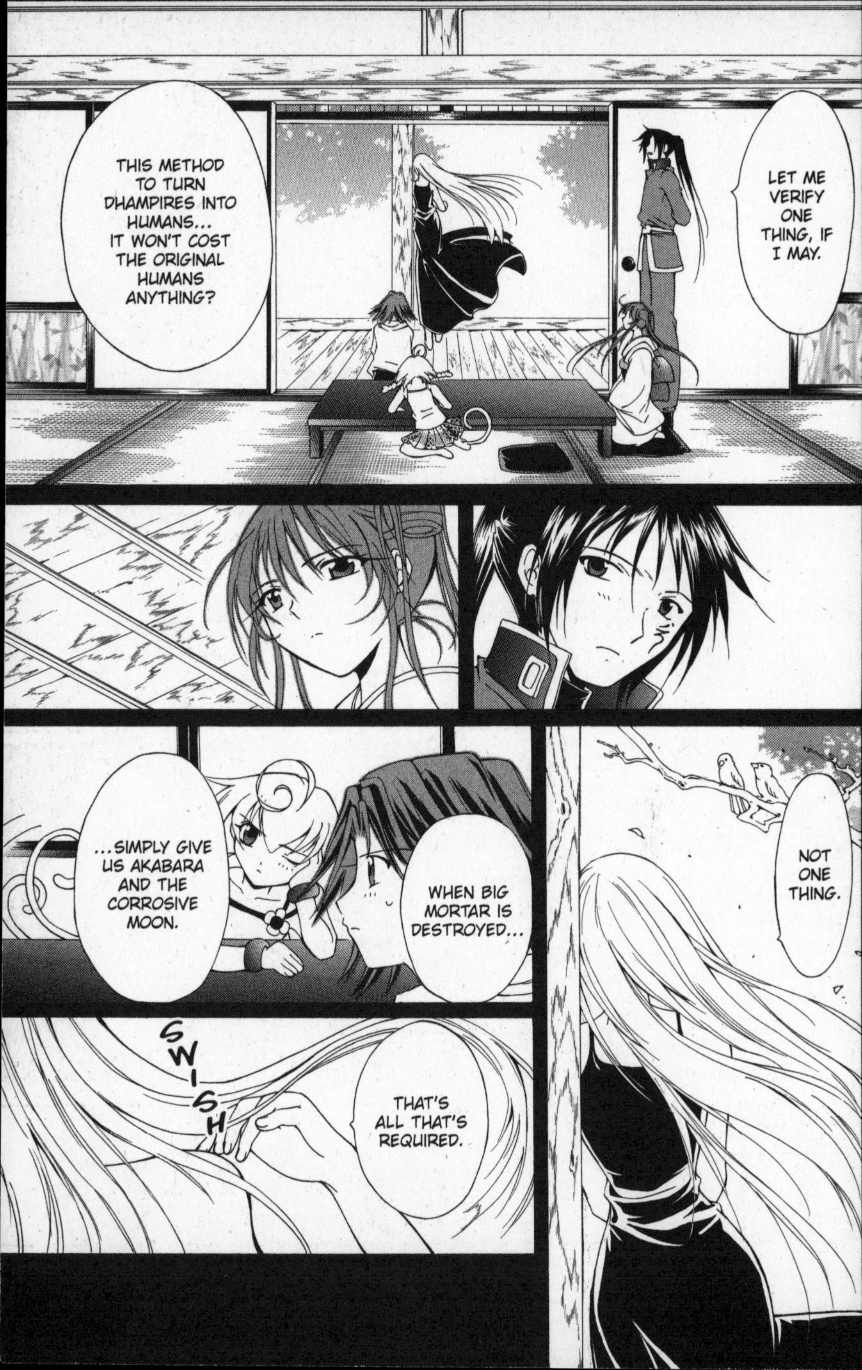
LET ME VERIFY ONE THING, IF I MAY.
THIS METHOD TO TURN DHAMPIRES INTO HUMANS... IT WON'T COST THE ORIGINAL HUMANS ANYTHING?
NOT ONE THING.
WHEN BIG MORTAR IS DESTROYED...
...SIMPLY GIVE US AKABARA AND THE CORROSIVE MOON.
SWISH
THAT'S ALL THAT'S REQUIRED.

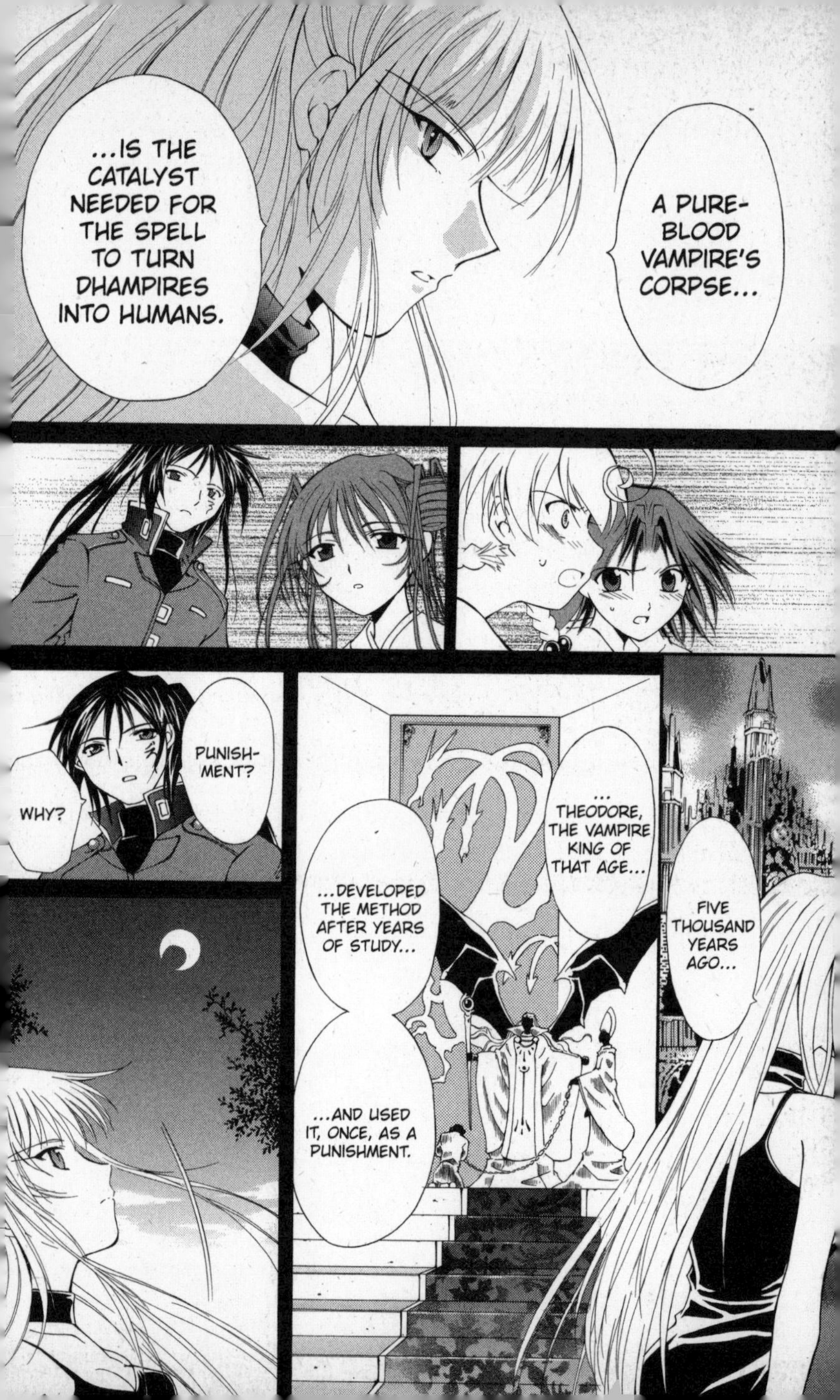
A PURE-BLOOD VAMPIRE'S CORPSE...
...IS THE CATALYST NEEDED FOR THE SPELL TO TURN DHAMPIRES INTO HUMANS.
FIVE THOUSAND YEARS AGO...
...THEODORE, THE VAMPIRE KING OF THAT AGE...
...DEVELOPED THE METHOD AFTER YEARS OF STUDY...
...AND USED IT, ONCE, AS A PUNISHMENT.
PUNISHMENT?
WHY?

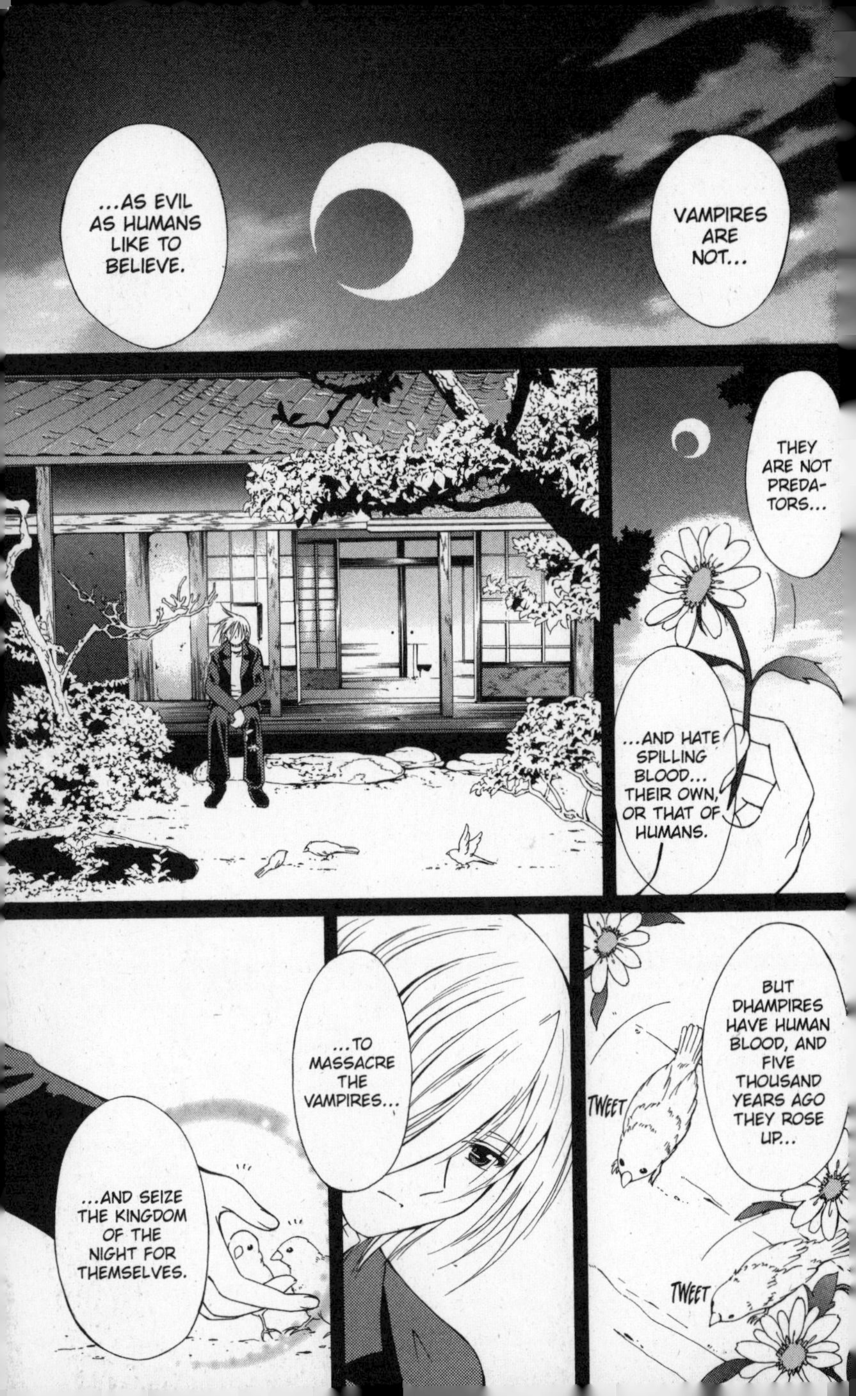
VAMPIRES ARE NOT...
...AS EVIL AS HUMANS LIKE TO BELIEVE.
THEY ARE NOT PREDATORS...
...AND HATE SPILLING BLOOD... THEIR OWN, OR THAT OF HUMANS.
BUT DHAMPIRES HAVE HUMAN BLOOD, AND FIVE THOUSAND YEARS AGO THEY ROSE UP...
TWEET
TWEET
...TO MASSACRE THE VAMPIRES...
...AND SEIZE THE KINGDOM OF THE NIGHT FOR THEMSELVES.

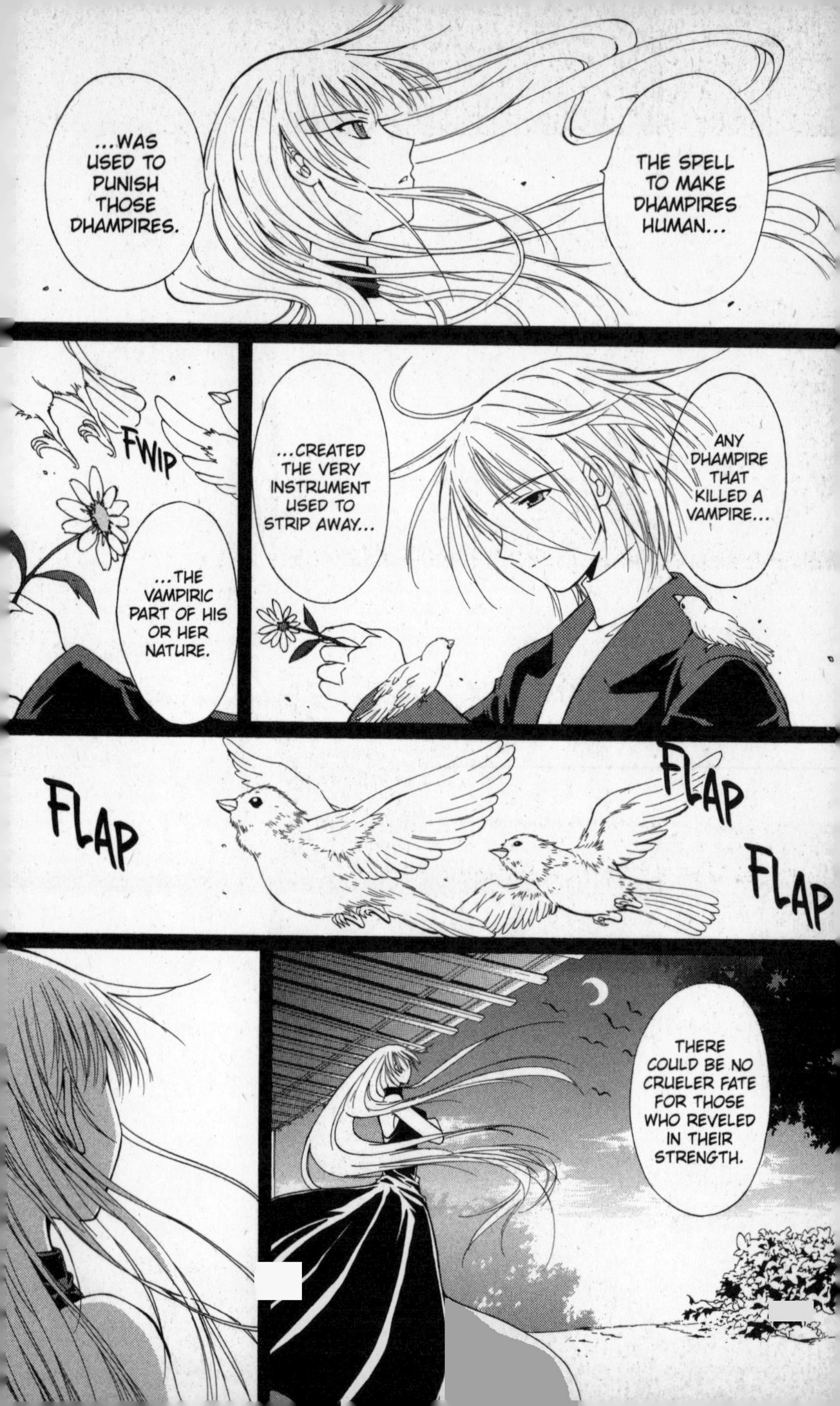
THE SPELL TO MAKE DHAMPIRES HUMAN...
...WAS USED TO PUNISH THOSE DHAMPIRES.
ANY DHAMPIRE THAT KILLED A VAMPIRE...
...CREATED THE VERY INSTRUMENT USED TO STRIP AWAY...
FWIP
...THE VAMPIRIC PART OF HIS OR HER NATURE.
FLAP
FLAP
FLAP
THERE COULD BE NO CRUELER FATE FOR THOSE WHO REVELED IN THEIR STRENGTH.

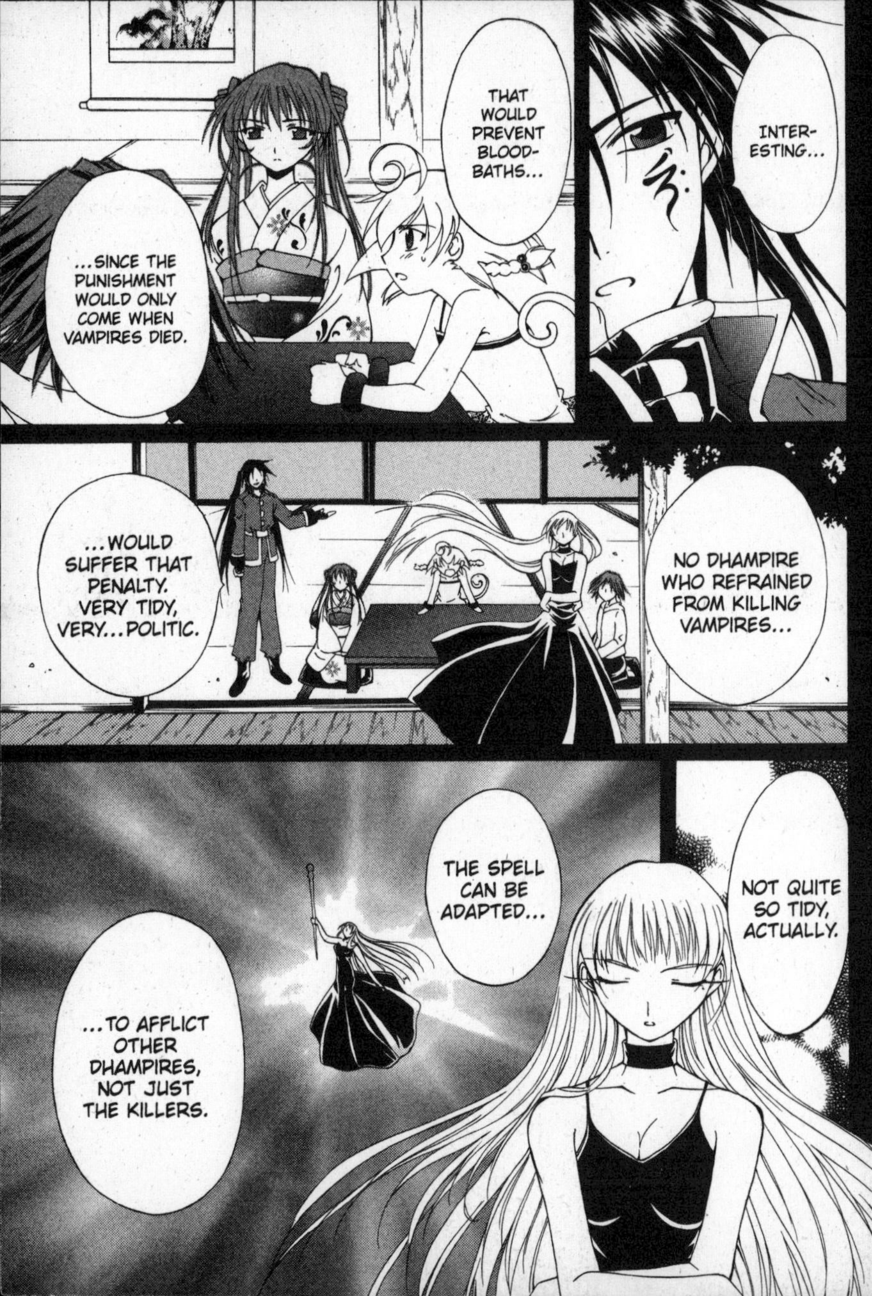
INTER-ESTING...
THAT WOULD PREVENT BLOOD-BATHS...
...SINCE THE PUNISHMENT WOULD ONLY COME WHEN VAMPIRES DIED.
NO DHAMPIRE WHO REFRAINED FROM KILLING VAMPIRES...
...WOULD SUFFER THAT PENALTY. VERY TIDY, VERY...POLITIC.
NOT QUITE SO TIDY, ACTUALLY.
THE SPELL CAN BE ADAPTED...
...TO AFFLICT OTHER DHAMPIRES, NOT JUST THE KILLERS.

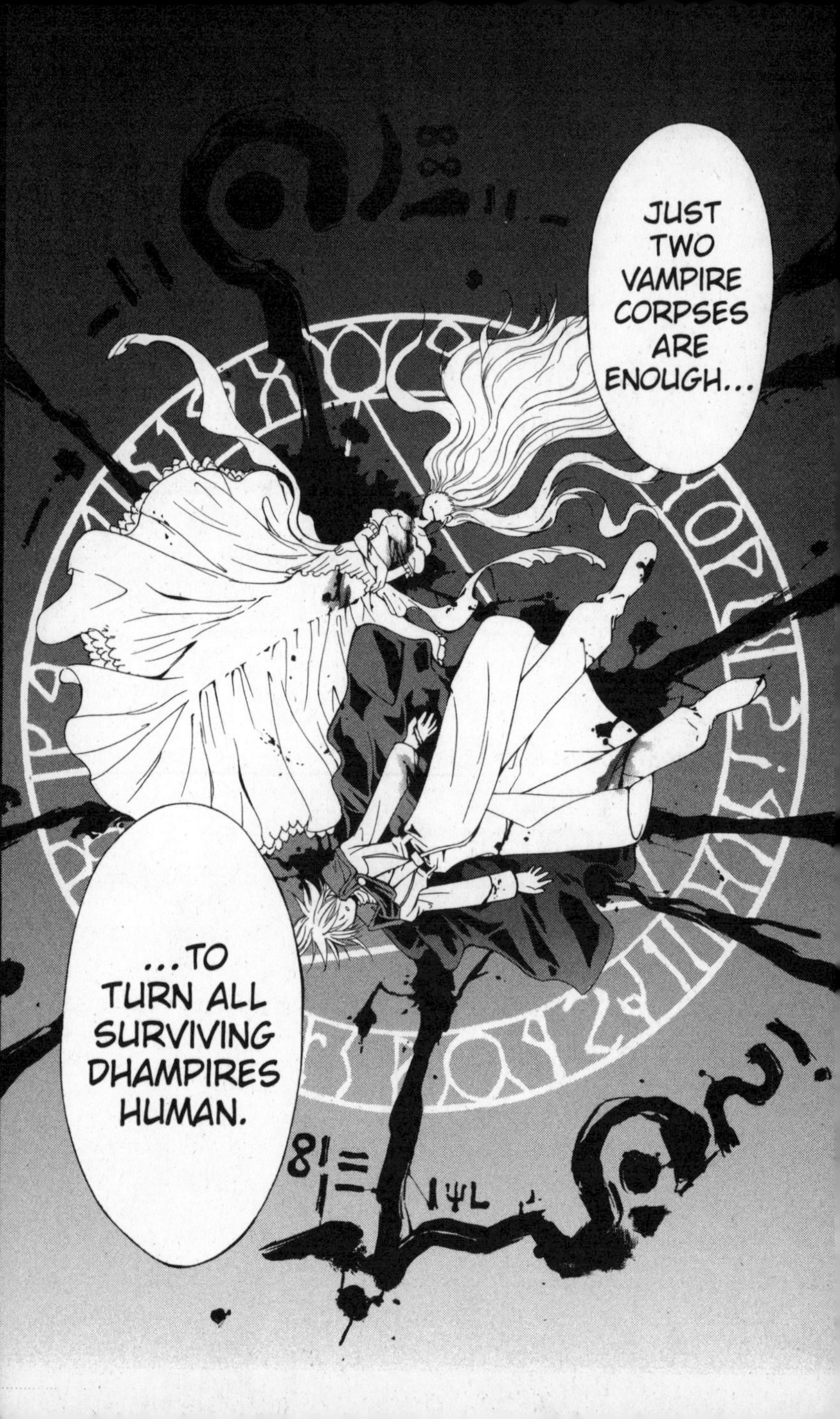
JUST TWO VAMPIRE CORPSES ARE ENOUGH...
...TO TURN ALL SURVIVING DHAMPIRES HUMAN.

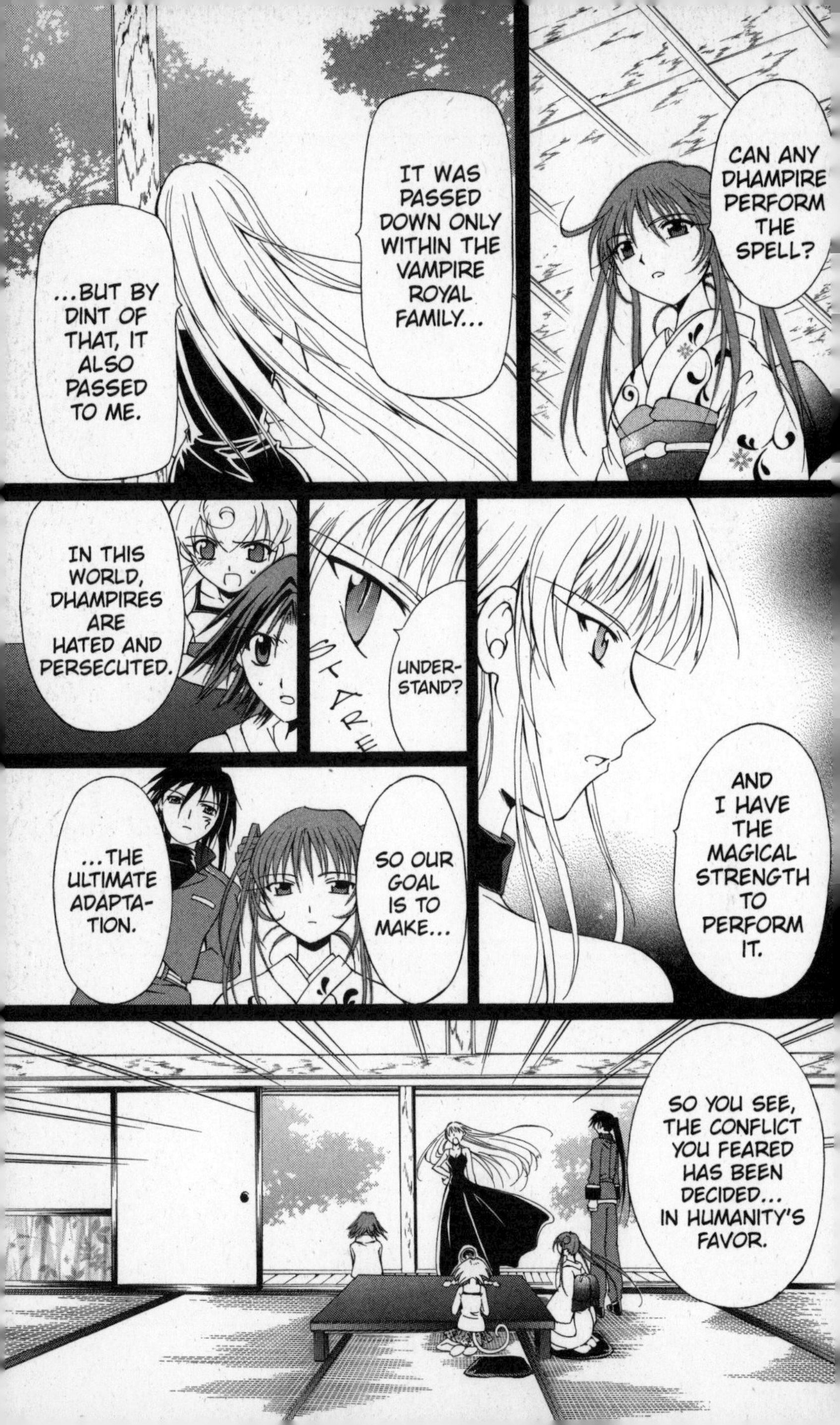
CAN ANY DHAMPIRE PERFORM THE SPELL?
IT WAS PASSED DOWN ONLY WITHIN THE VAMPIRE ROYAL FAMILY...
...BUT BY DINT OF THAT, IT ALSO PASSED TO ME.
AND I HAVE THE MAGICAL STRENGTH TO PERFORM IT.
UNDER-STAND?
STARE
IN THIS WORLD, DHAMPIRES ARE HATED AND PERSECUTED.
SO OUR GOAL IS TO MAKE...
...THE ULTIMATE ADAPTA-TION.
SO YOU SEE, THE CONFLICT YOU FEARED HAS BEEN DECIDED... IN HUMANITY'S FAVOR.

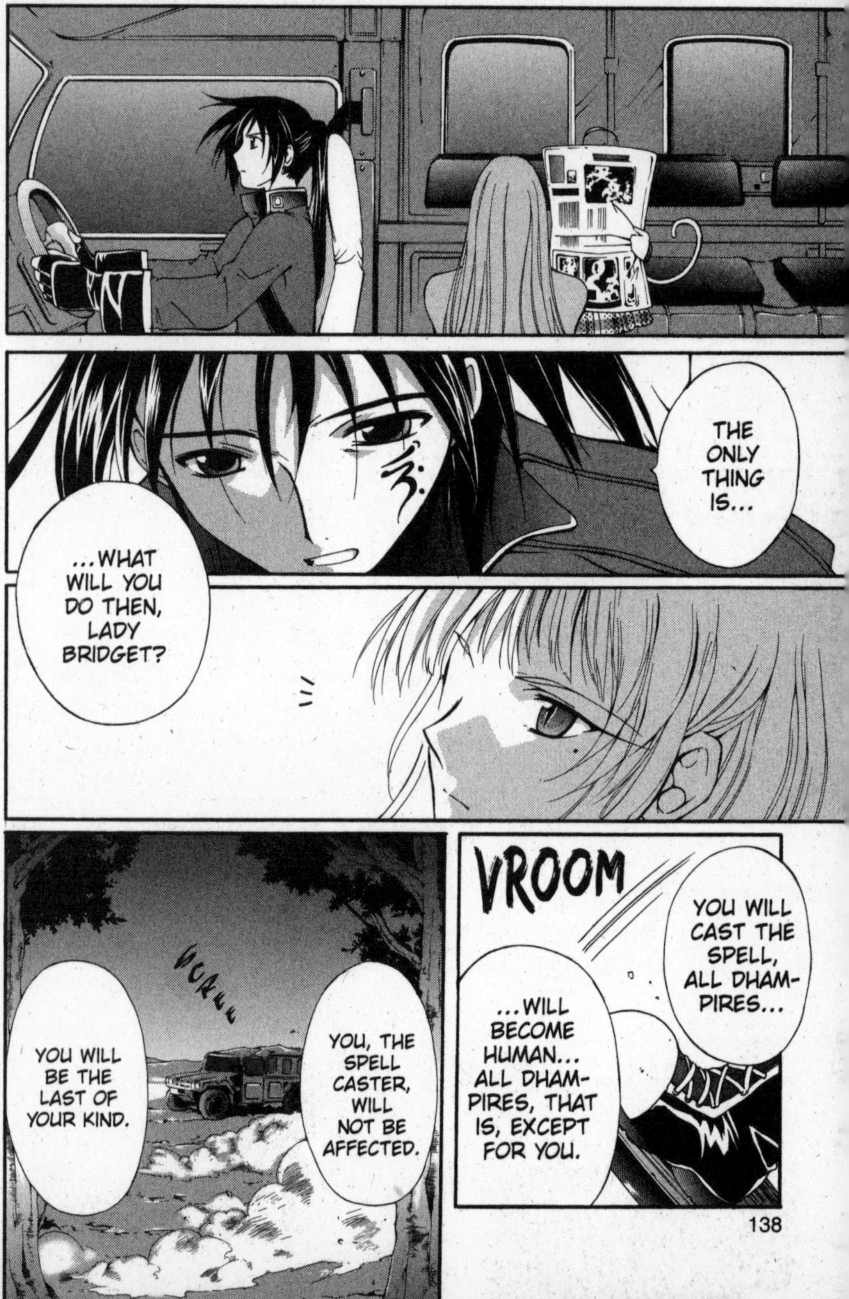
THE ONLY THING IS...
...WHAT WILL YOU DO THEN, LADY BRIDGET?
VROOM
YOU WILL CAST THE SPELL, ALL DHAM-PIRES...
...WILL BECOME HUMAN... ALL DHAM-PIRES, THAT IS, EXCEPT FOR YOU.
YOU, THE SPELL CASTER, WILL NOT BE AFFECTED.
YOU WILL BE THE LAST OF YOUR KIND.

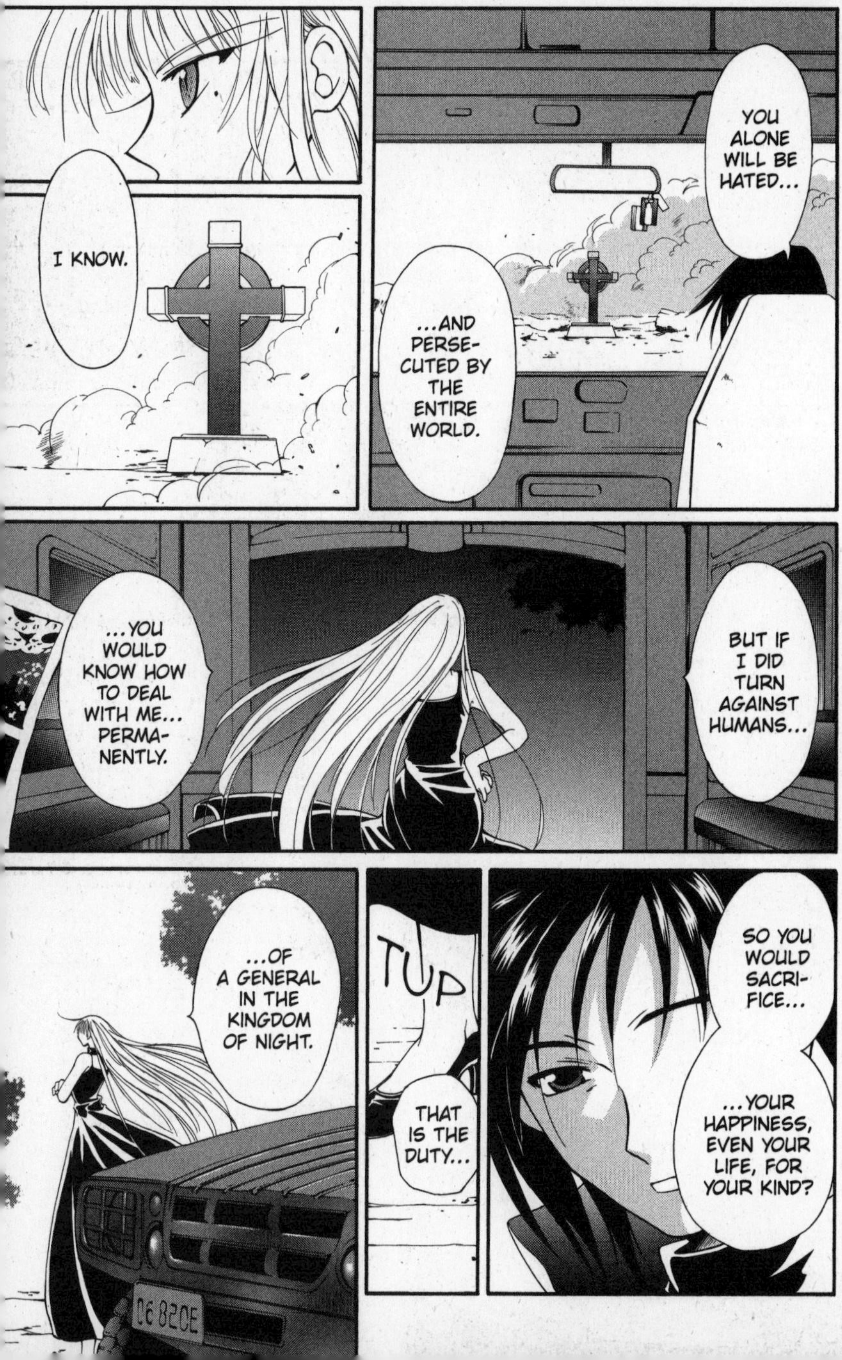
YOU ALONE WILL BE HATED...
...AND PERSE-CUTED BY THE ENTIRE WORLD.
I KNOW.
BUT IF I DID TURN AGAINST HUMANS...
...YOU WOULD KNOW HOW TO DEAL WITH ME... PERMA-NENTLY.
SO YOU WOULD SACRI-FICE...
...YOUR HAPPINESS, EVEN YOUR LIFE, FOR YOUR KIND?
TUP
THAT IS THE DUTY...
...OF A GENERAL IN THE KINGDOM OF NIGHT.

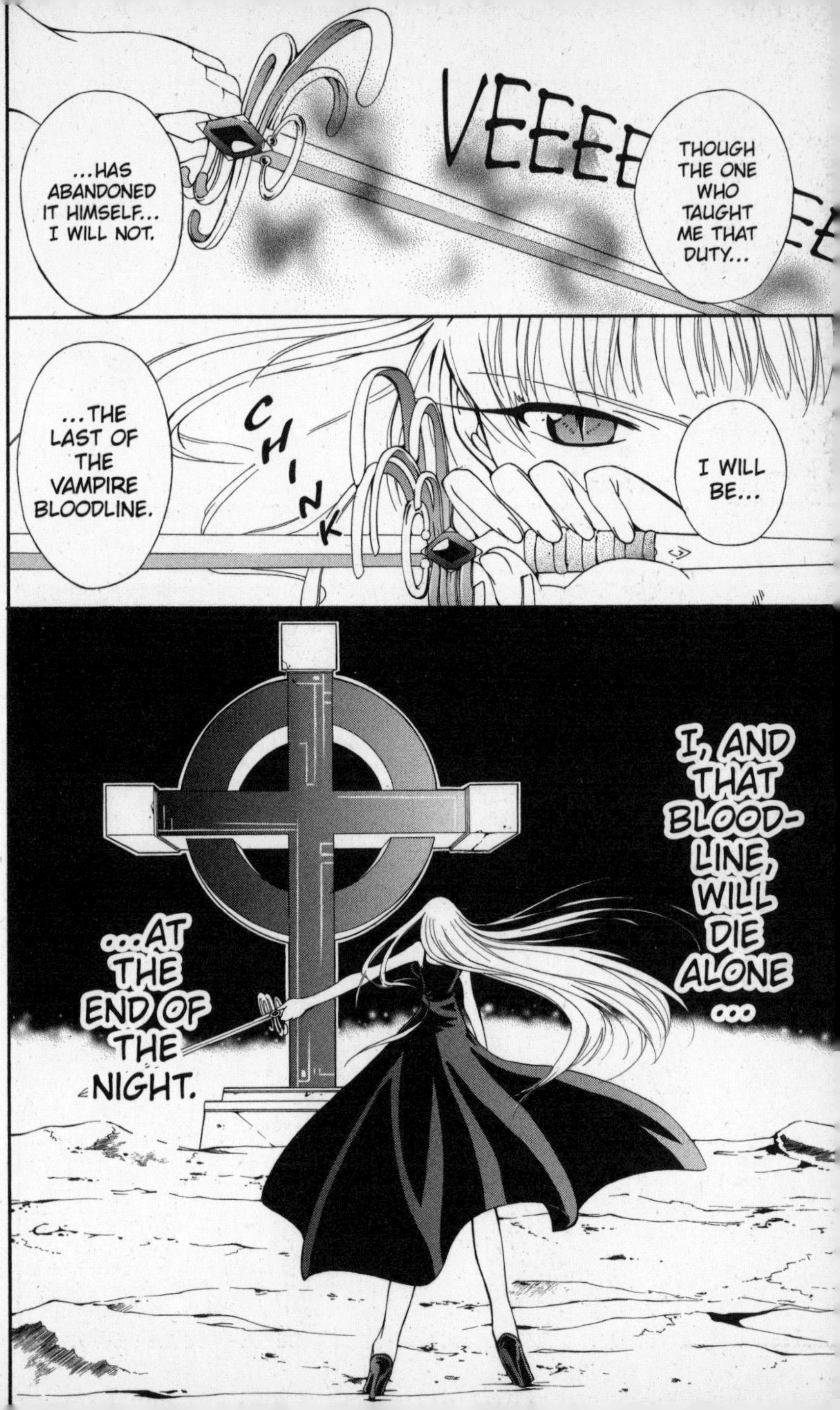
THOUGH THE ONE WHO TAUGHT ME THAT DUTY...
VEEEE
...HAS ABANDONED IT HIMSELF... I WILL NOT.
I WILL BE...
CHINK
...THE LAST OF THE VAMPIRE BLOODLINE.
I, AND THAT BLOOD-LINE, WILL DIE ALONE...
...AT THE END OF THE NIGHT.

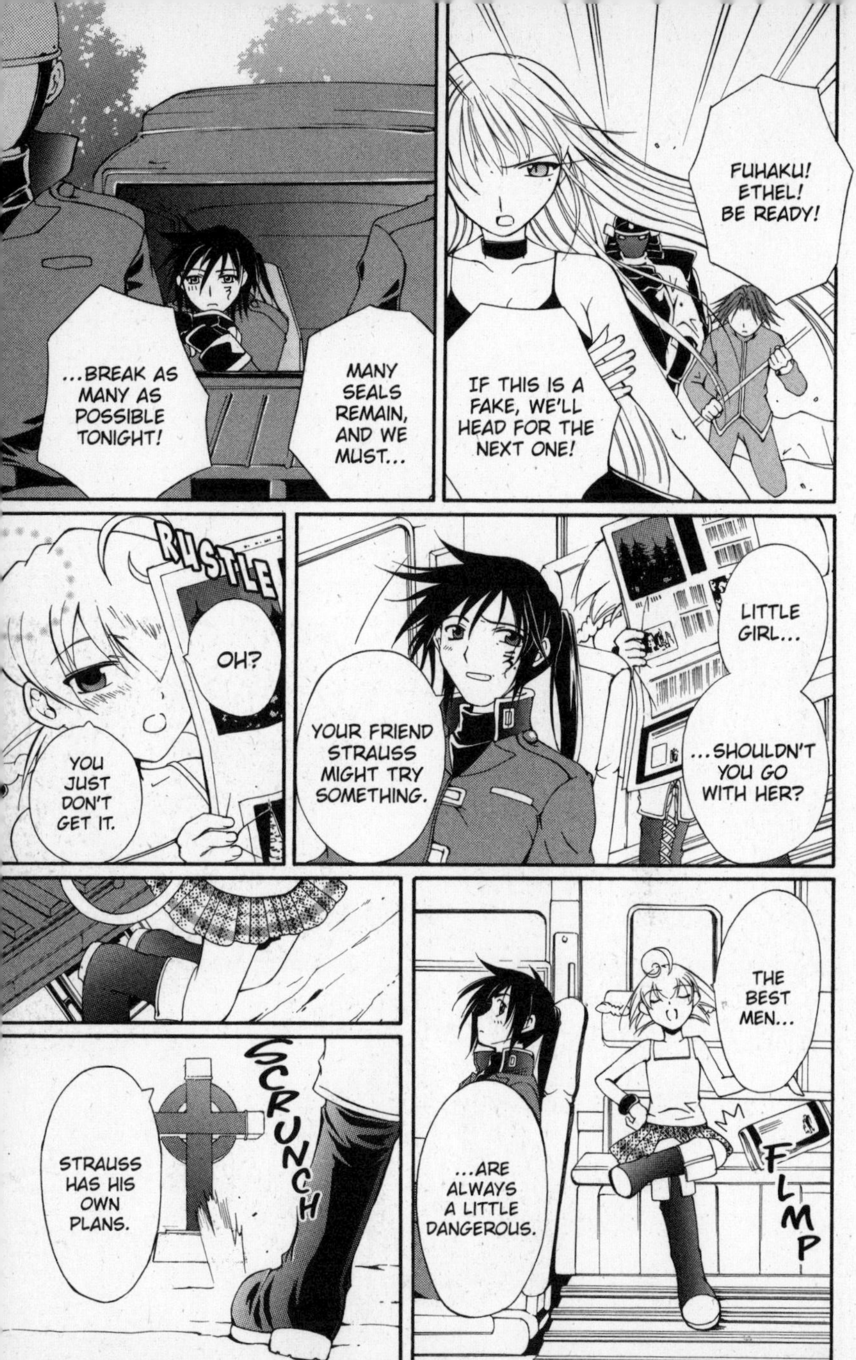
FUHAKU! ETHEL! BE READY!
IF THIS IS A FAKE, WE'LL HEAD FOR THE NEXT ONE!
MANY SEALS REMAIN, AND WE MUST...
...BREAK AS MANY AS POSSIBLE TONIGHT!
LITTLE GIRL...
...SHOULDN'T YOU GO WITH HER?
YOUR FRIEND STRAUSS MIGHT TRY SOMETHING.
RUSTLE
OH?
YOU JUST DON'T GET IT.
THE BEST MEN...
...ARE ALWAYS A LITTLE DANGEROUS.
FLMP
SCRUNCH
STRAUSS HAS HIS OWN PLANS.

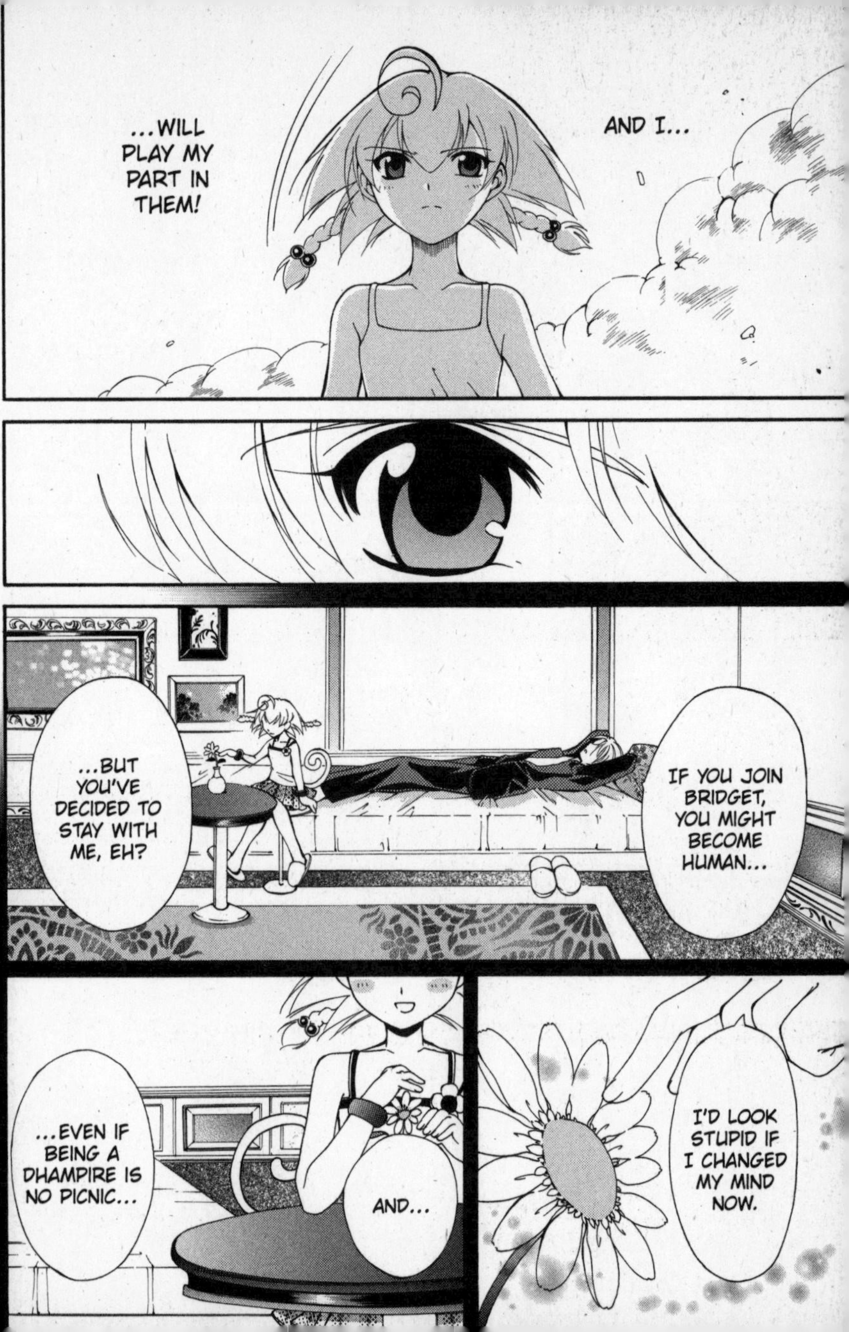
AND I...
...WILL PLAY MY PART IN THEM!
IF YOU JOIN BRIDGET, YOU MIGHT BECOME HUMAN...
...BUT YOU'VE DECIDED TO STAY WITH ME, EH?
I'D LOOK STUPID IF I CHANGED MY MIND NOW.
...EVEN IF BEING A DHAMPIRE IS NO PICNIC...
AND...

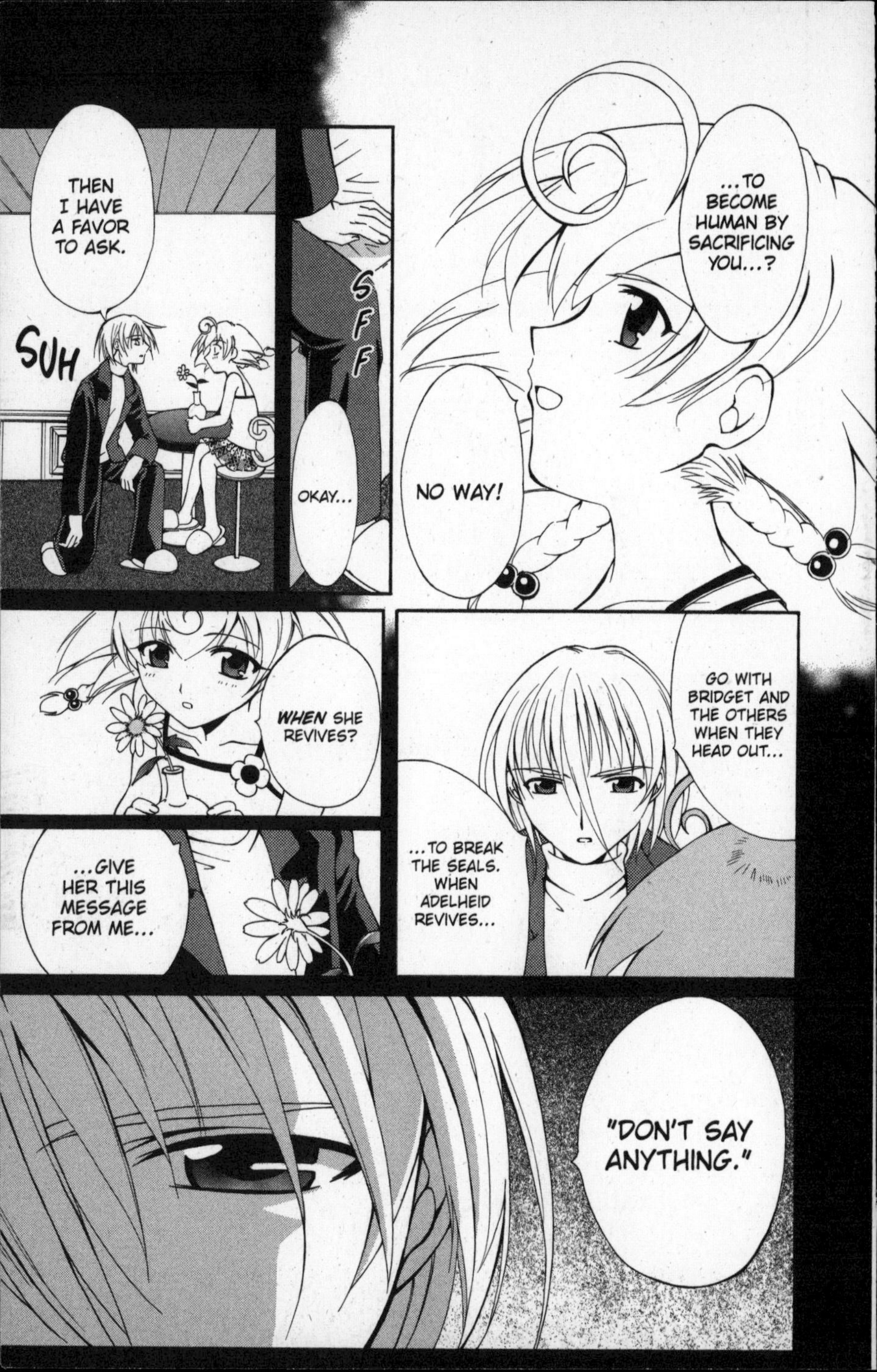
...TO BECOME HUMAN BY SACRIFICING YOU...?
NO WAY!
SFF
OKAY...
THEN I HAVE A FAVOR TO ASK.
SUH
GO WITH BRIDGET AND THE OTHERS WHEN THEY HEAD OUT...
...TO BREAK THE SEALS. WHEN ADELHEID REVIVES...
WHEN SHE REVIVES?
...GIVE HER THIS MESSAGE FROM ME...
"DON'T SAY ANYTHING."

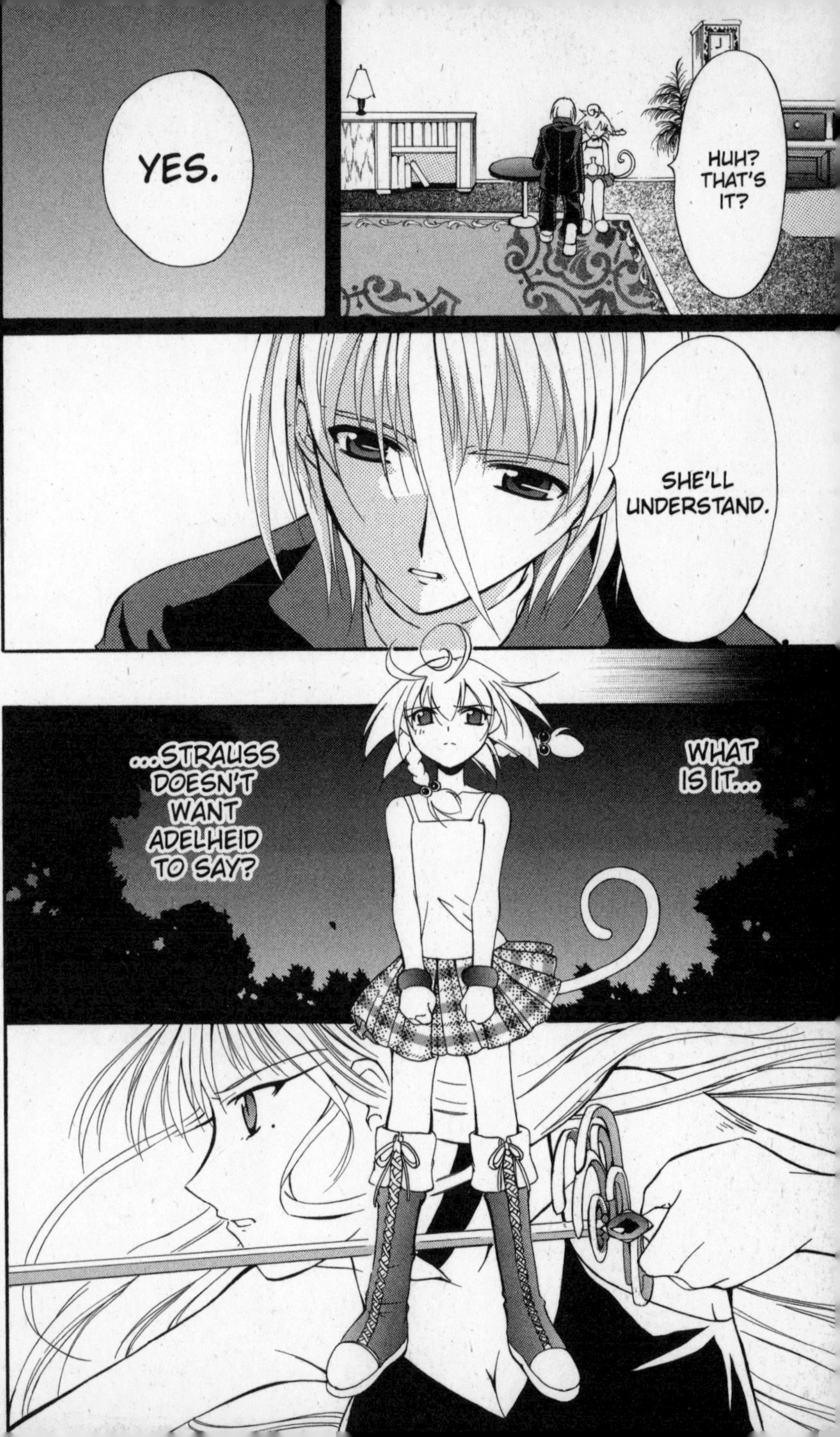
HUH? THAT'S IT?
YES.
SHE'LL UNDERSTAND.
WHAT IS IT...
...STRAUSS DOESN'T WANT ADELHEID TO SAY?

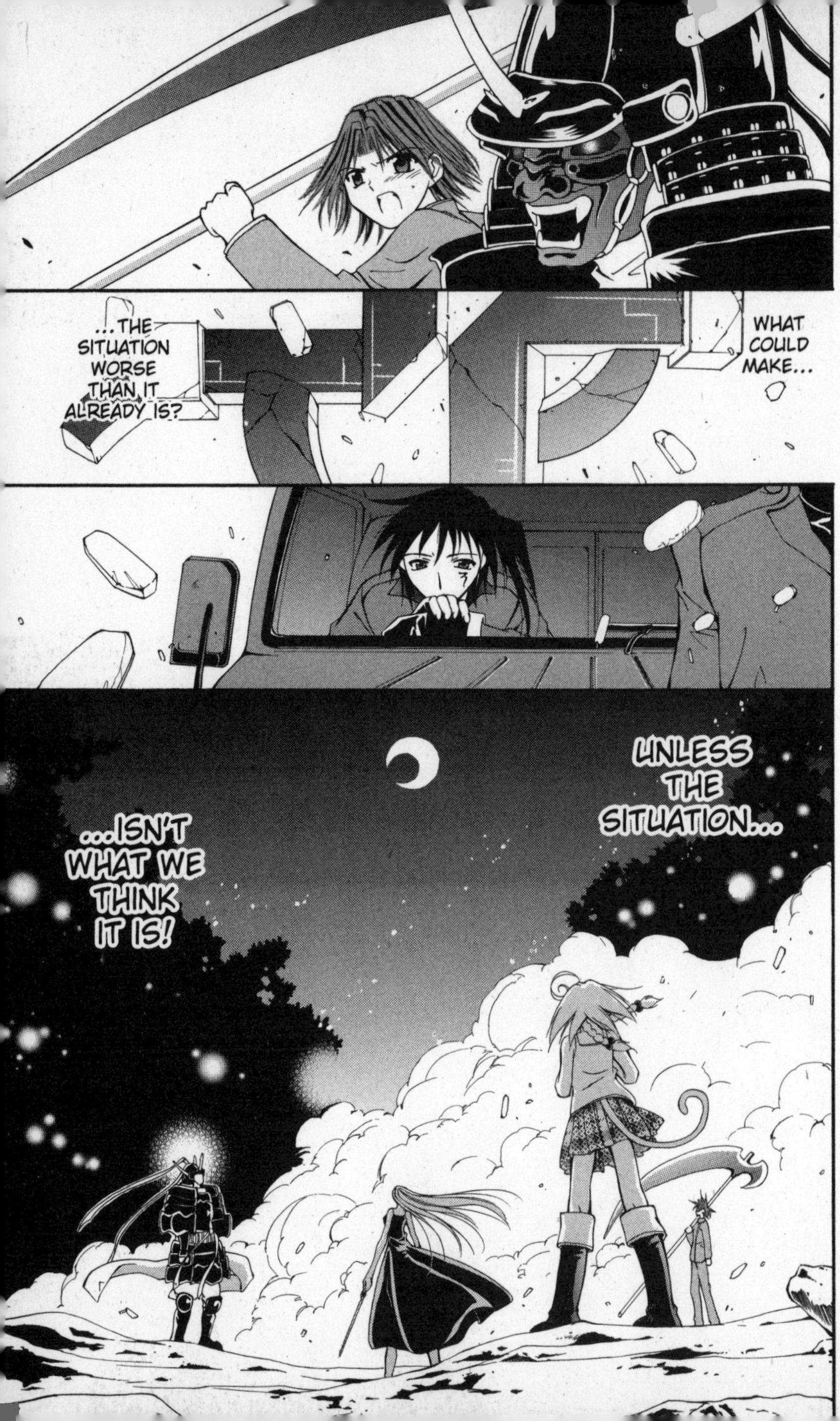
WHAT COULD MAKE...
...THE SITUATION WORSE THAN IT ALREADY IS?
UNLESS THE SITUATION...
...ISN'T WHAT WE THINK IT IS!

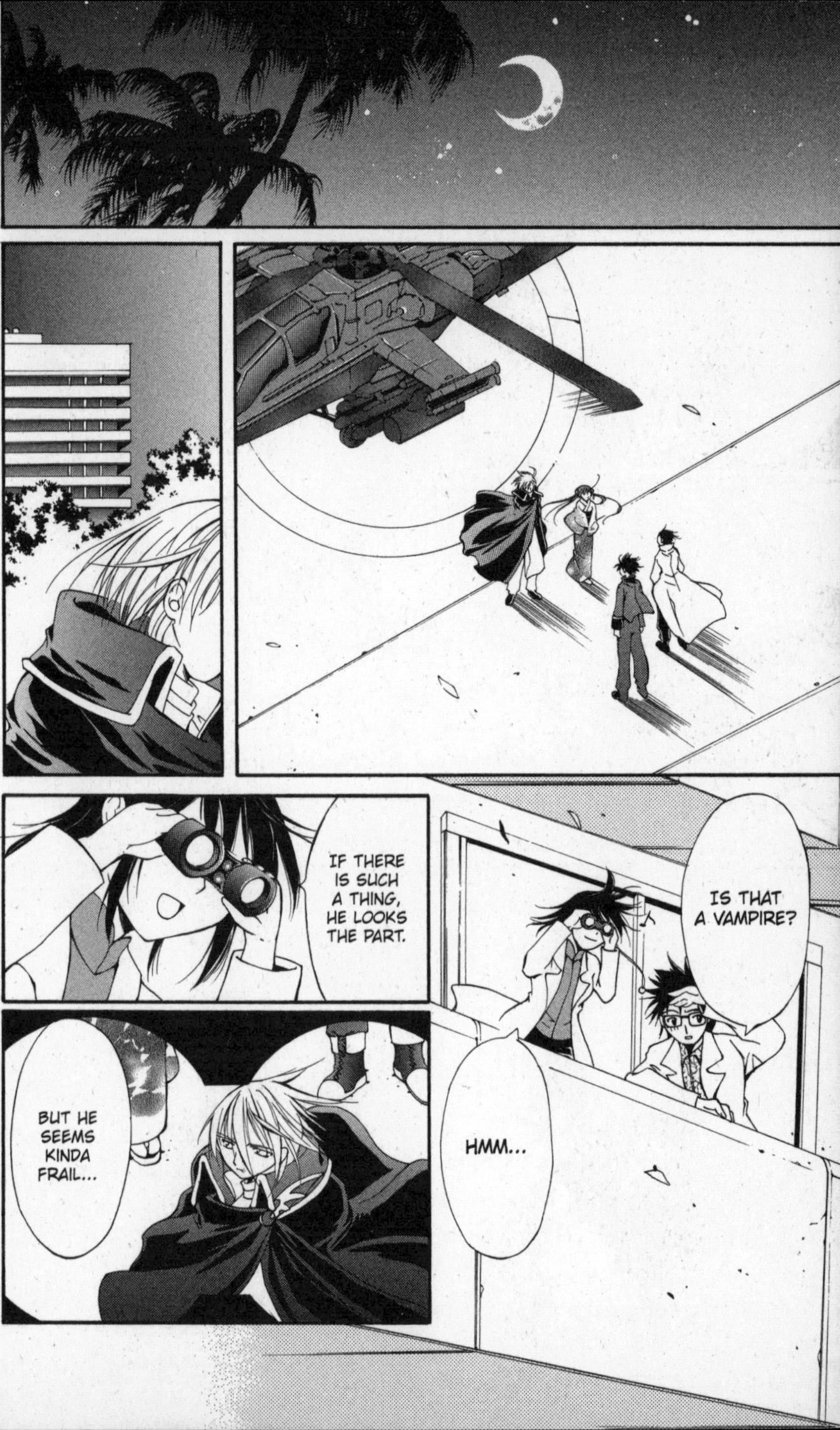
IS THAT A VAMPIRE?
HMM...
IF THERE IS SUCH A THING, HE LOOKS THE PART.
BUT HE SEEMS KINDA FRAIL...

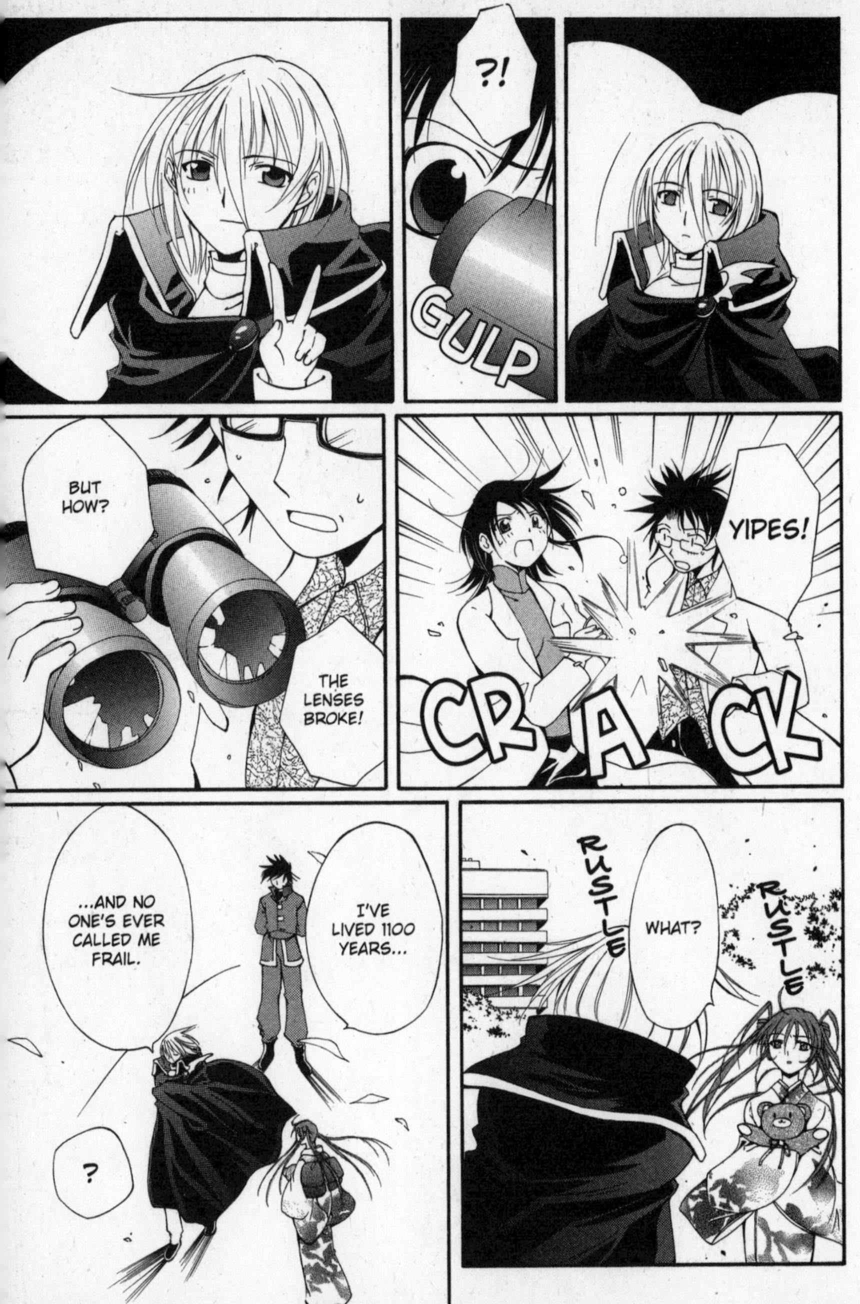
?!
GULP
YIPES!
CRACK
BUT HOW?
THE LENSES BROKE!
RUSTLE
WHAT?
RUSTLE
I'VE LIVED 1100 YEARS...
...AND NO ONE'S EVER CALLED ME FRAIL.
?

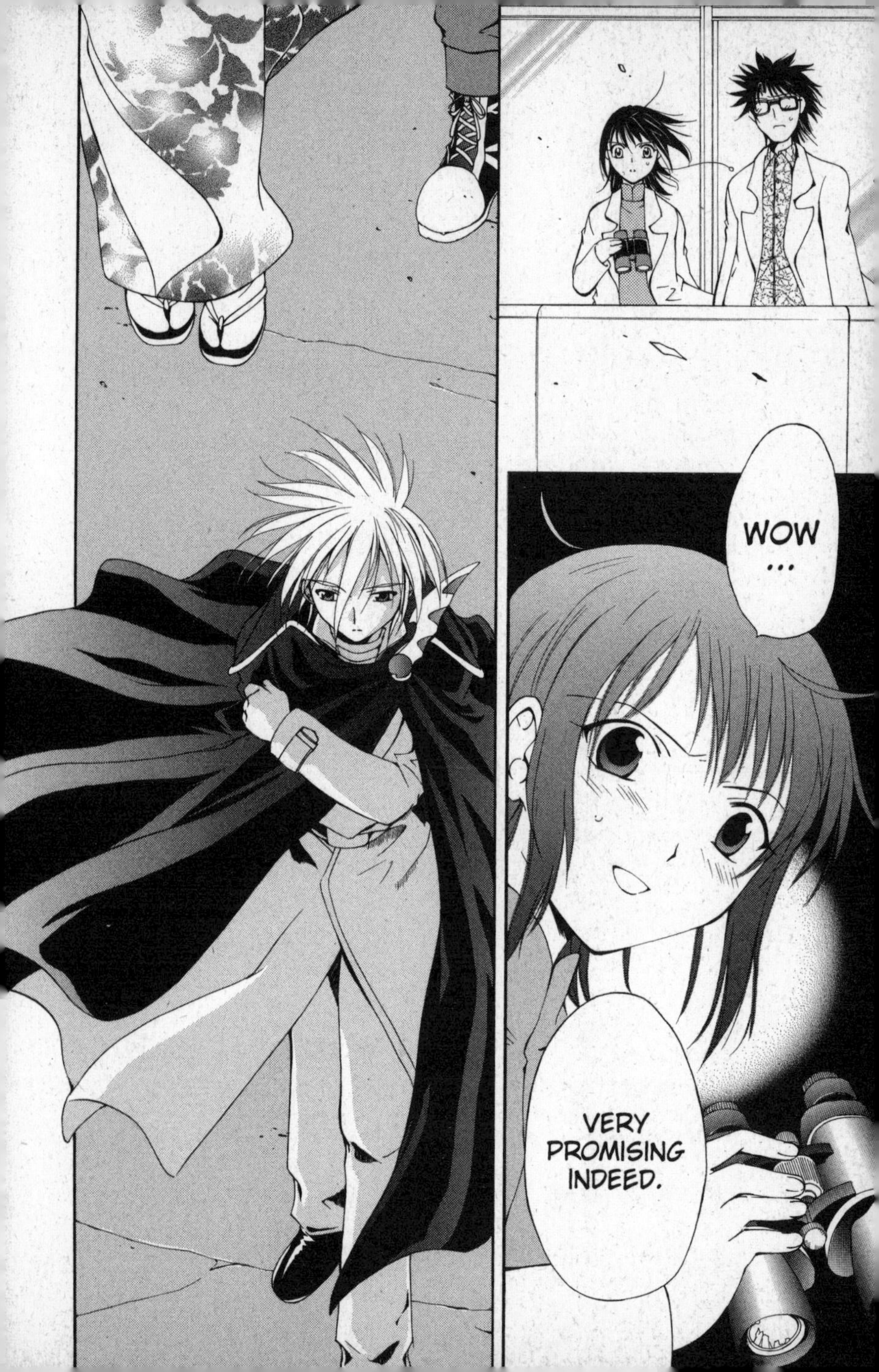
WOW ...
VERY PROMISING INDEED.

THE RECORD OF A

FALLEN VAMPIRE

THE RECORD OF A

FALLEN VAMPIRE

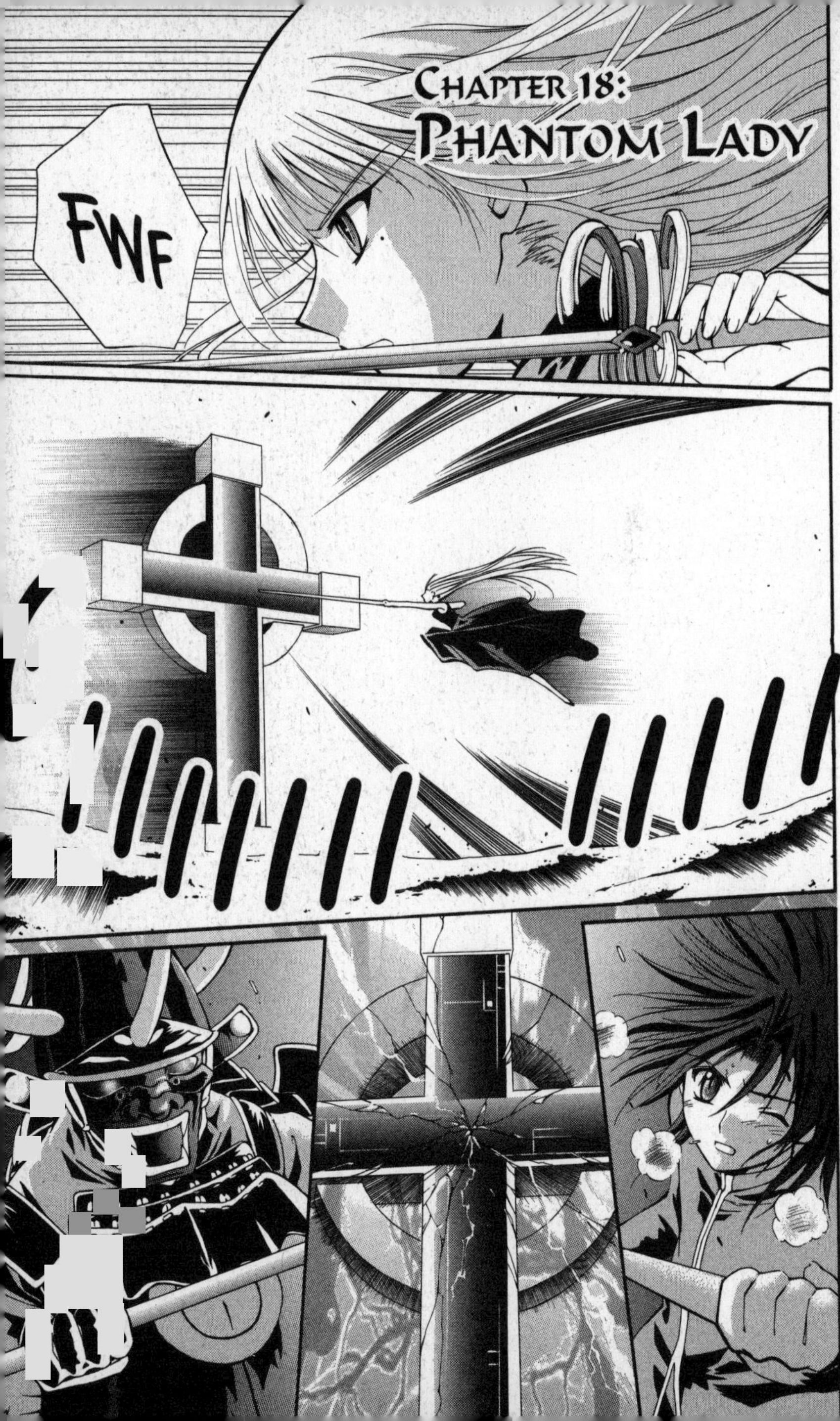
Chapter 18:
Phantom Lady
FWF

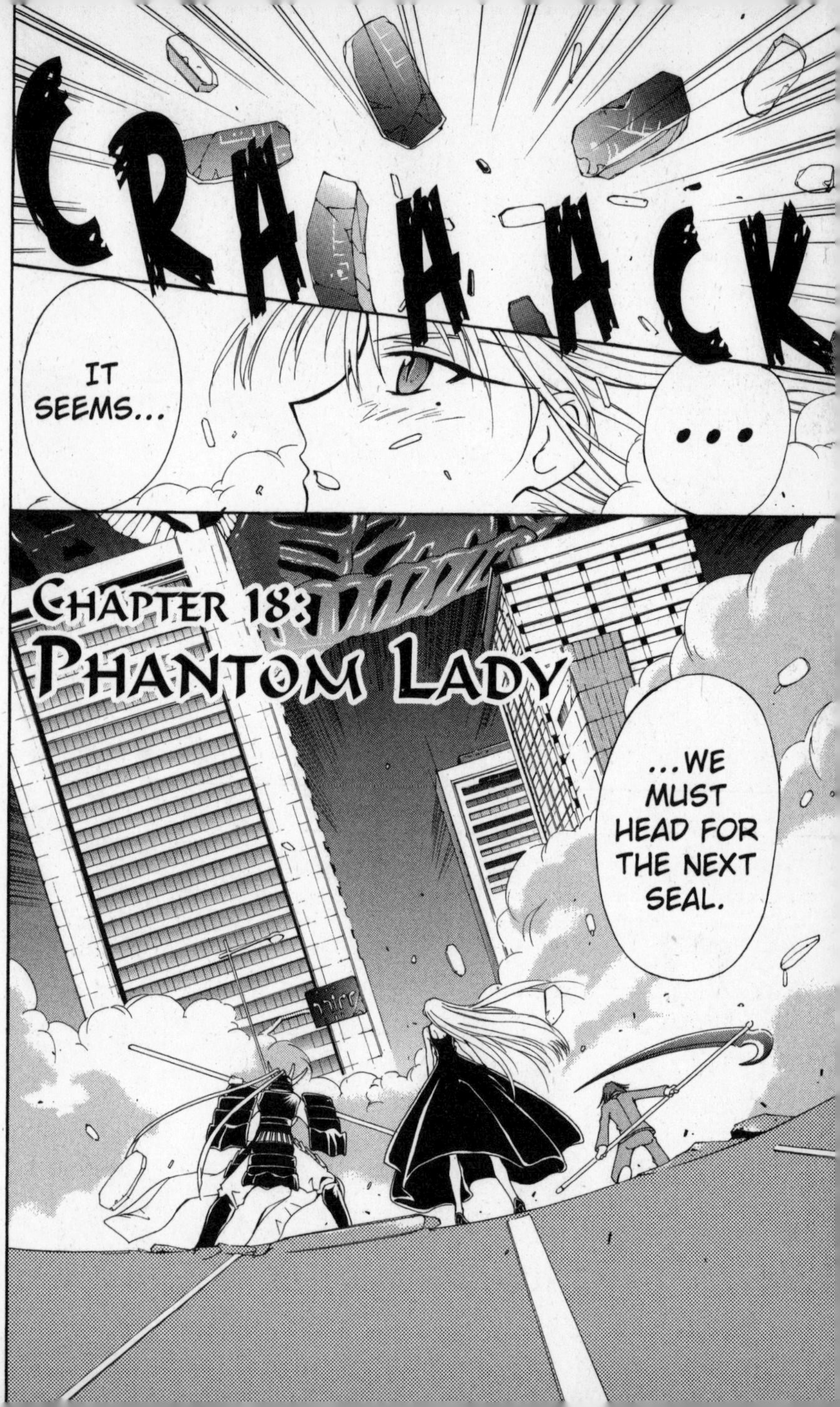
CRAAACK
IT SEEMS...
...
CHAPTER 18:
PHANTOM LADY
...WE MUST HEAD FOR THE NEXT SEAL.

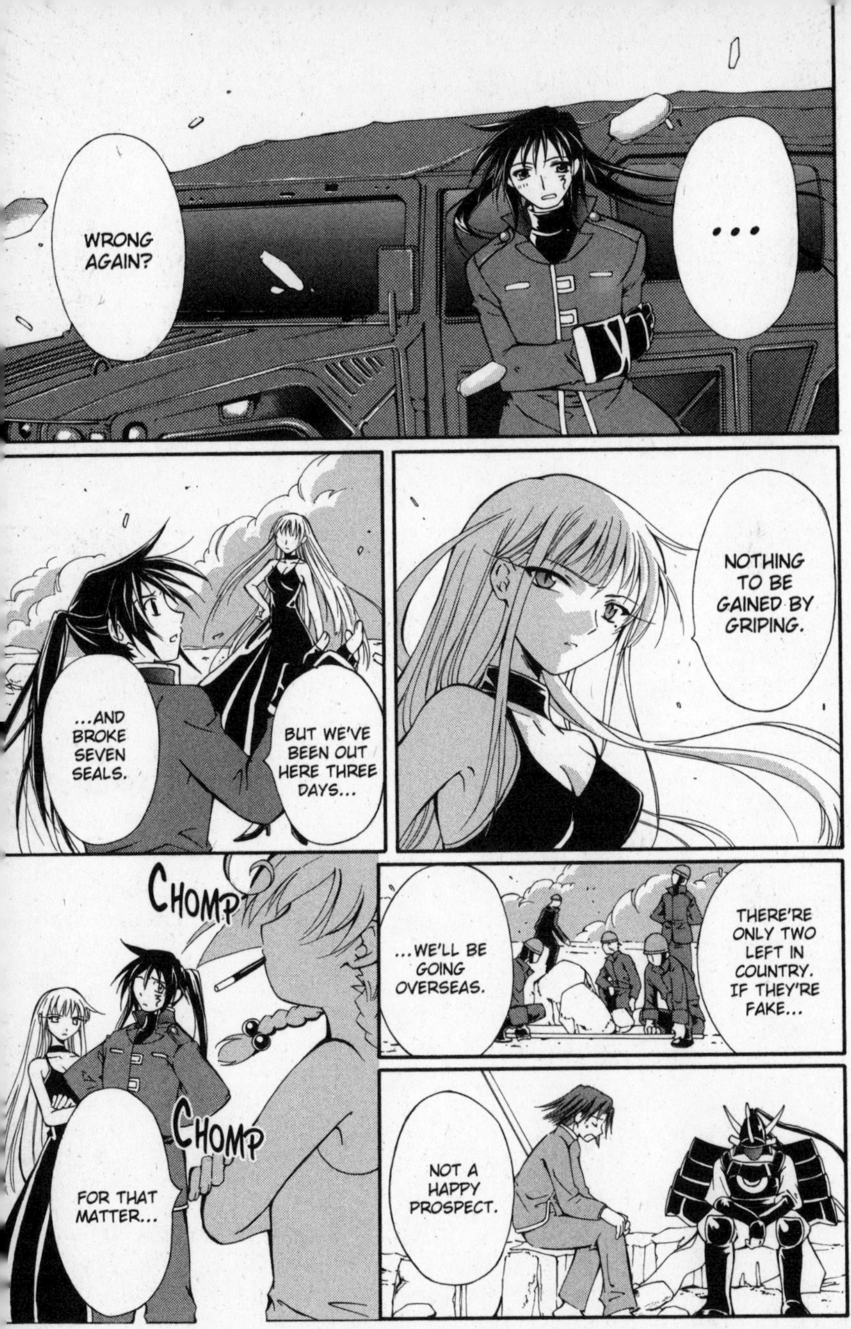
...
WRONG AGAIN?
NOTHING TO BE GAINED BY GRIPING.
BUT WE'VE BEEN OUT HERE THREE DAYS...
...AND BROKE SEVEN SEALS.
THERE'RE ONLY TWO LEFT IN COUNTRY. IF THEY'RE FAKE...
...WE'LL BE GOING OVERSEAS.
NOT A HAPPY PROSPECT.
CHOMP
CHOMP
FOR THAT MATTER...

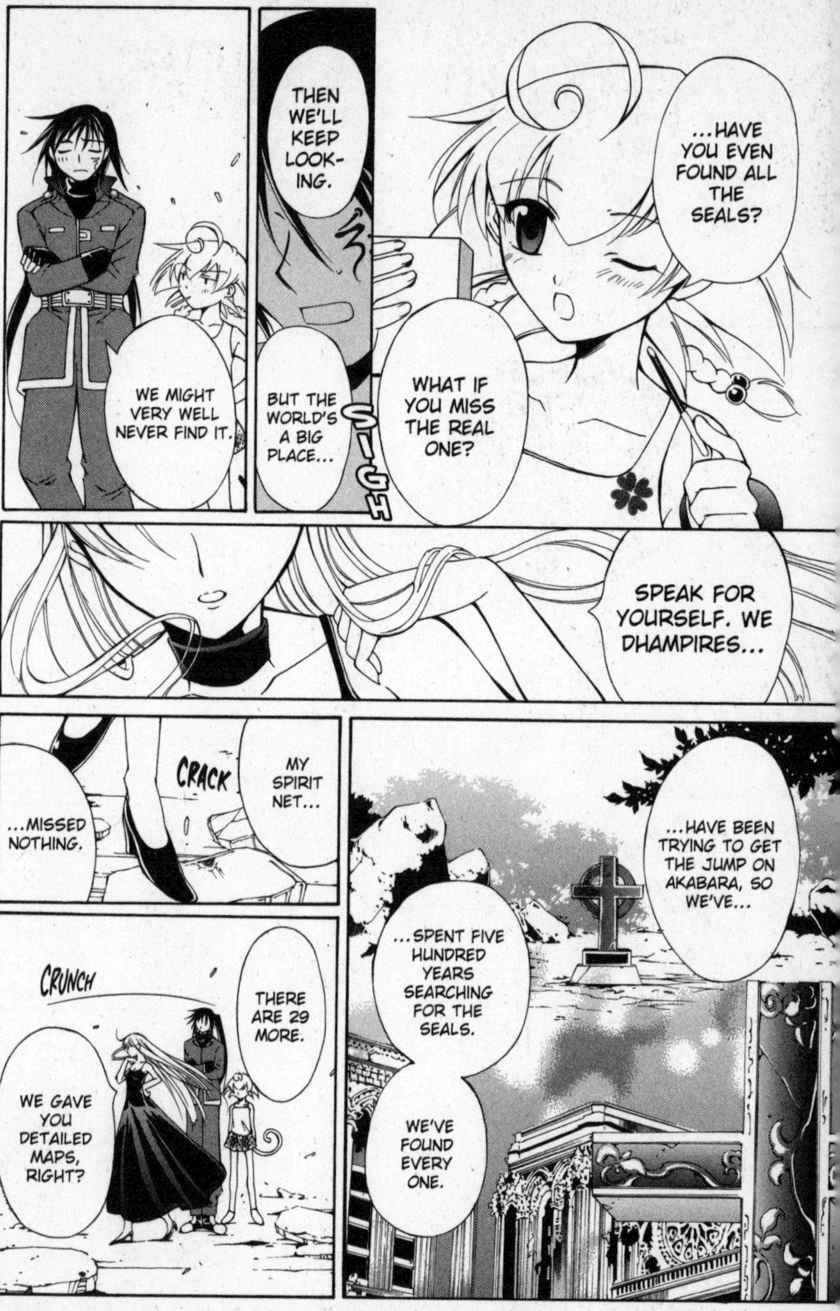
...HAVE YOU EVEN FOUND ALL THE SEALS?
WHAT IF YOU MISS THE REAL ONE?
THEN WE'LL KEEP LOOKING.
BUT THE WORLD'S A BIG PLACE...
SIGH
WE MIGHT VERY WELL NEVER FIND IT.
SPEAK FOR YOURSELF. WE DHAMPIRES...
...HAVE BEEN TRYING TO GET THE JUMP ON AKABARA, SO WE'VE...
...SPENT FIVE HUNDRED YEARS SEARCHING FOR THE SEALS.
WE'VE FOUND EVERY ONE.
MY SPIRIT NET...
CRACK
...MISSED NOTHING.
THERE ARE 29 MORE.
CRUNCH
WE GAVE YOU DETAILED MAPS, RIGHT?

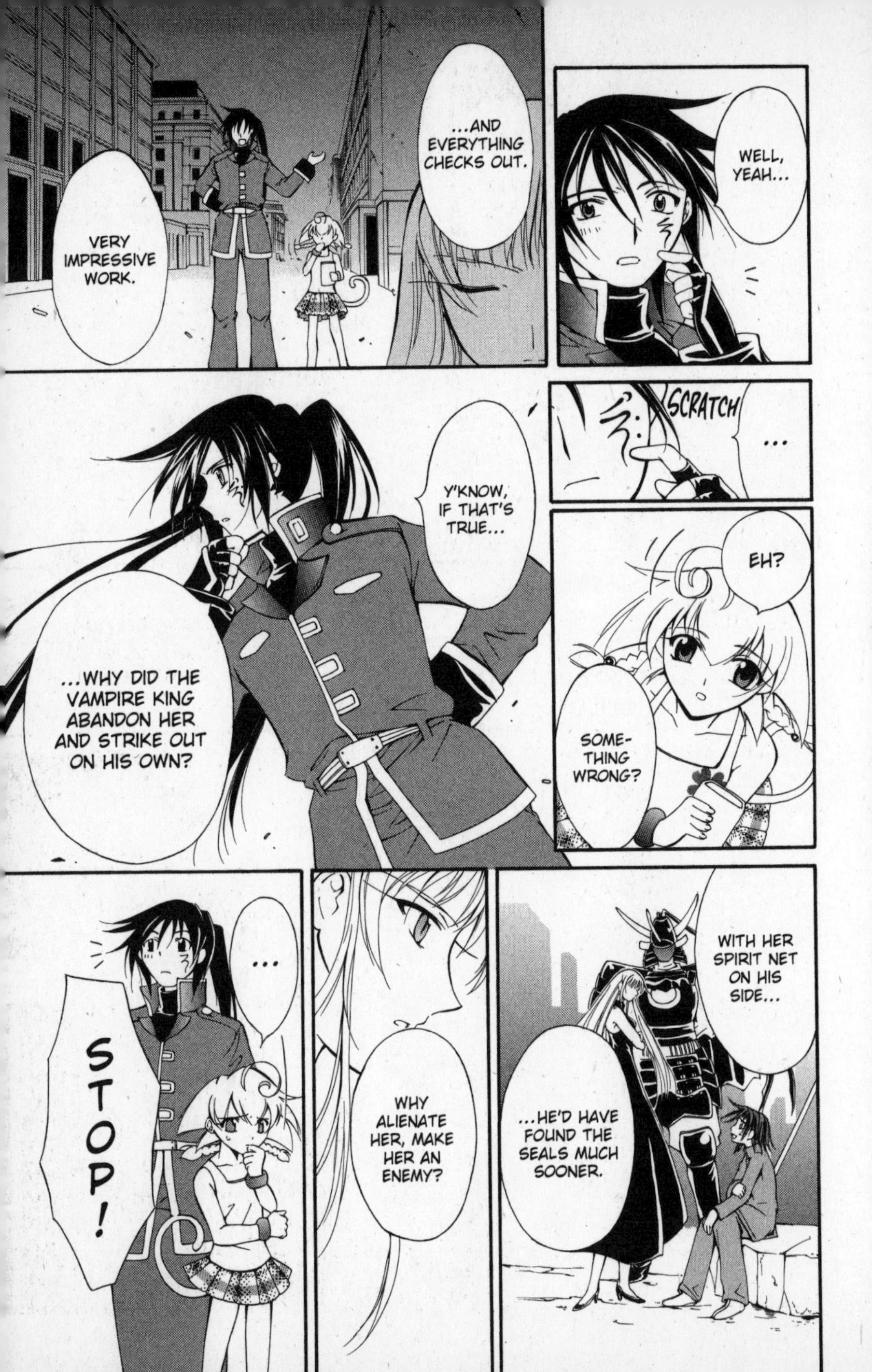
WELL, YEAH...
...AND EVERYTHING CHECKS OUT.
VERY IMPRESSIVE WORK.
SCRATCH
...
EH?
SOME-THING WRONG?
Y'KNOW, IF THAT'S TRUE...
...WHY DID THE VAMPIRE KING ABANDON HER AND STRIKE OUT ON HIS OWN?
WITH HER SPIRIT NET ON HIS SIDE...
...HE'D HAVE FOUND THE SEALS MUCH SOONER.
WHY ALIENATE HER, MAKE HER AN ENEMY?
...
STOP!

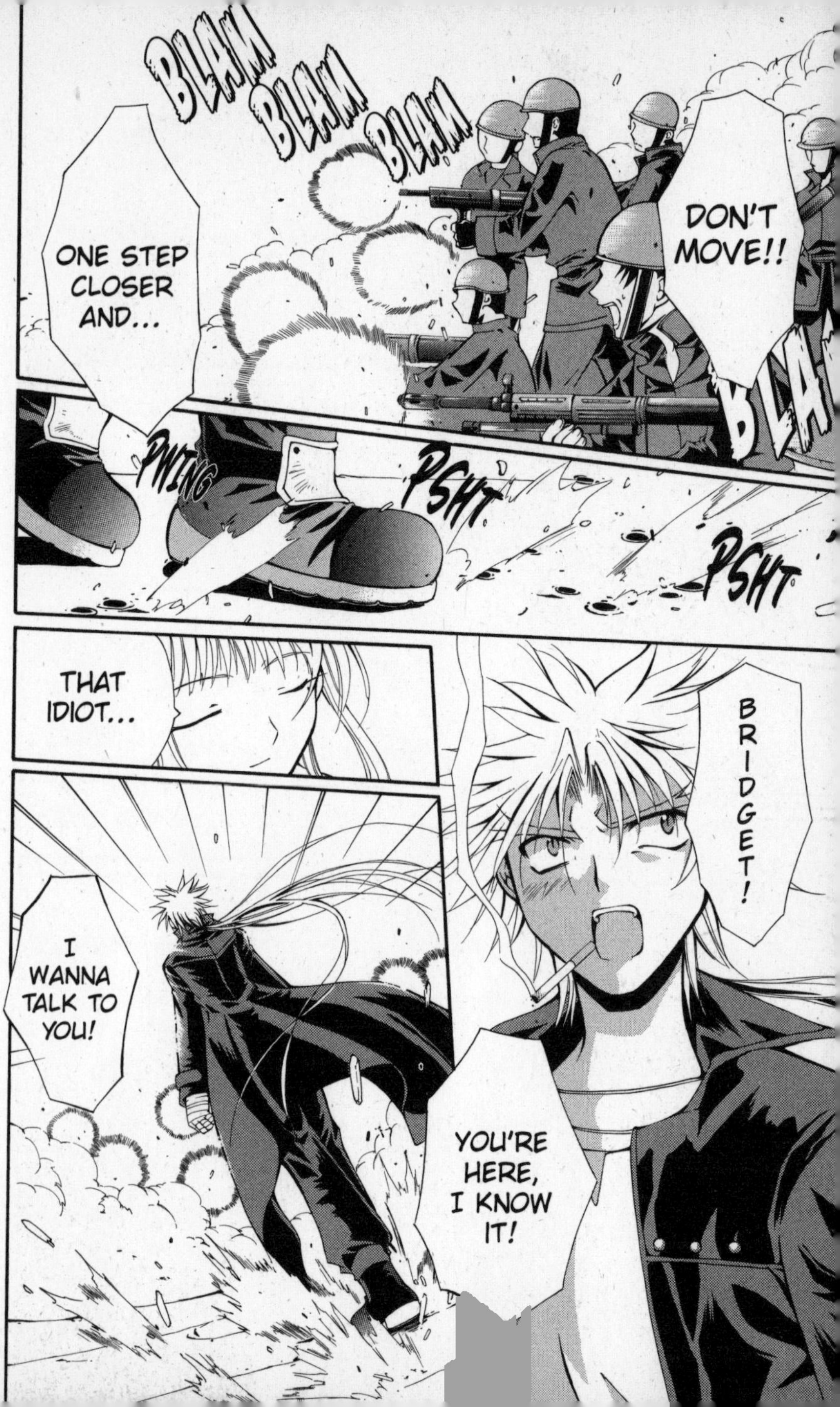
DON'T MOVE!!
BLA
ONE STEP CLOSER AND...
BLAM BLAM BLAM
PSHT
PSHT
PWING
BRIDGET!
YOU'RE HERE, I KNOW IT!
THAT IDIOT...
I WANNA TALK TO YOU!

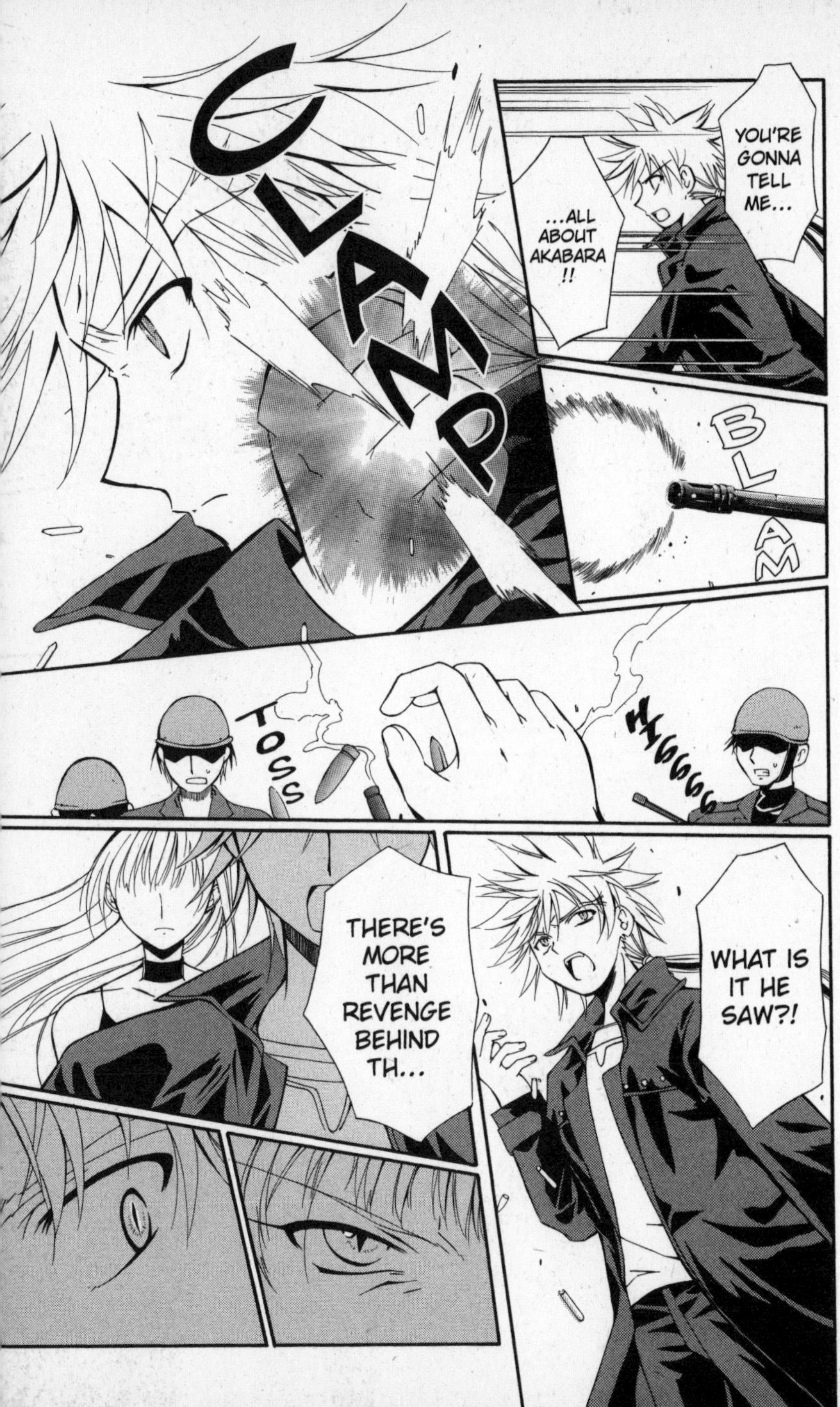
YOU'RE GONNA TELL ME...
...ALL ABOUT AKABARA!!
BLAM
CLAMP
TOSS
WHAT IS IT HE SAW?!
THERE'S MORE THAN REVENGE BEHIND TH...

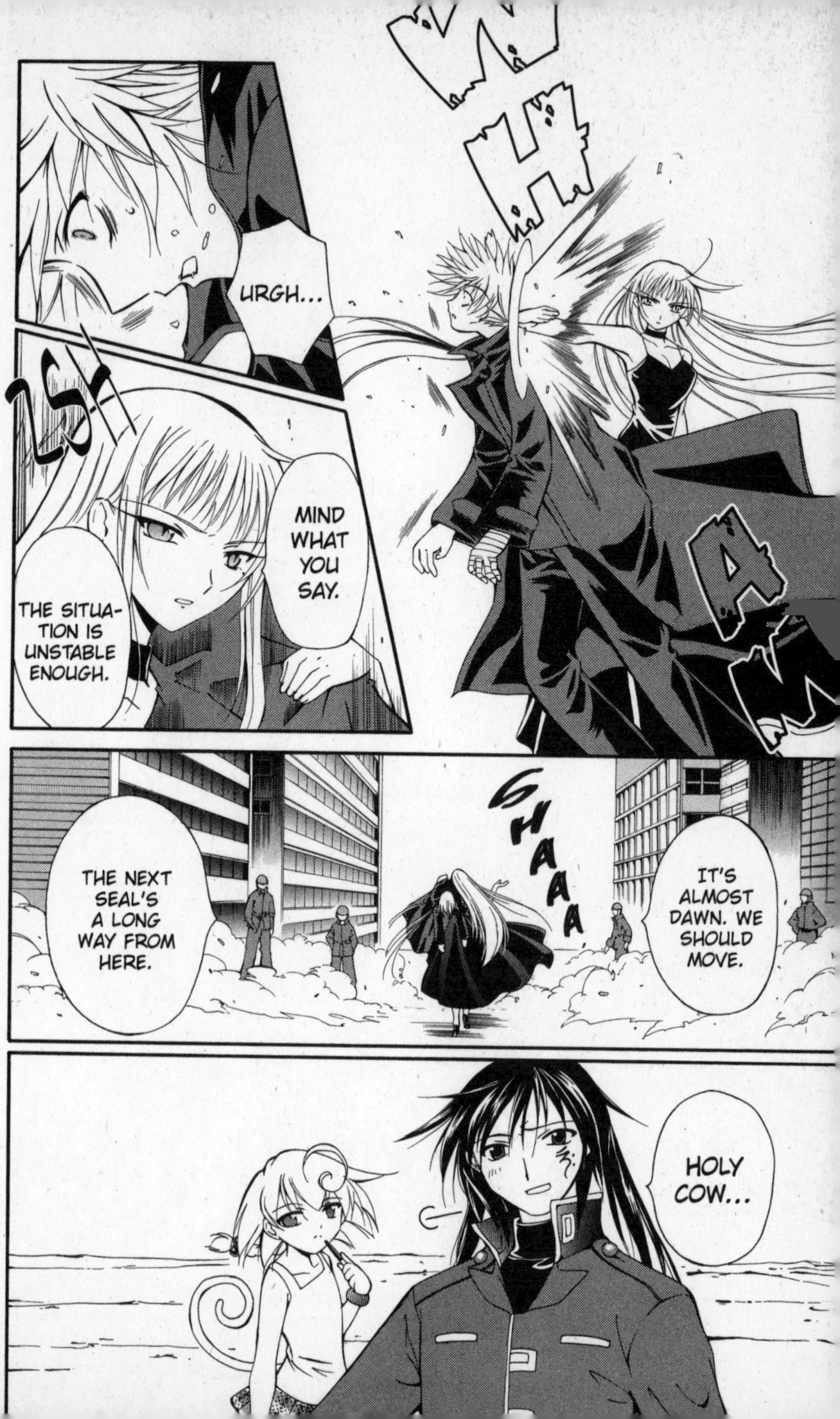
WHAM
URGH...
MIND WHAT YOU SAY.
THE SITUATION IS UNSTABLE ENOUGH.
SHAAA
IT'S ALMOST DAWN. WE SHOULD MOVE.
THE NEXT SEAL'S A LONG WAY FROM HERE.
HOLY COW...

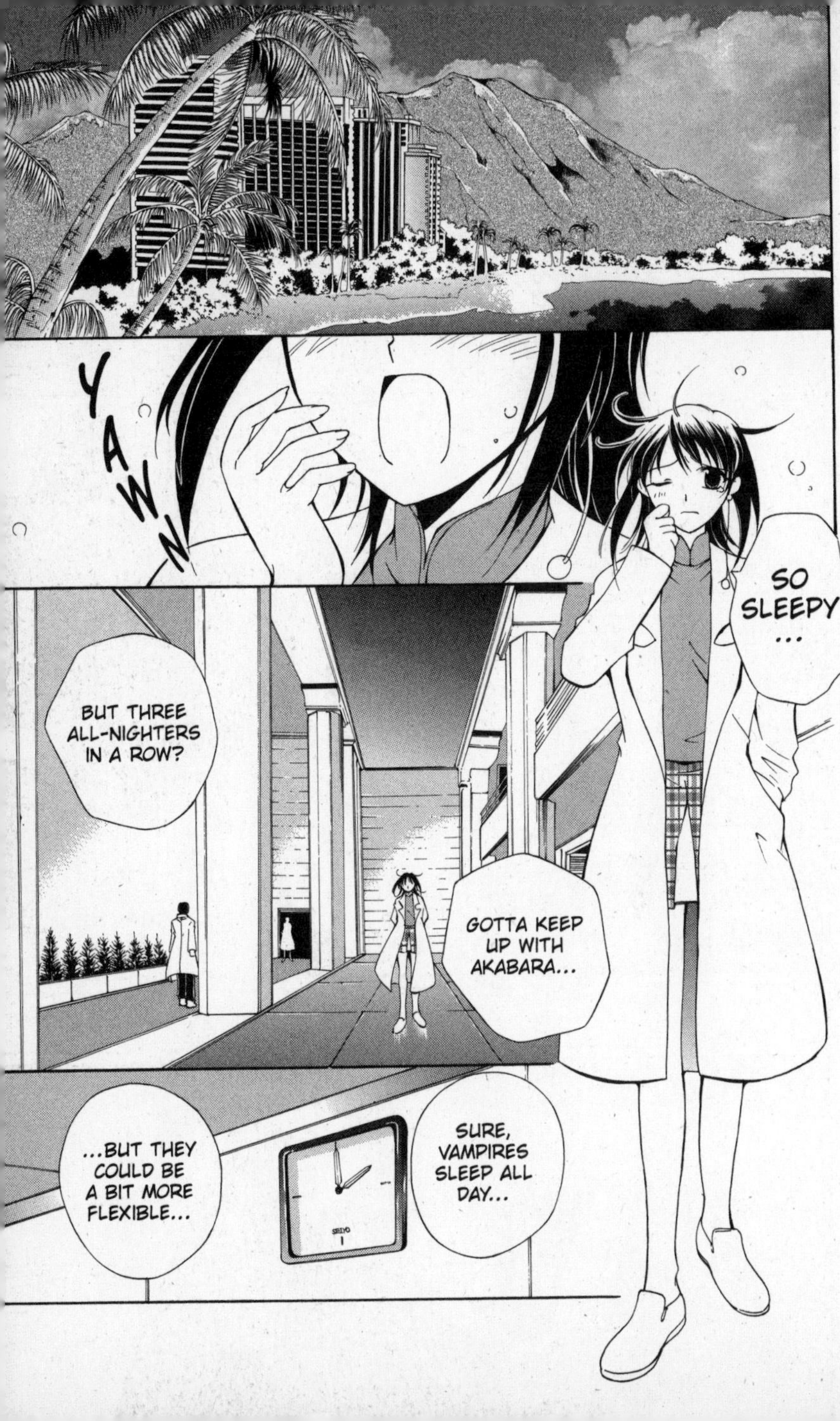
YAWN
SO SLEEPY...
GOTTA KEEP UP WITH AKABARA...
BUT THREE ALL-NIGHTERS IN A ROW?
SURE, VAMPIRES SLEEP ALL DAY...
...BUT THEY COULD BE A BIT MORE FLEXIBLE...

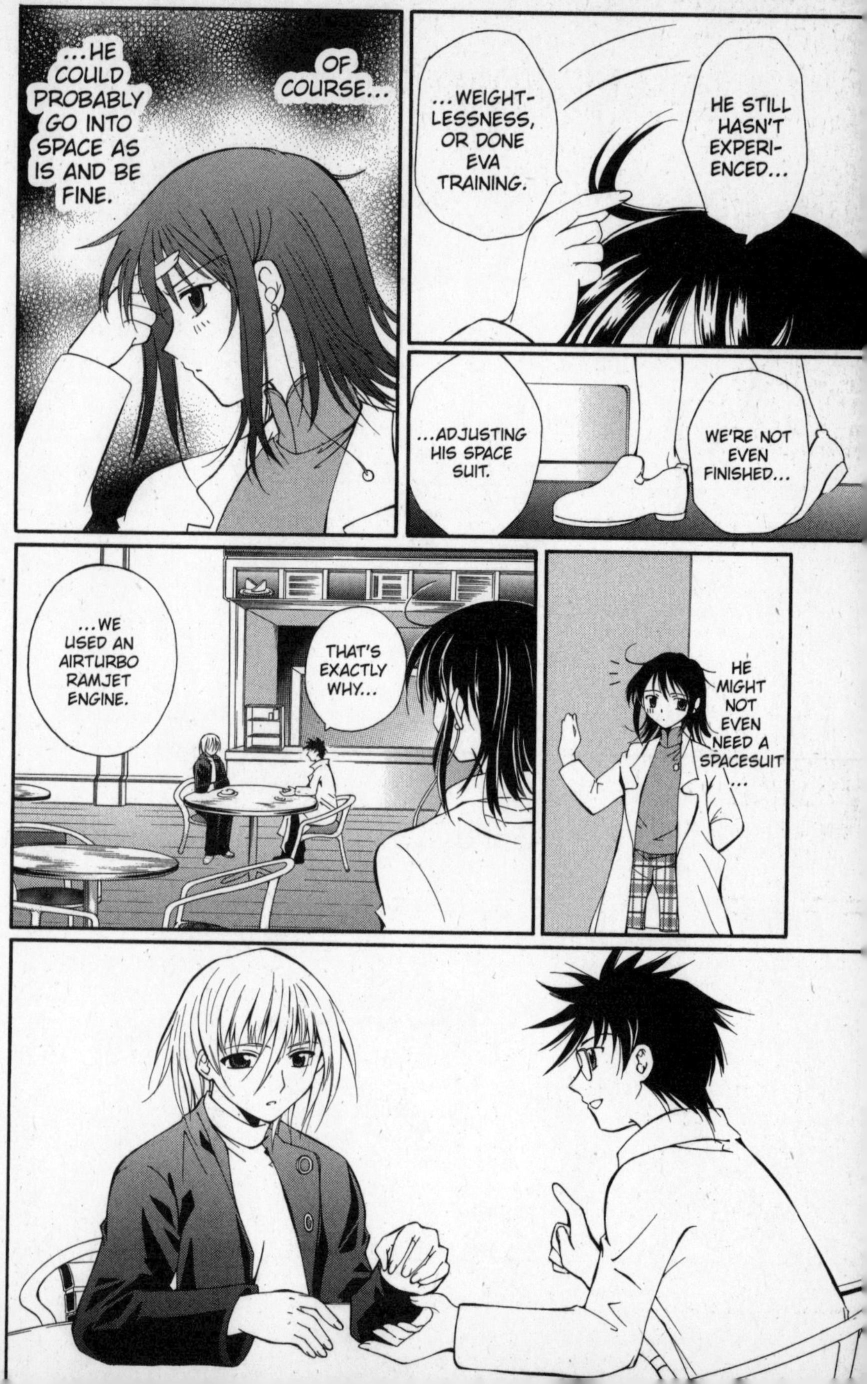
HE STILL HASN'T EXPERI-ENCED...
...WEIGHT-LESSNESS, OR DONE EVA TRAINING.
WE'RE NOT EVEN FINISHED...
...ADJUSTING HIS SPACE SUIT.
OF COURSE...
...HE COULD PROBABLY GO INTO SPACE AS IS AND BE FINE.
HE MIGHT NOT EVEN NEED A SPACESUIT...
THAT'S EXACTLY WHY...
...WE USED AN AIRTURBO RAMJET ENGINE.

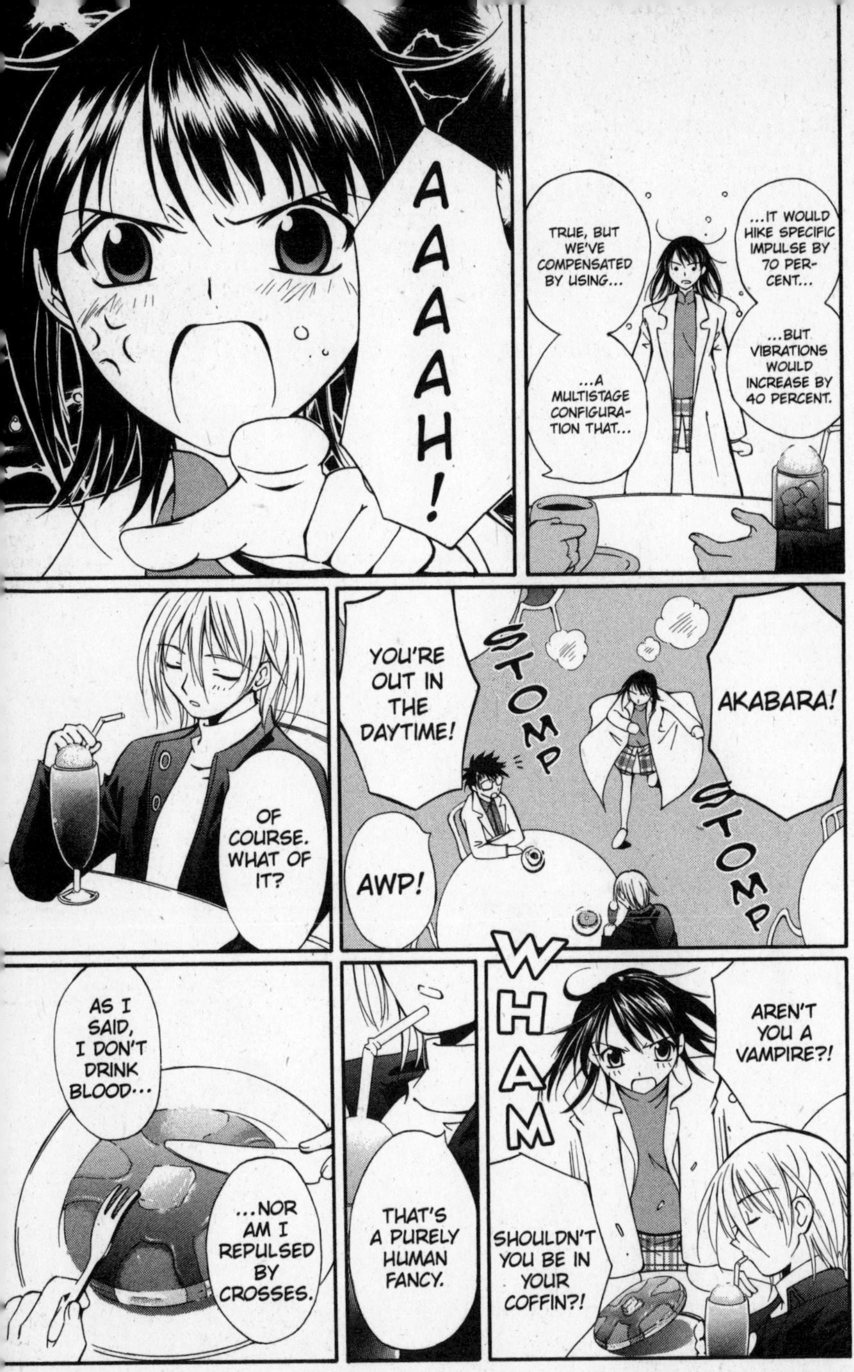
...IT WOULD HIKE SPECIFIC IMPULSE BY 70 PERCENT...
...BUT VIBRATIONS WOULD INCREASE BY 40 PERCENT.
TRUE, BUT WE'VE COMPENSATED BY USING...
...A MULTISTAGE CONFIGURATION THAT...
AAAAH!
AKABARA!
STOMP
STOMP
YOU'RE OUT IN THE DAYTIME!
AWP!
OF COURSE. WHAT OF IT?
WHAM
AREN'T YOU A VAMPIRE?!
SHOULDN'T YOU BE IN YOUR COFFIN?!
THAT'S A PURELY HUMAN FANCY.
AS I SAID, I DON'T DRINK BLOOD...
...NOR AM I REPULSED BY CROSSES.

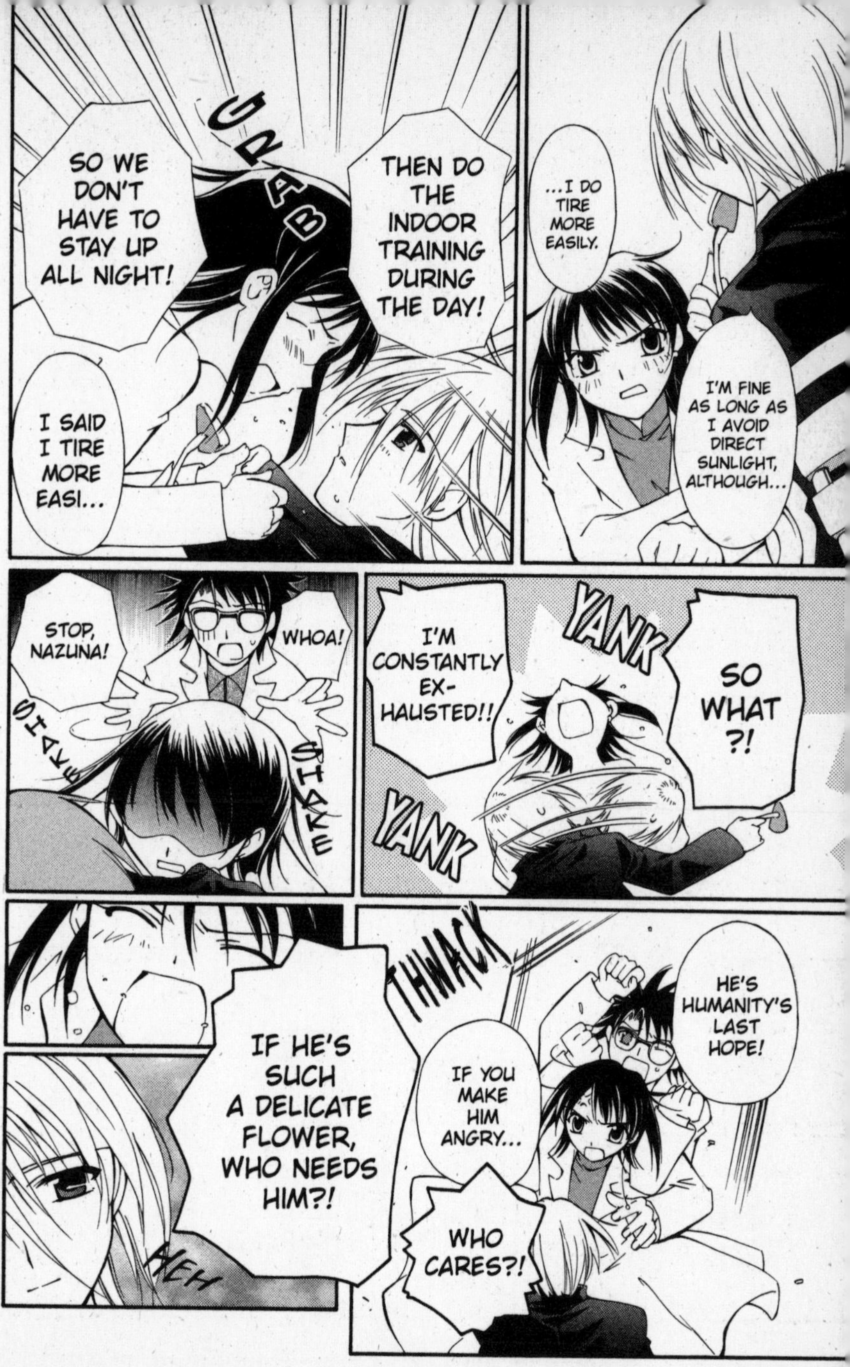
...I DO TIRE MORE EASILY.
I'M FINE AS LONG AS I AVOID DIRECT SUNLIGHT, ALTHOUGH...
THEN DO THE INDOOR TRAINING DURING THE DAY!
GRAB
SO WE DON'T HAVE TO STAY UP ALL NIGHT!
I SAID I TIRE MORE EASI...
YANK
SO WHAT?!
I'M CONSTANTLY EX-HAUSTED!!
YANK
WHOA!
STOP, NAZUNA!
SHAKE
SHAKE
HE'S HUMANITY'S LAST HOPE!
THWACK
IF YOU MAKE HIM ANGRY...
WHO CARES?!
IF HE'S SUCH A DELICATE FLOWER, WHO NEEDS HIM?!
HEH

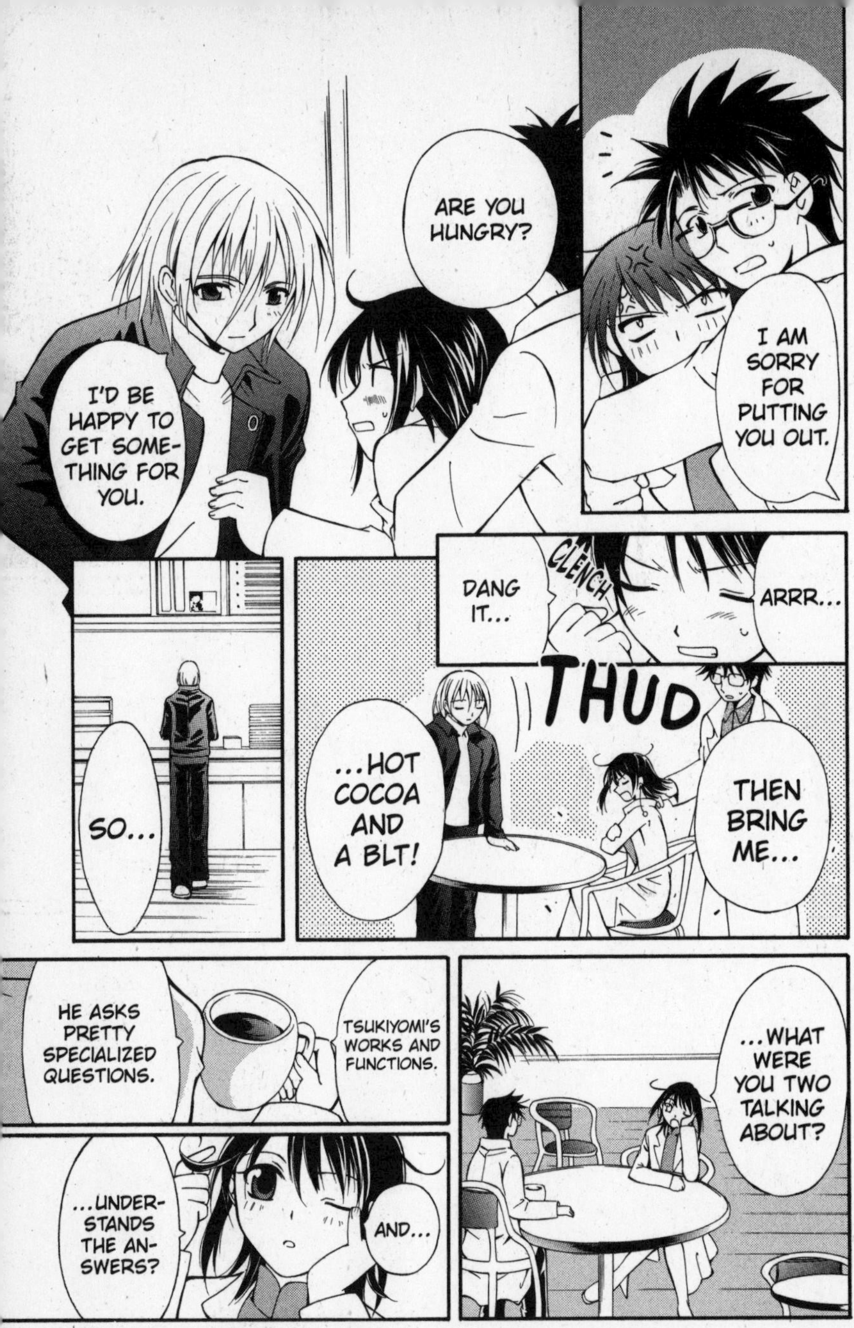

I AM SORRY FOR PUTTING YOU OUT.
ARE YOU HUNGRY?
I'D BE HAPPY TO GET SOMETHING FOR YOU.
ARRR...
CLENCH
DANG IT...
THUD
THEN BRING ME...
...HOT COCOA AND A BLT!
SO...
...WHAT WERE YOU TWO TALKING ABOUT?
TSUKIYOMI'S WORKS AND FUNCTIONS.
HE ASKS PRETTY SPECIALIZED QUESTIONS.
AND...
...UNDERSTANDS THE ANSWERS?

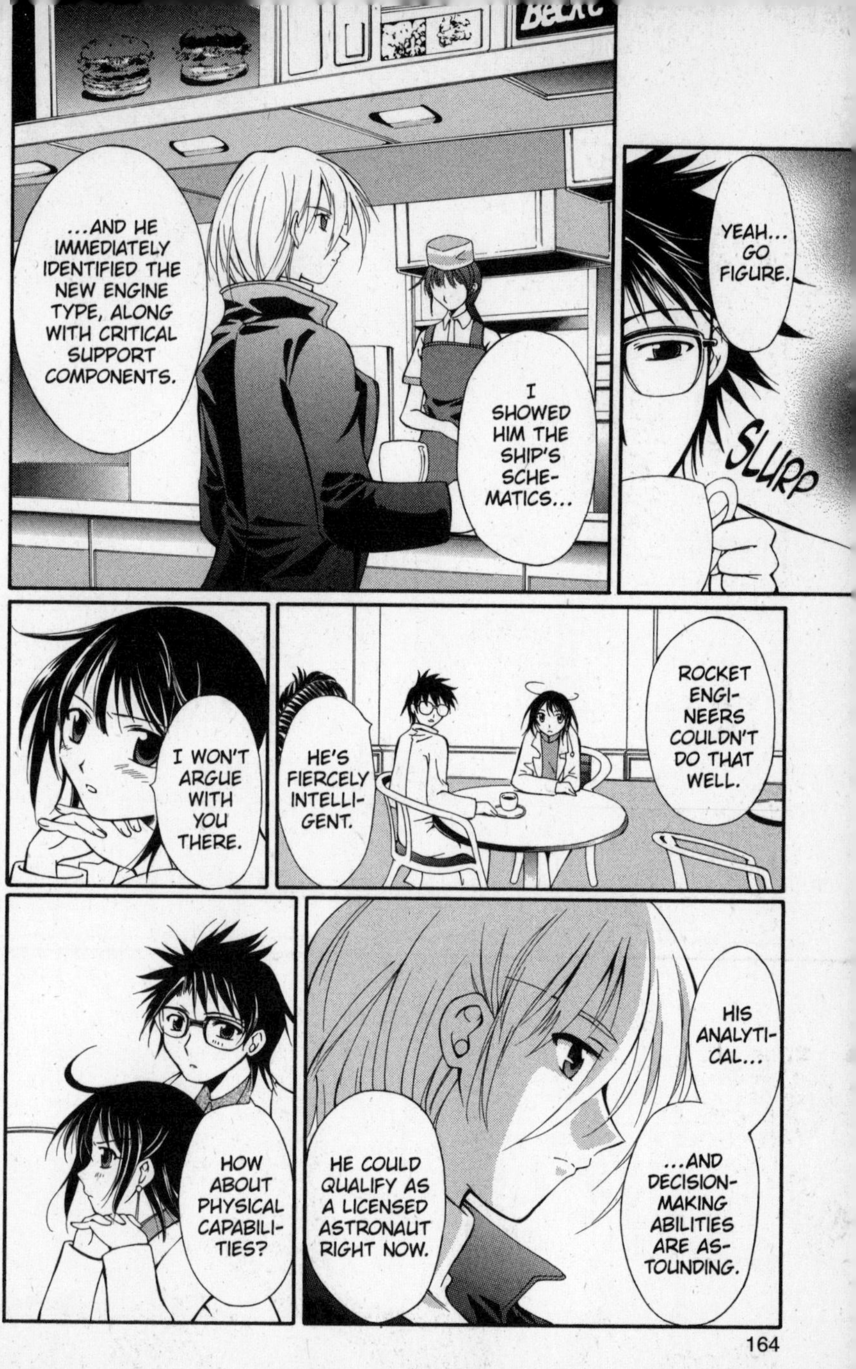
YEAH... GO FIGURE.
SLURP
I SHOWED HIM THE SHIP'S SCHE-MATICS...
...AND HE IMMEDIATELY IDENTIFIED THE NEW ENGINE TYPE, ALONG WITH CRITICAL SUPPORT COMPONENTS.
ROCKET ENGI-NEERS COULDN'T DO THAT WELL.
HE'S FIERCELY INTELLI-GENT.
I WON'T ARGUE WITH YOU THERE.
HIS ANALYTI-CAL...
...AND DECISION-MAKING ABILITIES ARE AS-TOUNDING.
HE COULD QUALIFY AS A LICENSED ASTRONAUT RIGHT NOW.
HOW ABOUT PHYSICAL CAPABILI-TIES?

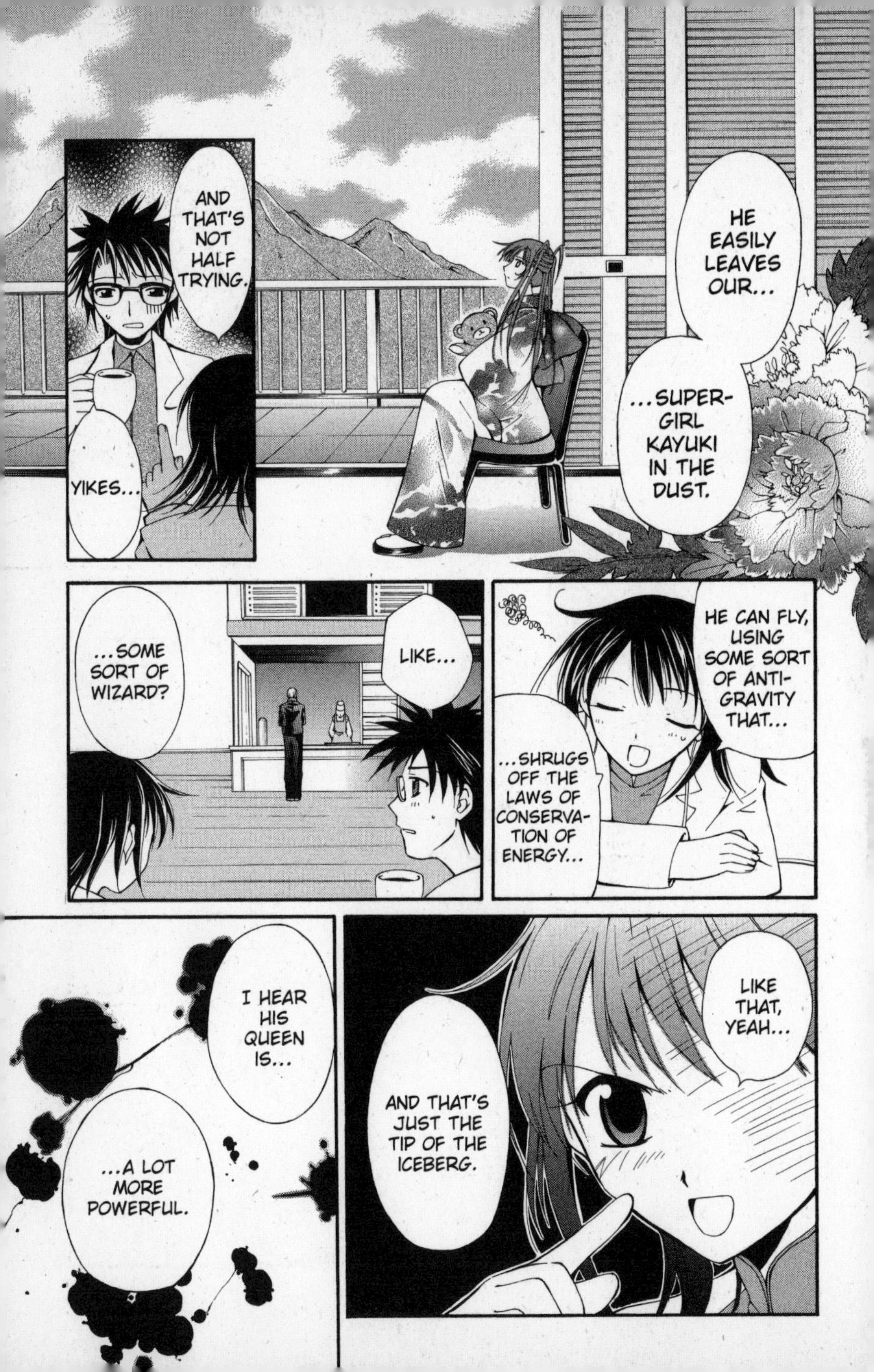
HE EASILY LEAVES OUR...
...SUPER-GIRL KAYUKI IN THE DUST.
AND THAT'S NOT HALF TRYING.
YIKES...
HE CAN FLY, USING SOME SORT OF ANTI-GRAVITY THAT...
...SHRUGS OFF THE LAWS OF CONSERVATION OF ENERGY...
LIKE...
...SOME SORT OF WIZARD?
LIKE THAT, YEAH...
AND THAT'S JUST THE TIP OF THE ICEBERG.
I HEAR HIS QUEEN IS...
...A LOT MORE POWERFUL.

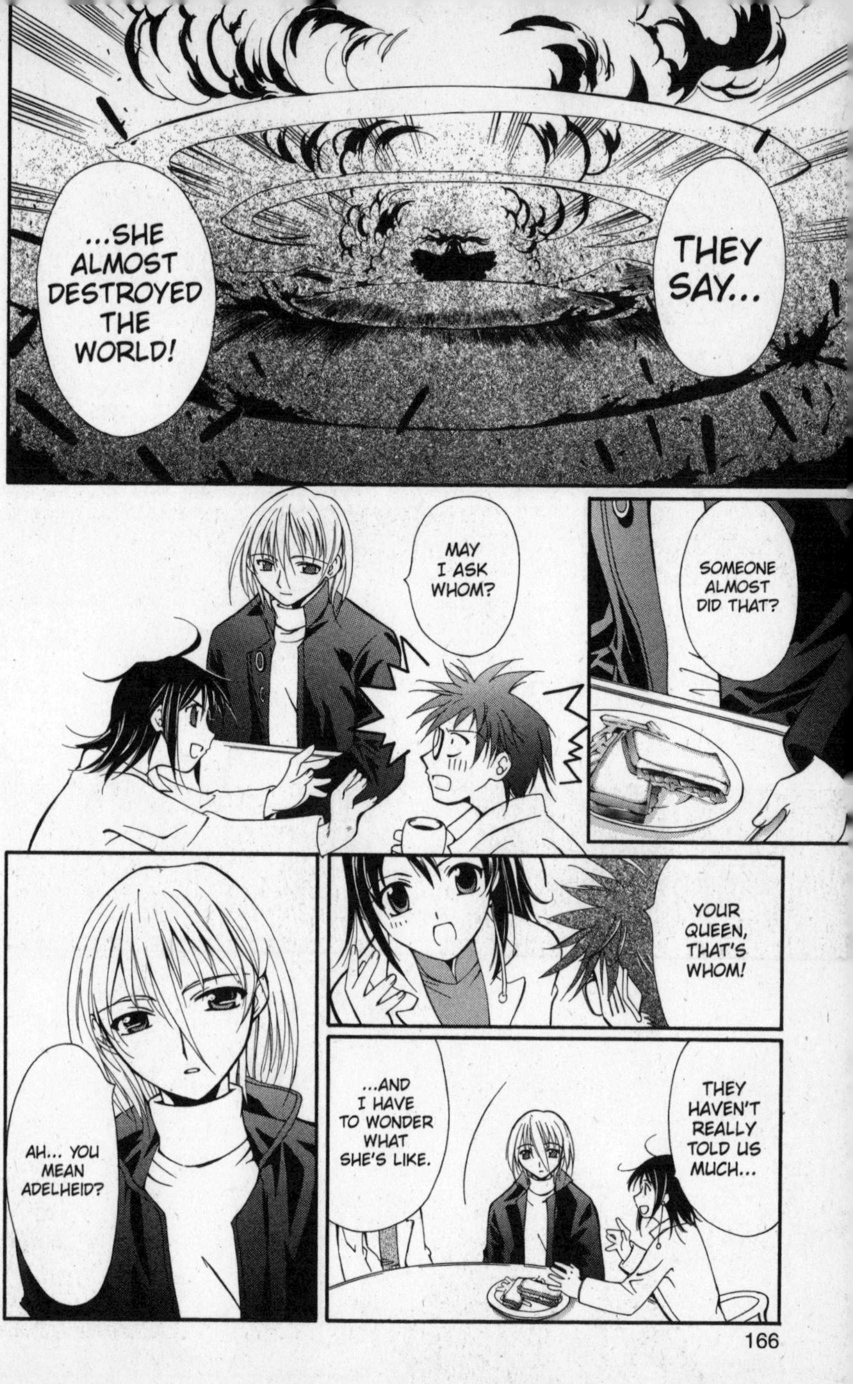
THEY SAY...
...SHE ALMOST DESTROYED THE WORLD!
SOMEONE ALMOST DID THAT?
MAY I ASK WHOM?
YOUR QUEEN, THAT'S WHOM!
THEY HAVEN'T REALLY TOLD US MUCH...
...AND I HAVE TO WONDER WHAT SHE'S LIKE.
AH... YOU MEAN ADELHEID?

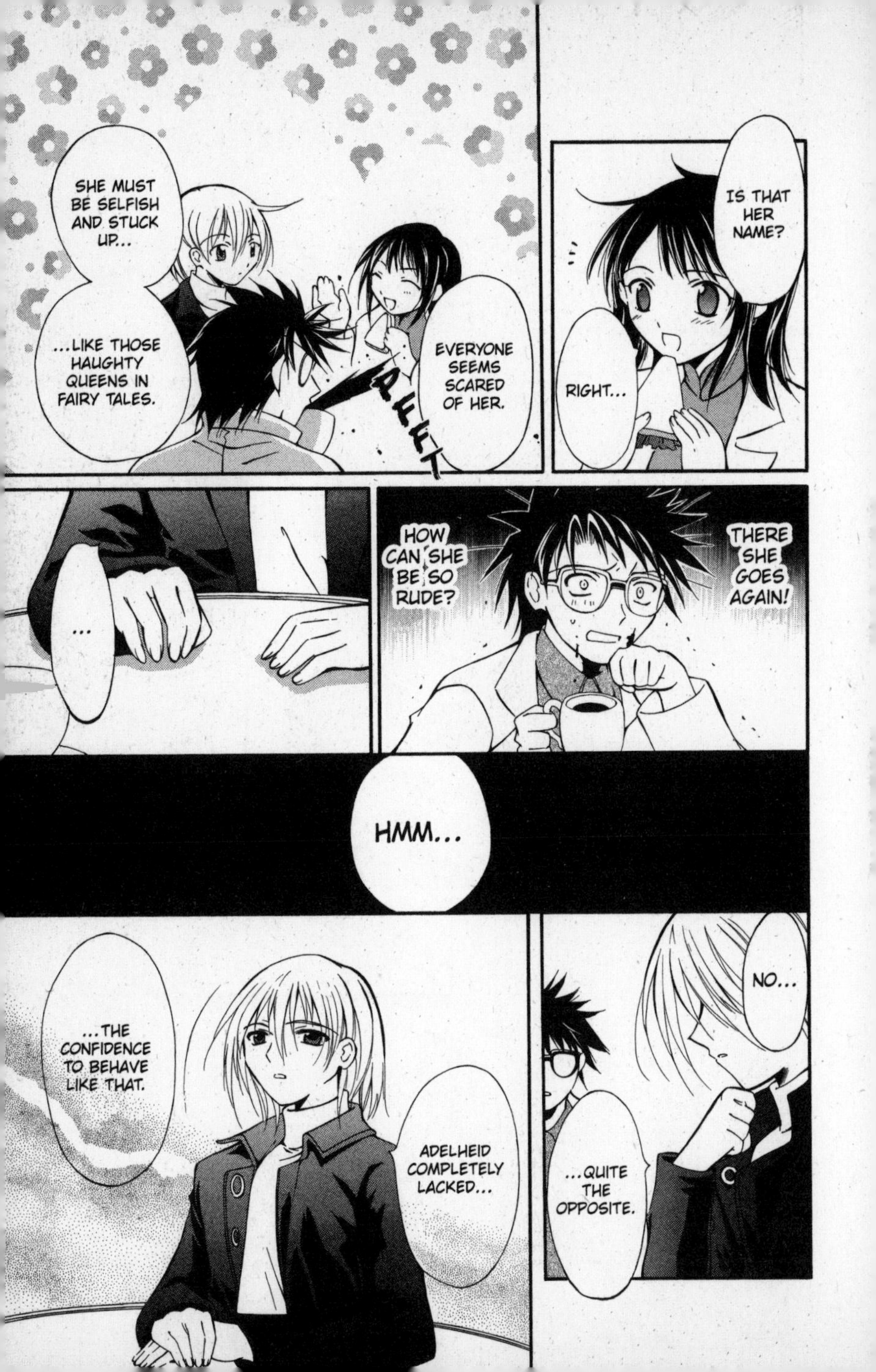
IS THAT HER NAME?
RIGHT...
EVERYONE SEEMS SCARED OF HER.
SHE MUST BE SELFISH AND STUCK UP...
...LIKE THOSE HAUGHTY QUEENS IN FAIRY TALES.
PFFT
THERE SHE GOES AGAIN!
HOW CAN SHE BE SO RUDE?
...
HMM...
NO...
...QUITE THE OPPOSITE.
ADELHEID COMPLETELY LACKED...
...THE CONFIDENCE TO BEHAVE LIKE THAT.

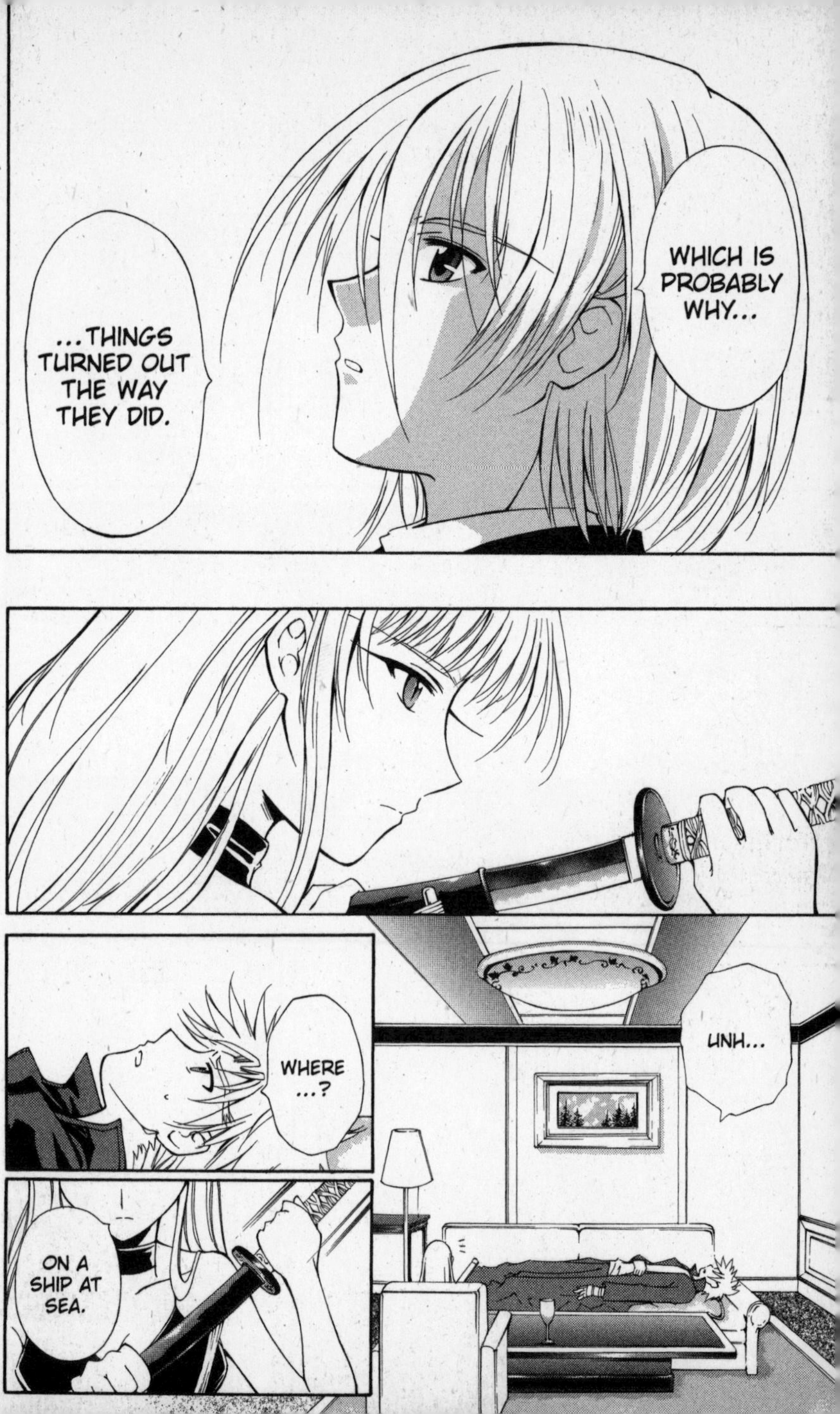
WHICH IS PROBABLY WHY...
...THINGS TURNED OUT THE WAY THEY DID.
UNH...
WHERE ...?
ON A SHIP AT SEA.

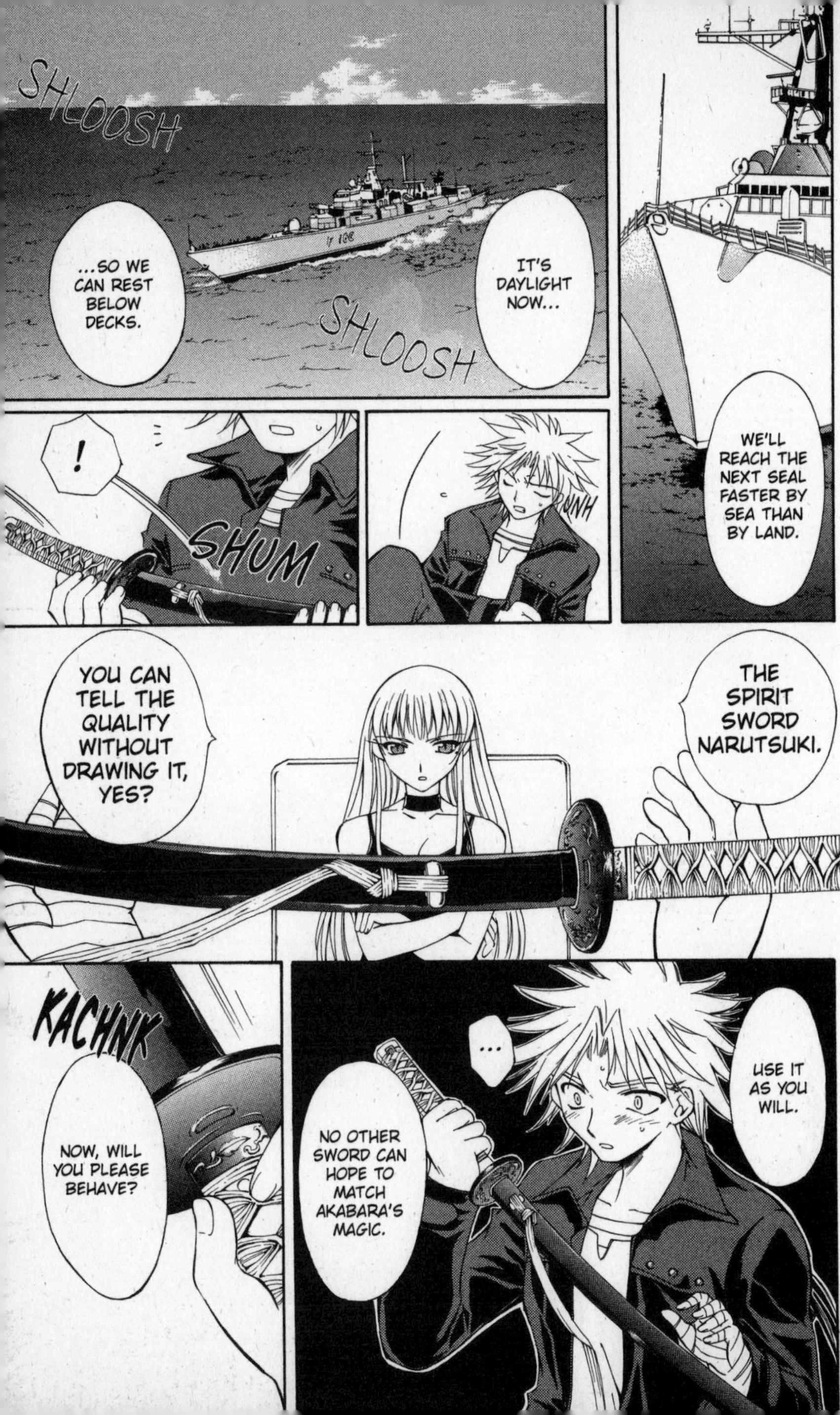
WE'LL REACH THE NEXT SEAL FASTER BY SEA THAN BY LAND.
SHLOOSH
IT'S DAYLIGHT NOW...
...SO WE CAN REST BELOW DECKS.
SHLOOSH
UNH
!
SHUM
THE SPIRIT SWORD NARUTSUKI.
YOU CAN TELL THE QUALITY WITHOUT DRAWING IT, YES?
USE IT AS YOU WILL.
...
NO OTHER SWORD CAN HOPE TO MATCH AKABARA'S MAGIC.
KACHNK
NOW, WILL YOU PLEASE BEHAVE?

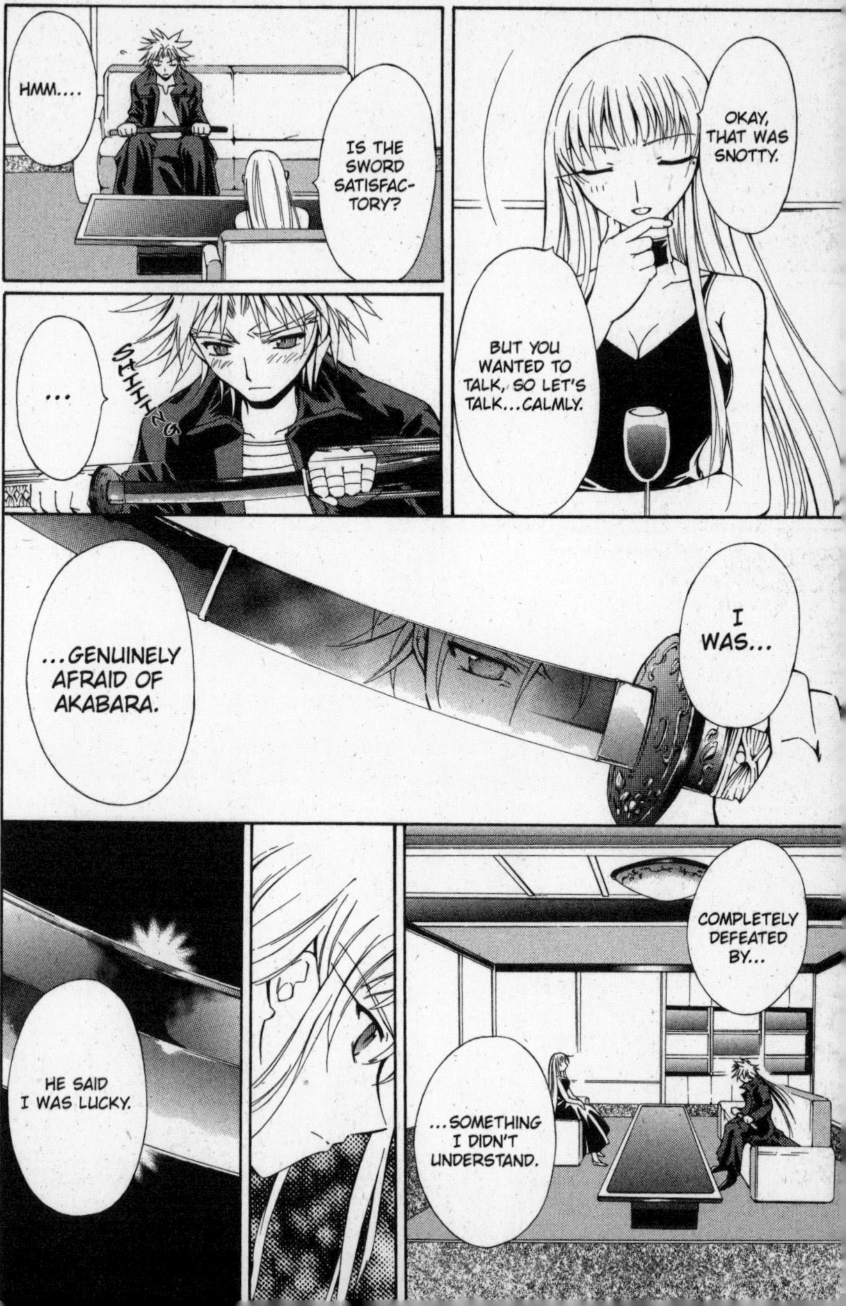
OKAY, THAT WAS SNOTTY.
BUT YOU WANTED TO TALK, SO LET'S TALK...CALMLY.
IS THE SWORD SATISFACTORY?
HMM....
SHIIIING
...
I WAS...
...GENUINELY AFRAID OF AKABARA.
COMPLETELY DEFEATED BY...
...SOMETHING I DIDN'T UNDERSTAND.
HE SAID I WAS LUCKY.

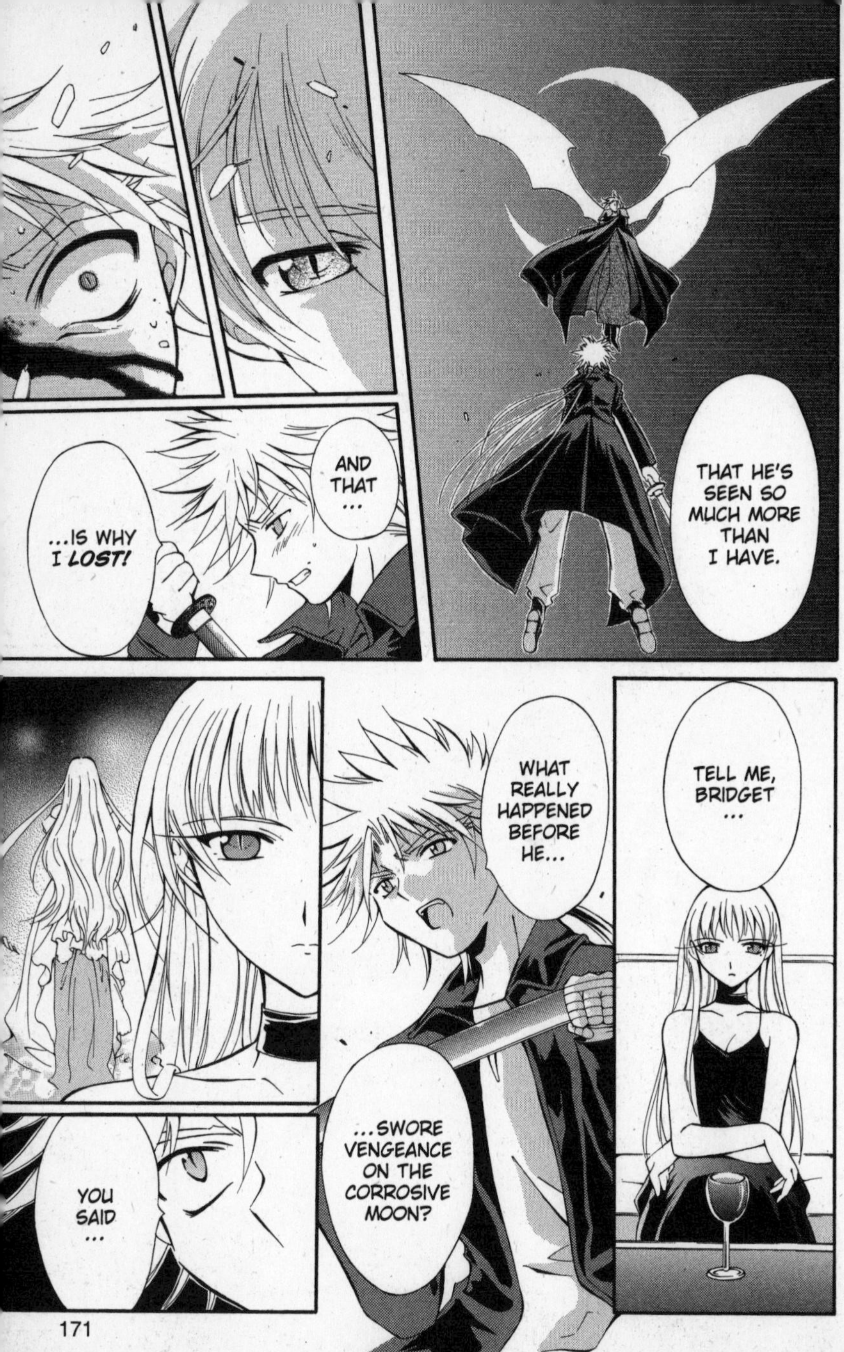
THAT HE'S SEEN SO MUCH MORE THAN I HAVE.
AND THAT ...
...IS WHY I *LOST!*
TELL ME, BRIDGET ...
WHAT REALLY HAPPENED BEFORE HE...
...SWORE VENGEANCE ON THE CORROSIVE MOON?
YOU SAID ...

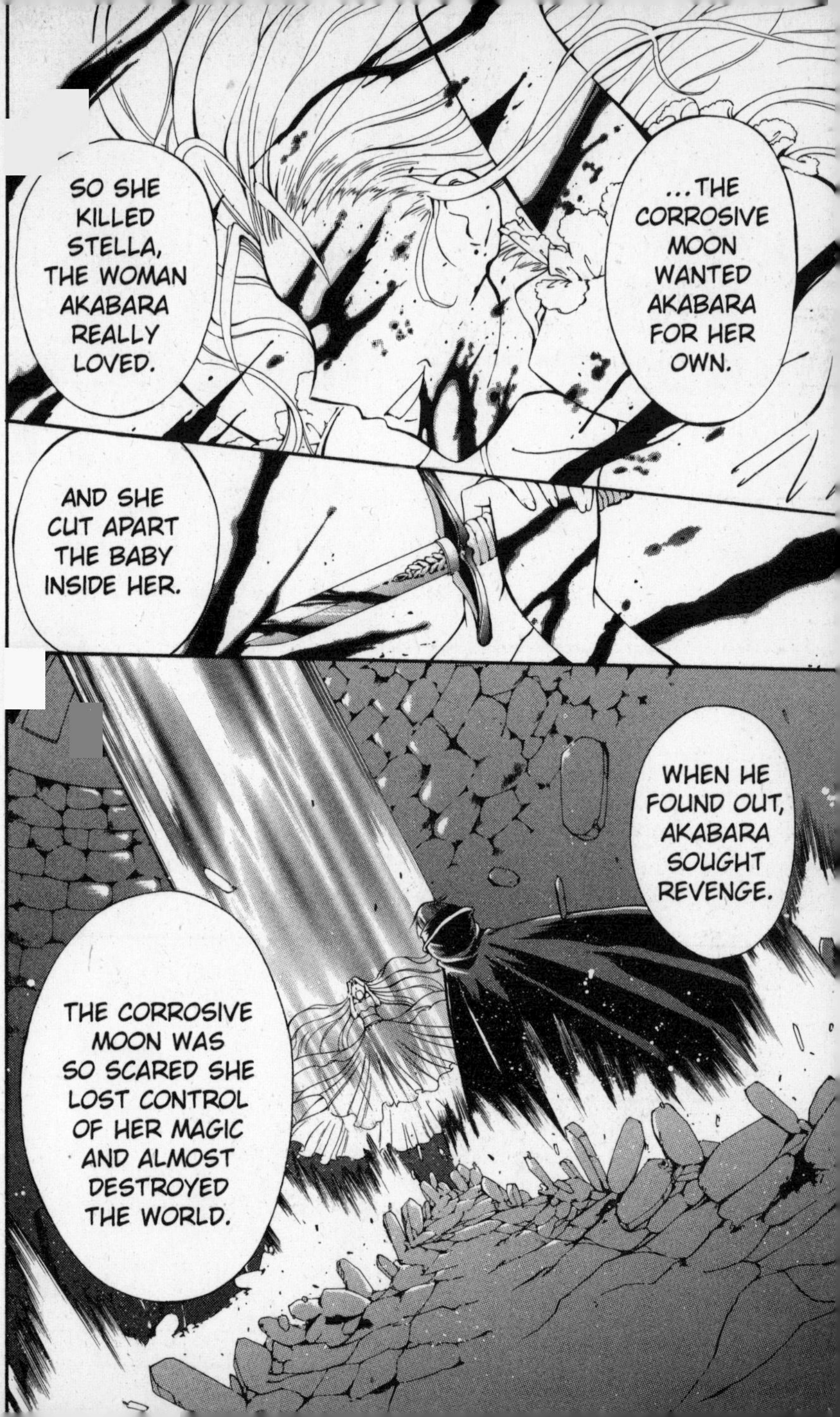
...THE CORROSIVE MOON WANTED AKABARA FOR HER OWN.
SO SHE KILLED STELLA, THE WOMAN AKABARA REALLY LOVED.
AND SHE CUT APART THE BABY INSIDE HER.
WHEN HE FOUND OUT, AKABARA SOUGHT REVENGE.
THE CORROSIVE MOON WAS SO SCARED SHE LOST CONTROL OF HER MAGIC AND ALMOST DESTROYED THE WORLD.

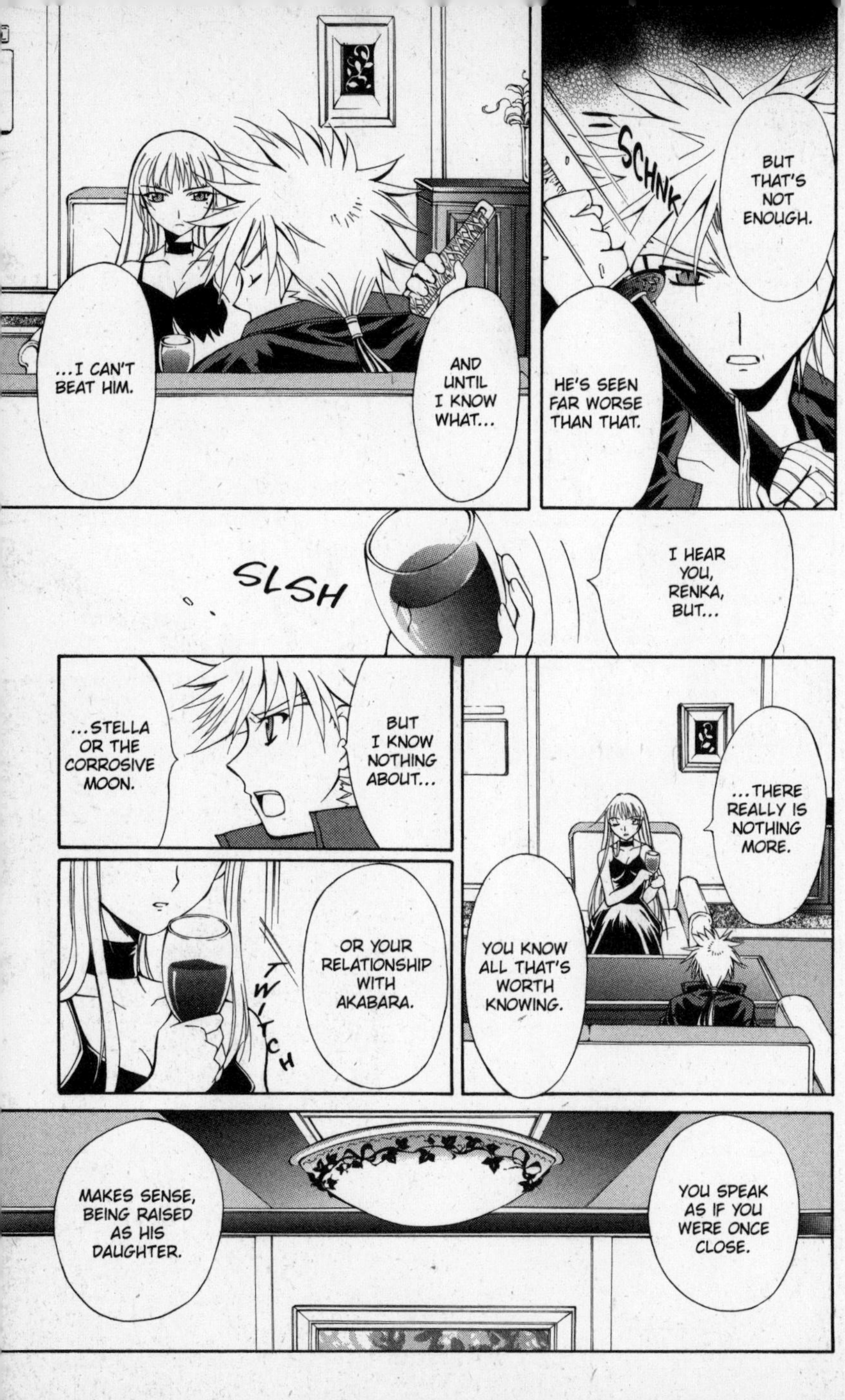
BUT THAT'S NOT ENOUGH.
SCHNK
HE'S SEEN FAR WORSE THAN THAT.
AND UNTIL I KNOW WHAT...
...I CAN'T BEAT HIM.
I HEAR YOU, RENKA, BUT...
SLSH
...THERE REALLY IS NOTHING MORE.
YOU KNOW ALL THAT'S WORTH KNOWING.
BUT I KNOW NOTHING ABOUT...
...STELLA OR THE CORROSIVE MOON.
OR YOUR RELATIONSHIP WITH AKABARA.
TWITCH
YOU SPEAK AS IF YOU WERE ONCE CLOSE.
MAKES SENSE, BEING RAISED AS HIS DAUGHTER.

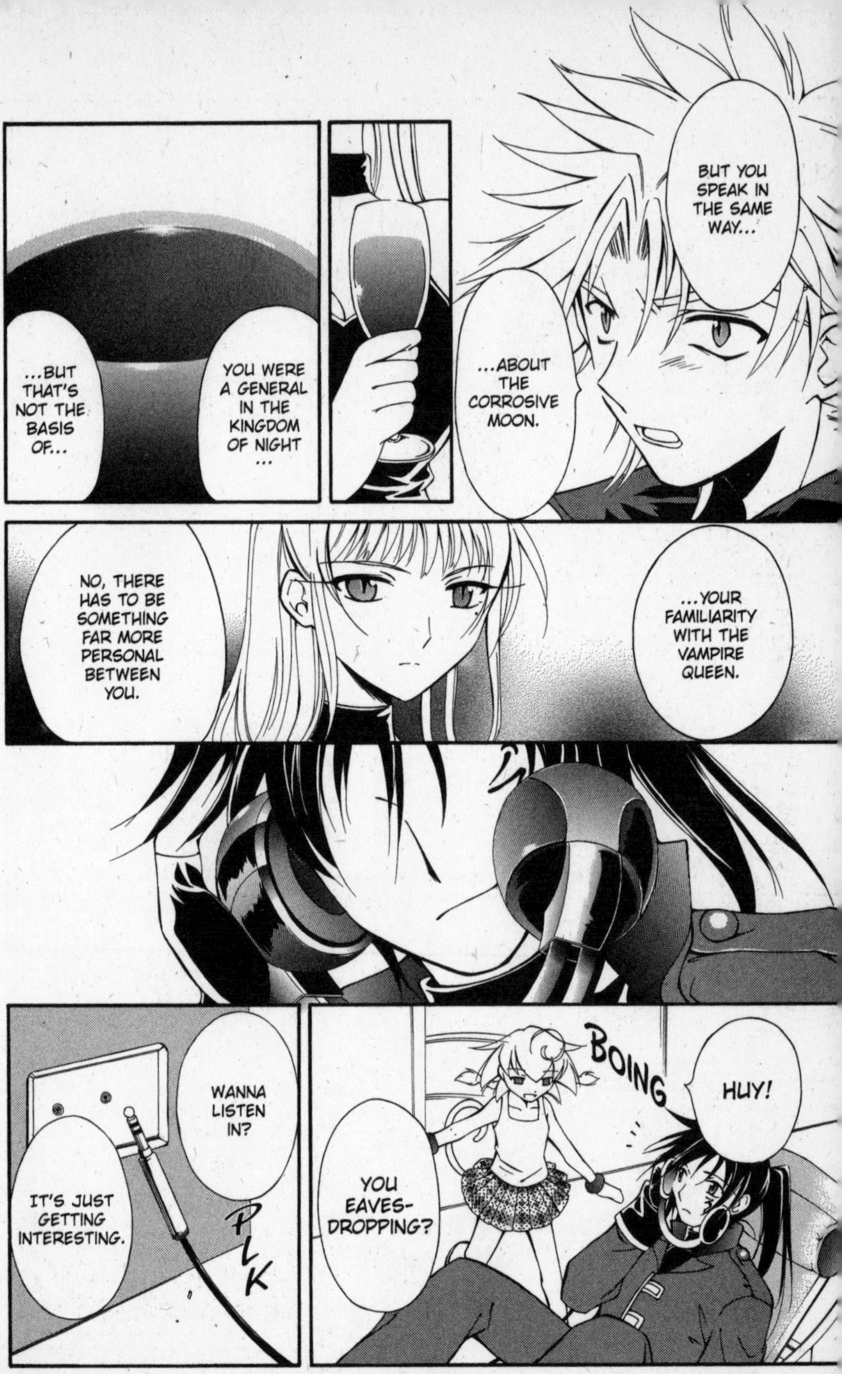
BUT YOU SPEAK IN THE SAME WAY...
...ABOUT THE CORROSIVE MOON.
YOU WERE A GENERAL IN THE KINGDOM OF NIGHT ...
...BUT THAT'S NOT THE BASIS OF...
...YOUR FAMILIARITY WITH THE VAMPIRE QUEEN.
NO, THERE HAS TO BE SOMETHING FAR MORE PERSONAL BETWEEN YOU.
BOING
HUY!
YOU EAVES-DROPPING?
PLK
WANNA LISTEN IN?
IT'S JUST GETTING INTERESTING.

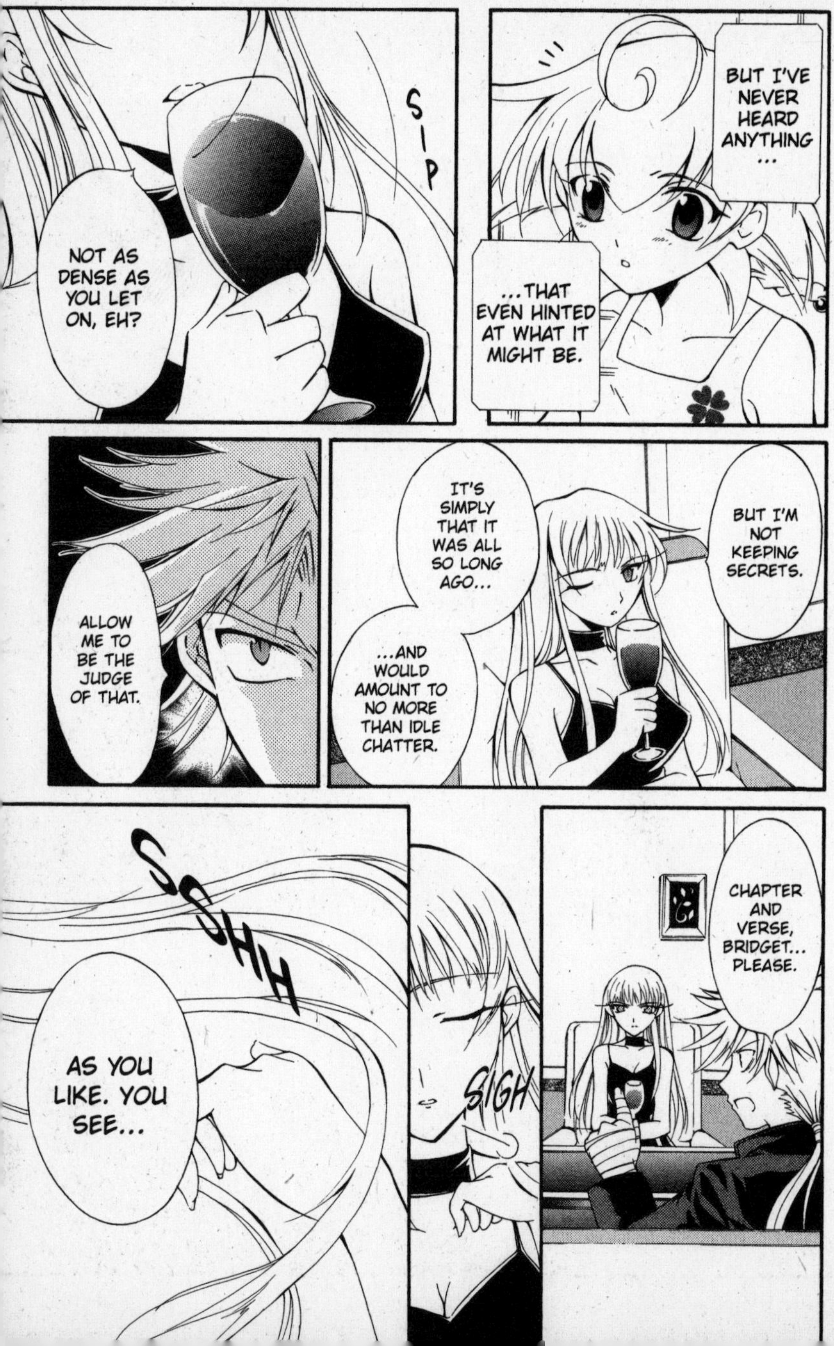
BUT I'VE NEVER HEARD ANYTHING ...
...THAT EVEN HINTED AT WHAT IT MIGHT BE.
SIP
NOT AS DENSE AS YOU LET ON, EH?
BUT I'M NOT KEEPING SECRETS.
IT'S SIMPLY THAT IT WAS ALL SO LONG AGO...
...AND WOULD AMOUNT TO NO MORE THAN IDLE CHATTER.
ALLOW ME TO BE THE JUDGE OF THAT.
CHAPTER AND VERSE, BRIDGET... PLEASE.
SIGH
SSHH
AS YOU LIKE. YOU SEE...

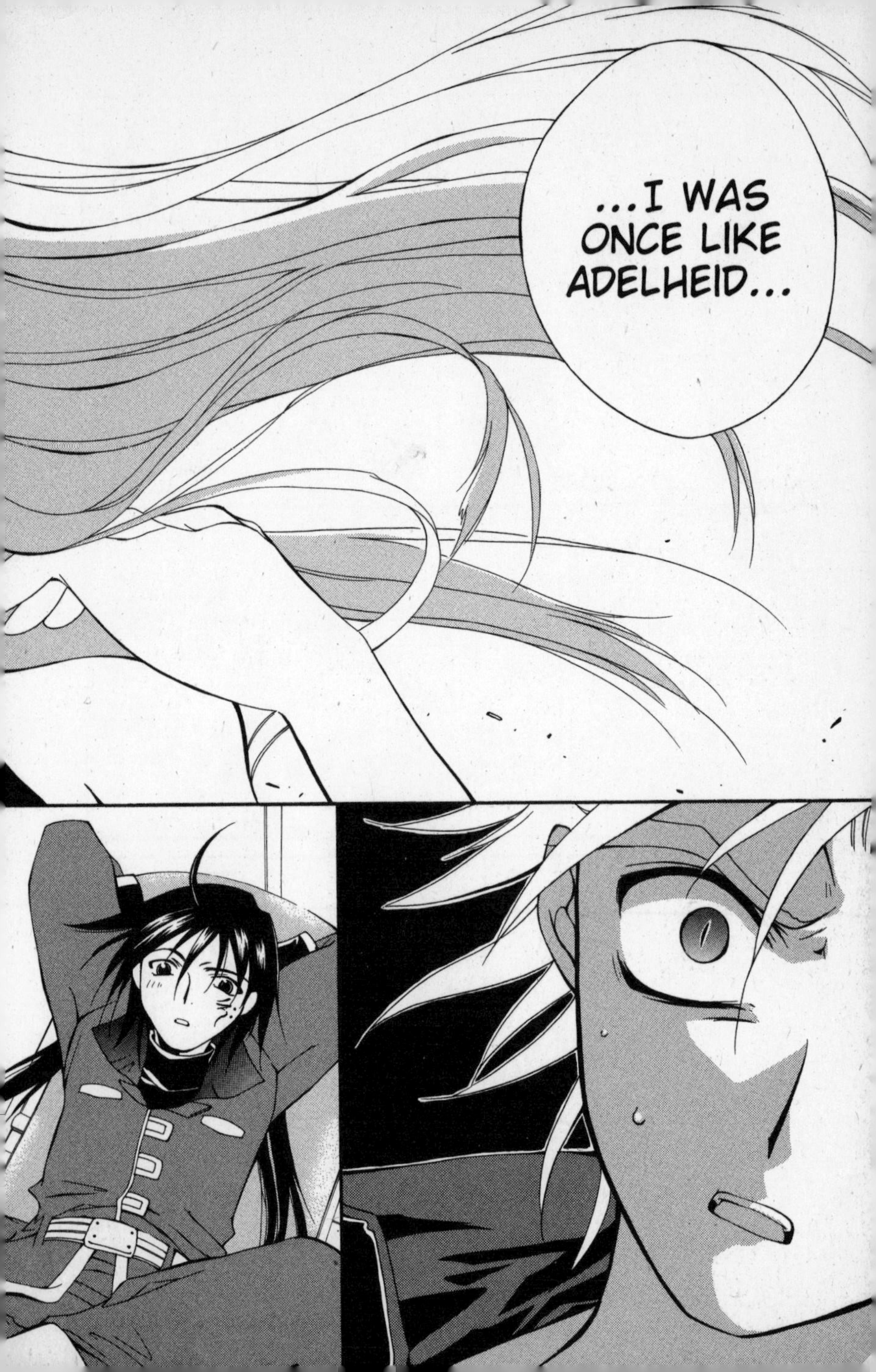
...I WAS ONCE LIKE ADELHEID...

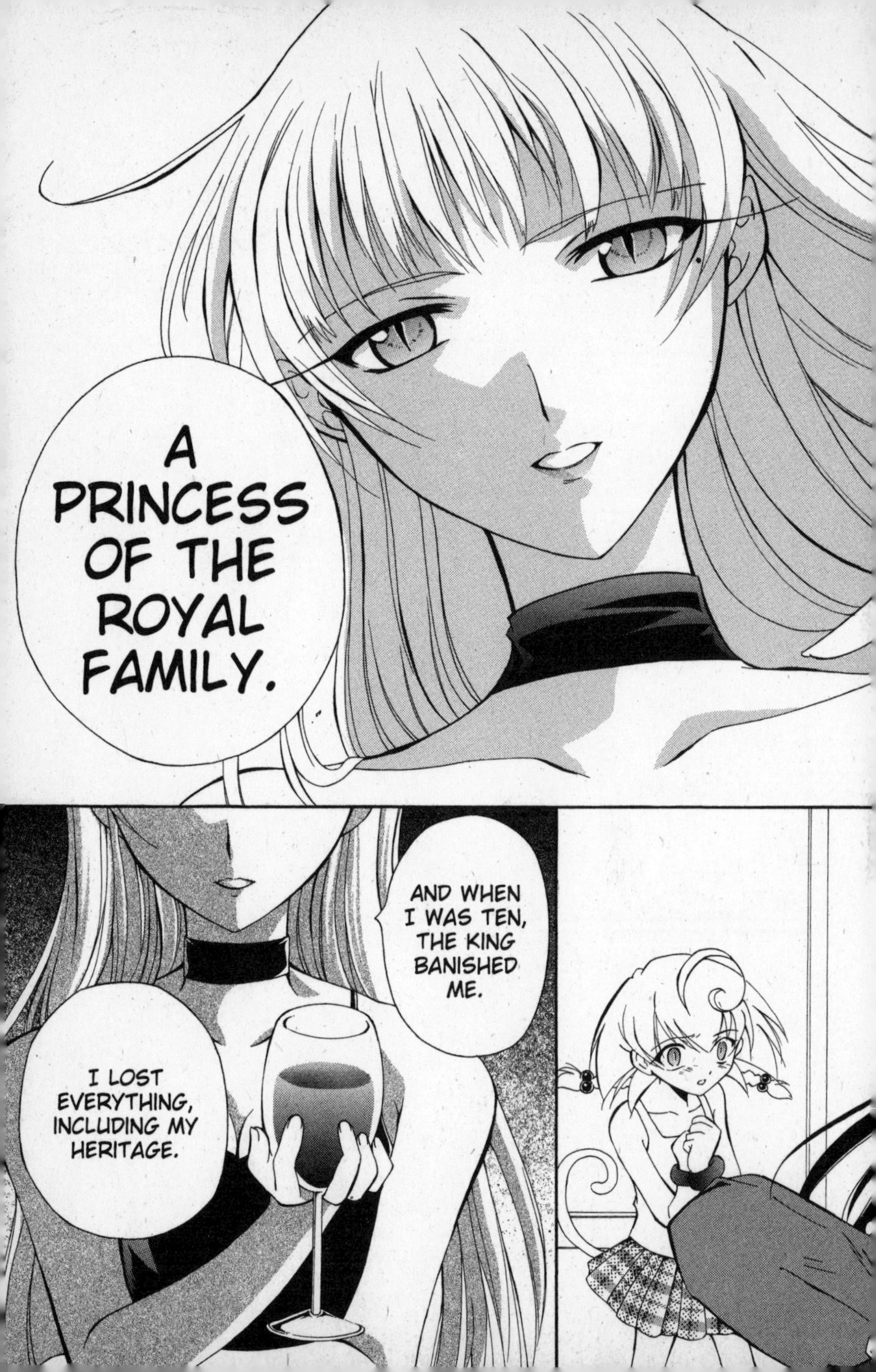
A PRINCESS OF THE ROYAL FAMILY.
AND WHEN I WAS TEN, THE KING BANISHED ME.
I LOST EVERYTHING, INCLUDING MY HERITAGE.

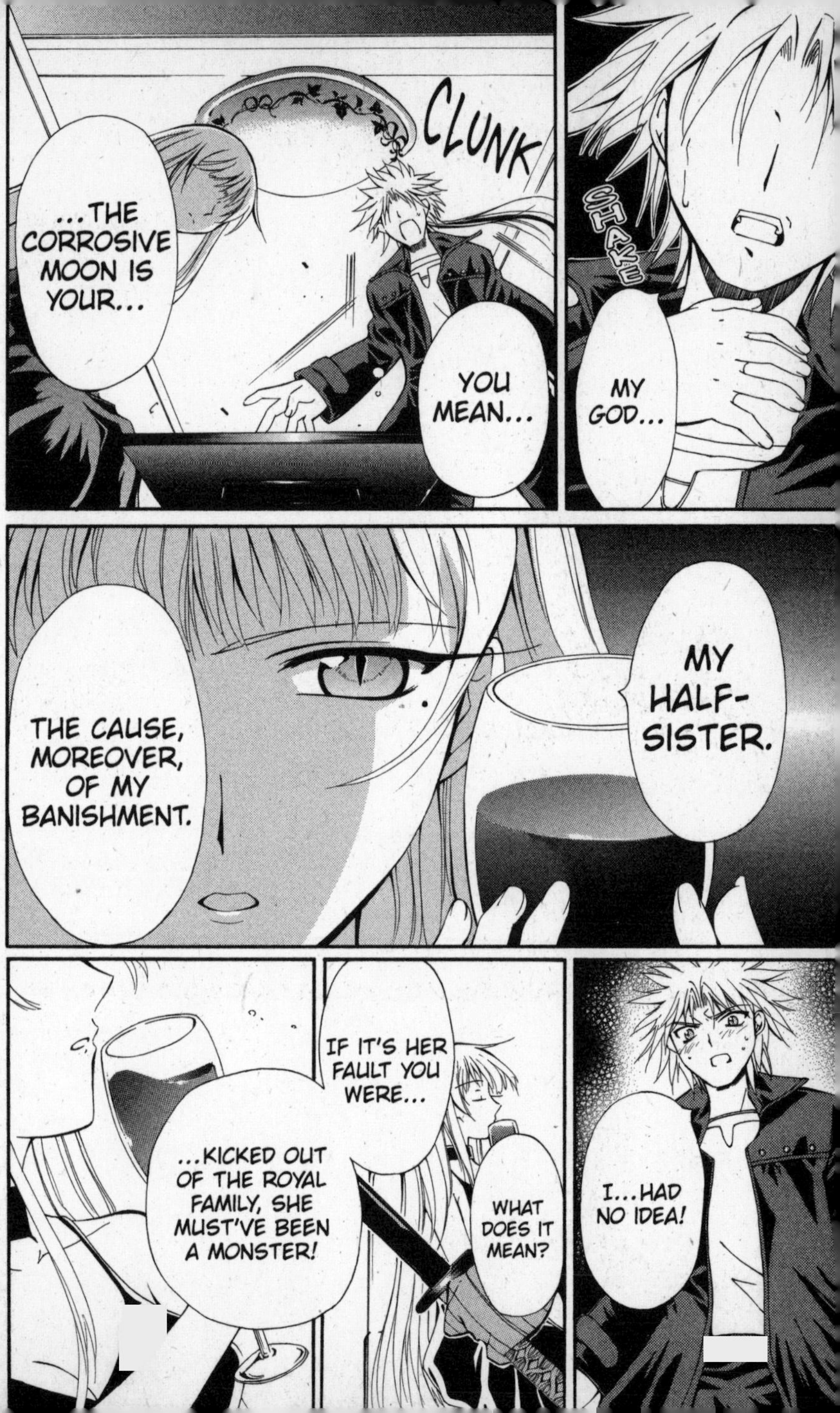
SHAKE
MY GOD...
CLUNK
...THE CORROSIVE MOON IS YOUR...
YOU MEAN...
MY HALF-SISTER.
THE CAUSE, MOREOVER, OF MY BANISHMENT.
I...HAD NO IDEA!
IF IT'S HER FAULT YOU WERE...
...KICKED OUT OF THE ROYAL FAMILY, SHE MUST'VE BEEN A MONSTER!
WHAT DOES IT MEAN?

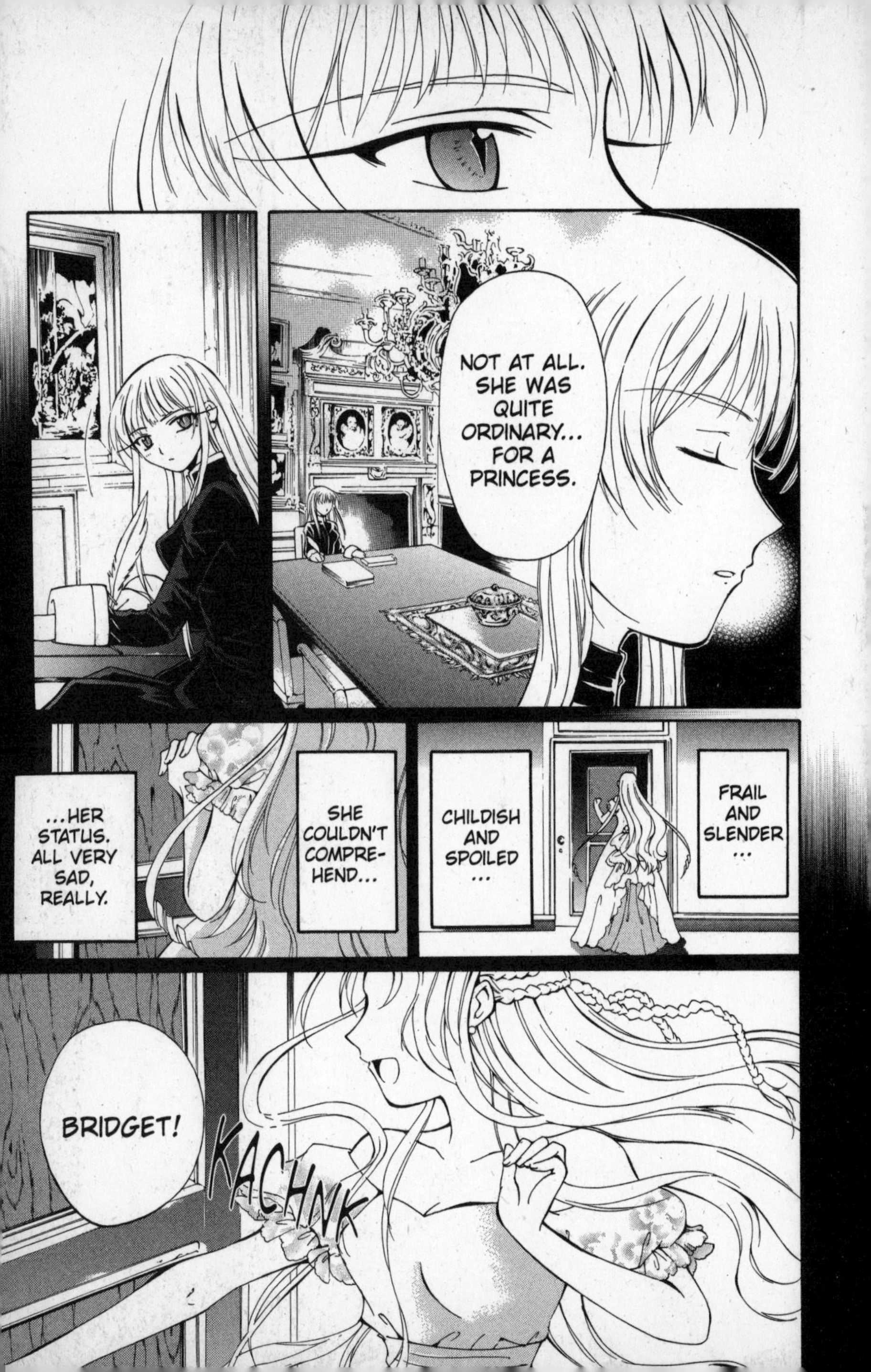
NOT AT ALL. SHE WAS QUITE ORDINARY... FOR A PRINCESS.
FRAIL AND SLENDER ...
CHILDISH AND SPOILED ...
SHE COULDN'T COMPRE- HEND...
...HER STATUS. ALL VERY SAD, REALLY.
BRIDGET!
KACHNK

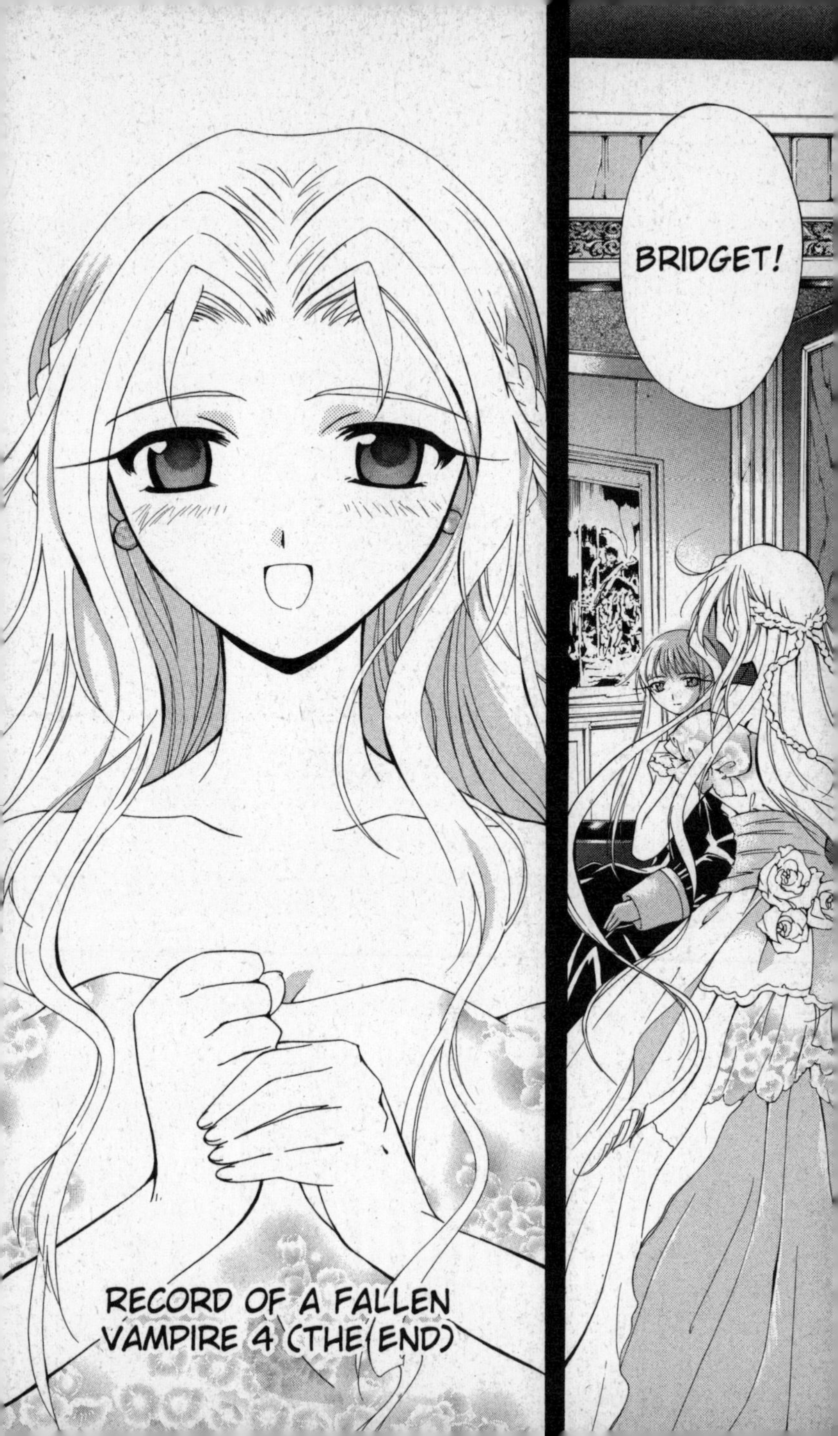
BRIDGET!
RECORD OF A FALLEN VAMPIRE 4 (THE END)

THE RECORD OF A

FALLEN VAMPIRE

ILLUSTRATION OF

THE RECORD OF A

FALLEN VAMPIRE

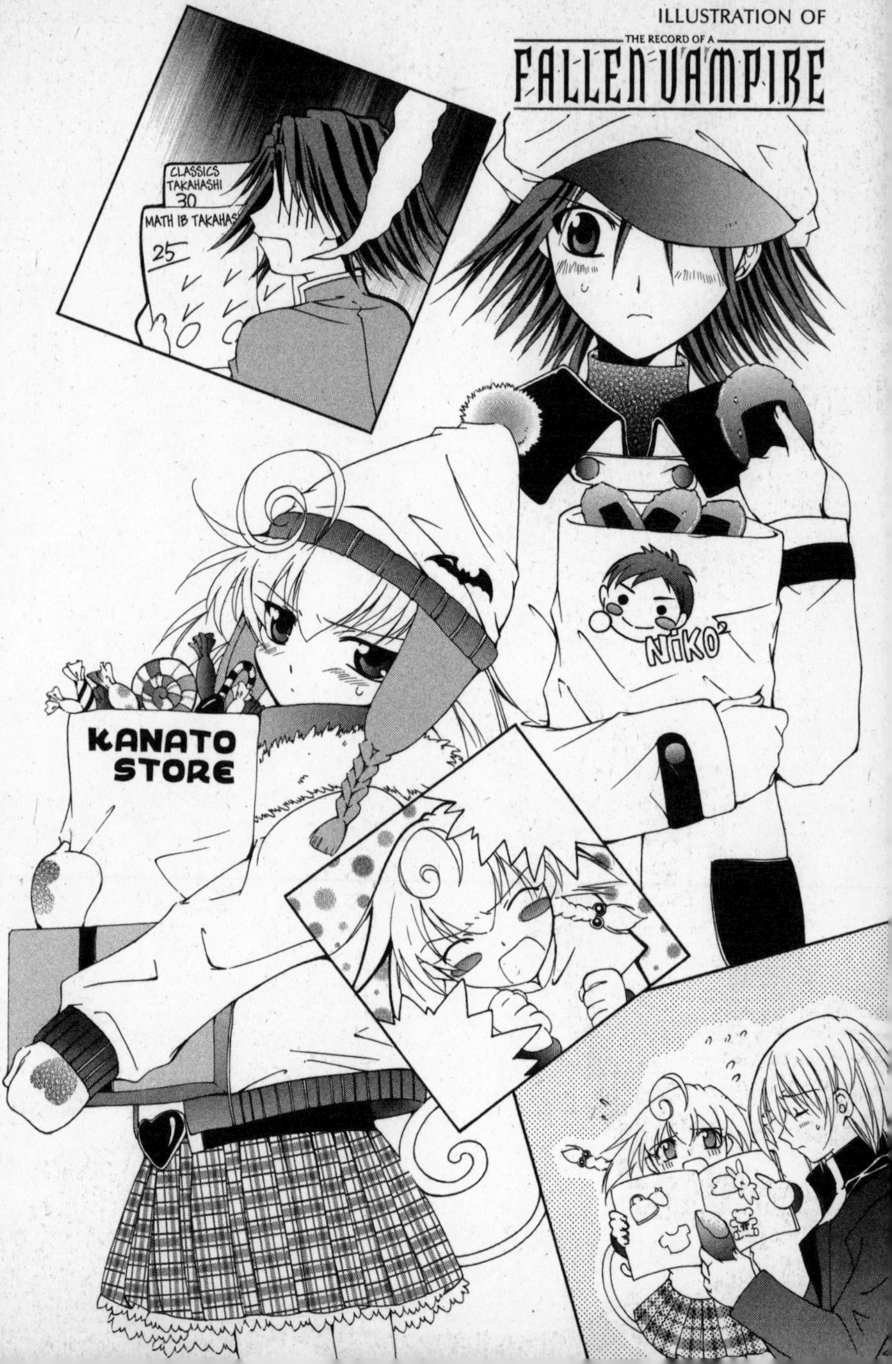
CLASSICS TAKAHASHI 30
MATH IB TAKAHAS
25
NIKO^{2}
KANATO STORE

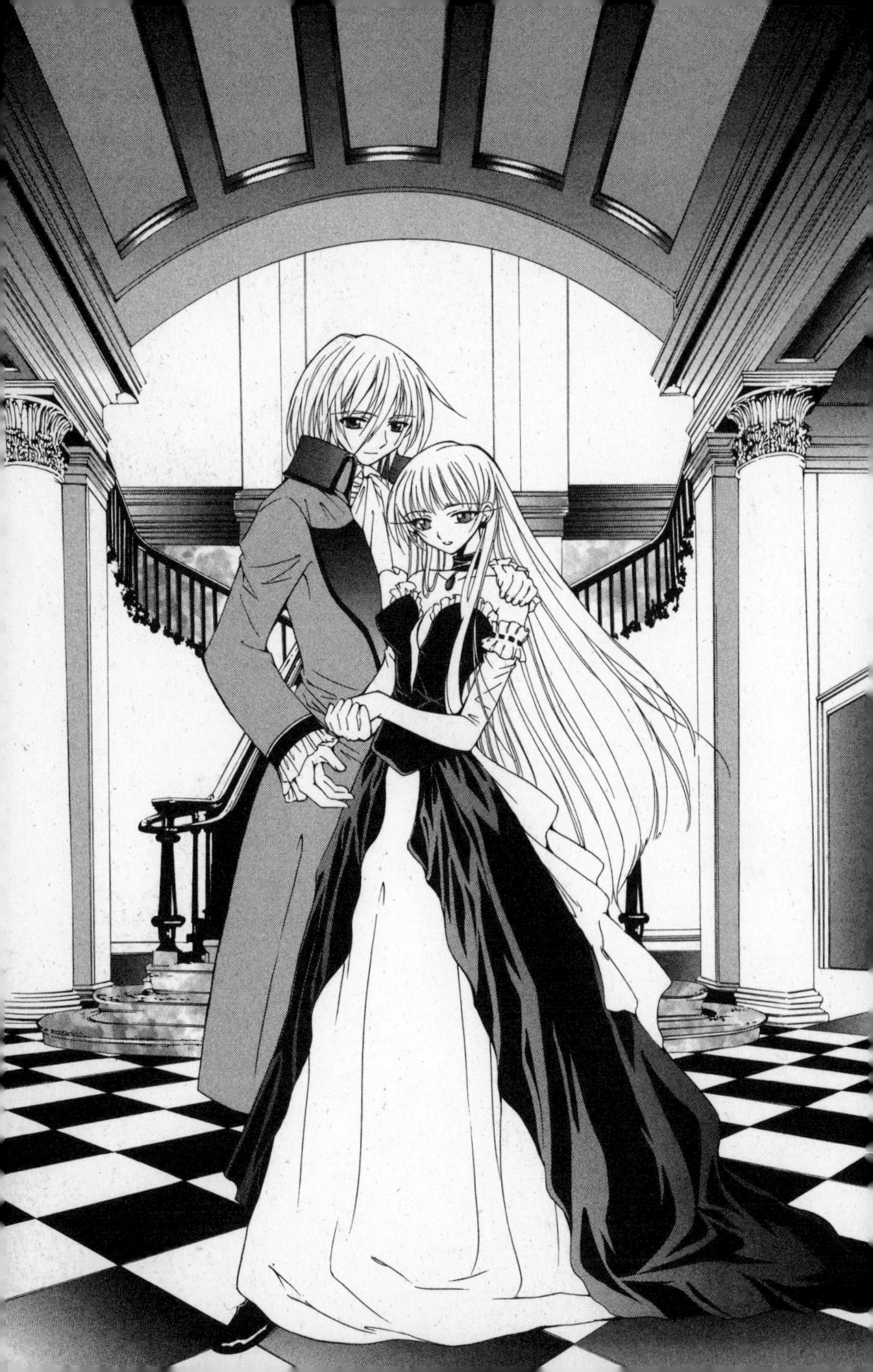

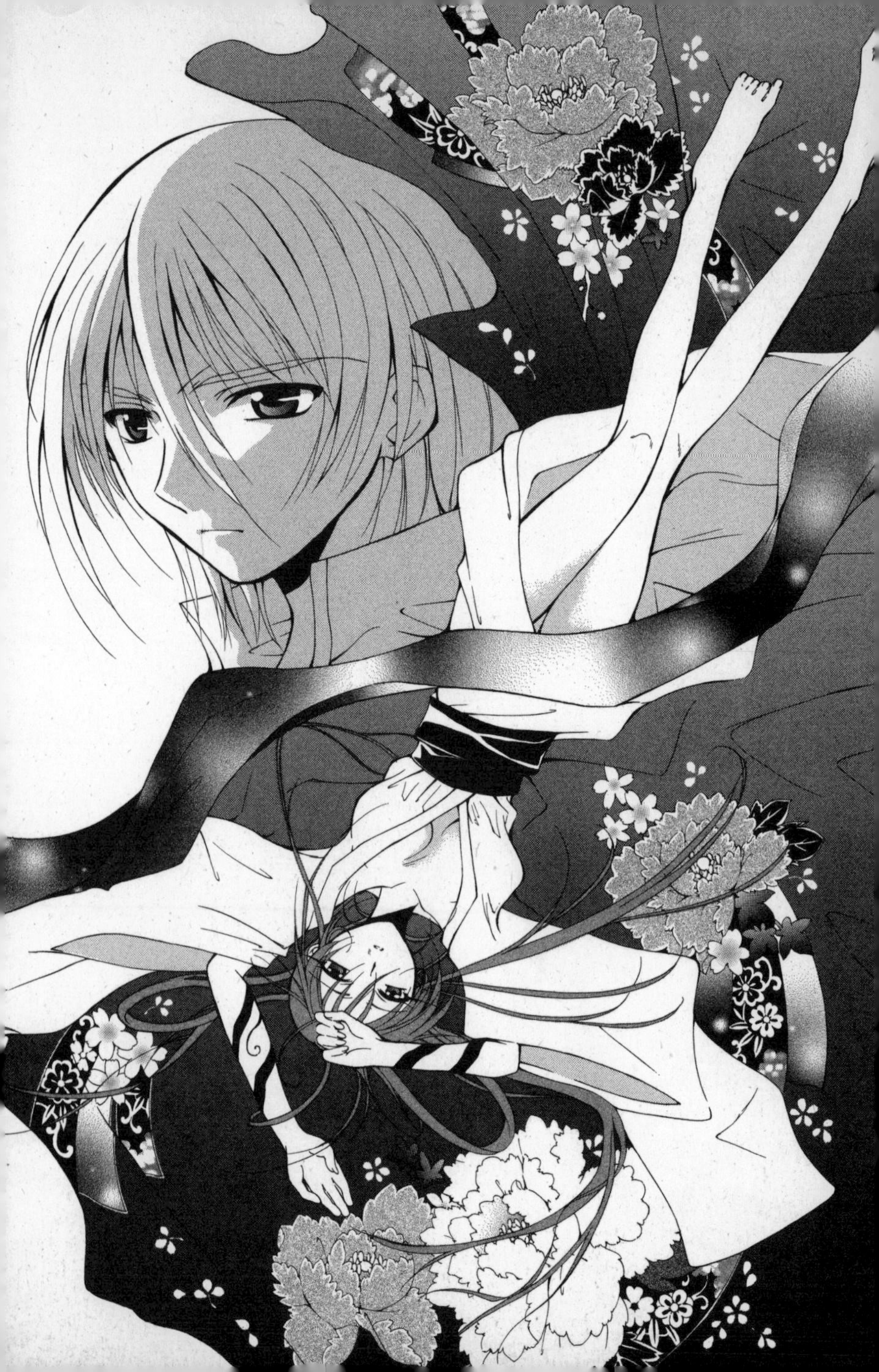

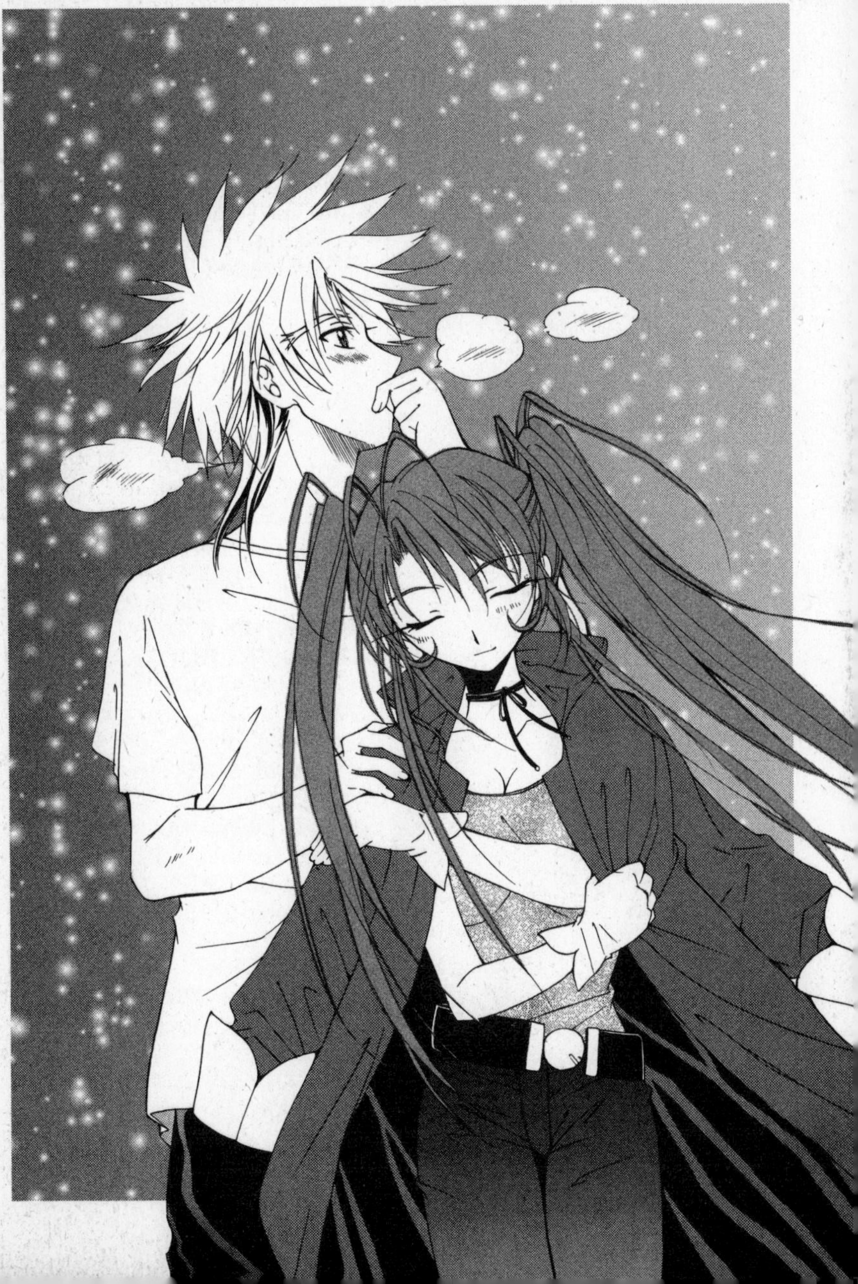

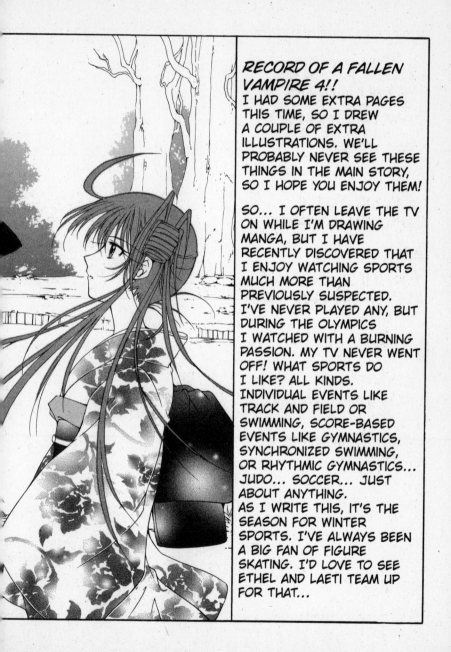

RECORD OF A FALLEN VAMPIRE 4!!
I HAD SOME EXTRA PAGES THIS TIME, SO I DREW A COUPLE OF EXTRA ILLUSTRATIONS. WE'LL PROBABLY NEVER SEE THESE THINGS IN THE MAIN STORY, SO I HOPE YOU ENJOY THEM!

SO... I OFTEN LEAVE THE TV ON WHILE I'M DRAWING MANGA, BUT I HAVE RECENTLY DISCOVERED THAT I ENJOY WATCHING SPORTS MUCH MORE THAN PREVIOUSLY SUSPECTED. I'VE NEVER PLAYED ANY, BUT DURING THE OLYMPICS I WATCHED WITH A BURNING PASSION. MY TV NEVER WENT OFF! WHAT SPORTS DO I LIKE? ALL KINDS. INDIVIDUAL EVENTS LIKE TRACK AND FIELD OR SWIMMING, SCORE-BASED EVENTS LIKE GYMNASTICS, SYNCHRONIZED SWIMMING, OR RHYTHMIC GYMNASTICS... JUDO... SOCCER... JUST ABOUT ANYTHING. AS I WRITE THIS, IT'S THE SEASON FOR WINTER SPORTS. I'VE ALWAYS BEEN A BIG FAN OF FIGURE SKATING. I'D LOVE TO SEE ETHEL AND LAETI TEAM UP FOR THAT...

NOT TO CHANGE THE SUBJECT, BUT THE NEXT VOLUME FOCUSES ON THE PAST. WHAT HAPPENED? WHAT DID STRAUSS SEE? I HOPE WE MEET AGAIN NEXT VOLUME.

-YURI KIMURA

RECORD OF A FALLEN VAMPIRE 4

SPECIAL THANKS

MARUKO ASAGAYA CHIKA HANAZAWA

·

KASUMI AKIRA

·

EDITOR: NOBUAKI YUMURA

AND TO ALL MY READERS

AUTHOR'S AFTERWORD

A FLEET OF FLYING SAUCERS FROM SPACE INVADING THE
EARTH, AND THE VAMPIRES AND DHAMPIRES FLYING UP TO
TAKE THEM DOWN...

IT WAS THIS IDEA THAT LED ME TO START *THE RECORD
OF A FALLEN VAMPIRE*. WHICH MEANS THE EVENTS OF
THIS VOLUME ARE, IN A SENSE, PART OF MY ORIGINAL
PLAN. I'M NOT JUST MAKING THIS UP AS I GO ALONG.
THE ALIENS DID NOT END UP ARRIVING IN FLYING SAUCERS,
BUT THEY ARE DEFINITELY HERE TO INVADE.

SO I AM KYO SHIRODAIRA, AND THIS IS VOLUME 4.
LET ME SAY THIS IN ADVANCE SO THERE'S NO MISUNDER-
STANDING—DESPITE ALL THE TALK ABOUT ALIENS AND
ROCKETS, I AM NOT ATTEMPTING WHAT MOST PEOPLE
THINK OF WHEN THEY HEAR THE TERM SCI-FI. I'M WORK-
ING MORE WITH IMAGINARY SCIENCE.

PERHAPS YOU DON'T PERCEIVE A GREAT DIFFERENCE, BUT
SCI-FI ALWAYS SEEMS TOO HARD LINE AND RESPECTABLE,
CONCERNED WITH THE SCIENTIFIC FACTS. I SUPPOSE THE
EXISTENCE OF THE TERM HARD SCI-FI MEANS SCI-FI-
EQUALS-SCIENCE IS NOT ALWAYS ACCURATE. (TO TELL
THE TRUTH, IT IS OBVIOUSLY NOT TRUE AT ALL!) BUT THE
TERM HAS COME TO IMPLY DENSE AND DIFFICULT. (AND A
LOT OF OBVIOUSLY SCI-FI STORIES HAVE TO PRETEND
THEY AREN'T SCI-FI.)

BUT THERE'S STILL SOME ROMANCE TO THE TERM IMAGINARY SCIENCE. WE USED TO MAKE A TON OF TOKUSATSU MOVIES HERE, WITH IMAGINARY SCIENCE ALL OVER THE PLACE. *GODZILLA* AND THE OTHER MONSTER MOVIES ARE NOT THE ONLY TOKUSATSU FILMS WE MADE. MOVIES LIKE *THE MYSTERIANS*, *BATTLE IN OUTER SPACE*, AND *GORATH* ALL HAVE STORIES AND SETTINGS THAT MODERN SCIENTIFIC COMMON SENSE WOULD HAVE A FEW PROBLEMS WITH (*GORATH* HAS MORE THAN A FEW), BUT THEY WERE IMAGINATIVE ROMANCES THAT USED SCIENCE AS A SPRINGBOARD, AND CAN STILL ENTERTAIN TODAY. PARTICULARLY EFFECTIVE WERE THE MARCOLIGHTS FROM *THE MYSTERIANS*.

SO *THE RECORD OF A FALLEN VAMPIRE* IS A VAMPIRE STORY WITH ELEMENTS OF IMAGINARY SCIENCE IN THE STYLE OF TOKUSATSU FILMS THROWN IN. I HAVE, THEREFORE, NOT GIVEN THE SCIENCE USED HERE A GREAT DEAL OF THOUGHT... OR ANY AT ALL. AS LONG AS IT ENTERTAINS, I HOPE YOU WILL WARMLY OVER-LOOK THE FACTS. PERHAPS THAT IS MY ONLY POINT HERE. THE STORY HAS MADE SOME MAJOR SHIFTS IN THE PRESENT, BUT THE NEXT VOLUME WILL FOCUS ON THE PAST. JUST AS IN THIS VOLUME WE SAW THE ALIEN INVADERS, NEXT VOLUME WE WILL LOOK AT TWO MYSTERIOUS WOMEN, ADELHEID AND STELLA.

WHAT SECRETS ARE THEY HIDING? THIS STORY OF THE PAST WILL, NATURALLY, BE LIGHT ON THE IMAGINARY SCIENCE, FOCUSING ON MATTERS OF THE HEART.

I PRAY WE WILL MEET AGAIN IN VOLUME 5.

- KYO SHIRODAIRA

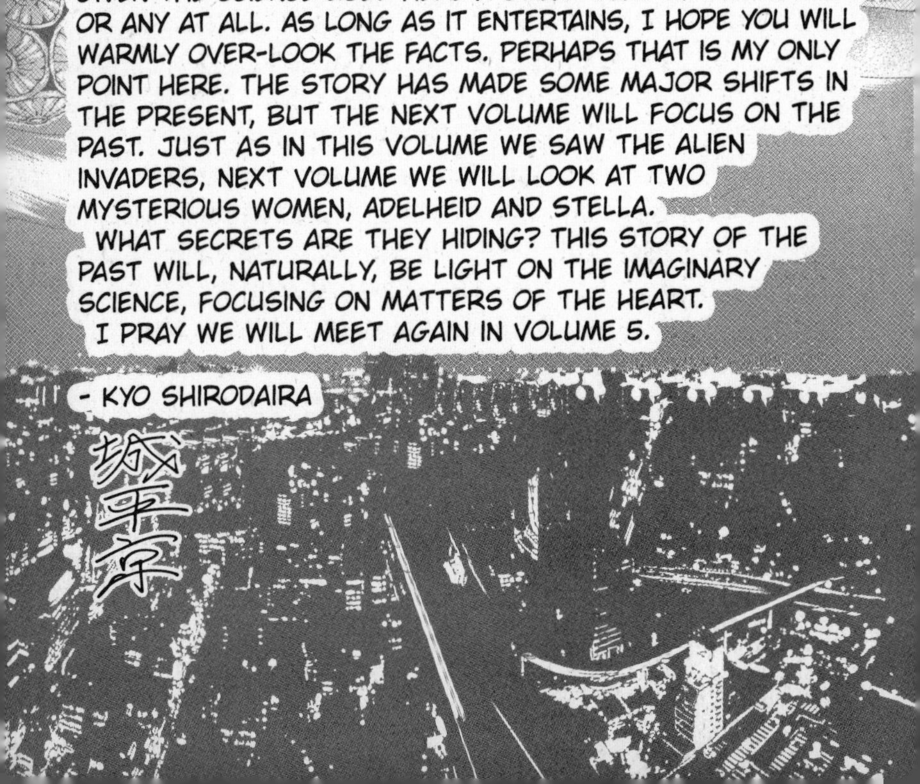

THE RECORD OF A FALLEN VAMPIRE
VOL. 4
VIZ MEDIA EDITION

STORY BY: **KYO SHIRODAIRA**   ART BY: **YURI KIMURA**

Translation & Adaptation...**Andrew Cunningham**
Touch-up Art & Lettering...**HudsonYards**
Cover Design...**Courtney Utt**
Interior Design...**Ronnie Casson**
Editor...**Gary Leach**

Editor in Chief, Books...**Alvin Lu**
Editor in Chief, Magazines...**Marc Weidenbaum**
VP, Publishing Licensing...**Rika Inouye**
VP, Sales & Product Marketing...**Gonzalo Ferreyra**
VP, Creative...**Linda Espinosa**
Publisher...**Hyoe Narita**

Printed in the U.S.A.

Published by VIZ Media, LLC
P.O. Box 77010
San Francisco, CA 94107

10 9 8 7 6 5 4 3 2 1
First printing, February 2009

store.viz.com

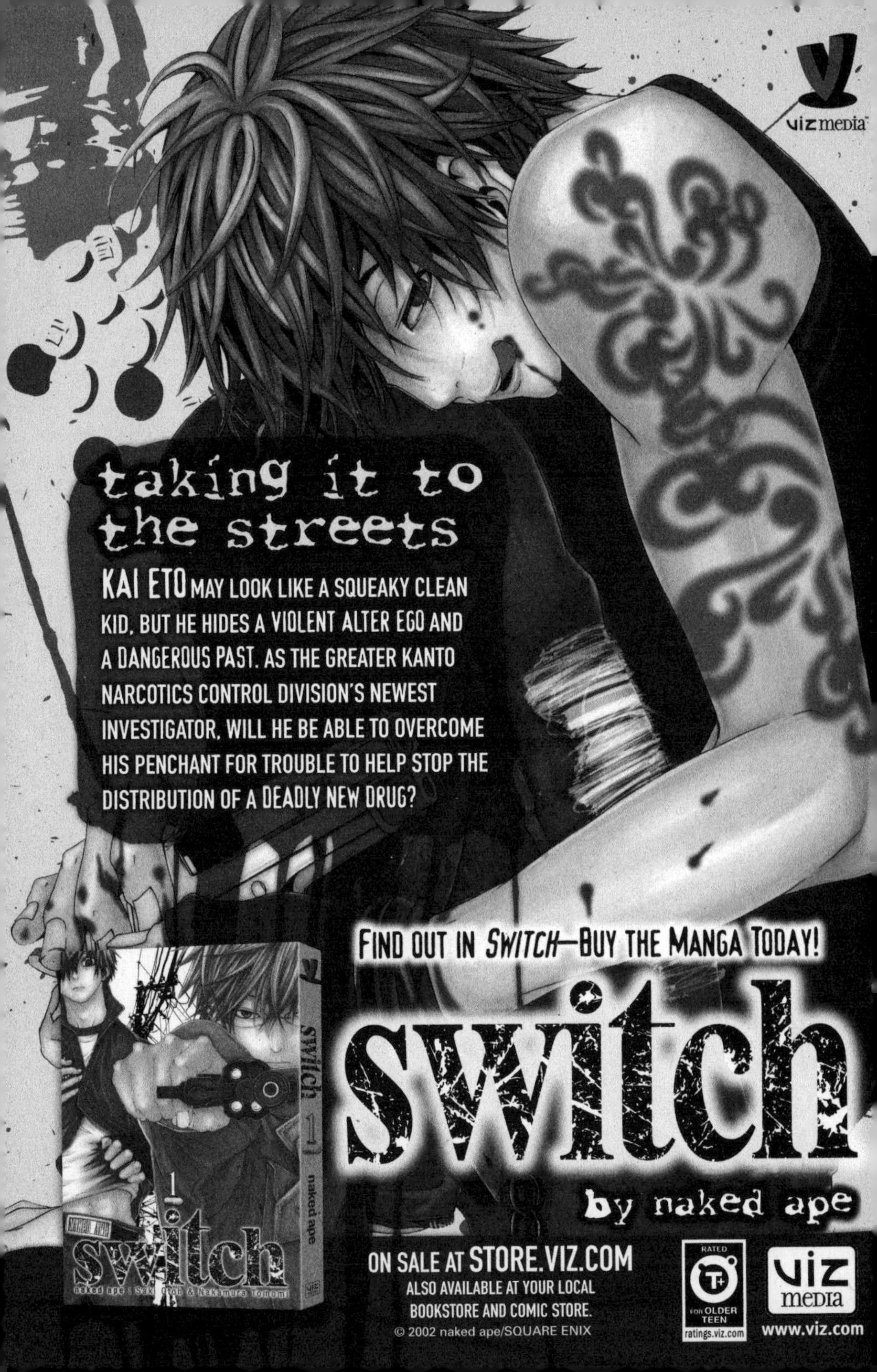

taking it to the streets
KAI ETO MAY LOOK LIKE A SQUEAKY CLEAN KID, BUT HE HIDES A VIOLENT ALTER EGO AND A DANGEROUS PAST. AS THE GREATER KANTO NARCOTICS CONTROL DIVISION'S NEWEST INVESTIGATOR, WILL HE BE ABLE TO OVERCOME HIS PENCHANT FOR TROUBLE TO HELP STOP THE DISTRIBUTION OF A DEADLY NEW DRUG?
FIND OUT IN SWITCH—BUY THE MANGA TODAY!
switch
by naked ape
switch 1 naked ape
1
switch
naked ape / Saki Otoh & Nakamura Tomomi
ON SALE AT STORE.VIZ.COM
ALSO AVAILABLE AT YOUR LOCAL BOOKSTORE AND COMIC STORE.
© 2002 naked ape/SQUARE ENIX
RATED T+ FOR OLDER TEEN
ratings.viz.com
VIZ media
www.viz.com
viz media